OVERRIDING MANDATORY RULES IN INTERNATIONAL COMMERCIAL DISPUTES

This open access book analyses how to identify and treat overriding mandatory rules in international commercial litigation and arbitration from a Korean and comparative law perspective.

In addition to providing a deeper understanding of the concept of overriding mandatory rules and setting out standards and factors to identify such rules, the book provides a solution to the problems that third-country mandatory provisions pose in international commercial disputes.

The book examines the jurisprudence of the European Court of Justice under the Rome Convention and the Rome I Regulation, Swiss IPRG, and German and English law to help interpret and propose an amendment to the Korean Act on Private International Law. The book also establishes tests to identify the overriding mandatory character and then empirically applies them to assess various provisions in ten different Acts in Korea.

Furthermore, the book provides a 'balancing interest test' for third country mandatory rules and suggests a new provision that harmonises the conflicting interests of the parties, the forum country, the third country and interests of international harmony of decisions. It also explores the arbitrability of disputes in relation to overriding mandatory rules, the validity of an arbitration agreement, the extent to which overriding mandatory rules should apply, and whether the national courts can refuse enforcement of or revoke arbitral awards which did not apply/consider overriding mandatory rules.

This book is an invaluable resource to legal practitioners, judges, arbitrators in international commercial dispute resolution, researchers in private international law and international commercial law, and parties to international commercial contracts.

Volume 10 in the series Studies in Private International Law – Asia

Studies in Private International Law – Asia

Editor: Anselmo Reyes
Advisory Editor: Paul Beaumont
Assistant editors: Kazuaki Nishioka and Wilson Lui

Much has been written about private international law in the EU and the US. Less is known about the conflict of laws in Asia. Thus, little attention has been paid so far to the modernisation of private international law codes and rules that has been taking place over the last decade all over Asia. That trend continues. Now is the time to take stock of those reforms that have already taken place and suggest further improvements for the future.

Published under the celebrated series *Studies in Private International Law*, this monograph sub-series provides a forum for discussion and analysis of private international law in Asia. The series is not solely a survey of jurisdictions for practitioners. Comprising in-depth thematic and country-specific studies, each volume considers the private international law of Asian countries from a variety of perspectives. An underlying assumption is that private international law in different jurisdictions follow broad discernible patterns. Each volume in this sub-series highlights those patterns and discusses how rules in different Asian jurisdictions are either converging with, or diverging from, the patterns identified. Such an analytical framework will assist academics, judges, lawyers and legislators to envisage ways in which laws affecting cross-border relationships can be harmonised across jurisdictions and be made more responsive to the needs of citizens in Asia and elsewhere.

Volume 1: Recognition and Enforcement of Judgments in Civil and Commercial Matters
Edited by Anselmo Reyes

Volume 2: Indonesian Private International Law
Afifah Kusumadara

Volume 3: Chinese Private International Law
Edited by Xiaohong Liu and Zhengyi Zhang

Volume 4: Direct Jurisdiction: Asian Perspectives
Edited by Anselmo Reyes and Wilson Lui

Volume 5: Japanese Private International Law
Kazuaki Nishioka and Yuko Nishitani

Volume 6: Indian Private International Law
Stellina Jolly and Saloni Khanderia

Volume 7: Treatment of Foreign Law in Asia
Edited by Kazuaki Nishioka

Volume 8: Choice of Law and Recognition in Asian Family Law
Edited by Anselmo Reyes, Wilson Lui and Kazuaki Nishioka

Volume 9: Private International Law in East Asia: From Imitation to Innovation and Exportation
Edited by Olivier Gaillard and Krista Nadakavukaren Schefer

Volume 10: Overriding Mandatory Rules in International Commercial Disputes: Korean and Comparative Law
Min Kyung KIM

Overriding Mandatory Rules in International Commercial Disputes

Korean and Comparative Law

Min Kyung KIM

•HART•
OXFORD • LONDON • NEW YORK • NEW DELHI • SYDNEY

HART PUBLISHING

Bloomsbury Publishing Plc

Kemp House, Chawley Park, Cumnor Hill, Oxford, OX2 9PH, UK

1385 Broadway, New York, NY 10018, USA

Bloomsbury Publishing Ireland Limited, 29 Earlsfort Terrace, Dublin 2, D02 AY28, Ireland

HART PUBLISHING, the Hart/Stag logo, BLOOMSBURY and the Diana logo are trademarks of Bloomsbury Publishing Plc

First published in Great Britain 2024

A catalogue record for this book is available from the British Library.

A catalogue record for this book is available from the Library of Congress.

Library of Congress Control Number: 2024944197

ISBN: HB: 978-1-50996-977-7
ePDF: 978-1-50996-979-1
ePub: 978-1-50996-978-4

Typeset by Compuscript Ltd, Shannon

For product safety related questions contact productsafety@bloomsbury.com

To John, Han and Luke

FOREWORD

The subject of this impressive new work could hardly be more important in international commercial law. The avoidance of risk is a primary, if elusive, objective in international commerce. Sometimes the risk is commercial, concerning perhaps a party's creditworthiness or currency fluctuations. But it can also be legal, often involving a transaction's regulatory framework and sometimes even its legality. Such legal risk can be mitigated by careful drafting, most importantly by expressly choosing both a favourable governing law and a benign forum for resolving any disputes, one which is unlikely to superimpose its own regulatory regime on the transaction. But this can never eliminate entirely the legal risk to cross border contracts from overriding mandatory rules, rules which are intended to oust the governing law. These rules may derive from the law of the forum or, more problematically, from the law of a third state, typically in contract cases the state where the contract is to be performed.

The operation of such overriding rules poses many difficult questions. It may be unclear whether a particular rule has overriding effect, a potential problem of construction in the absence of clear words. Or there may be doubt about the legal effect of overriding rules enacted after the conclusion of a contract, often in the place of performance. In this ambitious new book Min Kyung Kim examines comprehensively the many problems surrounding overriding mandatory rules in international commercial disputes, both in litigation and arbitration, with particular reference to Korean law but also more broadly from a comparative perspective.

The author brings to this enquiry a wealth of detail and practical insight but also confronts some important questions of principle, questions which expose fundamental issues in private international law. She is concerned with the legitimate scope and effect of overriding rules in the absence of clear words in a statute. She is also concerned with the apparently irreconcilable tensions between party autonomy and the national interest, and between the interests of the forum and those of any third states whose law is implicated. In her highly original analysis Dr Kim breaks new ground by bringing an international perspective to these problems. She seeks to transcend the apparent tensions underlying the operation of overriding rules by emphasising the importance of a cooperative approach and achieving harmony of result.

A particular feature of the work is its illuminating use of comparative material, which brings to a wider audience the approaches of different systems, and puts the underlying issues into sharper focus. Another is its treatment of mandatory rules in commercial arbitration and the distinct issues of principle this generates. Dr Kim addresses the intractable tension between the private, consensual nature of arbitration and the overriding effect of mandatory rules in national law. She questions whether the parties to an arbitration may properly insulate themselves from the reach of such rules, and offers a robust basis for denying effect to arbitral awards which fail to comply with them.

Overriding Mandatory Rules in International Commercial Disputes takes Korean law as its starting point but its scope and ambition are wider. It provides an invaluable comparative survey of the terrain and is full of insight into the methodology of private international law. Its comprehensiveness and practicality will be of value to judges and practitioners, but its broader approach and theoretical concerns offers much to the scholar and teacher as well. Dr Kim is to be congratulated on an impressively original work on an important topic which is sure to find a wide and appreciative audience.

Richard Fentiman

FOREWORD

This book by Dr Min Kyung KIM, a judge in Korea, discusses various issues concerning overriding mandatory rules raised in international commercial disputes from the perspective of Korean and comparative private international law. The concept of overriding mandatory rules may vary, but in general, it refers to mandatory provisions of law that the parties cannot exclude by agreement and that must be implemented regardless of the governing law of the legal relationship in light of their special legislative meaning and purpose. The concept has recently gained a firm position in private international law, as seen in the European Union's Rome Convention and Rome I Regulations, Switzerland's Private International Law Act, and private international legislation in Korea, Japan, and China that was influenced by the European codifications. Korea's Private International Law Act, which completely revised the choice of law rules in 2001 (international jurisdictional rules were completely revised in 2022), sets forth overriding mandatory rules, but only covers Korea's overriding mandatory rules, while leaving treatment of the overriding mandatory rules of third countries to the courts and academia. In order to solve the issues concerning overriding mandatory rules, Dr Kim reviews the private international law legislation and precedents of the European Union, the Switzerland, and the United Kingdom, among other jurisdictions, and then presents criteria for judging which Korean legal provisions are classified as overriding mandatory rules from the perspective of Korean law. She goes on to present theories for interpretation and propose future legislation concerning the treatment of the overriding mandatory rules of third countries. As the supervisor for Dr Kim's doctoral dissertation, on which this book is based, I welcome this book's publication and highly value her hard work in bringing it to print.

The 'global supply chain' that sustained the international division of labor in the past has recently been reorganized to focus on the national interests of individual countries, global supply chain blocs, and environmental, social, and governance (ESG) issues in response to changes in the international political situation, a phenomenon that is expected to continue for some time to come. Because the WTO system is not functioning properly, individual countries are tightening regulations on foreign businesses and imposing economic sanctions more often than before, and in Korea, an increasing number of laws specify extraterritorial application. If we are to understand such laws' impact on international transactions, it is necessary to analyse the implications of overriding mandatory rules. In this context, the author analyses, inter alia, the implications of provisions specifying extraterritorial application in the context of overriding mandatory rules (Chapter 4).

This book mainly deals with overriding mandatory rules from the perspective of Korean and comparative private international law, so it is firstly a useful resource for understanding Korean private international law. That is even more valuable because thus far there has been very little English literature addressing that topic. The book is also useful to lawyers around the world for elaborating the theory of overriding mandatory rules through specific court cases. Furthermore, Dr Kim presents guidelines for future legislation on overriding mandatory rules of third countries in the context of Korea's Private International Law Act (Chapter 6), which may also have implications for other countries seeking to modernise their private international law legislation. In addition, it could be helpful for European lawyers who are already familiar with the concept of overriding mandatory rules to better understand how related legal principles are actually received and developed in countries outside Europe, and particularly in Korea, a country in East Asia.

Last but not least, the author analyses the meaning of overriding mandatory rules in the context not only of litigation but also of international commercial arbitration from the perspective of Korean and comparative law (Chapter 7). Compared to litigation, choice of law rules on the merits and the treatment of overriding mandatory rules are less developed in international commercial arbitration, where there is no concept of forum as there is in litigation. In light of the practical importance of international commercial arbitration as a means of resolving international disputes, this is a very appropriate topic that increases the book's value.

In short, I believe this book is very useful to lawyers who deal with international transactions, and I recommend this book to them, as well as to anyone else interested in private international law.

Dr Kwang Hyun SUK
President Emeritus of the Korea Private International Law Association
Former Professor of Seoul National University School of Law
July 2024

SERIES EDITORS' PREFACE

Although ostensibly the second volume in the monograph sub-series of Hart's *Studies in Private International Law – Asia*, this book is actually the first monograph (in the sense of a work entirely written by one person) in that sub-series. Indeed, Judge Kim's study is the first book in the entire *Studies in Private International Law: Asia* series to be written by a single author from beginning to end. All other volumes have been the work of combinations of persons. The Editors therefore congratulate Judge Kim on her distinction.

As its title indicates, this study deals with overriding mandatory rules in the context of international commercial dispute resolution. One might be forgiven for wondering what the difference is between rules that are merely 'mandatory' and rules that are not only 'mandatory' but somehow also 'overriding'. Judge Kim succinctly explains the distinction in chapter one: 'Domestic mandatory rules can be excluded by the parties' choice of the law of another country, while overriding mandatory rules cannot be excluded even if the parties choose the law of another country or when the objective applicable law is the law of another country.' If so, how exactly does one tell whether a mandatory rule has attained 'overriding' status? Answering that eminently practical question lies at the heart of Judge Kim's study. She looks at the question from the vantage of legal history, legal theory and modern law. Nor does she shrink from venturing into areas of controversy, as she considers whether there is a doctrine of overriding mandatory law in international commercial arbitration, a mode of dispute resolution which is viewed by many as itself transcending domestic law.

The book bears the sub-title 'Korean and Comparative Law'. This should not lead would-be readers into thinking that this book is a narrow study of Korean law with little application outside of Korea. The Korean Act on Private International Law (KAPIL) as amended on 4 January 2022 and in force since 22 July 2022, is one of the most advanced codes of conflict of law rules in the world today. Jurisdictions in Asia and elsewhere seeking to modernise their private international law statutes can usefully kick-off their reform by studying KAPIL and assessing whether it can serve as a template for their law. Further, the reference to 'Comparative Law' in the subtitle, and the citation of common law cases and statutes throughout the book, should alert one to the fact that this book is not confined to readers in civil law countries. Judge Kim's study is more ambitious in that it also discusses overriding statutes at common law.

There is an additional feature of this volume to which we should draw attention. That is the book's availability on open access. The book shares this feature with the first volume in the monograph sub-series. We hope that this study will be a harbinger of future monographs being published on open access within Hart's sub-series.

The Editors
Kyoto
1 July 2024

PREFACE

Party autonomy is not absolute. Over the years I have spent sitting on the International Commercial List at the Seoul Central District Court, I have come to realise the huge impact that overriding mandatory rules can have on contractual rights and obligations. I became fascinated by provisions in domestic law that dictate application even when the parties to the contract agree that the applicable law is foreign law. In stark contrast to the usual principles for determining governing law, overriding mandatory rules by their very existence impose significant risks on contractual agreements, and those risks are particularly great when it is not easy to identify what provisions of law have an overriding mandatory character.

Established as the concept of overriding mandatory rules may be, those rules still pose vexing questions for international commercial dispute resolution: Which standards apply in ascertaining overriding mandatory character? How should we treat the overriding mandatory rules of a country that is not the country of *lex causae* or *lex fori*? And how are these rules applied or considered in the context of arbitration as opposed to litigation?

In this book, I have endeavored to provide answers to these three critical questions. Although there are certainly areas that require further development, I am committed to addressing these gaps in future research, especially as various jurisdictions adopt overriding mandatory rules in different areas of law (such as, most recently, sanctions and rules on cross-border data regulation). It is my hope that this book will contribute in some small way to the ongoing study of overriding mandatory rules.

When I first started my graduate studies in 2012, I did not anticipate that I would one day publish a book on international private law and international commercial law. I owe my progress to the priceless academic guidance and inspiration of my doctoral supervisor, Professor Kwang Hyun Suk at Seoul National University, and Professor Richard Fentiman at the University of Cambridge. I would also like to extend my heartfelt gratitude to Professors Seung Hwa Chang, Chang Min Chun, Bong Kyung Choi and Sunseop Jung for the invaluable insights they provided while I was writing my doctoral dissertation, which was originally written in Korean and on which this book is based. I am also sincerely grateful to Judge Anselmo Reyes, who encouraged me to publish this book in English, and to Mr. Justice Jonathan Harris and Mr. David Carruth who proofread the manuscript.

Lastly, I would like to express my endless love to my family and my gratitude for their support – and for putting up with me while I was grappling with this book.

Min Kyung KIM
September 2024

CONTENTS

LIST OF TABLES

LIST OF CASES

Arbitrations

Belgium

England and Wales

European Union

Germany

South Korea

Switzerland

The Netherlands

United States

LIST OF STATUTES

England and Wales

European Union

Germany

India

Nigeria

South Korea

Switzerland

United States

1

Introduction[1]

I. Significance and Objectives of the Study

It would be unusual these days for any contract for international trade or investment not to include clauses, which specify the law governing the transaction and specify the dispute resolution procedure; commonly specifying what court has jurisdiction to determine any dispute or providing for arbitration. However, party autonomy is not absolute. Although many jurisdictions respect the parties' rights to choose the governing law and dispute resolution process, which regulates their legal relationship, in most jurisdictions there will be matters in respect of which party autonomy is overridden by laws, which apply regardless of what the parties have agreed. These laws are known as overriding mandatory rules.[2] How they apply to international commercial disputes is the subject of this book.

In cases where disputes arise between the parties to an international contract, overriding mandatory rules can affect the enforcement of contractual rights in three ways: as a part of the *lex fori*; the *lex causae*; or the laws of a third country that is neither the forum of the litigation nor the country of the *lex causae*. This book aims to address three difficult questions regarding overriding mandatory rules.

First, it examines the question of *which provisions qualify as overriding mandatory rules*. This is a common issue arising the three aforementioned situations. This book will establish an interpretative framework for Article 20 of the Korean Act on Private International Law (KAPIL[3]), which pertains to 'Korea's mandatory rules that should be applied to the relevant legal relationship regardless of the governing law.' This author will propose a methodology for determining which provisions qualify as overriding mandatory rules and present factors to consider when making such determinations. Then, applying the suggested methodology, it will identify which provisions in Korean law are of overriding mandatory character.

[1] Chs 1–7 of this book are the revised and updated version of the author's doctoral dissertation, 'Overriding Mandatory Rules in International Contracts' (Seoul National University, 2022), originally written in Korean. The doctoral dissertation has been published as *International Contracts and Overriding Mandatory Rules* [Gukjekyeyakgwa gukjejeok ganghaenggyujeong] (Pakyoungsa, 2022) in Korean.

[2] These are also commonly referred to as 'overriding mandatory provisions'. The two terms are used interchangeably throughout this book.

[3] KAPIL was last amended on 4 January 2022 and has been in force since 22 July 2022. Before the amendment, Art 20 was located at Art 7. The English translation of the amended act can be accessed at www.law.go.kr/engLsSc.do?menuId=1&subMenuId=21&tabMenuId=117&query=%EA%B5%AD%EC%A0%9C%EC%82%AC%EB%B2%95#. English translation of Korean Acts can be generally accessed at www.law.go.kr/LSW/eng/engMain.do?eventGubun=060124 (translated by the Korean Law Information Centre, Ministry of Government Legislation), or at elaw.klri.re.kr/eng_service/main.do (translated by the Korea Legislative Research Institute).

The existing literature and precedents have traditionally acknowledged that the overriding mandatory provisions of both the forum state and the country of the *lex causae* apply to a contract. KAPIL contains provisions on the application of overriding mandatory rules in the *lex causae* (Article 19) and in the forum state (Article 20). However, Article 20 of KAPIL does not provide a comprehensive definition of overriding mandatory rules. Indeed, Article 20 only stipulates that:

> In the light of the purpose of legislation, irrespective of the applicable laws, the mandatory provisions of the Republic of Korea shall govern the corresponding legal relations even if foreign laws are designated as applicable laws thereof under this Act.

In the Korean legal literature, there is a consensus that laws with 'special purposes' envisaged in Article 20 correspond to overriding mandatory provisions. It is generally agreed that provisions protecting public or policy interests correspond to overriding mandatory provisions, while provisions mainly concerning private interests do not.[4] However, there is no established doctrine in Korean academia regarding whether legislative provisions that protect both public and private interests qualify as overriding mandatory provisions and, if so, what the criteria are. Additionally, previous studies in Korea have fallen short of presenting a comprehensive methodology for determining whether a provision qualifies as an overriding mandatory rule and the factors that should be considered in that assessment.

This lack of clarity is also evident in judicial precedents. Recently, Korean courts have been trying an increasing number of cases in which they are faced with the question whether a specific provision in Korean law applies to contracts governed by foreign law as an overriding mandatory provision. However, lower court decisions on what qualifies as an overriding mandatory provision have lacked consistency and coherence in the factors they have considered, which hampers predictability and legal certainty in international transactions. It is important that courts be able to identify overriding mandatory provisions based on consistent standards to ensure the predictability of the rules applicable for dispute resolution. Although this book focuses on Korean law provisions that may qualify as overriding mandatory provisions, the suggested methodology and factors to consider in determining whether a provision is overriding in nature not only apply to the *lex fori* (Korea), but may also apply to the *lex causae* and the law of a third country. Notably, as various countries implement regulations with similar regulatory purposes, inter alia, competition law, data protection, and consumer protection, examining whether specific provisions of Korean law qualify as overriding mandatory rules can also provide valuable insights for foreign law (whether that be the *lex causae* or the law of a third country).

Second, this book examines the legislative and interpretive aspects of KAPIL concerning *under what conditions the overriding mandatory provisions of a third country should be considered or applied*. The country of the *lex causae* and the forum state are determined according to clear criteria – the country to which the applicable law belongs and the country where the litigation is pending, respectively. However, by definition, the term 'third country' includes all countries except the country of the applicable law and the forum state.

[4] Kwang Hyun Suk, *Annotation to Private International Law* [Gukjesabeop haeseol] (Pakyoungsa, 2013) 141; Changseon Shin and Namsoon Yoon, *New Private International Law* [Singukjesabeop je2pan], 2nd edn (Fides, 2016) 275; Chang Seop Shin, *Private International Law* [Gukjesabeop je4pan], 4th edn (Sechang, 2018) 134.

It encompasses countries that have varying degrees of connection or relevance to the contract or the parties. As a result, there is no established rule on whether or under which circumstances the law of a third country should be considered or applied. This lack of uniform criteria undermines the predictability and legal certainty of international transactions because different jurisdictions may take different approaches in the application or non-application of a third country's overriding mandatory rule. Even within a single country, outcomes may differ from case to case if there are no established standards for considering or applying the overriding mandatory provisions of a third country.

KAPIL does not include any provisions regarding the overriding mandatory provisions of a third country, and the issue has not been actively discussed in academia. Against this backdrop, this book argues that Korean courts may consider or apply the overriding mandatory provisions of a third country even in the absence of explicit statutory provisions. It then establishes an interpretive theory (*de lege lata*) on the scope and conditions for considering or applying the overriding mandatory provisions of a third country and proposes legislative measures (*de lege ferenda*) to clarify the issue.

Third, the book aims to answer the unique questions that arise when disputes referred to international commercial arbitration are related to overriding mandatory provisions. There are doubts about the applicability of overriding mandatory provisions in arbitration procedures because arbitration is based on party autonomy while overriding mandatory provisions place a limit on party autonomy. It has been widely accepted that the overriding mandatory provisions of the applicable law or the forum state apply in the context of litigation.

However, international commercial arbitration differs from litigation in several aspects: first, arbitration gives more latitude to party autonomy than litigation. Regardless of the procedural rules of the seat of arbitration, arbitrators are generally not obliged to apply mandatory provisions from substantive law there. Secondly, there are no uniform rules regarding the principle of choice of law in arbitration. Thirdly, while judges can be considered guardians of the public interest, it is uncertain whether party-appointed arbitrators assume such a role. Since arbitration is essentially based on party autonomy and consent, the ability of arbitrators to apply overriding mandatory provisions without the parties' consent is debatable. Even if they can apply such rules, the scope of the rules that should be considered or applied is also unclear. Fourthly, if arbitrators' jurisdiction does not extend to determining whether mandatory overriding rules apply, the arbitrability of disputes that involve overriding mandatory rules is called into question. In the same vein, the validity of arbitration agreements regarding disputes related to overriding mandatory provisions may also be challenged. On the other hand, it is questionable whether a court can annul or refuse to recognise or enforce an arbitral award on the ground that the arbitrator erred in applying or not applying overriding mandatory rules.

II. Research Methods

To achieve the objectives stated above, the following research methods are employed. First, the foundational theories of overriding mandatory rules, examples from foreign legislation, and domestic and foreign precedents will be critically reviewed. This author selected the United Kingdom (UK), Germany, Switzerland, the 1980 Rome Convention on the Law

Applicable to Contractual Obligation ('Rome Convention'), and the Regulation (EC) No 593/2008 of the European Parliament and the Council of 17 June 2008 on the Law Applicable to Contractual Obligations ('Rome I Regulation') as the subjects of comparative legal research. The reasons for this choice are as follows:

In the European Union (EU), legal doctrines and precedents concerning overriding mandatory rules in the forum have developed since World War I. Different countries have taken varying stances towards this matter; in particular, Germany and the UK had adopted fundamentally different approaches to overriding mandatory rules. On the one hand, the UK has respected party autonomy to the greatest extent possible, and the concept of mandatory rules, let alone overriding mandatory rules, is not common there. On the other hand, Germany has had in a place a foundation for the concept of overriding mandatory rules since the time of Friedrich Carl von Savigny, and sought to establish theories justifying the application of Nazi Germany's foreign exchange laws in foreign courts.

Due to these opposing attitudes, the application of the overriding mandatory rules of third countries during the adoption of the Rome Convention, and Article 7(1) in particular was vigorously debated. The Rome I Regulation, which is the successor to the Rome Convention, includes provisions that limit the scope of application of overriding mandatory rules from third countries even further than Article 7(1) of the Rome Convention. That was the result of compromises by Member States. Meanwhile, Switzerland is a rare example of a country that explicitly incorporates provisions about overriding mandatory rules of third countries into its private international law. Switzerland's Federal Act on Private International Law (FAPIL) has had a significant influence on Korea's jurisprudence. In this regard, it is meaningful to examine Germany, the UK, Switzerland, the Rome Convention and the Rome I Regulation.

Secondly, a historical and comparative review of jurisprudence will allow for the derivation of the criteria to determine whether provisions of Korean law are overriding mandatory rules, the method of identifying overriding mandatory rules, and the factors to be considered in that process. As an empirical demonstration of their usefulness, the criteria, methods and considerations proposed herein will be applied to assess whether selected provisions of Korean laws meet the criteria for overriding mandatory rules.

Thirdly, this book will examine the substantive law approach and the conflict-of-laws approach, the two major methodologies for considering or applying overriding mandatory rules of third countries. It will critically review and analyse theories and laws to propose optimal solutions that complement the strengths and weaknesses of each approach before making *de lege lata* and *de lege ferenda* suggestions for KAPIL.

Fourthly, in the realm of international commercial arbitration, the book will consider situations where overriding mandatory rules are at issue, dividing them into three categories, and will examine how to answer the aforementioned questions in respect of each category. During this process, various court precedents and scholarly opinions will be critically reviewed.

III. Scope of the Research

First, this book focuses on overriding mandatory rules. Although conventionally assumed to be domestic mandatory rules, overriding mandatory rules are conceptually distinct from domestic mandatory rules.[5] Domestic mandatory rules can be excluded by the parties' choice of the law of another country, while overriding mandatory rules cannot be excluded even if the parties choose the law of another country or when the objective applicable law is the law of another country.[6] Thus, the mandatory nature of overriding mandatory rules applies at the conflicts-of-laws level. This book does not attempt to tackle how domestic mandatory rules should be identified in substantive laws.[7] As such, the issue of whether a certain provision is of domestic mandatory character and the criteria for assessing that will not be covered here.[8]

Secondly, this book focuses on the study of overriding mandatory provisions in the context of *contracts*. Although overriding mandatory provisions can also exist in areas such as tort law, property law, family law and bankruptcy law, the discussion of overriding mandatory provisions has mainly focused on contracts. This book specifically examines overriding mandatory provisions that affect the validity and performance of contracts. However, within the scope of contract-related matters, special tort laws are also considered. Provisions relating to tort, bankruptcy, family law, corporate law and property law will not be examined. The selected Korean legal provisions assessed in this book are primarily chosen on the basis that their application as overriding mandatory rules has been controversial in academia or practice, specifically in the context of international contracts.

Third, this book does not discuss consumer or employee protection laws. Although these are domestic mandatory provisions, they are subject to special treatment in private

[5] The Rome Convention and Rome I Regulation, as well as KAPIL, distinguish between overriding mandatory rules and domestic mandatory rules. Domestic mandatory rules refer to the mandatory rules in pure domestic contracts and those relating to consumer protection and worker protection, such as Arts 3(3), 5 and 6 of the Rome Convention, Arts 3(4), 6 and 8 of the Rome I Regulation, and Arts 45(4), 47(1) and 48(1) of KAPIL.

[6] Section by Renner in Gralf-Peter Calliess (ed), *Rome Regulations: Commentary*, 2nd edn (Kluwer Law International, 2015) 243; In-ho Kim, 'Limitations by Mandatory Rules on the Dominance of Party Autonomy in International Contracts' (2012) 60 *Advanced Commercial Law Review* 110, 114–15; section by Dieter Martiny in Kurt Rebmann, Kurt (ed), *Münchener Kommentar zum BGB* 4th edn (Verlag Beck München, 2006), EGBGB Art 34, Rn 7. It should be noted that Art 34 of the German EGBGB was removed around the implementation of the Rome I Regulation on 17 December 2009 to incorporate the Rome I Regulation into domestic law. This commentary dates to before that revision took place.

[7] On whether a regulation corresponds to a domestic mandatory rule and the criteria for judging such rules, see Jae Hyung Kim, 'Contracts Infringing Mandatory Rules' (2004) 26 *Journal of Private Case Law Studies* 1. This author does not deny that the criteria for distinguishing between domestic mandatory rules and non-mandatory rules may overlap with the criteria for distinguishing between overriding mandatory rules and domestic mandatory rules. For example, while the legislative purpose of certain regulations may be utilised as a criterion for judging domestic mandatory rules, as in Jae Hyung Kim 'Contracts Infringing Mandatory Rules (2004) 26 *Journal of Private Case Law Studies* 1, it also plays an important role in determining overriding mandatory rules, as seen in ch 3 of this book. While the former discussion relates to what legislative purpose must be present for a provision whose violation will be denied legal effect, the latter discussion is about what legislative purpose must be present for a regulation to be applied irrespective of the applicable law.

[8] Foreigner law (*Fremdenrecht, Ausländerrecht*) must be distinguished from overriding mandatory rules. 'Foreigner law' broadly refers to substantive laws that regulate matters concerning foreign nationals within the forum country and, in a narrower sense, to laws that regulate the status of foreign nationals in the country. Although foreigner laws that self-regulate their scope of application have similarities to overriding mandatory rules, foreigner laws can be distinguished from overriding mandatory rules by the fact that they aim to treat foreigners and domestic nationals differently. Professor Kwang Hyun Suk, 'Application of Korean Social Security Law to Aliens: Shift from Alien Law to Conflict of Laws Rules' (2021) 27 *Korea Private International Law Journal* 647, 679–680 explains that where a foreigner law provides its own conflict-of-laws rules and the situations under which they apply, it should not be assessed as an overriding mandatory rule.

international law. Determining which parts of consumer or employee protection laws should be defined as overriding mandatory rules will be task for future research.

IV. Contents of the Book

This book consists of eight chapters, the first of which introduces the purpose, significance, research methods, and scope of this study, as described above.

Chapter two introduces the historical background of overriding mandatory provisions, relevant terminology, and unique issues pertaining to the *lex fori*, the *lex causae* and the law of a third country, respectively.

Chapter three examines how to determine whether a given provision is overriding mandatory in character. First, the way that the EU and various countries define overriding mandatory provisions in their legislation will be examined, followed by the legislative history of Article 20 of KAPIL. The jurisprudence of the Rome Convention and Switzerland's FAPIL, which served as a model for KAPIL, will also be assessed. Chapter three presents criteria for assessing overriding mandatory provisions and, more specifically, delves into the meaning of 'legislative purposes' in Article 20 of KAPIL. It also presents a specific methodology for determining the overriding mandatory character and identifies the factors to be considered in the test.

Chapter four applies the criteria, methodology and factors proposed in chapter three in ascertaining the overriding mandatory character of specific provisions in Korean law. It covers examples that fall within the scope of overriding mandatory provisions and examples that do not. The former are divided into: (1) provisions with extraterritorial application; (2) provisions explicitly specifying the international or territorial scope of application; and (3) provisions with a strong public interest objective and their international/spatial scope of application can be ascertained through interpretation.

Chapter five details the results of a comparative legal study on the treatment of third-country overriding mandatory provisions, including an analysis of the theoretical basis for considering or applying such rules and the substantive and conflict-of-laws approaches. This chapter explains why the substantive law approach is not appropriate and argues that the conflict-of-laws approach is more desirable in terms of predictability and legal certainty for parties to international transactions.

Building upon the comparative research in chapter five, this author argues in chapter six that it is possible to consider or apply the overriding mandatory provisions of third countries within the framework of KAPIL. This chapter examines possible methodologies for considering or applying overriding mandatory provisions. In the same chapter, the author presents the requirements and effects of considering or applying the overriding mandatory provisions of third countries so that relevant interests can be harmoniously balanced before proposing a concrete draft clause for KAPIL.

In chapter seven, cases are considered involving overriding mandatory rules in international commercial arbitration. These are divided into three categories: (1) cases where a claim based on overriding mandatory provisions is the subject of an arbitration; (2) cases where the relevant laws stipulate that disputes related to overriding mandatory provisions must be exclusively resolved by a court; and (3) cases where determining the admissibility of a claim depends on the application of overriding mandatory provisions (ie, cases where overriding mandatory provisions serve as a ground of defence). This chapter examines: (1) the arbitrability of such disputes; (2) the validity of arbitration agreements; (3) whether the arbitrator can consider or apply overriding mandatory provisions; (4) the scope of overriding mandatory provisions that can be thus considered or applied; and (5) how judicial oversight should be conducted.

Chapter eight summarises and consolidates the research findings to present a conclusion.

2

Foundational Theory of Overriding Mandatory Rules

I. Historical Background of Overriding Mandatory Rules

Friedrich Carl von Savigny, known as the father of modern private international law, stated that the parties to a contract should be able to freely choose the applicable law. However, Savigny, writing in the mid-nineteenth century, argued that the freedom of choice of law was not unlimited. He claimed the existence of mandatory rules 'that cannot be excluded by the parties' choice due to their nature, which strictly compels their application irrespective of the boundaries of different states'.[1] He distinguished mandatory rules into those governing solely individual interests and those governing interests beyond individual interests, believing that the latter could undermine the choice-of-law rules. Thus, the modern concept of overriding mandatory rules can be traced back to Savigny.[2]

After the outbreak of World War I, a debate arose in Europe regarding how to apply foreign exchange and currency control laws and confiscation laws in international legal relationships. One issue was how to consider a law enacted by the Soviet Union following the 1917 Russian Revolution that prohibited foreign debt settlement in foreign countries.[3] During the 1930s, Nazi Germany's foreign exchange law (*Devisenrecht*) and the United States' freezing order of 9 April 1940 (which froze assets in response to Germany's invasion of Denmark and Norway) had a significant impact on international transactions. That led to vigorous discussions in academia on how to handle such foreign laws. The special rules theory (*Sonderstatuttheorie*) emerged in Germany, especially concerning the territorial scope of the application of Germany's foreign exchange law. Debate focused on whether the

[1] In the original, 'Gesetze von streng positiver zwingender Natur, die eben wegen dieser Natur zu jener freien Behandlung, unabhängig von den Gränzen verschiedender Staaten, nicht geeignet sind'. Friedrich Carl von Savigny, *System des heutigen römischen Rechts, Band 8* (Veit, 1849) 33–34. An overview of Savigny's theory of choice-of-laws rules can be found in Ho Jeong Lee, 'Savigny's Private International Law Theories' (1981) 22 *Seoul Law Review* 92 and Sagi Peari, 'Savigny's Theory of Choice-of-Laws as a Principle of 'Voluntary Submission'' (2014) 64 *University of Toronto Law Journal* 106, 111–122.

[2] Ivana Kunda, *Internationally Mandatory Rules of a Third Country in the European Contracts Conflict of Laws: The Rome Convention and the Proposed Rome 1 Regulation* (Rijeka, 2015) para 22.

[3] This issue arose in the following situation: prisoners of the war against Germany had borrowed money from foreigners residing in Siberia to escape to Germany, but when creditors brought lawsuits seeking debt repayment, the debtors claimed that they could not repay the debt due to foreign exchange regulations. For details on specific cases, refer to Kunda (n 2) para 24. For a detailed historical background on the concept of overriding mandatory rules from the nineteenth century to the 1940s, see Michael Hellner, 'Third Country Overriding Mandatory Rules in the Rome I Regulation: Old Wine in New Bottles?' (2009) 5 *Journal of Private International Law* 447, 447–450; Kunda (n 2) paras 23–34; Yong Dam Kim, 'The Governing Law of the International Contracts and Mandatory Rules' (1986) 33 *Trial Reference* 6, 16–19; and Kongwoong Choi, 'Extraterritorial Jurisdiction and Private International Law' (1994) 3 *Korea Private International Law Journal* 152, 165–66.

law should be applied extraterritorially, whether it was applicable to foreigners and whether its application would be contrary to public policy of the forum country.[4]

Different views were expressed. The theories of Wilhelm Wengler and Konrad Zweigert on 'special connections' developed in the context of economic control legislation, such as foreign exchange laws during and after World War I. Wengler argued that foreign mandatory law should be considered when: (1) foreign legal provisions are intended to apply; (2) there is a 'special connection' between private law relationships and public law; and (3) public policy of the forum does not exclude the application of such rules (Special Connection Theory, *Sonderanknüpfungtheorie*).[5] Zweigert advocated taking into account foreign economic regulations, especially export and import restrictions, due to the inability of contracting parties to perform contrary actions and the need to comply with international comity.[6]

Karl Neumayer and Louis I. De Winter also acknowledged mandatory rules that restrict parties' choice of law. Neumeyer raised the question of whether to respect legislative interventions that restrict contractual freedom after World War I, particularly those imposed by foreign legislators.[7] He classified mandatory rules into two types: first, those that are applicable only when the parties have chosen domestic law as the governing law; and secondly, those that are applicable even when the parties' chosen law is foreign. He argued that the legislative intent behind the second type of mandatory rules, which prescribe the law to be applied regardless of the autonomy of the contracting parties, should be broadly respected. De Winter argued that the parties' freedom to choose the governing law should be restricted by a norm 'so crucial to its social purpose that it should be applied even in international cases'. This theory was reflected in the Dutch court's *ALNATI* judgment of 13 May 1966,[8] which formed the basis for Article 7(1) of the Rome Convention. Meanwhile, in 1966, Franceskasis defined overriding mandatory rules as 'provisions that need to be observed to protect political, social, and economic organisations', which was reflected in the 1999 *Arblade* judgment[9] of the European Court of Justice(ECJ).[10]

Article VIII Section 2(b)[11] of the Articles of Agreement of the International Monetary Fund (IMF) has also historically generated significant discussion regarding the treatment of foreign overriding mandatory regulations.[12] The provision above stipulates that exchange contracts violating the exchange control regulations of a member country, as established

[4] Various perspectives are introduced in Hellner (n 3) 449–450; Kunda (n 2) para 30.

[5] Choi (n 3) 165. The origin of Wengler's concept of a special connection can be found in Savigny's '*Sitz*' (seat) and was later reflected in Art 7(1) of the Rome Convention.

[6] Wengler and Zweigert developed their special connection theories in the context of economic regulations, including foreign exchange controls during and after World War I. Choi (n 3) 163.

[7] Refer to Kim (n 3) 17 for a brief introduction to Neumeyer's theory.

[8] *Van Nievelt, Goudriaan and Co.'s Stoomvaartmij NV v NV Hollandische Assurantie Societeit and Others* (1967) 56 Rev Crit DIP 522; 1967 NJ 3, (1968) 15 Neths Int L Rev 82. An introduction to this judgment can be found in Trevor Hartley, 'Mandatory rules in international contracts: the common law approach' (1997) 266 *Recueil des Cours* 345, 357.

[9] Joined cases C-369/96 and C-376/96, ECLI:EU:C:1999:575, [1999] ECR I-8453.

[10] Michael Wilderspin, 'Overriding Mandatory Provisions' in *Encyclopedia of Private International Law* (Elgar Publishing, 2017) 1331.

[11] 'Exchange contracts which involve the currency of any member and which are contrary to the exchange control regulations of that member maintained or imposed consistently with this Agreement shall be unenforceable in the territories of any member.'

[12] References include Lawrence Collins (ed), *Dicey, Morris & Collins: The Conflict of Laws*, vol 2, 15th edn (Sweet & Maxwell, 2012) para 37R-61 ff; Charles Proctor, *Mann on the Legal Aspect of Money*, 7th edn (Oxford University Press, 2012) paras 15.01 ff, 16.04 ff.

and maintained in accordance with this agreement, cannot be enforced within the territory of any Member State. Since the exchange control laws of a country have traditionally been regarded as typical examples of overriding mandatory rules, when Article VIII Section 2(b) of the IMF Agreement is applicable, member countries are obliged under the agreement to implement the foreign exchange control laws of other member countries.[13] Thus, there has been much discussion about how to interpret the scope of the foreign exchange regulations that must be respected under Article VIII Section 2(b) of the IMF Agreement – or in other words, how to define 'exchange contracts' and how to treat foreign exchange control regulations that do not fall within its purview.[14]

II. Terminology

The terms for overriding mandatory rules differ between countries, and in many countries, separate terms are used for overriding mandatory rules and domestic mandatory rules. In the United Kingdom (UK), the terms 'overriding mandatory norms' or 'overriding statutes' have been used since the Rome I Regulation.[15] The concept of overriding mandatory rules was not well known in the UK until the adoption of the Rome Convention. But following the English language version of the Rome Convention, which defined these rules simply as 'mandatory rules' without distinguishing between overriding and domestic mandatory rules,[16] 'mandatory rules' has been used to refer to both domestic and overriding mandatory rules in English language literature.[17]

In Germany, the term '*Eingriffsnormen*', meaning 'interfering norms' or 'intervening norms', is used to refer to overriding mandatory rules, and was popularised by

[13] Kwang Hyun Suk, 'The Application of Foreign Exchange Control Law and Other Internationally Mandatory Rules of Third Countries in International Financial Transactions: Including Article VIII.2(b) of the Articles of Agreement of the International Monetary Fund' (2020) 26 *Korea Private International Law Journal* 353, 363 describes this as both a conflict-of-laws provision and a substantive law provision.

[14] The UK defines the concept of 'exchange contracts' narrowly as 'agreements for the exchange of currency between two countries'. *Wilson, Smithett and Cope Ltd v Terruzzi* (1976) QB 703, 714, 725 (CA). In contrast, civil law jurisdictions such as Germany, the Netherlands and France interpret 'exchange contracts' broadly as being any action that affects a country's foreign exchange resources. An introduction to these divergent positions can be found in Proctor (n 12) para 15.27; section by Martin Zwickel in Dieter Martiny (ed) *Internationales Vertragsrecht*, 9th edn (Ottoschmidt, 2022), Rn 5.162; and Suk (n 13) 364–65.

[15] Paul Torremans (ed), *Cheshire, North & Fawcett: Private International Law*, 15th edn (Oxford University Press, 2017) 744; *The Soldiers, Sailors, Airmen and Families Association Forces Help and another v Allgemeines Krankenhaus Viersen GmbH* [2022] UKSC 29 [34]. However, Jan Kleinheisterkamp, 'The Impact of Internationally Mandatory Rules on the Enforceability of Arbitration Agreements' (2009) 3 *World Arbitration & Mediation Review* 91 uses the term 'overriding mandatory rules'.

[16] The English, German, Danish and Portuguese versions of the Rome Convention did not distinguish between the terms for overriding and domestic mandatory rules. In contrast, the Dutch, French, Italian, Spanish and Swedish versions used distinct terms.

[17] Examples of the term 'mandatory rules' being used to refer to overriding mandatory rules can be found in references such as Lawrence Collins (ed), *Dicey, Morris & Collins*, vol 1 (2012) paras 1-053, 1-054; Richard Plender and Michael Wilderspin, *The European Contracts Convention: The Rome Convention on the Choice of Law for Contracts* (Sweet & Maxwell, 2001) para 9-01; and Peter Kaye, *The New Private International Law of Contract of the European Community* (Dartmouth, 1993) 240. The term 'mandatory rules' is also used in the United States. [Reference: Hossein Fazilatfar, *Overriding Mandatory Rules in International Commercial Arbitration* (Edward Elgar Publishing, 2019) 9; Jeffrey Maurice Waincymer, 'International Commercial Arbitration and the Application of Mandatory Rules of Law' (2009) 5 *Asian International Arbitration Journal* 1, 6].

Karl Neumayer in the 1950s.[18] In Article 34 of the former German Civil Code Enforcement Act (*Einführungsgesetz zum Bürgerlichen Gesetzbuche*, EGBGB) and Article 7 of the German version of the Rome Convention, the term '*zwingende Normen*', meaning 'mandatory rules', was used to refer to domestic mandatory rules. It signifies provisions that cannot be derogated from with the parties' agreement. On the other hand, '*international zwingende Normen*' (as opposed to '*einfach zwingende Normen*' for domestic mandatory rules) refers to overriding mandatory rules. In Germany, the *Ingmar* judgment[19] of the ECJ played a significant role in popularising this term. It is translated into English as 'internationally mandatory rules'.[20]

In Switzerland, the terms used for overriding mandatory rules are '*lois d'application immédiate*' or '*Eingriffsnormen*'.[21] In France, they are referred to as '*lois de police*' or '*lois d'application immédiate*'.[22] In the Rome I Regulation, they are referred to as 'overriding mandatory provisions'. The Hague Conference on Private International Law, in its Principles on Choice of Law in International Commercial Contracts, also uses the term 'overriding mandatory provision'. In Korea, depending on the context, overriding mandatory rules can be referred to as 'interfering norms' [ganseopgyubeom][23] or 'absolute mandatory rules' [jeoldaejeok ganghaenggyujeong].[24] However, the term 'international mandatory rules' [gukjejeok ganghaenggyugjoeng] is more commonly used.[25]

As the term 'overriding mandatory rules' properly reflects that such rules 'override' the usual choice-of-law principle, I will generally use the term 'overriding mandatory rules'

[18] Paul Hauser, *Eingriffsnormen in der Rom-I Verordnung* (Mohr Siebeck, 2012) 5–6.

[19] *Ingmar GB Ltd v Eaton Leonard Technologies Inc* Case C-381/98, ECLI:EU:C:2000:605, [2000] ECR I-09305.

[20] Andrea Bonomi, 'Mandatory Rules in Private International Law – The Quest for Uniformity of Decisions in a Global Environment' (1999) 1 *Yearbook of Private International Law* 215, 223.

[21] Section by Frank Vischer and Corinne Widmer Lüchinger in Markus Müller-Chen (ed), *Zürcher Kommentar zum IPRG*, Bd I-1, 3rd edn (Schulthess, 2018) Art 18, Rn 3; Art 19, Rn 5.

[22] Collins (n 17) para 1-054; Kunda (n 2) 11.

[23] Choi (n 3) 152, 153; Yongjin Kim, 'External Effect of Mandatory Rules' (1998) 3 *Korea Private International Law Journal* 703, 707.

[24] Choon Soo An, 'International zwingende Bestimmungen im IPR – Theorien und die Bedeutung von Artt. 6, 7 IPR Koreas' (2011) 23 *Kookmin Law Review* 189, 192.

[25] eg, Kwang Hyun Suk, 'Legal Issues in International Arbitration Related to International Guarantees That Are Unauthorized for Foreign Exchange' [Oehwanheogareul badji anihan gukjebojeunggwa gwallyeonhan gukjesa-beopsangui munjejeom] (1994) 429 *Korean Lawyers Association Journal* 142, 150; Kwang Hyun Suk, 'International Employment Contracts and Protection of Employees under the New Conflict of Laws Act' (2001) 13 *Journal of Labour Law* 1, 8; Kwang Hyun Suk, 'Some Issues on Korea's Accession to the UNIDROIT Convention on Stolen or Illegally Exported Cultural Objects' (2009) 15 *Korea Private International Law Journal* 324, 328; Kwang Hyun Suk, *Annotation to Private International Law* [Gukjesabeop haeseol] (Pakyoungsa, 2013) 140; Kwang Hyun Suk, 'The Role of the Private International Law Act and the Cultural Property Protection Act of Korea as Means of Protecting Cultural Property from International Illicit Transactions and the Proposal for Improvement' (2015) 56 *Seoul Law Journal* 117; Kwang Hyun Suk, 'Comment on a Lower Court Judgment Dealing with Law Applicable to International Acquisition Agreement – Are the Provisions of the Korean Commercial Code Requiring Resolution of Special Shareholders' Meeting Internationally Mandatory Rules?' (2018) 53 *Kyung Hee Law Journal* 119, 120; Suk (n 13) 353; Junhyok Jang, 'Internationally Mandatory Rules – A Comparative Study of Article 7 of the Rome Convention, Articles 18 and 19 of the Swiss Private International Law, and Article 7 of the Korean Private International Law' (2007) 75 *International Trade Law* 71; Junhyok Jang, 'Conflict's Mandatory Character as the Key Element of Internationally Mandatory Rules' (2007) 19 *SungKyunKwan Law Review* 563, 564; In-ho Kim, 'Limitations by Mandatory Rules on the Dominance of Party Autonomy in International Contracts' (2012) 60 *Advanced Commercial Law Review* 110; Seoung Jae Yu, 'Retirement Benefit Entitlement for Illegally Dispatched Foreign Workers' (2004) *Labour Law Monthly* 19; Hong Sik Chung, 'Applicability of Overriding Mandatory Rules in International Arbitration' (2013) 23 *Journal of Arbitration Studies* 3, 4.

in this book. But in the context of certain jurisdictions, I will also use the terms most commonly used there.

A separate but related matter is how to treat the 'application (*Anwendung*)' and 'consideration' of such rules. 'Application' refers to the enforcement of overriding mandatory rules as rules of law. 'Consideration' refers to the evaluation of overriding mandatory rules as factual circumstances under the provisions of general substantive law.[26] This is referred to as 'substantive law consideration' (*materielle Berücksichtigung*).

III. Specific Issues with Different Types of Overriding Mandatory Rules

Overriding mandatory rules can be classified by their originating country, either: (1) the forum country; (2) the country of governing law; or (3) a third country. The question of which rules of law are of overriding mandatory character is shared by all three categories. However, the grounds and requirements for application of such rules depend on the country to which they belong.

A. Overriding Mandatory Rules of the Forum

This section briefly examines the requirements and effects of the application of overriding mandatory rules of the forum as set out in the Rome Convention, the Rome I Regulation, German and English law before the Rome I Regulation, Switzerland's Federal Act on Private International Law (FAPIL) and Article 20 of Korean Act on Private International Law (KAPIL) (revised by Act No 18670, 4 January 2022).

i. Requirements for Application

a. Comparative Study

Most countries recognise the application of overriding mandatory rules of the forum, even in the absence of express provisions.[27]

Article 7(2) of the Rome Convention states that 'nothing in this Convention shall restrict the application of the rules of the law of the forum in a situation where they are mandatory

[26] Section by Dieter Martiny in Kurt Rebmann (ed), *Münchener Kommentar zum BGB*, 4th edn (Verlag Beck München, 2006), EGBGB Art 34, Rn 70; Lisa Günther, *Die Anwendbargkeit ausländischer Eingriffnormen im Lichter der Rom I- und Rom II Verordnungen* (Verlag Alma Mater, 2011) 27–28; Suk (n 13) 375; Fazilatfar (n 17) 138–39.

[27] Kwang Hyun Suk, 'Review of the Bill to Amend Private International Law – General Provisions and Corporations' [Seopoesabeop gaejeongbeomnyulanui geomto-chongchikgwa beopin] (2010) 6 *Korea Private International Law Journal* 181; Choon Soo An, 'Review of the Amendment Bill on the Private International Law – General Provisions and Corporations' (2001) 6 *Korea Private International Law Journal* 167, 211; Choon Soo An, *Private International Law* (Bobmunsa, 2017) 149; Heung Sub Choi, *Korean Private International Law I* (Korean Studies Information, 2019) 205. For detailed legislative examples of the application of overriding mandatory rules of the forum in various countries, see Daniel Girsberger, Thomas Kadner Graziano and Jan Neels (eds), *Choice of Law in International Commercial Contracts* (Oxford University Press, 2021) para 1.472.

irrespective of the law otherwise applicable to the contract'. This provision clarifies that the Convention does not affect the mandatory rules of the forum. Article 9(2) of the Rome I Regulation similarly states that 'nothing in this Regulation shall restrict the application of the overriding mandatory provisions of the law of the forum'. This provision establishes the applicability of the overriding mandatory rules of the forum. Although this is neither stipulated in Article 7(2) of the Rome Convention nor in Article 9(2) of the Rome I Regulation, the requirement of a connection between the case and the law of the forum is implied in the jurisprudence of both instruments.[28] This requirement is referred to as 'connection (proximity) to the forum (*Inlandsbeziehung*)', indicating that the matters regulated by the overriding mandatory rules of the forum fall within the legislative jurisdiction of the respective country.[29] In both the Rome Convention and the Rome I Regulation, therefore, the objective requirement of a connection to the forum is necessary for the application of the mandatory rules of the forum.

Before the adoption of the Rome Convention, the concepts of mandatory rules or overriding mandatory rules were not traditionally recognised in English law. However, English law did acknowledge that English rules of law could be applied irrespective of the governing law, which it explained as a 'crystallised public policy'.[30] Such provisions were seen to apply in cases where there is a territorial connection (place of work, residence, effects of transactions, etc) with the forum.[31] In Germany[32] and Switzerland, the application of mandatory rules of the forum has generally been recognised under the requirement of 'connection to the forum'.[33]

b. Article 20 of KAPIL

Article 20 of KAPIL states that:

> In the light of the purpose of legislation, irrespective of the applicable laws, the mandatory provisions of the Republic of Korea shall govern the corresponding legal relations even if foreign laws are designated as applicable laws thereof under this Act.

This indicates that the overriding mandatory provisions of the forum should apply, which is consistent with English, German and Swiss laws, and the Rome Convention and the Rome I Regulation. It is also possible to explain the application of overriding mandatory provisions

[28] Kaye (n 17) 262; Jang (n 25) 80, 84.

[29] Rebmann (n 26), Rom I-VO Art 9, Rn 124. For detailed description on legislative jurisdiction, see Kwang Hyun Suk, 'Cloud Computing: Regulation, Jurisdiction, and Applicable Law' [Keullaudeu keompyutingui gyuje mit gwanhalgwongwa jungeobeop] (2011) 7 *Law & Technology* 3, 16–25; Rebmann (ibid) Rn 5, 10; Ulrich Magnus and Peter Mankowski (eds), *Commentary: Rome I Regulation*, European Commentaries on Private International Law, vol 2 (Verlag Dr Otto Schmidt, 2017) para 96.

[30] Collins (n 17) para 1-061. The private international law of continental Europe followed a statute-centred approach, while the methodology of the common law system relied more on the flexible concept of public policy. Hartley (n 8) 350–56.

[31] Kaye (n 17) 245.

[32] EGBGB Art 34 *Zwingende Vorschriften* (before it was repealed to implement the Rome I Regulation): '*Dieser Unterabschnitt berührt nicht die Anwendung der Bestimmungen des deutschen Rechts, die ohne Rücksicht auf das auf den Vertrag anzuwendende Recht den Sachverhalt zwingend regeln*.' This provision was adopted in German law to implement Art 7(2) of the Rome Convention.

[33] Rebmann (n 26), EGBGB Art 34, Rn 134; Rebmann (n 29), Rom I-VO Art 9, Rn 124; section by Frank Vischer and Corinne Widmer Lüchinger in Müller-Chen (n 21) Art 18, Rn 8.

of the forum with the doctrine of territoriality in public international law. However, there may be overriding mandatory provisions of the forum that do not possess a public law character, and it is often difficult to distinguish between public law and private law. Therefore, the better approach is to consider the application of overriding mandatory provisions of the forum based on a 'close connection' to the forum.[34] This close connection is referred to as 'connection to the forum' [naegukgwanryunseong].[35] However, since most of the laws of the forum would fall within its legislative jurisdiction, there are likely to be few cases where the presence or absence of legislative jurisdiction is a problem. In cases where a certain provision does not explicitly define its scope of application, its scope should be interpreted on the limited basis of that 'connection to the forum'.[36]

ii. Effect

In applying overriding mandatory provisions of the forum, the question arises whether the effect of the disputed contract or legal act should be determined according to the *lex causae* or the *lex fori*.[37] One view is that the effect of an act violating the overriding mandatory provisions of the forum should be determined under the *lex fori* since it is related to the legislative intent of the forum.[38] On the other hand, it is also contended that the effect of applying overriding mandatory provisions of the forum should be determined according to *lex causae*.[39]

However, a more persuasive view is that whereas issues regarding the validity or invalidity of the contract should be assessed by the *lex fori*, other subsequent consequences of the rights arising from there (for example, restitution) should be determined according to the governing law of the contract.[40] This approach is plausible because it balances the parties' interests and the public interest. Determining the legal effect of the act that violated the overriding mandatory rules of the forum by *lex fori* ensures that the legislative purpose of the overriding mandatory rule is served.[41] On the other hand, issues such as restitution or damages arising from the nullification of the contract are meant to serve private interests. Therefore, it is considered reasonable to follow the governing law of the relevant legal relationship to ensure predictability and party autonomy.

[34] Kwang Hyun Suk, 'Comments on the Private International Law Cases of the Supreme Court of Korea in 2004' (2004) 10 *Korea Private International Law Journal* 429, 437; Kim (n 23) 710.

[35] Suk (n 34) 437; Kim (n 23) 710; Rebmann (n 26), EGBGB Art 34, Rn 136.

[36] This plays a significant role in determining whether a given rule is an overriding mandatory provision. See ch 3, II, B, ii for more details.

[37] A similar question arises in the application of a third-country overriding mandatory rules.

[38] Suk (1994) (n 25) 160; Kwang Hyun Suk, 'General Issues with Amended Private International Law' [Gaejeong gukjesabeopui chongnonjeok munje] (2001) 536 *Korean Lawyers Association Journal* 5, 40–41.

[39] Hauser (n 18) 103 takes this view regarding the application of a third country's overriding mandatory rules.

[40] Section by Ulrich Magnus in Julius von Staudinger and Norbert Habermann, *Staudingers Kommentar Zum Bürgerlichen Gesetzbuch Mit Einführungsgesetz Und Nebengesetzen: Einführungsgesetz zum Bürgerlichen Gesetzbuche/IPR* (Sellier-De Gruyter, 2002) Rn 82; Rebmann (n 26), EGBGB Art 34, Rn 73; Kim (n 25) 125; Jang (n 25) 87.

[41] In Korea, many laws with a public law character (which may be characterised as overriding mandatory rules) do not specify the private law effect when they are violated. Therefore, it is necessary to examine the legislative intent of the overriding mandatory provisions in the forum to assess the validity of contracts that violate those provisions.

B. Overriding Mandatory Provisions of the *Lex Causae*

It is generally recognised that overriding mandatory provisions of the *lex causae* apply, but there are conflicting views on the basis for their application.[42] After examining why the theory of the governing law ('*Schuldstatutstheorie*' or '*Einheitstheorie*') is a better approach than the Special Connection Theory (*Sonderanknüpfung* theory), this section will suggest how Article 19 of KAPIL should be interpreted.

i. *Conflicting Views:* Einheitstheorie *versus* Sonderanknüpfung

The Rome Convention and Rome I Regulation do not establish separate connecting principles regarding the overriding mandatory provisions of the *lex causae*. This raises the question of the basis for applying the overriding mandatory provisions of *lex causae*. According to *Einheitstheorie*, when the parties choose the law of a particular country as the governing law, the overriding mandatory provisions apply as a part of the governing law.[43] This view is persuasive considering the reality of international transactions. In the era of globalisation, when international commerce thrives, parties to international transactions are often aware of the limitations imposed by the overriding mandatory provisions of the country whose law they chose, such as foreign exchange laws, international trade laws and competition laws. It would be unnatural to ignore these provisions when considering the governing law.

Jurists in many different countries have also adopted this approach. In the past, the German courts considered that the overriding mandatory provisions of the governing law are applied as part of the governing law, regardless of whether they are of public or private law nature.[44] The English courts also held that when the parties choose the applicable law, they have chosen it as a whole including the overriding mandatory rules.[45] In this regard, foreign exchange controls, export controls, price controls and moratoriums have been applied as overriding mandatory provisions of the applicable law.[46] The Federal Court of Switzerland has stated that overriding mandatory rules that intervene in private law relationships should not be ruled inapplicable solely because they have a public law character.[47,48]

[42] For a detailed discussion of conflicting views, see Rebmann (n 26), EGBGB Art 34, Rn 39 et seq; Rebmann (n 29), Rome I Regulation Art 9, Rn 36 et seq; Günther (n 26) 15; Suk (2015) (n 25) 142; Jang (n 25) 571.

[43] Kim (n 23) 713.

[44] RG, 10 May 1884, RGZ 12, 34. Since in this case the law governing the consumer credit agreement was French law, the overriding mandatory provisions of French civil law declaring the nullity of gambling debts were applied as part of the governing law. However, this principle was abandoned when Germany's Federal Court of Justice declared in a leading case in 1959 that the foreign exchange control law of the governing law country cannot be applied because it is a foreign public law. BGHZ 31, 367.

[45] *Rex v International Trustee for the Protection of Bondholders Akt* [1937] 2 All ER 164, [1937] AC 500; *St Pierre v South American Stores (Gath & Chavels) Ltd* [1937] 3 ALL ER 407, 422 (CA); *Kahler v Midland Bank Ltd* [1950] AC 24.

[46] Frederick Alexander Mann, 'Conflict of laws and public law' (1971) 132 *Recueil des Cours* 109, 184–85.

[47] BGE 80 II 31, 367 et seq.

[48] This is the predominant view in France and Belgium. See section by Martin Zwickel in Dieter Martiny (ed) *Internationales Vertragsrecht*, 9th edn (Ottoschmidt, 2022), Rn 5.23.

Under the Rome Convention, *Einheitstheorie* was the prevailing view.[49] *Einheitstheorie* contends that while the Rome Convention assumed that the overriding mandatory rules of the country of applicable law were part of applicable law, it did not provide a connecting principle for such overriding mandatory rules. The same view prevails under the Rome I Regulation.[50] Although the Hague Principles on International Commercial Contracts do not explicitly provide for this, it is presumed that the overriding mandatory provisions of the country of *lex causae* are to be applied as part of the governing law.[51]

On the other hand, the Special Connection (*Sonderanknüpfung*) theory argues that since overriding mandatory provisions pursues the public interest and private international law pursues private interests, there must be a separate connecting principle for overriding mandatory provisions.[52] In Germany, the Special Connection Theory is the majority view,[53] and there is an opinion that the Rome Convention and Rome I Regulation have adopted the theory of special connection regarding the overriding mandatory provisions of the country of origin.[54] There have been conflicting views in Swiss law, but the view that overriding mandatory provisions of the governing law are specially connected has gained recognition.[55]

The Special Connection Theory presupposes that, apart from the law of the forum, the law of the country of *lex causae* or a third country should be treated equally. However, there is a significant difference in predictability between the law of the country of *lex causae* and the law of a third country from the parties' perspective. Therefore, it may be justified to apply the overriding mandatory provisions of the governing law under less stringent conditions than a third country's overriding mandatory rules. Moreover, when the overriding mandatory provisions of the *lex causae* have less of a connection to the case, they are less likely to apply: If the facts of the case are not related to the country of governing law, it is more likely that the case will not fall under the legislative jurisdiction of that country, so the facts may be out of the scope of application of the provisions in question.[56]

Therefore, explaining the basis for the application of the overriding mandatory provisions of the governing law through *Einheitstheorie* is more in line with the parties' intentions. It is also theoretically more concise.

[49] Staudinger and Habermann (n 40) Rn 20. Kwang Hyun Suk, 'International Contract Law' (1999) 4 *Korea Private International Law Journal* 330; Suk (1994) (n 25) 159; Suk (2015) (n 25) 139–40 also concludes that the Rome Convention takes the position that the overriding mandatory provisions of the country of the *lex causae* are applied as part of the governing law.

[50] An (n 24) 206; Proctor (n 12) paras 15.11, 16.02.

[51] Girsberger, Graziano and Neels (n 27) para 1.495; HCCH, 'Commentary on the Principles on Choice of Law in International Commercial Contracts' (2015) para 11.14.

[52] Frank Vischer, 'General course on private international law' (1992) 232 *Recueil des Cours* 21, 180.

[53] See section by Martin Zwickel in Dieter Martiny (ed), *Internationales Vertragsrecht* (2022) Rn 5.23.

[54] Günther (n 26) 16.

[55] Müller-Chen (n 21) Art 19, Rn 6. Conversely, Pascal Grolimund (ed), *Basler Kommentar Interntionales Privatrecht*, 4th edn (Helbnig Lichtenhahn Verlag, 2021) Art 19, Rn 16 adopts the *Einheitstheorie*.

[56] For example, the overriding mandatory provision of the Housing Grants, Construction and Regeneration Act 1996 in the UK, which is related to construction contracts, applies regardless of the governing law of the construction contract if the construction site is in the UK (Art 104(6) and (7), of the same act). Therefore, even if the governing law of the construction contract is determined as UK law, if the facts of the case do not have any connection to the UK (that is, if the construction site is not located in the UK) the aforementioned law will not apply.

ii. Article 19 of KAPIL

Article 19 of KAPIL states that when foreign provisions are designated as applicable laws under this Act, the application of such foreign provisions should not be excluded simply because they have the nature of public law.[57]

Traditionally, public law had been excluded from the scope of private international law. Therefore, foreign public law had no application in the forum (the so-called 'principle of non-application of foreign public law').[58] Article 19 explicitly excludes this principle. However, it should be noted that the application of foreign law in private international law does not mean that the direct enforcement of foreign legal regulations is allowed in the forum state. Applying foreign law as overriding mandatory rules means considering its effects on specific legal relationships (*Reflexwirkung*). In this context, foreign law can still be applied under Article 19 of KAPIL, even if it has a public nature, as long as it affects the relevant private legal relationship.[59]

Under Article 19 of KAPIL, the application of overriding mandatory rules of the country of *lex causae* can be explained by both *Einheitstheorie*[60] and the Special Connection Theory.[61] However, for reasons mentioned earlier, *Einheitstheorie* is more convincing. A lower court

[57] This is the same content as the Resolution adopted by the 20th Committee of the Institut de Droit International in Wiesbaden, Germany, on 11 August 1975. According to Art A.I.1. of this Resolution, the provisions of foreign laws with a public law character designated under the rule of conflict-of-laws shall not prevent the application of that provision, subject however to the fundamental reservation of public policy. The rationale behind this is that there is no persuasive theoretical or practical basis for the principles of non-application of foreign public laws or absolute territoriality. (The aforementioned resolution can be accessed at www.idi-iil.org/app/uploads/2017/06/1975_wies_04_en.pdf.)

[58] The principle of non-application of foreign public law was declared in the leading German case of BGHZ 31, 367. In the case, the defendant borrowed money from W, both being residents of East Germany at the time. But later, East Germany enacted a law stating that the transfer of claims would be invalid unless approved by the East German authorities if the assignee of the claim is a resident of West Germany. Subsequently, the defendant immigrated to West Germany, and W transferred the claim to the plaintiff, who was a resident of West Germany. When the plaintiff sought payment of the borrowed money from the defendant, the defendant argued that the transfer of the claim was invalid as it violated foreign exchange regulations in East Germany. The court stated that it is necessary to distinguish between conflict-of-laws of private and public laws. In the case of public law, the principle of territoriality applies, so foreign laws cannot be applied. However, as an exception, if an international treaty (such as the IMF Agreement) mandates the application of such laws or if a foreign country has the authority to enact such provisions, and if the provisions of foreign law serve to regulate the interests of individuals or private relationships wholly or partially, they may be applied under specific conditions. In this case, the court concluded that East Germany's foreign exchange regulations were intended for the economic and political purposes of East Germany and did not apply to the case in question. In Switzerland, there are precedents that deny the application of third-country law based on the theory of non-application of foreign public law or territoriality and Swiss public policy, such as BGE 68 II 203, BGE 76 II 33, and BGE 80 II 49.There is a similar principle in English law, which does not allow the enforcement of foreign law provisions related to criminal law, tax law, or other kinds of public law. This is known as the 'revenue rule'. For more details, refer to Collins (n 17) para 5R-003; Mann (n 46) 166–68. Relevant precedents include *Huntington v Attrill*, (1893) AC 150, 155–56; *Government of India v Taylor* (1955) AC 491; *Attorney General of New Zealand v Ortiz* (1984) AC 1, 2; *Williams and Humbert v W & H Trade Marks (Jersey) Ltd* (1986) AC 386, 394, 401; *Re State of Norway's Application* (1987) QB 433, 477–78 (CA), (1990) 1 AC 273.

[59] Suk (n 27) 179; Choi (n 27) 208.

[60] Ho Young Song, 'Study on the Legal Policy for Restitution of Illegally Exported Cultural Properties in Foreign Countries' (2004) 11 *Journal of Comparative Private Law* 229, 254; Hong Sik Chung (n 25) 7; Jong Hyeok Lee, 'Prospectus Liability in Cross-border Securities Offering: Focusing on the Choice-of-law Rules' (Doctorate degree dissertation, Seoul National University, 2019) 204–05.

[61] An (n 24) 210.

in Korea held that Argentina's foreign exchange controls would naturally be applied as part of the governing law,[62] which can be explained from the perspective of *Einheitstheorie*.

As seen here, when applying the overriding mandatory provisions of the country of *lex causae*, there is no issue regarding which country's law should apply to determine the effects of the contract. That is true because the overriding mandatory rules of the country of *lex causae* and the governing law of the contract belong to the same legal system.

C. The Specificity of a Third Country's Overriding Mandatory Rules

As seen in the previous subsections, the overriding mandatory rules of the forum must apply as a matter of the forum's policy, while the overriding mandatory rules of the governing law must apply as part of the governing law. Therefore, there is less doubt about the requirement for applying those rules. In those cases, it is more critical to identify which legal rules are overriding mandatory provisions.[63]

On the other hand, third country overriding mandatory provisions, by definition, do not inherently have a strong connection to either the forum state or the country of *lex causae*. The category of third country encompasses both countries related to the contract or the case and countries unrelated to them. That raises the question of whether the forum court should consider or apply the overriding mandatory provisions of a third country at all, and if so, under what conditions. That issue will be examined in chapters five and six.

[62] Seoul High Court, Judgment of 6 March 2009, Case No 2007Na122966. In this case, after the Argentinian Government abolished the fixed exchange rate between the peso and the US dollar, causing the peso to plummet to one-third of the dollar's value, an Argentinian financial institution demanded repayment of a loan denominated in dollars at a 1:1 exchange rate. The Seoul High Court applied Argentinian law as part of the governing law without specifying any additional requirements (it did not examine whether there was a special connection between the case and the regulation). For an introduction and analysis of this judgment, refer to Suk (n 13) 386.

[63] In relation to the task of identification, see chs 3 and 4.

3

Identifying Overriding Mandatory Rules

Article 20 of the Korean Act on Private International Law (KAPIL) does not explicitly define 'overriding mandatory rules'. In Europe, however, efforts have been made to define such rules in legislation. Since Article 20 of KAPIL reflects the Rome Convention and Swiss Federal Act on Private International Law (FAPIL), discussions in Europe serve as a reference for the interpretation of Article 20 of KAPIL. In this chapter, I will first examine how the Rome Convention, the European Court of Justice (ECJ) and the Rome I Regulation define overriding mandatory rules. Based on that, I will suggest the definition and criteria for determining overriding mandatory provisions and will also suggest the methodology and factors to be considered in such a determination under KAPIL.

I. Comparative Review of the Definition of 'Overriding Mandatory Rules'

A. The Rome Convention

The Rome Convention does not provide a direct definition of 'overriding mandatory rules'. However, an indirect definition can be derived from Article 7, which deals with third country overriding mandatory rules. Article 7(1) provides that:

> When applying under this Convention the law of a country, effect may be given to the mandatory rules of the law of another country with which the situation has a close connection, if and in so far as, under the law of the latter country, those rules must be applied whatever the law applicable to the contract. In considering whether to give effect to these mandatory rules, regard shall be had to their nature and purpose and to the consequences of their application or non-application.

Article 7(2) of the Rome Convention, which deals with overriding mandatory rules of the forum, states that 'Nothing in this Convention shall restrict the application of the rules of the law of the forum in a situation where they are mandatory irrespective of the law otherwise applicable to the contract.'

Considering both Article 7(1) and Article 7(2) of the Rome Convention, overriding mandatory rules refer to 'mandatory rules that should be applied regardless of the governing law which cannot be derogated from by the parties' agreement, and take precedence over the chosen governing law and the law determined by the Rome Convention.'[1]

[1] Richard Plender and Michael Wilderspin, *The European Contracts Convention: The Rome Convention on the Choice of Law for* Contracts (Sweet & Maxwell, 2001) para 9-07; Paul Torremans (ed), Cheshire, North & Fawcett: Private International Law, 15th edn (Oxford University Press, 2017) 744.

B. Case Law at the European Court of Justice

The issue dealt with in the *Arblade* case[2] was the extent to which Belgium's mandatory laws could limit the freedom of services under the Treaty Establishing the European Community. The ECJ classified the Belgian provisions as '*ordre public* legislation' of the Member State that could be deemed necessary to protect its political, social and economic order, thus requiring compliance from all individuals present in its national territory and all legal relationships within the state.[3] The Court found that the Treaty explicitly provides exceptions to the freedom of the community and that the value of the Member State's domestic law can be considered when deemed appropriate and when there is a paramount reason relating to the public interest.[4] This interpretation of '*ordre public* legislation' by the ECJ had a significant impact on the definition provided in Article 9(1) of the Rome I Regulation.[5]

Subsequently, the ECJ addressed the definition of overriding mandatory provisions directly in *United Antwerp Maritime Agencies NV v Navigation Maritime Bulgare (Unamar)*.[6] In *Unamar*, the question arose as to whether a law enacted by Belgium to implement the EU Agency Directive[7] provided stronger protection than expected by the Directive and could qualify as an overriding mandatory provision.[8] The ECJ affirmed that it could.[9] In this regard, the ECJ stated that a provision may qualify as an overriding mandatory provision when it 'protects an interest judged to be essential by the member state concerned'.[10] The Court considered 'not only the exact terms of the law, but also of its general structure and of all the circumstances in which that law was adopted'.[11] It further emphasised that the interpretation of overriding mandatory provisions should be restrictive.[12]

C. Rome I Regulation

Article 9(1) Rome I Regulation defines overriding mandatory rules as

> provisions the respect for which is regarded as crucial by a country for safeguarding its public interests, such as its political, social or economic organisation, to such an extent that they are

[2] Joined cases C-369/96 and C-376/96, ECLI:EU:C:1999:575, [1999] ECR I-8453.

[3] At [30].

[4] At [31].

[5] Michael Wilderspin, 'Overriding Mandatory Provisions' in Encyclopedia of Private International Law (Elgar Publishing, 2017) 1331. However, the main purpose of the *Arblade* judgment was to declare the primacy of European Community law over the 'ordre public legislation' of Member States rather than to define overriding mandatory provisions. The definition of 'ordre public legislation' made in Arblade was based on Belgian law submitted to the ECJ in this case, specifically relying on Phocion Francescakis' 'lois d'application immediate' in French law. Section by Andrea Bonomi in Ulrich Magnus and Peter Mankowski (eds), Commentary: Rome I Regulation, European Commentaries on Private International Law, vol 2 (Verlag Dr Otto Schmidt, 2017) Art 9(55).

[6] Case C-184/12, ECLI:EU:C:2013:663.

[7] Council Directive 86/653/EEC of 18 December 1986 on the coordination of the laws of the Member States relating to self-employed commercial agents.

[8] Whereas the Directive applied only to agents for the sale or purchase of goods, the Belgian law concerned with agents in shipping service. This could have been seen as falling outside the scope of the Directive. Michael Wilderspin, *The European Private International Law of Obligations*, 6th edn (Sweet & Maxwell, 2023) para 12-009.

[9] At [51]–[52].

[10] At [49]–[50].

[11] At [49]–[50].

[12] At [49].

applicable to any situation falling within their scope, irrespective of the law otherwise applicable to the contract under this Regulation.[13]

This definition draws on the *Arblade* case[14] while adding the term 'public interests', which was not present in *Arblade*. It is contended that this wording should be seen as an exhaustive list and that provisions that aim to regulate only private interests should not fall within the category of overriding mandatory provisions.[15]

Article 9(1) requires that the provision be 'regarded as crucial by a country' to be considered an overriding mandatory provision. Consequently, determining whether a provision is an overriding mandatory provision depends on whether protecting that interest is essential for the member state when the law was enacted.[16] That restriction aims to block Member States from adopting overriding mandatory provisions that are overly broad.[17]

II. Article 20 of KAPIL

Article 20 of KAPIL states in a section titled 'Mandatory Application of Acts of the Republic of Korea' that

> in the light of the purpose of legislation, irrespective of the applicable laws, the mandatory provisions of the Republic of Korea shall govern the corresponding legal relations even if foreign laws are designated as applicable laws thereof under this Act.

Although the term 'overriding mandatory provision' is not used in Article 20, the provision is still understood to refer to overriding mandatory provisions.[18] To determine whether

[13] The term 'mandatory rules' used in the English version of the Rome I Regulation created confusion as it encompassed both domestic and overriding mandatory provisions. To address this, the Rome I Regulation distinguished the terms. Section by Moritz Renner in Gralf-Peter Calliess (ed), *Rome Regulations: Commentary*, 2nd edn (Kluwer Law International, 2015) 243; Torremans (n 1) 745; Michael Wilderspin, 'Overriding Mandatory Provisions' in *Encyclopedia of Private International Law* (Elgar Publishing, 2017) 1331; Ivana Kunda, *Internationally Mandatory Rules of a Third Country in the European Contracts Conflict of Laws: The Rome Convention and the Proposed Rome 1 Regulation* (Rijeka, 2015) 7.

[14] Section by Moritz Renner in Calliess (n 13) Art 9(9); section by Dieter Martiny in Franz Jürgen Säcker (ed), *Münchener Kommentar zum BGB*, 8th edn (Verlag Beck München, 2021) Rom I-VO Art 9, Rn 9; Torremans (n 1) 746; Bonomi (n 5) Art 9(55). However, Paul Hauser, *Eingriffsnormen in der Rom-I Verordnung* (Mohr Siebeck, 2012) criticises Art 9(1) Rome I Regulation for closely imitating the *Arblade* judgment when the European legislators were not prepared to create new wording or define the concept of overriding mandatory provisions.

[15] According to Briggs, the Rome Convention Art 7(1) and Rome I Regulation Art 9(1) are essentially the same. Adrian Briggs, *Private International Law in English Courts* (Oxford University Press, 2014) para 7.303. Hellner also states that the Rome I Regulation did not intend to change the scope of the Convention regarding international mandatory provisions. Michael Hellner, 'Third Country Overriding Mandatory Rules in the Rome I Regulation: Old Wine in New Bottles?' (2009) 5 *Journal of Private International Law* 447, 455–57. However, the argument has been made that even provisions that only protect private interests can fall within the category of overriding mandatory provisions, interpreting the examples of 'political, social or economic organisation' as merely illustrative. For a detailed discussion of that position, see Wilderspin (n 13) 1333.

[16] Torremans (n 1) 746.

[17] Wilderspin (n 13) 1333. There are conflicting evaluations regarding the definition in the Rome I Regulation. Some criticise Art 9(1) for defining the scope of overriding mandatory provisions too broadly and allowing significant room for interpretation by member states. Lisa Günther, *Die Anwendbargkeit ausländischer Eingriffnormen im Lichter der Rom I- und Rom II Verordnungen* (Verlag Alma Mater, 2011) 146. Others praise it for minimising the role of overriding mandatory provisions. Briggs (n 15) para 7.245; Renner (n 13) 242.

[18] Kwang Hyun Suk, 'General Issues with Amended Private International Law' [Gaejeong gukjesabeopui chongnonjeok munje] (2001) 536 *Korean Lawyers Association Journal* 5, 18; Kwang Hyun Suk, *Annotation to Private International Law* [Gukjesabeop haeseol] (Pakyoungsa, 2013) 140; Kwang Hyun Suk, 'The Application of Foreign

a provision of law is of an overriding mandatory nature, it is necessary to interpret what is meant by 'mandatory provisions that shall apply, in light of their legislative purpose, irrespective of the applicable law'. In doing so, it is necessary to assess each provision in question individually, rather than making a uniform judgment of the entire Act in which the provision is contained.[19]

The important issues in the interpretation of Article 20 of KAPIL can be summarised as follows.

The first issue is what legislative purpose should be required for recognition as an overriding mandatory provision. It is generally agreed in academia that provisions protecting national and economic interests constitute overriding mandatory provisions, while provisions regulating private interests are only domestic mandatory provisions.[20] However, there are differing views on the criteria for determining whether a provision that protects both public and private interests qualifies as an overriding mandatory provision. In the following subsections A and B, I will analyse the wording and legislative history of Article 20 of KAPIL and then present the criteria for determining overriding mandatory provisions that protect both public and private interests.

The second issue is how to ascertain whether a specific provision applies 'irrespective of the applicable law'.[21] In Sections B and C, I will first present the method of determining overriding mandatory nature and then propose which specific factors should be considered in the determination process.

A. Criteria for Determining Overriding Mandatory Provisions: Legislative Purpose

Article 20 of KAPIL is modelled on Article 18 of the Swiss FAPIL and Article 7(2) of the Rome Convention. Therefore, interpretations under the Swiss FAPIL and the Rome Convention have significant implications for the interpretation of Article 20 of KAPIL.

Exchange Control Law and Other Internationally Mandatory Rules of Third Countries in International Financial Transactions: Including Article VIII2(b) of the Articles of Agreement of the International Monetary Fund' (2020) 26 *Korea Private International Law Journal* 353, 358; Junhyok Jang, 'Internationally Mandatory Rules – A Comparative Study of Article 7 of the Rome Convention, Articles 18 and 19 of the Swiss Private International Law, and Article 7 of the Korean Private International Law' (2007) 75 *International Trade Law* 71, 74.

[19] Kwang Hyun Suk, 'Is the Act on the Regulation of Terms and Conditions Overriding Mandatory Rules?' *Law Times* (21 March 2011) 13; Heung Sub Choi, *Korean Private International Law I* (Korean Studies Information, 2019) 208.

[20] Suk (2013) (n 18) 141; Changseon Shin and Namsoon Yoon, *New Private International Law* [Singukjesabeop je2pan], 2nd edn (Fides, 2016) 275; Chang Seop Shin, *Private International Law* [Gukjesabeop je4pan], 4th edn (Sechang, 2018) 134. This is the prevailing view in Germany. Julius Von Staudinger and Norbert Habermann, *Staudingers Kommentar Zum Bürgerlichen Gesetzbuch Mit Einführungsgesetz Und Nebengesetzen: Einführungsgesetz zum Bürgerlichen Gesetzbuche/IPR* (Sellier-De Gruyter, 2002) Rn 57.

[21] The term 'legislative intention to apply certain provisions of the law regardless of the governing law of the relevant legal relationship' is sometimes referred to in legal literature as '*international zwingender Anwendungswille*' (intent for international mandatory application), '*Geltungswille*' (intent for legal effect), '*Anwendungsinteresse*' (interest in application), '*Geltungsanspruch*' (claim for legal effect) or '*Geltungsinteresse*' (interest in legal effect). Yong Dam Kim, 'The Governing Law of the International Contracts and Mandatory Rules' (1986) 33 *Trial Reference* 6, 22; Pascal Grolimund (ed), *Basler Kommentar Interntionales Privatrecht*, 4th edn (Helbnig Lichtenhahn Verlag, 2021) Art 19, Rn 17. Choi (n 19) 209 describes the requirement for an 'intent to apply mandatory norms even in cases with foreign elements' as 'extraterritorial application'. However, since 'application irrespective of the governing' law is a distinct concept from extraterritorial application, that description may be misleading.

Article 18 of the Swiss FAPIL[22] states that 'provisions of Swiss law that must be mandatorily applied due to their special purpose, irrespective of the law designated by this statute, are reserved'. The wording of Article 18 of the Swiss FAPIL used in regard to the purpose of legislation is 'due to' (*wegen*) instead of 'in light of', as appears in KAPIL. It is difficult to ascertain why Article 20 of KAPIL adopted a different wording from its Swiss model. Although the use of 'due to' in Article 18 of the Swiss law suggests a stronger relevance between legislative purpose and application intent than the term 'in light of', the formulation of the respective provisions are similar in that both explicitly specify legislative purpose as the basis for application intent. Therefore, the jurisprudence of Article 18 of the Swiss FAPIL is still relevant in the interpretation of Article 20 of KAPIL.

According to the annotation on the draft amendment during the deliberation of Article 18 of the Swiss FAPIL, the concept of overriding mandatory provisions is defined as 'provisions that require mandatory application due to the special purpose of maintaining public order'.[23] This emphasises a special legislative purpose that is of fundamental importance to the state and legal community and recognises the mandatory effect of maintaining public order. Thus, overriding mandatory provisions in the Swiss FAPIL are understood as requiring application regardless of the governing law because they pursue a special purpose.[24]

It is understood that the Rome Convention requires a special legislative purpose for an overriding mandatory rule. Article 7(2) of the Rome Convention states that 'nothing in this Convention shall restrict the application of the rules of the law of the forum in a situation where they are mandatory irrespective of the law otherwise applicable to the contract'. Although this provision does not explicitly mention the 'legislative purpose', it is generally agreed that the concept of overriding mandatory rules refers to norms that have a specific regulatory purpose rather than merely indicating the intention of applying the rules.[25] This interpretation aligns with de Winter's theory, which forms the basis of Article 7 of the Rome Convention. De Winter defines overriding mandatory rules as 'rules that are crucial to be applied even in international situations due to their significant social purpose'.[26]

This point is supported by the definition of overriding mandatory rules in Article 9(1) of the Rome I Regulation:

> Overriding mandatory provisions are provisions the respect for which is regarded as crucial by a country for safeguarding its public interests, such as its political, social or economic organisation, to such an extent that they are applicable to any situation falling within their scope, irrespective of the law otherwise applicable to the contract under this Regulation.

This emphasises the special legislative purpose of overriding mandatory rules. Considering that this provision was not intended to change the scope of overriding mandatory rules under the Rome Convention, it can be said that the overriding mandatory rules under the

[22] Art 18. Vorbehalten bleiben Bestimmungen des schweizerischen Rechts, die wegen ihres besonderen Zweckes, unabhängig von dem durch dieses Gesetz bezeichneten Recht, zwingend anzuwenden sind.

[23] Schweizerische Bundesrat, Botschaft zum Bundesgesetz über das internationale Privatrecht (IPR-Gesetz) vom 10 November 1982 (1983), 82.072, accessible at www.amtsdruckschriften.bar.admin.ch/viewOrigDoc.do?id=10048889.

[24] Jang (n 18) 93.

[25] Renner (n 13) Art 9(13).

[26] See ch 2, I.

Rome Convention were also required to pursue a special legislative purpose.[27] This means that even if a provision explicitly states that it applies irrespective of the governing law of the contract, the court must scrutinise whether the provision serves the interests it protects and determine whether there are valid reasons for the legislator to apply the provision irrespective of the governing law.

In summary, considering that Article 20 of KAPIL was adopted with reference to the provisions of Article 7(2) of the Rome Convention and Article 18 of the Swiss FAPIL, it is reasonable to view overriding mandatory rules as norms that pursue a specific legislative purpose. This provides two methodological insights for determining the existence of these rules. Firstly, even if a provision seems to apply irrespective of the governing law, it is necessary to examine whether a specific legislative purpose is pursued. This aims to limit the excessive expansion of the number of overriding mandatory rules. Some scholars have suggested that if a provision explicitly states that it applies irrespective of the governing law of a contract, it can be considered an overriding mandatory rule because it serves a specific legislative purpose in itself.[28] However, that interpretation contradicts the wording of Article 20 of KAPIL, which requires a legislative purpose to be the basis for application irrespective of the governing law. If Article 20 of KAPIL indeed intended to define any provision as an overriding mandatory rule irrespective of its legislative purpose, it would not have needed the phrase 'in light of the legislative purpose'. Furthermore, Article 20 of KAPIL was enacted with reference to the Rome Convention and the Swiss FAPIL, both of which emphasise a specific legislative purpose as being a component of overriding mandatory rules.[29] Secondly, in cases where a provision does not appear to apply irrespective of the governing law, such a provision may still be identified as an overriding mandatory rule. As long as the interpretation of the relevant legislative purpose and the relevant provisions suggest that the said provision should apply irrespective of the governing law under certain circumstances, it may be of overriding mandatory character. Based on these two points, the method of determining whether a provision constitutes an overriding mandatory rule will be presented in Section C below.

Now, I will examine what constitutes a special legislative purpose. It is generally agreed that when the legislative purpose of a provision is to intervene in legal relationships between individuals for the implementation of essential political, economic and social purposes of the state, the said provisions are of overriding mandatory nature, whereas regulations that only regulate private interests constitute domestic mandatory regulations.[30,31] The difficulty

[27] Wilderspin (n 13) 1333 combines the wording of Art 9(1) of the Rome I Regulation and the judgment of the ECJ in the *Unamar* case (Case C-184/12 *United Antwerp Maritime Agencies (Unamar) NV v Navigation Maritime Bulgare* ECLI:EU:C:2013:663) to reach this interpretation of the purpose of Art 9(1).

[28] Hun Mook Lee, 'Elements to Determine Internationally Mandatory Provisions' (2014) 442 *Human Right and Justice* 83, 85.

[29] Wilderspin takes a similar view under the Rome I Regulation. He suggests that *Arblade* judgment should be read as the court has to consider both whether the relevant provision applies irrespective of the governing law of the contract and whether respect for the provision is crucial for safeguarding the country's public interests. Wilderspin (n 8) paras 12-020–022.

[30] Section by Frank Vischer and Corrine Widmer Lüchinger in Markus Müller-Chen (ed), *Zürcher Kommentar zum IPRG*, Bd I-1, 3rd edn (Schulthess, 2018) Art 18(3); Kurt Rebmann (ed), *Münchener Kommentar zum BGB*, 4th edn (Verlag Beck München, 2006) EGBGB Art 34, Rn 11, 13; Martiny (n 14), Rome I Regulation, Art 9, Rn 11, 13; Renner (n 13) 247; Günther (n 17) 33; Suk (2013) (n 18) 141; Choi (n 19) 207.

[31] The Seoul High Court's judgment of 20 June 2017, Case No 2015 Na 2070479 concluded that the provision in Art 15 of the Commercial Law (concerning the authority of an employee with limited general agency power) is not

lies in the fact that there are few norms that solely protect either public or private interests. For example, Korea's Housing Lease Protection Act can be considered a regulation aimed at adjusting the imparity between landlords and tenants while pursuing the public interest of providing a stable housing supply.[32] Therefore, questions arise about whether the so-called special private law (*Sonderprivatrecht*) that intervenes in legal relationships between individuals with social and political objectives is overriding in nature. There are different views on this matter.[33] Commentators suggest that the test should be 'whether the provision primarily protects public or private interest'[34] or that 'the degree of anticipated social harm resulting from the violation of the provision' should be assessed.[35] However, these perspectives are unsatisfactory when it is difficult to distinguish which interest a provision primarily protects. Also, it is unclear how much social harm must be anticipated from the violation of the said rule for it to be identified as an overriding mandatory rule. It has also been argued that 'if the public order and morals protected by the regulation are superior to party autonomy, then it constitutes an overriding mandatory rule'.[36] However, this view also fails to provide a standard for determining when public order and morals should be considered superior to party autonomy. Moreover, the view that 'provisions aimed at protecting weaker parties from social policy objectives'[37] constitute overriding mandatory rules would lead to an overly broad recognition of overriding mandatory rules as most provisions protecting the weaker party would then have a certain social purpose. That could result in excessive restrictions on party autonomy.

Against this backdrop, I will set out specific criteria for determining overriding mandatory rules that protect both private and public interests. The ECJ's *Ingmar* judgment[38] is instructive for setting such standards in a way that does not unduly restrict party autonomy. In this case, the ECJ stipulated that Articles 17 and 18 of the Council Directive (Commercial Agent) Regulations of 1993[39] ('Commercial Agent Directive'), which guarantees commercial

an overriding mandatory rule because it is meant to regulate the relationships between individual contractual parties. Furthermore, the Seoul High Court's judgment of 22 August 2014, Case No 2013Na35063, concluded that the legislative purpose of the Product Liability Act, specifically when an importer asks a manufacturer for liability, was based on the need to protect consumers. This need arose due to disparities between consumers and businesses, which resulted from mass production and distribution. Therefore, this was deemed a domestic mandatory rule aiming to adjust the interests of parties and not an overriding mandatory rule.

[32] Hellner (n 15) 458–59.

[33] Hauser (n 14) 10–11 believes that a special private law that protects both public and private interests can also be considered an overriding mandatory provision. In contrast, Andrea Bonomi, 'Overriding Mandatory Provisions in the Rome 1 Regulation on the Law Applicable to Contracts' (2008) 10 *Yearbook of Private International Law* 215, 291; Wilderspin (n 13) 1331; Martiny (n 14) Art 9(16) argue that considering such regulations as overriding mandatory rules would excessively restrict party autonomy.

[34] Suk (2013) (n 18) 141. This is the prevailing view in the German literature. See section by Martin Zwickel in Dieter Martiny (ed) *Internationales Vertragsrecht*, 9th edn (Ottoschmidt, 2022) Rn 5.22; BGH NJW 2006, 230, 233; BGH NJW 2006, 762. The German Federal Court of Justice held that the Consumer Credit Act (*Verbraucherkreditgesetz*) is not an overriding mandatory rule because it is intended to protect individual interests, and public interest is only protected reflexively.

[35] Rebmann (n 30), EGBGB Art 34(14)–(15), (17); Kerstin Ann-Susann Schäfer, *Application of Mandatory Rules in the Private International Law of Contracts* (Peter Lang, 2010) 103; Günther (n 17) 34.

[36] Lee (n 28) 87.

[37] Choi (n 19) 207.

[38] *Ingmar GB Ltd v Eaton Leonard Technologies Inc* Case C-381/98, ECLI:EU:C:2000:605, [2000] ECR I-09305.

[39] Council Directive 86/653/EEC of 17 December 1986 on the coordination of the Member States relating to self-employed commercial agents.

agents certain rights to compensation after termination of agency contracts, must be applied when the commercial agent conducts their activities in a Member State, even if the principal is established in a non-Member State and the contract includes a clause stipulating that the law of the non-Member State applies.[40] The ECJ held that the uniform measures provided for in the Commercial Agent Directive aim to harmonise the conditions of competition in the European Community and to enhance the security of commercial transactions by removing restrictions on commercial agents' activities.[41] The Court stated that since Articles 17 and 19 of the Commercial Agency Directive aim to guarantee freedom of establishment to all agents and to protect undistorted competition in the internal market, those provisions must be observed throughout the Community in order to achieve their objectives.[42] It therefore held that the Commercial Agency Directive applies irrespective of the governing law of the agency contract, provided that the purpose served by the provisions in question requires that they be applied where the situation is closely related to the Community, and in particular where the principal is based in a non-member state but the agent has carried out business in a Member State.[43]

There is a different possible reading of this judgment. One commentator has suggested that *Ingmar*'s implication is that rules concerning private interests can also be recognised as overriding rules.[44] However, considering the reasons given in *Ingmar*, the correct reading of the case is that the court was not simply aiming to protect the weaker party in the contract (ie the commercial agent).[45] The Court found that the purpose of the Commercial Agency Directive was to 'guarantee freedom of establishment to all agents and to ensure undistorted competition in the internal market' and that, to achieve that purpose, the Directive should apply throughout the European Community. That amounts to an economic policy objective of maintaining competition in the market, which goes beyond protecting the weak or correcting imbalances in the position of private parties. Thus, the *Ingmar* judgment seems to indicate that for a provision to be recognised as overriding, it must have a public purpose that transcends the protection of private interests.

This issue is intertwined with the debate over whether to adopt a liberal or interventionist approach. In the realm of private law, there has been a recent trend to limit the principle of freedom of contract in order to correct the imbalance of information and bargaining power between businesses and individuals.[46] In response, an argument has been made in

[40] *Ingmar* (n 38) [26].
[41] ibid [23].
[42] ibid [24].
[43] ibid [24]–[25]. Although Arts 17 and 18 do not stipulate the spatial scope of application, the Court limited the scope of application of the Commercial Agent Directive to cases 'where the situation is closely connected with the European Community' after interpreting the purpose of the provision. This is a useful tool for identifying the overriding mandatory nature of a given provision.
[44] Namsoon Yoon, 'International Trade and Protection of Commercial Agents' (2006) 17 *Journal of Business Administration & Law* 97, 113.
[45] This view is shared by Renner (n 13) 251 and Günther (n 17) 138, who see the judgment as recognising that norms that protect both public and private interests can be overriding rules. See also Jan Kleinheisterkamp, 'The Impact of Internationally Mandatory Rules on the Enforceability of Arbitration Agreements' (2009) 3 *World Arbitration & Mediation Review* 91, 113; Audley Sheppard, 'Mandatory Rules in International Commercial Arbitration: An English Law Perspective' in George A Berman and Loukas A Mistelis (eds), *Mandatory Rules in International Arbitration* (Juris, 2011) 201; Hellner (n 15) 460.
[46] Youngjoon Kwon, 'The Philosophical Foundation of Contract Law – From the Perspective of Autonomy and Paternalism' (2011) 124 *Justice* 187–88.

private international law for limiting the freedom of choice of law.[47] In the same vein, it is argued that the value-neutralism (*Wertneutralität*) and 'tendency towards depoliticisation' (*Tendenz zur Entpolitisierung*) of private international law in the traditional sense of being detached from substantive legal assessment – except for in the application of public policy or overriding mandatory rules – should be corrected.[48] This approach could support the idea that overriding mandatory rules should be extensively adopted to help the weaker party.

However, this author suggests that a more cautious approach would be plausible. Overriding mandatory rules should be adopted under restricted circumstances for the following reasons. First, the freedom of contract is an effective way to implement party autonomy in substantive law. That is to say, domestic mandatory rules are an exception to the freedom of contract, and therefore the party contending that a certain provision is of domestic mandatory character bears the burden of proof. Considering that overriding mandatory rules are narrower in scope than domestic mandatory rules, there must be a higher hurdle for a provision to be identified as an overriding mandatory rule. The strict approach taken by Recital (37) of the Rome I Regulation[49] and the *Unmar* judgment[50] by the ECJ also support this view.

Secondly, since the interventionist approach is widely reflected in substantive laws,[51] there will ironically be less of a need to adopt overriding mandatory rules. The reason that Friedrich Carl von Savigny recognised the concept of overriding mandatory provisions in the first place was that there were provisions that could not be substituted by an equivalent foreign provision due to the unique policy interests of the adopting state. However, if there are provisions in foreign law that provide similar or equivalent protection to that afforded by domestic law, such domestic law provisions do not need to have an overriding mandatory character. For example, the interventionist approach in substantive laws endorses wider protection of weaker parties such as consumers and employees. Accordingly, there is widespread acceptance of the principle in private international law that the parties' choice of law does not preclude the protection that is provided by the national law of the consumer's habitual residence or the employee's habitual place of work. Even when the provisions of the country of habitual residence or habitual work that protect the consumers or employees do not 'override' the parties' choice of law agreement, the parties will still be protected by

[47] Shin and Yoon (n 20) 278 argue that the principle of party autonomy was established by projecting the principle of freedom of contract in substantive law into private international law, so if the principle of freedom of contract is modified, the freedom of the parties to choose applicable law should also be modified.

[48] Kwang Hyun Suk, 'A Study on the Revised German Private International Law' (2021) 27 *Korea Private International Law Journal* 662–63 lists human rights, climate change, refugee integration, modern family issues (such as same-sex marriage and surrogacy) and anti-discrimination (including anti-Semitism) as specific examples of how private international law has recently been used to implement political values in various areas.

[49] Art 37 states that 'Considerations of public interest justify giving the courts of the Member States the possibility, in exceptional circumstances, of applying exceptions based on public policy and overriding mandatory provisions. The concept of "overriding mandatory provisions" should be distinguished from the expression "provisions which cannot be derogated from by agreement" and should be construed more restrictively.'

[50] *United Antwerp Maritime Agencies (Unamar) NV v Navigation Maritime Bulgare (Unamar)* Case C-184/12 ECLI:EU:C:2013:663. The Court specified that overriding mandatory provisions should be interpreted more restrictively than domestic mandatory rules.

[51] Some good examples of this trend are found in the Principles of European Contract Law (PECL) and the Draft Common Frame of Reference (DCFR). Kwon (n 46) 189–90.

those provisions through the aforementioned principles of private international law as well as similarly protective substantive law provisions in foreign law.[52]

Therefore, this author believes that provisions that protect both private and public interests can be recognised as overriding mandatory provisions only when they protect essential political, social and economic interests that transcend private interests.[53] A provision may be considered an overriding mandatory provision as long as it seeks to correct the unfairness and imbalance stemming from the political, social and economic order, rather than merely adjusting the typical imbalance between parties in individual legal relationships.[54] Specifically, provisions that implement important constitutional values, such as the right to equality (Article 11[55] of the Korean Constitution), provisions that protect the dignity of workers and provisions against discrimination (Article 32(3) and (4) of the Korean Constitution[56]), and provisions that protect the market economy and economic justice (Article 119 of the Korean Constitution[57]) fall into this category.[58]

B. Method of Determining Overriding Mandatory Provisions

It is noteworthy that the legislative purpose plays a key role in determining whether a provision counts as an overriding mandatory rule, regardless of whether the wording of the relevant provision appears or does not appear to apply irrespective of the applicable law to the relevant legal relationship. This interpretation is consistent with the wording of Article 20 of KAPIL, which defines 'overriding mandatory rules' as those that should be applied regardless of the applicable law 'in light of the legislative purpose'.

However, when applying such a standard, it is necessary to take into account that various laws and regulations are being enacted in different forms in practice. Depending on the

[52] There are divergent approaches in the EU. Wilderspin (n 8) para 12-028 ff introduces the different approaches of the Member States. The German courts have taken a more restrictive approach than the ECJ in *Arblade* and *Unamar*, and have held that laws for consumer protection or employee protection are not necessarily of overriding mandatory character.

[53] The recent judgment by the European Court of Justice seems to support this view. In the case of *E.N.I., Y.K.I. v HUK-COBURG-Allgemeine Versicherung AG*, Case C-86/23 (2024) ECLI:EU:C:2024:689, the Court stated at [46] that national courts in the forum cannot apply provisions intended to protect individual rights as overriding mandatory provisions, unless the individual interests of a category of persons correspond to an essential public interest that those provisions are meant to safeguard.

[54] Specific examples are given in ch 4.

[55] Art 11(1): 'All citizens shall be equal before the law. No citizen shall be discriminated against in political, economic, social, or cultural life, on account of sex, religion, or social status.'

[56] Art 32: '(3) Standards of working conditions shall be determined by Act in such a way as to guarantee human dignity. (4) Special protection shall be accorded to working women, and they shall not be subject to unjust discrimination in terms of employment, wages and working conditions.'

[57] Art 119: '(1) The economic order of the Republic of Korea shall be based on a respect for the freedom and creative initiative of enterprises and individuals in economic affairs. (2) The State may regulate and coordinate economic affairs in order to maintain the balanced growth and stability of the national economy, to ensure proper distribution of income, to prevent the domination of the market and the abuse of economic power and to democratise the economy through harmony among the economic agents.'

[58] In relation to the overriding mandatory nature of consumer protection laws, a test has been proposed by Phil-Bok Lee, 'International Transaction of Cultural Heritage and Overriding Mandatory Provisions – Focused on the Overriding Mandatory Provisions of *Lex Originis*' (2021) 27 *Korea Private International Law Journal* 119, who states that to be recognised as an overriding mandatory provision of the Consumer Protection Law, a specific provision must be a 'necessary legal provision for the realisation of the public interest of consumer protection that would be practically deprived without its application'. But since the fundamental purpose of the Consumer Protection Law is to protect consumers as a weaker party in society (that is, to reconcile private interests), the purpose of 'consumer protection' by itself is insufficient to find a necessary public interest here.

laws and regulations in question, if there are easily identifiable indicators of an overriding mandatory provision, it would be methodologically better to start by reviewing those. For example, it is relatively straightforward to tell whether the wording of the provision in question appears to be applicable regardless of the governing law of the contract, or whether there is an extraterritorial application clause.[59] Thus, this author suggests to first check for the presence of these two elements above, and then, if there are none, to determine whether the international or spatial scope of application can be ascertained by interpreting the legislative purpose of the provision.

i. When the Wording of the Provision in Question Appears to be Applicable Regardless of the Governing Law of the Legal Relationship

If the wording of the relevant provision suggests that the provision is applicable irrespective of the governing law of the legal relationship in question, the first step is to examine elements that indicate the legislator's intention. First, if a regulation explicitly states that it is applicable regardless of the governing law, that can be considered a clear expression of the legislators' intention. However, it is rare for a provision to explicitly make such a statement. Second, in cases where a provision defines the scope of its international or spatial application, there is a strong possibility that the legislator intended the provision to apply regardless of the governing law of the legal relationship. Examples include provisions concerning the import or export of goods, transactions between nationals and foreigners, transactions conducted by foreigners in the domestic currency, transactions by nationals in foreign countries, provisions regarding international bidding, and regulations concerning suppliers of workers who will be employed domestically. Third, extraterritorial application also has significant meaning.[60] As extraterritorial application of a provision presupposes

[59] I argue that the legislative purpose should be separately examined even if a provision, from the wording, appears to apply regardless of the applicable law of the relevant legal relationship or contains an extraterritorial application clause.

[60] The principle of extraterritorial application developed in the US based on the Effect Doctrine. The development of US precedents regarding extraterritorial application and the Effect Doctrine is detailed by Min Cheol Jeon, 'A Study on the Extraterritorial Application of Competition Law – Focused on Legislations and Judicial Decisions of US and EU' (2017) 29 *Yonsei Law Journal* 209, and Jeehyun Choi, 'Standards of Extraterritorial Application of Competition Law: Case Study of Air Cargo' (2016) 15 *Korean Journal of International Economic Law* 35, 44–45. The development of the extraterritorial application of domestic law has mainly been based on the US's competition law, the Sherman Antitrust Act. In the context of expanding international trade and global economic integration, relying solely on the principle of territoriality is problematic for ensuring effective regulation. Therefore, the United States Court of Appeals for the Second Circuit recognised the extraterritorial application based on the effects doctrine in the case of *United States v Aluminum Co of America et al*, 148 F 2d 416 (2nd Cir) in 1945. The case involved whether Aluminum Ltd, a Canadian subsidiary of US company Alcoa, had violated the Sherman Act by forming a cartel with European companies to restrict the production of aluminum intermediates and block European companies' exports to the US. The Court of Appeals declared the legal principle that if foreign conduct (1) was intended to affect US commerce and (2) actually had an impact on the US market, US law could be applied. 'Extraterritorial application' refers to the application of domestic laws to acts conducted abroad, whether or not the actor is foreign, based on the place where the act occurred, as argued by Seon Heo, 'Experience and Logic of Extraterritorial Application of Fair Trade Laws to International Cartels: Focusing on the Graphite Electrode Rod International Cartel Case' (2003) 9 *Journal of Competition Law* 207, and Min Cheol Jeon (ibid) 209. On the other hand, it is also used to mean applying domestic laws to acts conducted abroad by foreigners, as argued by Kwang Hyun Suk, *Private International Law and International Litigation*, vol 5 (Pakyoungsa, 2012) 161; O Seung Kwon, 'Extraterritorial Application of the Korean Monopoly Regulation Act – With a Focus on the Air Cargo Cartel Case' (2011) 24 *Journal of Competition Law* 149; Bong-Eui Lee, 'Jurisdictional Issues of Extraterritorial M&A Regulation

situations involving foreign elements, it can serve as an indicator of overriding mandatory nature. Provisions with extraterritorial application can be regarded as the manifestation of the legislative intent for a law to apply regardless of the governing law.[61] The next step is to examine whether a special legislative purpose is recognised when one of these three criteria is met. If the relevant provision had a special legislative purpose, that provision has an overriding mandatory character.

ii. When the Wording of the Provision in Question does not Appear to be Applicable Regardless of the Governing Law of the Legal Relationship

If the relevant law does not fall under i. as described above, its legislative purpose should be examined. The first question to ask is whether the special legislative purpose is recognised as a conceptual element of an overriding mandatory rule. But even if a special legislative purpose is recognised, applying Korean law to all cases involving foreign elements regardless of the applicable law of the relevant legal relationship would exceed the limit of legislative jurisdiction.[62] It follows that the interpretation of a provision should be conducted in a manner that limits the scope of international or spatial application within the legislative jurisdiction. Whether the relevant statute applies irrespective of the governing law can be identified by assessing whether the international or spatial scope of application can be ascertained by interpreting legislative purpose.[63,64] A connection (or proximity) to the forum country (*Inlandsbeziehung*) could provide useful guidance by interpreting the relevant provision to apply to cases where there are connections to the forum. In such cases, the policies and values that form the basis of the relevant provision should be considered.[65] Not only the provision itself,[66] but also the structure of the statute that contains the provision, the circumstances of that statute's enactment[67] and its overall purpose should be taken into account.[68]

under Korean Competition Law' (2016) 33 *Journal of Korean Competition Law* 165, 168. Traditionally, it is used in the former sense in the US, as in Peter Hay, Patrick Borchers and Symeon C Symeonides, *Conflict of Laws*, 5th edn (West, 2010) 258–84. That is the sense in which extraterritorial application will be defined in this book.

[61] Some scholars refer to provisions with extraterritorial application as overriding mandatory rules, such as Matthias Lehmann, 'New challenges of extraterritoriality: superposing laws' in Franco Ferrari and DP Fernández Arroyo (eds), *Private International Law: Contemporary Challenges and Continuing Relevance* (Elgar, 2019) 258, and Kleinheisterkamp (n 45) 91, 92. However, this can be misleading as it cannot be said that all overriding mandatory rules have extraterritorial application. Even if a certain provision limits its application to nationals and domestic territory, it may still be considered an overriding mandatory rule if it is intended to be applied regardless of the governing law of the legal relationship.

[62] Rebmann (n 30), EGBGB Art 34, Rn 9; Suk (n 19) 13.

[63] Wengler also argued that the spatial scope of the 'mandatory obligation law (*zwingendes obligationsrecht*)' should be determined from the purpose of the relevant provision (*aus dem Zweck der betreffenden Vorschrift*). See Kim (n 21) 16.

[64] In the aforementioned *Ingmar* judgment, the ECJ has also confirmed the spatial scope of the provision's application in light of legislative purpose and recognised the intention for it to apply. See n 43. The Supreme Court of Korea has interpreted the spatial scope of Art 82(1) of the Medical Service Act, which requires those who intend to engage in the massage business to obtain accreditation from the mayor or provincial governor in light of its legislative purpose. Supreme Court of Korea, Judgment of 8 February 2018, Case No 2014Do10051.

[65] Junhyok Jang, 'Conflict's Mandatory Character as the Key Element of Internationally Mandatory Rules' (2007) 19 *SungKyunKwan Law Review* 563, 575.

[66] Yongjin Kim, 'External Effect of Mandatory Rules' (1998) 3 *Korea Private International Law Journal* 703, 709.

[67] Torremans (n 1) 746.

[68] Renner (n 13) 247.

On the other hand, even if there is a need to apply a given provision irrespective of the governing law of the legal relationship to achieve certain legislative purposes, the provision cannot be considered an overriding mandatory rule when there are no grounds for limiting the scope of *in personam* or spatial application based on the requirements of proximity to the forum.[69]

In this regard, some hold that when examining the purpose of a rule to determine whether it is an overriding mandatory rule, it should not be approached from the perspective of maximising the regulatory purpose of the relevant substantive law itself.[70] This view, instead, contends that a given provision should allow interpretation of the legislators' 'actual' intent for the substantive law to always apply within a certain international scope determined by themselves regardless of the governing law of the legal relationship. However, there is a question as to whether the maximisation of legislative purposes and the legislator's intent about actual application can be completely separated. Considering the reality that laws are often enacted without sufficient consideration of private international law, it seems unrealistic to expect legislators to explicitly stipulate that it shall apply regardless of the governing law or to leave materials indicating such an intent (for example, in their reasons for enacting or amending the law). In this situation, clarifying whether the legislator intended its application is a matter of interpretation. If, therefore, the relevant provision is so essential to achieve important legislative purposes that those purposes will be undermined if it does not apply irrespective of the governing law of the relevant legal relationship, it is more likely that legislators intended for the provision to apply regardless of the applicable law.[71] However, in case of doubts, the provision should be presumed not to be an overriding mandatory rule because overriding mandatory rules are exceptions to the general connection principle in private international law.[72]

C. Factors to Consider in Determining Overriding Mandatory Rules

There is a question of what factors one should consider when determining whether a given provision is an overriding mandatory rule in accordance with the criteria presented in section A and the method of determination presented in section B. In short, the legislative purpose of Article 20 of KAPIL is to protect public interests, such as the political, social and economic order of the state, and important constitutional values. Below I present the factors one should specifically consider in subsequent determination and evaluate the perspective of previous studies and lower court precedents to the extent necessary.

[69] The specific examples are examined in ch 4 I, C. Jang (n 64) 575 also points out how an overriding mandatory rule does not 'necessarily' apply regardless of whether there was *in personam* or spatial contact. He suggests that there are many examples of overriding mandatory rules that are intended to apply within a limited spatial scope based on *in personam* and/or territorial contact as a requirement.

[70] Jang (n 64) 575.

[71] The judgment of the ECJ in *Arblade* and Art 9(1) of the Rome I Regulation purport the same.

[72] Suk (2013) (n 18) 142.

i. Factors to Consider Regarding Legislative Intent

The factors to consider in determining whether legislators intended for the provision to apply regardless of the applicable law of the legal relationship in question can be summarised as (1) and (2) below. If the answer to questions (1) and (2) is 'yes', then there is a case where the intention of application is explicitly expressed in the wording, and in addition, where one should review whether the legislative purpose is recognised in accordance with the criteria set forth in section A. If the answer to questions (1) and (2) is 'no', the factors below in subsection ii. should be considered.

(1) *Does the relevant provision stipulate its applicability regardless of the applicable law, or does it directly stipulate the scope of international/spatial application?*
This question was considered in Seoul High Court, Judgment of 12 October 2007, Case No 2007Na16900; Seoul High Court, Judgment of 9 July 2019, Case No.2018Na2052472, 2018Na2052489;[73] Seoul High Court, Judgment of 16 February 2017, Case No 2015Na2065729;[74] and Seoul Central District Court, Judgment of 1 April 2020, Case No 2018Na63343.[75]

(2) *Is there an extraterritorial application clause?*
This was taken into account by Seoul Central District Court, Judgment of 24 October 2019, Case No 2018GaHap576876;[76] and Seoul Central District Court, Judgment of 1 April 2020, Case No 2018Na63343.[77]

ii. Factors to Consider Regarding whether Legislative Intent about Application can be Derived from Legislative Purpose[78]

If elements (1) and (2) in subsection i. above are not present, it means that there are no apparent indicators as to the application intention by the legislators. In this case, further investigation is necessary to identify such intention by considering the legislative purpose and other factors. The question of whether the provision in question has a special legislative

[73] This ruling found that the Act on the Regulation of Terms and Conditions, which stipulates the obligation to specify and explain terms and conditions, does not constitute an overriding mandatory provision.

[74] This ruling denied the overriding mandatory nature of Art 30(2) and (4) of the Act on Promotion of Information and Communications Network Utilisation and Information Protection.

[75] This ruling denied the overriding mandatory nature of Art 12 of the Fair Transactions in Franchise Business Act.

[76] At issue in this ruling was whether Art 14 of the Fair Transactions in Franchise Business Act was an overriding mandatory rule. The Court has determined that the provision in question does not qualify as an overriding mandatory rule on the ground that the provision does not share the same legislative purposes and intent as the Monopoly Regulation and Fair Trade Act, which possesses an overriding mandatory character. The Monopoly Regulation and Fair Trade Act stipulates its extraterritorial application (Art 2), restricts the execution of international contracts that violate the Act (Art 32) and imposes sanctions for violation of the Act (Art 34). From the foregoing, the Court interpreted that the legislators intended for the Monopoly Regulation and Fair Trade Act to apply in contracts with foreign elements. However, these were not found in Art 14 of the Fair Transactions in Franchise Business Act.

[77] After simply repeating the legislative purpose of Art 12 of the Fair Transactions in Franchise Business Act, the court declined to recognise legislators' intention to intervene in international transactions and did not specify its rationale except for stating that there is no extraterritorial application clause in the Fair Transactions in Franchise Business Act.

[78] Many lower court precedents have ruled that a specific provision would not constitute an overriding mandatory rule in light of the legislative purpose, without presenting specific standards for reaching that conclusion. Supreme Court of Korea, Judgment of 30 March 2015, Case No 2012Da11846, 18853 and Judgment of 26 August 2010, Case No 2010Da28185 held that 'in consideration of the legislative purpose of the Act on the Regulation of Terms and Conditions', it cannot be recognised as an overriding mandatory rule. The Seoul High Court, Judgment

purpose that merits recognition as an overriding mandatory rule shall be determined in accordance with the criteria set forth in section A. If the legislative purpose of that provision meets the criteria in section A, the next step should be to examine whether that purpose can be used to derive the legislators' intention for the rule to be applied regardless of the applicable law of the legal relationship. In that case, questions (1) to (4) are to be considered.

(1) *Is the relevant statute deemed essential for implementing important public interests, and would the legislative intent be undermined if the statute were not applied regardless of the governing law?*

If the answer to this question is positive, it may be possible to derive a legislative intent for the provision to be applied irrespective of the governing law.[79] Some lower court precedents have delivered rulings in consideration of similar purposes. Seoul High Court, Judgment of 17 January 2017, Case No 2016Na2015158, and Intellectual Property High Court, Judgment of 10 November 2017, Case No 2017Na1919 determined whether Article 374(1) of the Commercial Act constitutes an overriding mandatory rule, taking into account 'whether the order to be maintained and established by the relevant provision is an order/system essential in leading the development of the national economy and society, and whether it is a necessary provision for maintaining such an order'.[80]

of 5 February 2015, Case No 2013Na2006955, held that Art 56 of the Monopoly Regulation and Fair Trade Act, which stipulates the obligation to compensate for damages due to violations of Art 23(1) and (2) of the same Act, constitutes an overriding mandatory provision. That was echoed in Seoul Central District Court, Judgment of 17 April 2019, Case No 2017GaHap32348. Seoul High Court, Judgment of 14 January, Case No 2004Na14040 held that Art 92(2) of the Commercial Act cannot be seen as a provision that should be applied to the relevant legal relationship regardless of the applicable law 'in light of legislative purposes such as fair transactions and consumer protection' in determining whether the indemnity rights of a commercial agent under Art 92(2) of the same Act constitute an overriding mandatory rule. This decision seems to list the Monopoly Regulation and Fair Trade Act and the Consumer Protection Act as examples of provisions whose overriding mandatory nature can be deduced from their legislative purposes. Seoul Central District Court, Judgment of 29 March 2013, Case No. 2012Gahap83969 denied the overriding mandatory nature of Arts 4 and 11 of the Special Act on the Protection of Guarantors. The court found that the reason for the enactment of the Act was 'to establish reasonable financial transaction practices by specifying the scope of guarantees, as guarantees in Korea are often agreed to without consideration of or economic benefit to the guarantor'.

[79] The UK Supreme Court adopted a similar standard in *Cox v Ergo Versicherung AC* [2014] UKSC 22. Lord Sumption explained at [29] that 'implied extraterritorial effect' of a provision will arise 'only if (i) the terms of the legislation cannot effectually be applied or its purpose cannot be applied or its purpose cannot effectually be achieved unless it has extraterritorial effect; or (ii) the legislation gives effect to a policy so significant in the law of the forum that Parliament must be assumed to have intended that policy to apply to any one resorting to an English court regardless of the law that would otherwise apply.' Although it may be confusing that it is referred to as 'extra-territorial effect', meaning that a provision in the forum law should apply outside of the forum, in this case, these standards are helpful in deciding whether a provision should apply irrespective of the choice of law. *The Soldiers, Sailors, Airman and Families Association – Forces Help and another v Allgemeines Krankenhaus Viersen GMbH* [2022] UKSC 29 also examined whether the legislative purpose of the Civil Liability (Contribution) Act 1978 can be achieved without giving the legislation overriding effect in determining whether the relevant provision has an overriding mandatory nature. At [49]. The recent judgment by the European Court of Justice expressed a similar view, by stating the application of the relevant provision must be 'absolutely necessary in order to protect the essential interest concerned in the particular case', which cannot be achieved by applying the law designated pursuant to the usual conflict-of-laws rules. *E.N.I., Y.K.I. v HUK-COBURG-Allgemeine Versicherung AG* Case C-86/23 (2024) ECLI:EU:C:2024:689, at [42–43].

[80] This ruling viewed Art 374(1) of the Commercial Act as an overriding mandatory provision on the grounds that it is essential for maintaining the overall corporate law order and the public interest of the Republic of Korea. The Court's reason was that the provision separates ownership and management of a company and establishes a reasonable management system while also promoting and ensuring the investment and recovery of physical capital. This ruling was criticised, however, by Kwang Hyun Suk, 'Comment on a Lower Court Judgment Dealing with Law Applicable to International Acquisition Agreement – Are the Provisions of the Korean Commercial Code Requiring Resolution of Special Shareholders' Meeting Internationally Mandatory Rules?' (2018) 53 *Kyung Hee Law Journal* 119, 140 who argues that, in light of Art 374(1), the Commercial Act of Korea should have been applied as a personal law of the company and not as an overriding mandatory rule. This is a valid criticism.

In addition, there are lower court precedents where the courts applied the test to determine 'whether there is a possibility that a significantly unreasonable result will occur in light of our legal system, social policy, and transactional safety when the legal provision is not applied and it needs to be applied mandatorily'.[81] This seems to be in the same vein as the considerations this author has presented. However, the meaning of the 'possibility that a significantly unreasonable result will be caused' is ambiguous. Considering that overriding mandatory rules should be interpreted in a restrictive manner, the questions of 'whether a statute is essential for protecting social and economic order' and 'whether the legislative intent would be undermined if that statute were not applied regardless of the applicable law' seem to be better criteria.

(2) *Is the relevant provision equivalent to or substitutable with a foreign provision?*

The equivalence and substitutability of a provision can serve as a meaningful test to determine the overriding mandatory nature of that provision. If the legislative purpose of the provision in question can be achieved with a similar foreign law, it may not be an overriding mandatory rule. On the other hand, if there is no equivalent provision in foreign law and the interests intended to be protected by the provision cannot be safeguarded by any other foreign law, the provision may possess an overriding mandatory nature.

Seoul Central District Court, Judgment of 23 August 2013, Case No 2012GaHap10763 denied the overriding mandatory nature of the principle of piercing the corporate veil. The Court ruled that

> piercing the corporate veil is a legal principle that has been developed through theories and precedents in various countries around the world, and its requirements and effect vary depending on the needs of each country. Furthermore, in Korea, piercing the corporate veil is not a statutory rule, but a legal principle recognised as a theory and in precedent, so its requirements and effect are different from piercing the corporate veil under the laws of the British Virgin Islands.

This ruling can be seen to have used equivalence and substitutability to determine whether a legal principle counts as an overriding mandatory rule.

This is similar to Seoul Administrative Court, Judgment of 6 October 2016, Case No 2016GuHap54565, which examined whether the Korean Labour Standards Act was to apply as an overriding mandatory rule to an employment contract governed by German law. The Court found that the Labor Standards Act did not possess the overriding mandatory character for the following reasons:

> In relation to employee protection law, it is reasonable to develop a system tailored to the specific situation of each country. In doing so, the level of social welfare systems, including employment service agency, and the characteristics of the labour market, such as employment flexibility should

[81] Seoul High Court, Judgment of 12 October, Case No 2007Na16990, and Seoul High Court, Judgment of 9 July 2019, Case No 2018Na20524272, 2018Na2052489 held that the rules on the obligation to clarify and explain terms and conditions under the Act on the Regulation of Terms and Conditions do not correspond to overriding mandatory rules. Seoul High Court, Judgment of 16 February 2017, Case No 2015Na2065729 denied the overriding mandatory nature of the Act on Promotion of Information and Communications Network Utilisation and Information Protection. Seoul Central District Court, Judgment of 1 April 2020, Case No 2018Na63343 denied that Art 12 of the Fair Transaction in Franchise Business Act was an overriding mandatory rule. Seoul Central District Court, Judgment of 23 August 2013, Case No 2012GaHap10763 denied the overriding mandatory nature of the legal principle of piercing the corporate veil.

be taken into account. Therefore, it is not appropriate to apply one country's labour law to an employment contract governed by foreign law.

(3) *Are administrative or criminal sanctions imposed on violations of the provision in question?*
If a provision specifies administrative or criminal penalties for its violation, it may signify a strong public purpose and legislative intent to enforce the rule regardless of the applicable law. This is different from cases where the provision only has an impact on private legal matters when violated. Some lower court precedents have adopted this test. Seoul High Court, Judgment of 11 February 2010, Case No 2009Na31323 and Seoul High Court, Judgment of 4 July 2013, Case No 2012Na73822 acknowledged the overriding mandatory nature of the Monopoly Regulation and Fair Trade Act, inter alia, on this basis. Seoul High Court, Judgment of 12 October 2007, Case No 2007Na16900 also adopted this test when it decided Article 3[82] of the Act on the Regulation of Terms and Conditions was not an overriding mandatory provision.

(4) *Are there clues to limit the scope of personal or spatial application of the relevant provision?*
If it is possible to determine that a particular provision applies to a specific group of people or facts pertaining to a specific region through the interpretation of relevant provisions based on their connection (proximity) to the forum (*Inalndsbezhiehung*), it may be inferred that the legislative intent was for the provision to apply irrespective of the governing law. For instance, if the relevant provision regulates a specific type of business, and the region or location of the business holds significant importance under the relevant law, it can be assumed that legislators intended for the provision to apply to businesses situated in that area, regardless of the governing law.

D. Evaluation of Other Factors to Consider in Precedents and Previous Studies

In the following section, I discuss additional factors cited in lower court precedents and previous studies that I deem as unsuitable.

(1) *Are there separate provisions for protection under KAPIL?*
Supreme Court of Korea, Judgment of 26 August 2010, Case No 2010Da28185 and Judgment of 2012Da118846 and 118853 20 March 2015 adopted this test. In denying the overriding mandatory character of Article 3 of the Act on the Regulation of Terms and Conditions, which outlines the obligation of business entities to explain the details or important parts of standardised terms and conditions, the Court cited one of the grounds as the fact that 'Article 27 of KAPIL (before it was amended on 4 January 2022)[83] separately provides

[82] Art 3 of the Act provides for a business entities' obligation to explain the details or important parts of standardised terms and conditions to the other party.

[83] This Article corresponds to Art 47 of the current KAPIL (as amended on 4 January 2022) and in force from 22 July 2022. Art 27 (Consumer Contracts) (before the amendment on 4 January 2022): '(1) Where a consumer who has a habitual residence in the Republic of Korea concludes a contract for a purpose other than his or her

mandatory choice-of-law rules on consumer contracts to protect consumers'. The Court took the view that, therefore, it was unnecessary to interpret Article 3 of the Act on the Regulation of Terms and Conditions as overriding. The protection provided by Article 27 KAPIL at that time would be sufficient to protect consumers.

In the same vein, Seoul Administrative Court, Judgment of 6 October 2016, Case No 2016GuHap54565 noted that Article 28(1) of KAPIL[84] (before it was amended on 4 January 2022) provides that 'in the case of a labour contract, even if the parties choose the applicable law, the protection granted to workers by the mandatory rules belonging to the applicable law designated under Article 28(2) shall not be deprived'. The Court considered that this Article of KAPIL provides rules on the protection of employees and found that the provisions in Labour Standards Act are not of overriding mandatory nature.

However, whether there are special private international law rules on consumer protection or employee protection cannot be a decisive factor in determining a provision's overriding mandatory nature. The purpose of Articles 27 and 28 of KAPIL (before the amendment on 4 January 2022) is to ensure that domestic mandatory provisions of the consumer's habitual residence, or the country from with the employee habitually carries out work, are applied in order to protect consumers and workers thoroughly. It does not necessarily follow that the existence of such special choice-of-laws rules precludes provisions on consumer/employee protection from being an overriding mandatory rule. As seen in Article 27 of KAPIL (before the amendment on 4 January 2022), these special private international law rules set out specific requirements for the domestic mandatory rules to apply. For example, they may require the business entities to direct their activities towards consumers, and if the facts of the case do not meet these requirements, the domestic mandatory rules on consumer protection would not apply. However, if a provision is classified as an overriding mandatory rule, it would still apply even if the relevant facts do not meet the requirements provided in Article 27 of KAPIL (before the amendment on 4 January 2022).[85]

(2) *Is the provision a universal or representative form of legislation?*

Seoul Administrative Court, in its judgment of 6 October 2016, Case No 2016GuHap54565, inter alia, found that the Labour Standards Act is not a universal or representative form of legislation for employees and denied its overriding character. Conversely, a provision can

occupation or business activities, he or she may file a lawsuit with the court against the other party to the contract (referring to a person who concludes a contract for his or her occupation or business activities; hereinafter referred to as 'business entity') in any of the following cases: 1. Where a business entity engages in occupation or business activities, such as solicitation for transactions through advertising, before the conclusion of a contract in a country in which a consumer has a habitual residence (hereinafter referred to as 'country of habitual residence') or where a business entity engages in occupation or business activities, such as solicitation for transactions through advertising in a territory not included in the consumer's country of habitual residence toward the country of habitual residence, and where the contract falls under the scope of the business entity's occupation or business activities; 2. Where a business entity receives an order from a consumer in the consumer's country of habitual residence; 3. Where a business entity encourages a consumer to place an order in a country other than his or her country of habitual residence.'

[84] Art 28 of KAPIL (before it was amended on 4 January 2022) corresponds to Art 48 of KAPIL (as it was amended on 4 January 2022).

[85] This aligns with the interpretation of the Rome I Regulation. The prevailing view of the Rome I Regulation is that Art 9 is not excluded by Art 8, which is a special conflicts-of-laws rule to protect employees.

only be deemed an overriding mandatory rule if it can be regarded as a universal or representative legislative form. However, such a viewpoint is not plausible, as legislation that is universal or representative in all countries need not be considered an overriding mandatory rule, since it can be substituted by an equivalent provision in foreign law.

On the other hand, if the aforementioned ruling intended to require that overriding mandatory rules should protect universal values in various countries around the world, such a requirement can be included in the consideration of whether the provision protects vital political, social, and economic interests, as this author has already presented. Thus, this consideration would not have to be examined separately.

(3) *Is the relevant provision of a public or private law nature?*
Seoul High Court, Judgment of 20 June2017, Case No 2015Na2070479, examined Article 15 of the Commercial Act, and Seoul High Court, Judgment of 22 August 2014, Case No 2013Na35063 examined the Product Liability Act, with both decisions reviewing those provisions' applicability as overriding mandatory rules. The Courts decided that they do not constitute overriding mandatory rules by applying the criterion of 'public nature' – that is, whether the said provisions serve national or economic policy interests.

Although the courts correctly assessed whether the relevant provision protects national or economic policy interests, the reference to the 'public law nature' can be mistaken to mean whether the provision belongs to public law or private law. However, the distinction between public law and private law is not clear, and the standards of public and public law vary in different jurisdictions. The better view, thus, is that whether a provision is public law or private law cannot be a decisive criterion in determining whether it is an overriding mandatory rule.[86]

(4) *Does the non-application of the provision run counter to good morals and other social order of Korea?*
Seoul High Court Judgment of 15 November 2012, Case No 2012Na14816, held that Article 450(2) of the Civil Act does not constitute an overriding mandatory rule. The defendants asserted that the non-application of the provision to a contract governed by English law would go against good morals and other social orders of Korea. The Court held that the requisites for counteraction against the transfer of claims in a manner that does not conform with Article 450(2) of the Civil Act[87] does not violate good morals or other social order of Korea.

Seoul Central District Court, Judgment of 19 July 2017, Case No 2016Gahap527665 ruled similarly and denied the overriding mandatory nature of Article 449(2) of the Civil Act.[88]

[86] Suk (2013) (n 18) 138; Choon Soo An, 'International zwingende Bestimmungen im IPR – Theorien und die Bedeutung von Artt. 6, 7 IPR Koreas' (2011) 23 *Kookmin Law Review* 189, 192; Günther (n 17) 31, 131; Renner (n 13) 247.

[87] Art 450 (Requisite for Setting up Assignment of Nominative Claim against Obligor): '(2) The notice or consent mentioned in the preceding paragraph cannot be set up against a third person other than the obligor, unless it is put in writing with a certified fixed date.'

[88] Art 449 (Assignability Nature of Claim): '(2) Where the parties have declared a contrary intention, a claim shall not be assigned: Provided, that such declaration of intention cannot be set up against a third person acting in good faith.'

It is not entirely clear if the courts intended to adopt the test of 'would good morals or other social order of Korea be infringed upon if the said provision does not apply irrespective of the applicable law' in determining the overriding mandatory nature. If so, the courts may have misunderstood the relationship between overriding mandatory rules and public policy.[89] Public policy and overriding mandatory rules are related to some extent,[90] and if the overriding mandatory rules of the forum protect the principles of the fundamental legal system of the forum, they may overlap with public policy.[91] However, public policy and overriding mandatory rules are distinct concepts in private international law. While public policy focuses on the results of the application of foreign laws and examines their violation of the public policy of the forum, the overriding mandatory rules of the forum apply regardless of the results of the application of the governing law.[92] Overriding mandatory rules concern the selection of the applicable law (that is, a positive function), while public policy serves an exceptional, defensive, and negative function by denying the application of the governing law.[93] In the past, the grounds for applying the overriding mandatory rules of the forum was at times explained as a positive function of public policy,[94] but today, the positive function is generally not recognised. Since Article 20 of KAPIL serves as a basis for applying the overriding mandatory rules of the forum, separately from its public policy provision (Article 23[95]), this need not be explained as an active function of public policy.[96]

In addition, the scope of public policy is narrower than that of overriding mandatory rules, as it is used only in exceptional circumstances, for instance, when it would

[89] 'Good morals or other social order' is referred to as 'public policy' in Korean legal literature. The same wording appears in Art 23 of KAPIL, which provides for the non-application of foreign law in cases where it would violate the public policy of Korea.

[90] Savigny also recognised that 'provisions of a strongly active and compulsory nature' protect public policy. Friedrich Carl von Savigny, *System des heutigen römischen Rechts*, Band 8 (Veit, 1849) 36. Paragraph 37 of the preamble to the Rome I Regulation also implies the connection between public policy and overriding mandatory rules by stipulating that the consideration of public interests justifies the court's application of exceptions based on public policy and overriding rules in exceptional circumstances.

[91] Peter Kaye, *The New Private International Law of Contract of the European Community* (Dartmouth, 1993) 265; Adeline Chong, 'The Public Policy and Mandatory Rules of Third Countries in International Contracts' (2006) 2 *Journal of Private International Law* 27, 31.

[92] Plender and Wilderspin (n 1) paras 9–23.

[93] ibid, paras 9–22; Kaye (n 90) 265; Lawrence Collins (ed), *Dicey, Morris & Collins: The Conflict of Laws*, 15th edn (Sweet & Maxwell, 2012) vol 2, para 32-182; Torremans (n 1) 144, 748–49; Frank Vischer, 'General course on private international law' (1992) 232 *Recueil des Cours* 21, 165; Daniel Girsberger, Thomas Kadner Graziano and Jan Neels (eds), *Choice of Law in International Commercial Contracts* (Oxford University Press, 2021) paras 1.444, 1.492; Kwang Hyun Suk, 'Protection of Commercial Agents in International Transactions – Scope of Application of Article 92bis of the Commercial Code' (2006) 55 *Korean Lawyers Association Journal* 19, 47; In-ho Kim, 'Limitations by Mandatory Rules on the Dominance of Party Autonomy in International Contracts' (2012) 60 *Advanced Commercial Law Review* 110, 139.

[94] Trevor Hartley, 'Mandatory rules in international contracts: the common law approach' (1997) 266 *Recueil des Cours* 345, 353. Common law traditionally did not clearly distinguish between public policy and mandatory provisions. See Girsberger, Graziano, and Neels (n 92) paras 1.451–1.452. England has considered the overriding mandatory rules of third countries in accordance with the public policy-comity rule, one of the principles of public policy. For details, see ch 5, II, C.

[95] Art 10 (Provisions of Foreign Law Contrary to Social Order): 'Where a foreign law shall govern but the application of the provisions of the foreign law is clearly contrary to good morals and other public order of the Republic of Korea, the provisions shall not apply.'

[96] Suk (n 92) 47.

be repugnant[97] to apply foreign law as the governing law because the effect of doing so would clearly be contrary to the forum's public policy.[98] Accordingly, not all overriding mandatory rules automatically have the nature of public policy.[99,100] Therefore, the consideration of whether the non-application of the provision would violate public policy of Korea cannot be deemed an appropriate factor in determining its overriding mandatory nature.

[97] Plender and Wilderspin (n 1) paras 9–24.

[98] Kwang Hyun Suk, 'Laws Applicable to International Construction Contracts Using FIDIC Conditions and their Practical Consequences' (2014) 29 *Juris* 3, 50 also purports the same. In contrast, Lee (n 28) 89 seems to believe that overriding mandatory rules are identical to international public policy, simply because public policy is the genuine basis for overriding mandatory rules and, at the same time, the criterion for their determination. While recognising the difficulty in quantifying the concepts of public policy and overriding mandatory rules, some claim that the 'fundamental policy of the country to which the objective governing law belongs' under the United States Restatement (Second) of Conflict of Laws is a more relaxed concept than that of overriding mandatory rules under the Rome I Regulation and that the threshold of public policy under Art 21 of the Rome I Regulation is higher than that of overriding mandatory rules. Symeon C Symeonides, 'Party Autonomy in Rome I and II From a Comparative Perspective' in Katarina Boele-Woelki (ed), *Convergence and Divergence in Private International Law – Liber Amicorum Kurt Siehr* (Shulthess, 2010) 530, 539.

[99] Girsberger, Graziano, and Neels (n 92) para 1.492. Müller-Chen (n 30) Art 18, Rn 4.

[100] As such, most domestic laws distinguish between public policy and overriding mandatory rules, and govern them separately. See Girsberger, Graziano and Neels (n 92) paras 1.445–1.467 for legislative examples of public policy and overriding mandatory rules in different jurisdictions. Despite the unusual treatment of overriding mandatory rules and public policy in the same article, the above explanation of the functions of overriding mandatory rules and public policy is also in accordance with the Hague Principles on Choice of Law in International Commercial Contracts. HCCH, 'Commentary on the Principles on Choice of Law in International Commercial Contracts' (2015) para 11.11.

4

Overriding Mandatory Rules in Korean Law

This chapter examines which provisions of Korean law are of overriding mandatory nature by applying the criteria, methods and factors to consider presented in chapter three. Since the Korean court must apply the overriding mandatory rules of Korean law (*lex fori*) even when the applicable law of the relevant legal relationship is foreign,[1] the courts must familiarise themselves with the laws of the forum that serve as overriding mandatory rules.

Provisions from the following categories will be analysed as to whether they qualify as overriding mandatory rules: (1) provisions concerning international commercial contracts; (2) provisions of which overriding mandatory character has been disputed in the precedents and prior legal studies; (3) provisions on special torts insofar as they are connected to contracts; and (4) a need for a timely assessment.

From the first and second categories, the Foreign Trade Act, Foreign Exchange Transactions Act, Employment Security Act, Act on Contracts to which the State is a Party (hereinafter 'State Contracts Act'), Act on Conservation and Utilisation of Cultural Heritage (hereinafter 'Cultural Heritage Act'), Equal Employment Opportunity and Work-Family Balance Assistance Act (hereinafter 'Equal Employment Act'), Act on the Regulation of Terms and Conditions (hereinafter 'Terms and Conditions Regulation Act'), Article 799 of the Commercial Act, and Article 92-2 of the Commercial Act will be reviewed. The Equal Employment Act was also selected for review even though its status as an overriding mandatory rule has not been challenged in the precedents, because it has been mentioned as possibly being an overriding mandatory rule in previous studies without any detailed reasons.

The third category includes the Monopoly Regulation and Fair Trade Act (hereinafter 'Fair Trade Act'), the Fair Transactions in Subcontract Act (hereinafter 'Subcontract Act'), and the Fair Transactions in Franchise Business Act (hereinafter 'Franchise Act'). In recent years, there has been an increase in the number of laws enacted in Korea whose title begins with 'fair transactions', and the Subcontract Act and the Franchise Act were adopted as part of that trend. Therefore, reviewing these Acts would be timely. These Acts can be viewed as extensions of the Fair Trade Act, which has traditionally been regarded as an overriding mandatory rule.

Fourthly, although the State Contracts Act's status as an overriding mandatory rule has not been challenged in precedents, in recent years, and in light of the COVID-19 pandemic, it seems timely to review whether the State Contracts Act applies[2] when the Republic of Korea enters into a vaccine supply contract governed by foreign law with a foreign company.

[1] See ch 2, III, A for the application requirements.

[2] For a brief introduction to the vaccine supply agreement between the EU and AstraZeneca, see Jung Hwa You, 'The Vaccine Purchase Agreement Signed by South Korea and the United Nations Convention on Contracts for the International Sale of Goods (CISG)' [Daehanminguki chegyeolhan baeksingumaegyeyakgwa UNtongilmaemaebeop(CISG)] *Law Times* (26 August 2021).

The order of classification and review of the regulations was decided in accordance with the criteria for determination and factors for consideration presented in chapter three. First, I will look at examples of overriding mandatory rules (section I) and then at examples that are not (section II). The former will be classified based on whether the legislators' intention to have the provision apply regardless of the governing law of the legal relationship is explicit. More specifically, that refers to cases where: (1) there are extraterritorial application clauses (Fair Trade Act, Foreign Exchange Transactions Act[3]); (2) where there are no extraterritorial application clauses, but the law explicitly provides for its international or spatial scope application (Foreign Trade Act, Employment Security Act, State Contracts Act); and (3) where there are no extraterritorial application clauses, nor explicit provisions on international or spatial scope of application but there is a strong public purpose and the scope of application can be inferred through the interpretation of relevant provisions. Category (3) is further segmented into whether the public interest protected by the relevant laws is economic (Subcontract Act, Franchise Act), or social (Equal Employment Act, Cultural Heritage Act[4]) and reviewed in that order. The implications of the results of my review are summarised and presented in section III.

I. Examples of Overriding Mandatory Rules

A. Laws with Extraterritorial Application

As discussed in chapter three, if a certain provision stipulates that it shall be applied extraterritorially, it sets out the international or spatial scope of application and it can be seen to apply regardless of the governing law of the relevant legal relationship. Extraterritorial application clauses were introduced to Article 2(2) of the Fair Trade Act, which was amended by Act No 7289 on 31 December 2004,[5] and Article 2(2) of the Foreign Exchange Transactions Act.[6] The following sections discuss whether the Fair Trade Act and Foreign Exchange

[3] Art 2 of the Foreign Exchange Transactions Act not only has an extraterritorial application clause but also stipulates international or spatial scope of application.

[4] Provisions subject to review under the Cultural Heritage Act include some that stipulate an international or spatial scope of application and some that do not, but they will be reviewed together under this section.

[5] There was no extraterritorial application clause under the Fair Trade Act in the past, but the Supreme Court of Korea accepted the Effect Doctrine of the United States in its Judgment of 24 March 2006, Case No 2004Du11275 (*Graphite Electrode*) and ruled that the provisions under the Fair Trade Act on illegal cartel conduct may apply to foreign business entities if their illegal cartel conduct in a foreign country affects the Korean market. The Supreme Court pointed out that the purpose of the Fair Trade Act is to promote fair and free competition by regulating illegal cartels, to encourage creative corporate activities, to protect consumers, and to lead to the balanced development of the national economy. The Court considered that the wording of the law stated 'manufacturing business, service business, or other business' and did not limit the business entities to domestic entities. The express grounds for the extraterritorial application were established in Art2(2) of the Fair Trade Act by the amendment of the Fair Trade Act on 31 December 2004, while the Supreme Court case was pending.

[6] Extraterritorial application clauses were also introduced to the Financial Investment Services and Capital Markets Act (hereinafter 'Capital Markets Act'), Telecommunications Business Act, Act on Promotion of Information and Communications Network Utilisation and Information Protection (hereinafter 'Information and Communications Network Act'), and the recently amended Act on Consumer Protection in Electronic Commerce, etc (hereinafter 'e-Commerce Act').

Transactions Act are overriding mandatory rules. In addition, as a relevant issue, I briefly introduce principles for resolving overlapping regulations with extraterritorial effect.

i. Fair Trade Act[7]

Article 3 of the Fair Trade Act (Article 2(2) before amendment on 29 December 2020) stipulates that 'This Act shall apply even to an act conducted overseas if such act affects the domestic market.' The Supreme Court of Korea stated that 'cases affecting the domestic market' under Article 3 of the Fair Trade Act should be interpreted narrowly as 'problematic foreign activities with direct, significant, and reasonably foreseeable effect on the domestic market'.[8] Article 3 does not specify provisions subject to extraterritorial application. However, there is controversy over whether the unique provisions of Korea, such as the prohibition of unfair trade practices, also apply extraterritorially, in addition to the prohibition of illegal cartel conduct or anti-competitive business mergers and acquisitions and the abuse of market dominant position, for which there are international standards in place for determining illegality.[9]

The regulations of the Fair Trade Act are mainly focused on restricting or prohibiting the abuse of market dominant position (Article 5), anti-competitive business mergers and acquisitions (Article 9), illegal cartel conduct (Article 40) and unfair trade practices (Article 45). The abuse of market dominant position, anti-competitive business mergers and acquisitions and illegal cartel conduct have traditionally been regulated by competition law from a comparative legal point of view[10] and are subject to extraterritorial application.[11]

[7] The Fair Trade Act, which was wholly amended by Act No 17799 on 29 December 2020, entered into force on 30 December 2021, and the organisation of the previous provisions was changed. The article numbers in this book are based on the wholly amended Fair Trade Act.

[8] After the Supreme Court's ruling in *Graphite Electrode* (n 5), there was criticism that the ruling did not set restrictions or limitations on extraterritorial application of the Fair Trade Act. The Supreme Court stated in a series of rulings concerning cargo fare collusion between 26 airlines that the issue of whether the case 'has a direct, substantial and reasonably predictable effect on the domestic market' should be determined specifically and individually by comprehensively considering the content and intent of the act in question, the characteristics of the goods or services that are the subject of the act, the transaction structure, and the content and extent of the effect on the domestic markets. Supreme Court of Korea, Judgment of 16 May 2014, Case No 2012Du5466; Judgment of 24 December 2014, Case No 2012Du13412; Judgment of 16 May 2014, Case No 2012Du5237 (all three cases regarding flight routes from Korea); Supreme Court of Korea, Judgment of 24 December 2014, Case No 2012Du6216 regarding flight routes from Europe; Supreme Court of Korea, Judgment of 16 May 2014, Case No 2012Du14545 regarding flight routes from Hong Kong; and Supreme Court of Korea, Judgment of 16 May 2014, Case No 2012Du13665 and Judgment of 16 May 2014, Case No 2012Du13269, along with others, regarding flight routes from Japan. These cases are referred to as the *Air Carrier Collusion* cases.

[9] Section by Sung Kuk Cho in Iksoo Park (ed), *ONJU Monopoly Regulation and Fair Trade Act* (Thomson Reuters, 2015) Art 2(2), § 4 explains that the prohibition of 'unfair trade practices' is unique in the Korean Fair Trade Act and this is not enforced in the US or EU, which have led major trends in competition laws. Considering that the extraterritorial application has been mainly discussed in those jurisdictions in relation to illegal cartels, it follows that the scope of extraterritorial application may inevitably face restrictions, even if the Korean Fair Trade Act does not stipulate it.

[10] Dae-sik Hong, 'Korean Competition Law from a Private Law Perspective – Focused on Abuse of Market-dominant Position' (2008) 18 *Journal of Competition Law* 203, 214.

[11] Hun-je Suh, 'Extraterritorial Application of Fair Trade Act – Focusing on the Extraterritorial Application of Substantive Rules' (1998) 23 *International Trade Law* 6, 27; Young Han Ko, 'Extraterritorial Application of Fair Trade Law, Various Issues Economic Law' [Dokjeomgyujebeopui yeokoejeokyong, gyeongjebeopui jemunje] (2000) 87 *Trial References* 765, 850. In *Intel v Commission* Case C-413/14 P, ECLI:EU:C:2017:632, the European Court of Justice recognised the extraterritorial application of TFEU on Intel's abuse of market dominant position.

However, unfair trade practices are different from other types of practices in terms of anti-competitiveness in that they regulate 'unfair' acts.[12] Regulation of unfair trade practices can be seen as being 'located on a spectrum between relevance to private autonomy on one end and relevance to competition on the other'.[13] The prohibition of unfair trade practices touches upon rules adjusting private interests arising from the imbalance of the parties' tangible status; therefore, there is a fine line between 'unfair acts' under the Fair Trade Act and unfair legal acts under the Korean Civil Act (Article 104 of the Civil Act), acts contrary to good customs (Article 103 of the Civil Act) and the prohibition of abuse of rights (Article 2 of the Civil Act). Therefore, it is necessary to review separately from other types of acts whether Article 45 of the Fair Trade Act, which prohibits unfair trade practices, constitutes an overriding mandatory rule.

On the other hand, the regulations of the Fair Trade Act consist of administrative regulations with public law regulations, as well as civil liability and criminal punishment for violations. However, since extraterritorial application has been mainly discussed in the context of administrative regulations, in relation to civil liability, it is unclear how extraterritorial application clauses are related to the conflict-of-laws rules of private law and whether indemnity liability clauses (Article 109 of the Fair Trade Act) can be recognised as overriding mandatory rules. This shall be explored hereafter.

a. Articles 5, 9, 11 and 40

Pursuant to Article 3 of the Fair Trade Act, Articles 5, 9 and 40 of the Fair Trade Act are applied extraterritorially, so the legislators' intention to have these provisions applied can be read even when the applicable law of the relevant contract or tort is foreign. Now it should be examined whether each of the above provisions of the Fair Trade Act has a special legislative purpose under Article 20 of KAPIL.

Article 1 of the Fair Trade Act states:

> The purpose of this Act is to prevent the abuse of market dominance by business entities and excessive concentration of economic power and to promote fair and free competition by regulating illegal cartel conduct and unfair trade practices, thereby encouraging creative business activities, protecting consumers, and promoting the balanced development of the national economy.

This is to protect the essential public interest of the economic order of the nation, and Articles 5, 19, 11, 40 are an essential means to protect such a strong public interest.

The Fair Trade Act governs administrative regulations, criminal punishment and civil liability for damages (Article 109) in all cases of violation of the prohibition on the three

For extraterterritorial appplication of anti-competitive business merger and provisions, see Bong-Eui Lee, 'Jurisdictional Issues of Extraterritorial M&A Regulation under Korean Competition Law' (2016) 33 *Journal of Korean Competition Law* 165; O Seung Kwon, 'Extraterritorial Application of the Korean Monopoly Regulation Act – With a Focus on the Air Cargo Cartel Case' (2011) 24 *Journal of Competition Law* 159; *Gencor Ltd v Commission* Case T-102/96 (1999) ECR II-753; 4CMLR 971 [90], [92]. See the Supreme Court's ruling on *Graphite Electrodes* (n 5) and the *Air Carrier Collusion* cases (n 8) for illegal cartel conduct.

[12] Cho (n 9) Art 2(2), § 4.

[13] Hong (n 10) 215 and Dae-sik Hong, 'Revisiting the Standard for Determining Illegality of Unfair Trade Practices under the Monopoly Regulation and Fair Trade Act of Korea – Centered on Relevance to Competitive Order' (2018) 37 *Journal of Competition Law* 188, 189 refer to the rules of unfair trade practices as 'hybrid', referring to their mixture of competition law and other viewpoints.

types of conduct. In the event of abuse of market dominant position, corrective measures (Article 7) and fines (Article 8) may be imposed, and criminal punishment shall be imposed (Article 124(1)(1)). Corrective measures (Article 14) may be imposed in the event of anti-competitive mergers and acquisitions, and enforcement fines (Article 16) may be imposed if the corrective measures are not implemented; criminal punishment shall also be imposed (Article 125(1)). If a merger and acquisition report is not made or is falsely made, administrative fines shall be imposed (Article 130(1)). In the event of illegal cartel conduct, corrective measures (Article 42), penalty surcharges (Article 43) and criminal penalties (Article 124(1)(10)) may be imposed. This is also a situation in which a strong public purpose can be inferred.

In short, Articles 5, 9, 11 and 40 of the Fair Trade Act correspond to overriding mandatory rules.

b. Article 45

As discussed above, there is controversy over whether Article 45 of the Fair Trade Act applies extraterritorially. However, in light of the deletion of Articles 32 and 34 of the former Fair Trade Act (which was amended by Act No 14137 of 29 March 2016), it seems that legislators intended at least to have Article 45 of the Fair Trade Act apply to legal relationships with foreign elements. Article 32 of the former Fair Trade Act provides that:

> No business entity or trade association shall enter into an international agreement or international contract prescribed by Presidential Decree containing matters concerning unfair collaborative acts, unfair trade practices or resale price maintenance, provided, that this shall not apply where the Fair Trade Commission deems the effect of the said international contract upon competition in a particular business area to be negligible or deems that there are other unavoidable reasons for the said contract.

Corrective measures were imposed in cases of violation (Article 34). Articles 32 and 34 of the former Fair Trade Act were subsequently deleted in the amendment procedure, but not because there was a legislative determination that the Fair Trade Act should not apply to international legal relationships. Rather, it was because no cases of corrective measures had been based on the relevant provisions and there was no practical benefit of establishing a separate provision restricting the execution of international agreements since there was already an extraterritorial application clause. It follows that it is possible to derive the legislators' intention that the legislative purpose of the Fair Trade Act should also be complied with in international agreements. Therefore, it can be acknowledged that legislators intended for Article 45 of the Fair Trade Act to apply even when the law governing contracts or torts was not Korean law.

Next, whether Article 45 of the Fair Trade Act has a special legislative purpose in terms of Article 20 of KAPIL. Unlike Articles 5, 9, 11, 40 of the Fair Trade Act, which focus on 'competition restrictions', the prohibition of unfair trade practices focuses on whether 'fair trade' is undermined. The Enforcement Decree of the Fair Trade Act, Table 2 further categorises unfair trade practices into: (1) refusal to trade; (2) discriminatory treatment; (3) exclusion of competitors; (4) unfair inducement of customers; (5) coercion of trade; (6) abuse of a bargaining positon; (7) conditional transactions; (8) interference with business activities; and (9) unfair support. Table 2 categorises (6) 'the abuse of bargaining position' into (1) coercion to purchase, (2) coercion to provide profits, (3) coercion of sales targets, (4) imposition of disadvantages and (5) management interference. These types of acts are clearly different from those that restrict competition. Therefore, it is questionable whether the purpose of regulating this type of act can be distinguished from the adjustment of interests between private persons that Articles 103 and 104 of the Civil Act aims for, or in other words, whether the purpose of such regulation can be recognised as the protection of essential public interests going beyond the adjustment of private interests.

The competition law nature of the types of unfair trade practices prohibited by Article 45 of the Fair Trade Act, is relatively weak (except for (6) abuse of a bargaining position) compared to abuse of a market dominant status, anti-competitive business mergers and acquisitions, and illegal cartel conduct. Still, the objective of Article of the Fair Trade Act is to protect the competition rather than other business entities.[14] The protection of competition presupposes that an individual is practically guaranteed the 'freedom to participate in the competition' in the market. Accordingly, regulating unfair trade practices is designed to guarantee the 'freedom to participate in competition' and thus related to competition order.[15]

Granting variations depending on the specific type stipulated in Table 2 of the Enforcement Decree of the Fair Trade Act, a similar explanation can be given regarding 'abuse of a bargaining position'. The Supreme Court of Korea ruled that:

> [T]he relevant provisions on unfair trade practices in the Fair Trad Act define the other party to the unfair conduct as a business entity or a competitor, or the interpretation of the wording requires relevance to the trade order or competition order. Article 23(1)(4) of the former Fair Trade Act,[16] by stipulating "an act of unfairly using one's bargaining position to trade with the other party", does not limit the other party to 'a business entity or competitor'. However, considering the structure of the relevant provisions, relevance to trade order is required for the abuse of bargaining position.[17]

In light of the Supreme Court's ruling that the act of abuse of a bargaining position is relevant to the competition order, it can be seen that the purpose of the Fair Trade Act's prohibition of unfair trade practices is to regulate and adjust the economy in order to establish a fair trade order or competition order, which is distinct from the purpose of correcting the imbalance in the parties' position under private law.[18] The Supreme Court's ruling that 'trade' in unfair trade practices does not refer to individual contracts such as sales contracts, but rather to the general trade order as a means for business activities in a broader sense also supports the same.[19] Based on this point of view, the Supreme Court sets standards for cases where the counterparty to an abuse of a bargaining position is the general consumer (as opposed to a competitor or business entity). In these cases, the Supreme Court takes the

[14] Hong (n 13) 210.
[15] ibid 211.
[16] This provision corresponds to Art 45(1)(6) of the current Fair Trade Act.
[17] Supreme Court of Korea, Judgment of 10 September 2015, Case No 2012Du18325.
[18] Supreme Court of Korea, Judgment of 10 September 2015, Case No 2012Du18325; Dae-sik Hong, 'Unfair Trade Practices in Relation to Public Order and Good Morals' (2007) 14 *Journal of Comparative Private Law* 109, 115; Hong (n 13) 211 also purport the same.
[19] Supreme Court of Korea, Judgment of 14 January 2010,Case No 2008Du14739.

view that fair transactions will be impeded as long as some relevance to the trade order can be found, such as in cases where the business entity may harm many unspecified consumers by abusing its bargaining power or by similar types of violations that occur continuously and repeatedly, which could have a great ripple effect on the trade order.[20] Commentators also support the positions that, in order for abuse of a bargaining position to be recognised, there is a need for relevance to the trade order in addition to unfairness[21] and that the standard for determining illegality should require relevance to the trade order or competition order, which is different from the standard for examining the unfairness of a contract.[22]

In short, competition law is intended to protect competition, not competitors. Article 45 of the Fair Trade Act, which prohibits unfair trade practices, including abuse of a bargaining position, has the essential public purpose of protecting the competition order or trade order beyond protecting the weak or adjusting the imbalance of status between the parties. This is also intended to implement the constitutional value of economic justice. In addition, prohibiting unfair trade practices is an essential means to protect such a strong public interest. In the event of unfair trade practices, corrective measures (Article 49) and fines (Article 50) may be imposed, and the potential criminal penalties (Article 124(1)(10) and Article 125(4)) also support the strong public interest.[23]

Therefore, Article 45 of the Fair Trade Act can be seen as an overriding mandatory rule on the premise that it targets unfair trade practices that are closely related to the trade order.

c. Article 109

Article 109 of the Fair Trade Act stipulates liability for damages due to violations of the Fair Trade Act. This is to deter violations of the Fair Trade Act and contribute to providing tangible relief for victims.[24] During the period when only administrative and criminal sanctions were imposed under the Fair Trade Act, there was still an incentive to violate the Fair Trade Act where the excess revenue obtained by a company through anti-competitive activities was greater than monetary sanctions.[25] In civil law jurisdictions, the enforcement of economic laws has been carried out by public supervisory authorities, but in the US, most proceedings for violations of antitrust laws have been led by private parties.[26] Article 109 of the current Fair Trade Act introduced a private enforcement system for a stronger deterrent effect.[27]

[20] Supreme Court of Korea, Judgment of 10 September 2015, Case No 2012Du18325.

[21] Hong (n 13) 210; Myungsoo Hong, 'A Study on the Determination of Illegality According to Types of Unfair Trade Practices – Focusing on Unfairness' (2015) 50 *Kyung Hee Law Journal* 43, 68.

[22] Hong (n 13) 190.

[23] ibid 205.

[24] Byung Duck Chung, 'A Study on the Treble Damage Compensation System under the Korean Fair Trade Act' (2019) 43 *Dankook Law Review* 374, 377.

[25] Yongjin Kim, 'Pro Opt In Class Action in Antitrust Law' (2014) 21 *Journal of Comparative Private Law* 157, 176.

[26] ibid 160.

[27] ibid 176. Accordingly, treble damages was introduced under the Fair Trade Act. Such multiple damages should be distinguished from punitive damages in the US. The decisive difference is that punitive damages are designed to punish the offender for an illicit act, while treble damage compensation is designed to deter violations and compensate for the damages caused. Byung Duck Chung, 'A Study on the Treble Damage Compensation System under the Korean Fair Trade Act' (2019) 43 *Dankook Law Review* 373, 394; Young Su Shin, 'Issues and Prospects for the Introduction of Punitive Damages under Fair Trade Act' (2017) 163 *Justice* 36, 48.

Before reviewing whether Article 109 of the Fair Trade Act is an overriding mandatory rule, it is necessary to examine the relationship between the extraterritorial application clause of Article 3 of the Fair Trade Act and Article 52 of KAPIL,[28] which is the connecting principle for torts. If Article 3 of the Fair Trade Act is a special rule to Article 52 of KAPIL, Article 109 of the Fair Trade Law will prevail; if not, general principles apply and then it must be determined whether Article 3 of the Fair Trade Act would still apply as an overriding mandatory rule. This would be relevant in practice, for example, when domestic consumers claim compensation in Korean courts for damages due to illegal cartel conduct overseas by foreign companies. This will involve the question of how to determine the applicable law to the liability for damages.

There may be two possible views. The view that the extraterritorial application clause of Article 3 of the Fair Trade Act is *lex specialis* to Article 52 of KAPIL aligns the connection principle of civil liability with the connection principle of administrative and criminal sanctions (Theory 1).[29] Based on Theory 1, if administrative or criminal sanctions under the Fair Trade Act apply according to the extraterritorial application clause, Article 109 of the Fair Trade Law clearly applies to the consequent liability for damages. Consequently, the effectiveness of the regulation can be maximised by combining administrative, criminal sanctions and civil liabilities of the Fair Trade Act. Thoery 1 is persuasive.

On the other hand, Theory 2 argues that civil liability should be governed by the traditional conflict-of-laws principle on torts. According to Theory 2, the extraterritorial application of the Fair Trade Act was mainly discussed in terms of administrative or criminal sanctions and which did not consider a principle for determining the governing law of civil liability.[30] In addition, Theory 1 would not conform to the sophisticated connection principles under private international law.[31]

However, the following rebuttal is possible from the standpoint of Theory 1 on the grounds asserted for Theory 2.[32] Even if the extraterritorial application of the Fair Trade Act was mainly focused on administrative or criminal sanctions, the cause of civil liability under Article 109 is a 'violation of the provisions of this Act'. In other words, the violation of the Fair Trade Act as the premise of liability for damages is what is subject to the Act's administrative and criminal sanctions. There is no doubt that rules on public law regulations apply extraterritorially in accordance with Article 3. If illegal cartel conduct by a

[28] Art 52 (Torts): '(1) A tort shall be governed by the law of the place where it is committed or the consequences thereof occur. (2) Where the habitual residences of the tortfeasor and the injured party are in the same country while a tort is committed, the law of such country shall govern, notwithstanding paragraph (1). (3) Where a tort violates an existing legal relationship between the tortfeasor and the injured party, the law applicable to such legal relationship shall govern, notwithstanding paragraphs (1) and (2). (4) In cases of application of a foreign law under paragraphs (1) through (3), the right to claim compensation for damage resulting from a tort shall not be recognized, where the nature of such right is not evidently for the purpose of payment of due compensation to the injured party or where such right is exercised beyond the scope essentially necessary for the payment of due compensation to the injured party.'

[29] Kim (n 25) 802, 810. Kwang Hyun Suk, *Annotation to Private International Law* [Gukjesabeop haeseol] (Pakyoungsa, 2013) 414 supposes that this theory and Theory 2 below are feasible.

[30] Kwang Hyun Suk, *Private International Law* (2012) 184 presents this as the basis for Theory 2.

[31] Jong Hyeok Lee supported Theory 2 in the context of the extraterritorial application of the Capital Market and Investor Protection Act, suggesting that extraterritorial application is different on civil liability, administrative sanctions, and criminal liability. Jong Hyeok Lee, 'Prospectus Liability in Cross-border Securities Offering: Focusing on the Choice-of-law Rules' (Doctorate degree dissertation, Seoul National University, 2019) 63–66.

[32] Suk (n 30) 185.

foreigner in a foreign country affects Korea, it constitutes an act of illegal cartel conduct under the Fair Trade Act, and a person who suffers in Korea may claim damages under Article 109. Therefore, it may not be plausible to separate civil liability under Article 109 of the Fair Trade Act from the extraterritorial application clause in Article 3 of the same Act.

In addition, this author presents the following challenge to Theory 2. Article 3 of the Fair Trade Act stipulates that its provisions shall apply to cases that affect the domestic market, even if the act is committed outside the country; according to the Effect Doctrine, this can be interpreted as having stipulated the choice of law theory for special torts caused by anti-competitive acts. It is widely recognised that the applicable law is chosen by having the market as the connecting point with respect to anti-competitive activities. For instance, Article 6(3)(a)[33] of Regulation (EC) No 864/2007 of the European Parliament and of the council of 11 July 2007 on the law applicable to non-contractual obligations (hereinafter the Rome II Regulation) sets out that the law applicable to non-contractual obligations arising out of restrictions on competition is the law of the country in which the market is affected or likely to be affected. Likewise, Article 137(1) of the Swiss Federal Act on Private International Law (FAPIL) also states, 'Claims based on a restraint of competition are governed by the law of the state in whose market the restraint has direct effects on the injured party'[34] and determines the applicable law of civil liability arising from anti-competitive acts using the market as the connecting point. In the US, the Sherman Act is applied extraterritorially according to the Effect Doctrine, and US courts only rule on domestic damages regarding civil liability arising from anti-competitive acts committed in a foreign country and apply US law without applying the foreign antitrust law as the governing law.[35] This also establishes the connection principle by setting the market as the connecting point.

However, it is worth paying attention to some of Theory 2's criticisms of Theory 1; namely, that Article 3 of the Fair Trade Act is not a 'sophisticated' connecting principle. In a situation where major blocs and countries around the world, such as the EU and the US, are applying their own competition laws extraterritorially, the rules under Article 3 cannot help identify which of the overlapping competition laws of each country should be applied. In other words, if both the Korean market and the foreign market are affected by illegal cartel conduct committed in a foreign country, and if a Korean individual claims compensation for damages due to such illegal cartel conduct in a Korean court, it may be unclear whether to apply the Korean Fair Trade Act or foreign competition laws (representing a 'true conflict of laws').[36]

Nevertheless, the 'overlap of civil liability itself' may not be a major issue.[37] In practice, it is unusual for foreign competition laws to purport to apply in disputes over civil liability in the forum country.[38] The EU and the US recognise their international jurisdiction based

[33] Art 6 (Unfair Competition and Acts Restricting Free Competition): '3. (a) The law applicable to a non-contractual obligation arising out of a restriction of competition shall be the law of the country where the market is, or is likely to be, affected.

[34] An unofficial English translation of the FAPIL can be accessed at: www.fedlex.admin.ch/eli/cc/1988/1776_1776_1776/en.

[35] Yongjin Kim, 'Choice of Law in International Antitrust Law' (2013) 44 *Journal of Legislation Research* 801, 803.

[36] Suk (n 29) 183.

[37] In contrast, overlapping administrative or criminal sanctions related to international cartels by multiple jurisdictions are recognised as an important issue. See subsection d. below.

[38] Kim (n 35) 803.

on the impact of anti-competitive acts on their domestic markets and adopt the so-called 'mosaic theory', determining only the damages incurred within their own countries.[39] Given this, there will not be many cases in which courts of one country make decisions on damages incurred in another country by applying the civil liability provisions of another country, or apply the civil liability provisions of another country to damages incurred in their own country.

On the other hand, as I will discuss in subsection d. below, there have been attempts to resolve the overlap of administrative sanctions, which is the prerequisite of civil liability, by limiting extraterritorial application of competition laws or adopting a conflict-of-laws approach in determining which law to apply. With such methodology, it is possible to design a more nuanced conflict-of-laws principle based on Article 3 of the Fair Trade Act. Therefore, arguably, Article 3 of the Fair Trade Act is the special rule to Article 52 of KAPIL. Article 109 of the Fair Trade Act applies to liability for damages for acts violating the Fair Trade Act, regardless of Article 52 of KAPIL. Consequently, from this point of Theory 1, reviewing whether Article 109 of the Fair Trade Act is an overriding mandatory rule may not be seen as considerably useful as it will apply as *lex specialis*.

However, even if one takes the view that Theory 2 is correct, a similar result can be achieved if Article 109 of the Fair Trade Act is an overriding mandatory rule. Even according to the viewpoint of Theory 2, Article 3 of the Fair Trade Act nevertheless can be seen to stipulate the scope of the Act's *in personam* and spatial application. It can be inferred that legislators intended Article 109 of the Fair Trade Act to apply to torts with foreign elements, even when their governing law is foreign. Next, whether Article 109 has a special legislative purpose in connection with Article 20 of KAPIL should be examined.

Liability for damages under Article 109 of the Fair Trade Act is intended to compensate the victims, but at the same time, it represents private enforcement of competition law.[40] This is essential for the national economic interest of protecting the competition in the market and corresponds to the special legislative purpose of Article 20 of KAPIL. Therefore, Article 109 of the Fair Trade Act constitutes an overriding mandatory rule.[41]

d. Resolving the Issue of Overlapping Regulations Due to Extraterritorial Application

If domestic laws are applied extraterritorially without restrictions, there will be problems such as conflicts between jurisdictions with overlapping regulations. Therefore, jurisdictions that recognise the extraterritorial application of competition laws have also been developing legal principles to tackle this issue.[42]

[39] ibid, 803–17. The 'mosaic theory' is a legal principle recognised in the *Shevill v Pressee Alliance* Case C-68/93, ECLI:EU:C:1995:61, ECR [1995] I-00415 at the European Court of Justice, a case where the plaintiff's reputation was damaged in many countries by the defendant's actions. On the other hand, Art 6(3)(b) of the Rome II Regulation recognises the exception that if the claimant is affected by the market in the country where the defendant's business is located, the court of that country may render judgments on damages incurred outside that country in accordance with the law of the country where the market is located.

[40] Section by Kyungpil No, in Iksoo Park (ed), *ONJU Fair Trade Act* (Thomson Reuters, 2015) Art 56, § 1.

[41] Kyung Han Sohn purports the same. Kyung Han Sohn, 'Recent Case Law Developments in Governing Law of Contractual Obligation in Korea' (2016) 22 *Korea Private International Law Journal* 103, 129.

[42] This issue is not limited to competition laws but arises from the extraterritorial application of laws.

In the US, the so-called 'interest balancing theory' or 'jurisdictional rule of reason' was adopted in *Timberland Lumber Co v Bank of America National Trust & Savings Association*.[43] This means that, as a matter of international comity and fairness, domestic law should be applied extraterritorially only when the degree to which the domestic competition order is violated by the foreign anti-competitive act is greater than the degree to which foreign sovereignty is restricted when domestic law is applied extraterritorially. Thereafter, the US Supreme Court ruled in *Hartford Fire Insurance Co v California (Hartford Fire)*[44] that there is a true conflict of laws only if the law of the foreign country – the place of action – requires a violation of US law or renders it impossible to comply with both the foreign law and US law, and that only in the case of such a conflict is it necessary to compare the various factors between foreign law and US law. It is also worth noting that the US Supreme Court declared that the securities laws should be presumed to have been excluded from extraterritorial application in the *Morrison*[45] and *Nabisco*.[46]

The Supreme Court of Korea rendered a similar ruling to *Hartford Fire*. The Court, in the judgment of 24 December 2014, Case No 2012Du6216 declared 'direct, significant and reasonably foreseeable effects' as the principle of restriction on extraterritorial application of the Fair Trade Act. The Court, in the judgment of 16 May 2014, Case No 2012Du13689 stated factors to consider in limiting the extraterritorial application of the Fair Trade Act in cases where a certain act is permitted under foreign law whereas it is not allowed under the Korean Fair Trade Act:

> If domestic law and foreign law conflict regarding the same conduct to the extent that the business entity cannot choose a legitimate action, the application of only domestic law cannot be enforced in such a case; thus, if a request to respect foreign law is significantly greater than a enforcing the Fair Trade Act, the application of the Fair Trade Act may be restricted. Whether a case falls under such a scenario should be determined by comprehensively considering the impact of the relevant conduct on the domestic market, the degree of the foreign government's involvement in the relevant conduct, the extent of conflict between domestic and foreign laws, the extent of disadvantage to foreign business entities and the degree of harm to foreign government's legitimate interests when applying domestic law to the relevant act.[47]

In addition to the traditional restrictions on extraterritorial application, it is interesting that many arguments have recently been presented that overlaps of administrative or criminal sanctions due to extraterritorial application of competitions laws should be resolved by applying the connection principle of private international law. First, there is the argument that the principles of private international law – such as the separation of jurisdiction and governing law; characterisation, *depéçage*, adaptation, *renvoi* and public policy; and the choice-of-laws rule for torts that connect the place of tort and the place of damages – should

[43] 549 F 2d 597 (9th Cir 1976).

[44] 509 US 764(1993).

[45] *Morrison v National Australia Bank Ltd* 547 F 3d 167 (2d Cir 2008).

[46] *RJR Nabisco v European Community* 136 S Ct 2090 (2016). See Seonuk Park, 'Standards of Extraterritoriality of US Antitrust Law: Applying the US Supreme Court's Analysis in RJR Nabisco to Foreign Component Cartels' (2020) 30 *Dong-A Journal of International Business Transactions Law* 227.

[47] This is reminiscent of legal doctrine on the true conflict of laws, as used in the decision by the US Supreme Court in *Hartford Fire* (n 44).

be applied to resolve the issue of overlapping regulations.[48] However, this argument, as acknowledged by its supporter, is difficult to be immediately put into practice and needs more detailed principles of application.[49]

Others call for the application of the legal principle of 'substitution' from private international law while emphasising that each country needs to refrain from overregulating.[50] Recognising that what is required under the substantial law of a particular country may conflict with the substantial law of another country, those who hold this view believe that compliance with country A's financial regulations (for example) should be deemed the same as compliance with country B's regulations. Thus, if country A's regulations are complied with, country B's regulations can be ignored. This approach is already being used in the current practice of financial regulations.[51]

Regarding overlaps in public law regulations, the movement to adopt private international law methodology is consistent with Savigny's predictions. Savigny said that if the purpose of mandatory rules or interfering norms were internationally recognised, the connecting principles for overriding mandatory rules would become meaningless, and consequently, unilateral conflict-of-laws rules would change into multilateral ones.[52,53] Each country's adoption of provisions with similar regulatory purposes that apply extraterritorially may be perceived as a pathway to a place where the 'objective of the overriding mandatory rules is internationally recognised', as Savigny predicted. In this author's view, however, the mere fact that various countries are establishing overlapping regulations in certain areas of law does not necessarily mean that the concept of overriding mandatory rules should be abandoned yet.

The issue of overlapping regulations may be effectively resolved if equivalence and substitutability for laws that pursue essential national public interests can be secured. In the area of competition law, major countries and blocs such as the US, the EU, Germany and Japan regulate similarly anti-competitive activities and recognise the extraterritorial application of competition law based on the same connecting point of the market location. Therefore, it can be said that the equivalence and substitutability of regulations have been secured to some extent, and there are examples of legislation that introduced two-sided conflict-of-laws principles on claims due to restrictions on competition. This is the case in Article 137(1) of FAPIL and Article 6(3) of the Rome II Regulation.

[48] Ralf Michaels, 'Towards a private international law for regulatory conflicts?' (2016) 59 *Japanese Yearbook of International Law* 175, 175 ff.

[49] ibid 191–95.

[50] Matthias Lehmann, 'New challenges of extraterritoriality: superposing laws' in Franco Ferrari and Diego Fernández Arroyo (eds), *Private International Law: Contemporary Challenges and Continuing Relevance* (Elgar, 2019) 288.

[51] Annelise Riles, 'Managing Regulatory Arbitrage: A Conflict of Laws Approach' (2014) 47 *Cornell International Law Journal* (2014) 63, 103.

[52] Changseon Shin, 'The Objectives and Ideals of Private International Law: Focusing on the Relationship between Private International Law Justice and Substantive Law Justice' (2000) 5 *Korea Private International Law Journal* 86.

[53] In line with this, Kongwoong Choi, 'Extraterritorial Jurisdiction and Private International Law' (1994) 3 *Korea Private International Law Journal* 152, 163, 174 also argues that public law should also be applied under the traditional connecting principles in private international law. He contended that it is possible to apply public law with Savigny's choice of law rules based on the closest connection.

However, it is difficult practically to tackle regulation overlaps in the same way as two-sided conflict-of-laws rules in areas where each country's regulations are not homogeneous. It would also be very time-consuming and costly to standardise the practical laws of statutes.[54] In response to this situation, an attempt has been made in the US to present private international law solutions that are based on Currie's interest analysis theory.[55,56] This approach offers the following explanation of the advantages of taking private international law solutions rather than standardising laws, especially in the area of international finance laws. First, it is possible to take a multilateral approach as an alternative to choosing political regulations led by a few leading countries in finance. Due to the technical characteristics of private international law, it is easier to standardise the principles of private international law rather than harmonising the substantive laws of each country whose political interests may conflict. That the connecting principles in private international law are already somewhat uniform is another advantage. Secondly, adopting a private international law methodology can lead to a valid conclusion in specific cases by encouraging careful consideration of what the relevant regulatory authority is, how each regulatory principle differs, and what national and party interests are involved.[57] Rather than applying uniform principles to certain types of transactions, different conclusions may be reached depending on what interfaces there are between certain parties and relevant regulatory authorities. The essence of the solution suggested by this view is to analyse various conflicting interests in the case of overlapping regulations and apply the regulations of the countries with the greater interests.[58] As such, it is claimed that this approach can prevent regulatory arbitrage.

This view offers valuable and specific guidance about how to apply the principles of private international law to resolve the problem of regulation overlaps. However, Currie's interest theory, which forms the basis of this methodology, seeks to derive conflict-of-laws principles based on the interests protected by each substantive legal norm and the applicable facts, which is substantially different from the connecting principle of KAPIL. Under KAPIL, the connecting principle, as in other civil law countries, determines the applicable law based on the connecting point, so such a methodology would be out of place in the Korean legal system.[59]

[54] Riles (n 51) 63–64.

[55] Brainerd Currie, 'Married Women's Contracts: A Study in Conflict-of-Law Method' (1958) 25 *University of Chicago Law Review* 227, 234 ff.

[56] Riles (n 51) 63 ff.

[57] ibid 100–05.

[58] Riles shows how cases can be resolved by applying the methodology of interest analysis with a hypothetical case where the regulations of the UK and the US financial services overlap in their application. ibid 106–14.

[59] For a discussion of this issue in Japan, see Nobuo Fujikawa, 'Toward Unification and Order Formation of Extraterritorial Application Rules in International Transactions', (2013) 79 *Japanese Legal Studies* 1, 15, 23 and thereafter (藤川信夫, 「國際取引における域外適用ル-ル統一化ならびに秩序形成に向 けて」, 日本法學 第79巻 第1号 (2013)) [Kokusaitoryū ni okeru iki-gai tekiyō rūru tōitsu-ka narabini chitsujo keisei ni mukete," Nihon Hōgaku, Dai 79-kan Dai 1-gō (2013)]. Nobuo says that extraterritorial application that interferes with the economic policies of other countries is not permitted under international law and that three principles derived from international law would be critical: (1) there is a substantial and genuine connection between the subject of jurisdiction and the origin of jurisdiction; (2) there is no interference with matters within the jurisdiction of other countries; and (3) it is in accordance with the principles of suitability, reciprocity and proportionality. (2) is of particular importance according to this view. However, it is questionable whether a criterion like (2) would actually be useful. When the extraterritorial application of various countries' provisions overlaps, asserting that one country shall not interfere when another country has jurisdiction cannot be an adequate solution to the question of which country's laws shall apply when all countries have jurisdiction.

Currently, it seems difficult to present a universally valid and uniform solution to the issue of overlapping public law regulations regarding all types of extraterritorial application in all areas of law. This is because the extent to which substantive law regulations are unified and the need for standardisation depend on the specific area of law. Considering that the legislative situation and the focus of regulations differ with the country, standardising the substantive law of regulations worldwide may not be the best approach. In this situation, this author believes a more practical way to resolve the regulation overlap issue would be by utilising various legal principles of private international law in consideration of the legal areas where regulations are challenged and the nature of regulations.

First, when the substantive laws of regulations are unified to some extent, as with restrictions on competition, overlapping public administrative or criminal sanctions can be tackled in the same way as two-sided conflict-of-laws principles. Determining the connecting point according to which country has a greater regulatory interest would guarantee the predictability of the applicable law without any need to analyse interests on a case-by-case basis. If it is believed that a country other than those selected through the two-sided conflict provisions has a greater regulatory interest, the same principle as the exception provision in Article 21[60] of KAPIL may be established. Second, when the overlapping administrative or criminal sanctions have a similar focus despite the substantive law not having been standardised, the legal principle of 'substitute' from private international law can be adopted. For example, if a financial institution's licence requirements are met in one jurisdiction, its licence can also be recognised in other jurisdictions. Third, when the substantive laws of regulations are not standardised and focus on different things, there is no great need to tackle the regulation overlap itself.

ii. Foreign Exchange Transactions Act

Although the foreign exchange laws of countries are cited as a typical example of overriding mandatory rules,[61] it is difficult to find literature that examines which specific provisions of the Foreign Exchange Transactions Act correspond to overriding mandatory rules. In the past, Korea prohibited the creation, alteration, repayment and extinction of bonds between residents and non-residents in principle under the Foreign Exchange Management Act. But as a result of gradual foreign exchange liberalisation and deregulation in accordance with policies aimed at revitalising foreign transactions, the Foreign Exchange Management Act,

[60] Art 21 (Exception to Designation of Applicable Law): '(1) Where the applicable law designated under this Act is slightly related to the corresponding legal relationship and where the law of another country most closely related to such legal relationship obviously exists, the law of the other country shall govern. (2) Paragraph (1) shall not apply if the parties choose the applicable law by agreement.'

[61] For discussions of English law, see Lawrence Collins (ed), *Dicey, Morris & Collins: The Conflict of Laws*, 15th edn (Sweet & Maxwell, 2012) vol 2, para 37-067; for discussions of Swiss law, see section by Frank Vischer and Corrine Widmer Lüchinger in Markus Müller-Chen (ed), *Zürcher Kommentar zum IPRG*, Bd I-1, 3rd edn (Schulthess, 2018) Art 18, Rn 42; for discussions of German law, see section by Dieter Martiny in Franz Jürgen Säcker (ed), *Münchener Kommentar zum BGB*, 8th edn (Verlag Beck München, 2021) Rom I-VO Art 9, Rn 68; section by Martin Zwickel in Dieter Martiny (ed) *Internationales Vertragsrecht*, 9th edn (Ottoschmidt, 2022), Rn 5.115. Suk (n 29) 142; Kwang Hyun Suk, 'The General Contract Terms Control Act of Korea and Its Application to Hull Insurance Contract between Two Korean Companies Governed by English Law' (2015) 149 *Justice* 207–08; Chang Seop Shin, *Private International Law* [Gukjesabeop je4pan], 4th edn (Sechang, 2018) 134; Changseon Shin and Namsoon Yoon, *New Private International Law* [Singukjesabeop je2pan], 2nd edn (Fides, 2016) 274–75.

which was of a strongly regulatory nature, was abolished, and the current Foreign Exchange Transactions Act now allows foreign exchange transactions to be freely conducted in principle and only imposes restrictions exceptionally.[62]

Among the provisions of the Foreign Exchange Transactions Act, foreign exchange regulations in the traditional sense[63] are the obligations to pay/receive, temporarily suspend transactions in whole or in part, deposit or sell means of payment or precious metals in or to the Bank of Korea following a grave and sudden changes in domestic and foreign economic conditions; for nationals to collect claims from non-nationals (Article 6(1)); to receive permission for capital transactions where the balance of payments or international finance are confronted with serious difficulty or where serious obstacles exist in carrying out currency policies, exchange rate policies and other macroeconomic policies (Article 6(2)).

The Foreign Exchange Transactions Act also stipulates payment and receipt methods (Article 16), export and import of payment means (Article 17)' and capital transactions (Article 18) as transactions subject to reporting even though none of them have been traditionally considered key types of foreign exchange regulations. According to each of the above provisions, many types of international transactions, such as offsetting, mutual accounts, overseas deposits, overseas borrowings, issuance of securities, acquisition of overseas real estate by residents, acquisition of domestic real estate by non-residents, foreign direct investment, establishment of overseas branches and leases between residents and non-residents, are subject to the Foreign Exchange Transactions Act; it is therefore necessary to examine whether any are overriding mandatory rules. In addition, Article 15 of the Foreign Exchange Transactions Act provides that if necessitated by the implementation of international treaties and international laws, a resident or non-resident may obtain permission to make a payment from the Republic of Korea to a foreign country and a resident may also obtain permission to make a payment to or receive one from a non-resident, which also directly affects international transactions. In the following section, this author will examine whether each of the aforementioned provisions constitutes an overriding mandatory rule.

Article 2 of the Foreign Exchange Transactions Act states that its provisions shall be applicable to 'foreign exchange in the Republic of Korea, foreign exchange transactions conducted therein, or other acts related thereto' (Article 2(1)), 'transactions, payments or receipts between the Republic of Korea and any foreign country, or other acts related thereto (including those which are performed in any foreign country and which have an effect in the Republic of Korea)' (Article 2(2)), 'transactions between an individual having a domicile

[62] Minwoo Kang, 'The Redesign of Enforcement System on the Violation of Foreign Exchange Transactions Regulation' (2016) 13 *Korea Financial Law Association* 139, 141. The Foreign Exchange Transactions Act categorises the relevant transactions into reporting exemptions, reported matters and permitted matters in consideration of the transactions' impact on the market. The Foreign Exchange Transactions Regulations as announced by the Ministry of Strategy and Finance further specifies the types of transactions subject to reporting or reporting exemptions. See Kang (ibid) 149 for further details.

[63] Traditionally, foreign exchange regulations were focused on providing for the obligation to waive foreign currency in exchange for an amount calculated at a specific exchange rate for the national currency or a moratorium on payments by domestic debtors to foreign creditors. Charles Proctor, *Mann on the Legal Aspect of Money*, 7th edn (Oxford University Press, 2012) para 16.14 refers to Art 2 of the UK Exchange Control Act 1948 as an example. The foreign exchange regulation of Argentina, which was at issue in Seoul High Court, Judgment of 6 March 2009, Case No 2007Na122966 also falls under this case. See Kwang Hyun Suk, 'The Application of Foreign Exchange Control Law and Other Internationally Mandatory Rules of Third Countries in International Financial Transactions: Including Article VIII2(b) of the Articles of Agreement of the International Monetary Fund' (2020) 26 *Korea Private International Law Journal* 353, 386 and thereafter for comments on the foregoing judgment.

or residence in a foreign country and a legal entity having a main office in a foreign country, which are denominated or payable in the currency of the Republic of Korea, or other acts related thereto' (Article 2(3)), 'acts conducted by an individual having a domicile or residence in the Republic of Korea, or his or her agents, employers or other employees in connection with his or her assets or business in a foreign country' (Article 2(4)) and 'acts conducted by a representative, agents, employers or other employees of a legal entity having its main office in the Republic of Korea in connection with assets or business of the legal entity in a foreign country' (Article 2(5)). Article 2(2) of the Foreign Exchange Transactions Act corresponds to an extraterritorial application clause, and Article 2(1), (3), (4) and (5) stipulates the international and spatial scope of application for cases with foreign elements. Therefore, the legislator's intention to apply the said provision regardless of the governing law of the relevant legal relationship may be derived.

It is now important to examine whether the Foreign Exchange Transactions Act recognises the special legislative purpose of Article 20 of KAPIL. Under Article 1(1), the purpose of the Foreign Exchange Transactions Act is

> to contribute to the sound development of the national economy by striving to facilitate foreign transactions, to maintain equilibrium in the balance of payments and to stabilise the value of the currency by ensuring liberalisation of foreign exchange transactions and of other foreign transactions, and by invigorating market function.

Articles 6 and 15 through 18 of the Foreign Exchange Transactions Act are concerned with achieving the economic purpose of the state; requiring permission or reporting for acts subject to regulation in each of the provisions therein are essential means for achieving such important public interests. The purpose sought by each of these provisions cannot be achieved through similar provisions in foreign exchange laws of other countries, so there is no equivalence or substitutability of provisions. Any violation of Article 6 of the Foreign Exchange Transactions Act shall be subject to criminal punishment (as stipulated in Article 27), and any violation of Articles 15–18 shall also be subject to administrative warning, suspension or restriction of transactions, revocation of permission, and criminal punishment (Articles 19, 27(2), and 29). The very existence of these sanctions also supports strong public purposes.

In sum, Articles 6, 15 and 18 of the Foreign Exchange Transactions Act are all overriding mandatory rules.[64,65]

[64] The Supreme Court of Korea, the *en banc* Judgment of 22 April 1975, Case No 72Da2161 applied Art 21(1)(2) of the former Foreign Exchange Management Act (before amended by Act No 4447 of 1 September 1992), which in principle prohibited a resident from paying a non-resident, and Art 23, which in principle prohibited the creation, modification, repayment or extinction of claims between a resident and a non-resident, irrespective of the applicable of the relevant legal relationship. Supreme Court of Korea, Judgment of 10 February 1981, Case No 80Da1670 also applied Art 30 of the former Foreign Exchange Management Act which prohibits non-residents from acquiring domestic real estate without permission from the Minister of Finance and Economy, not having determined whether the applicable law was Korean law. The Supreme Court's application of each of the above provision seems to represent the application of overriding mandatory rules of the forum.

[65] On the other hand, there is also a view that the Foreign Exchange Management Act was deemed a domestic mandatory rule, based on how the Supreme Court regarded the former Foreign Exchange Management Act as containing crackdown provisions (*Ordnungsvorschriften*). See Supreme Court of Korea, Judgment of 20 April 1972, Case No 72Da428. Choon Soo An, *Private International Law* (Bobmunsa, 2017) 156. However, whether the provision is an overriding mandatory rule and whether it contains crackdown provisions are different discussions altogether, and being a crackdown provision does not necessarily preclude it from being an overriding mandatory rule. Suk (n 29) 141 purports the same.

B. Provisions Defining International or Spatial Scope of Application

Even if a provision does not explicitly stipulate its applicability irrespective of the relevant legal relationship's applicable law, the inclusion of international or spatial scope may suggest the legislator's intention to that effect. The Foreign Trade Act, Employment Security Act and State Contracts Act are examples of that.

i. *Foreign Trade Act*

Legislations restricting certain imports and exports with foreign countries (import and export restrictions) have historically existed in various jurisdictions.[66] Currently, countries around the world are controlling exports through multilateral systems to prevent the leakage and spread of technologies that may pose risks to world peace and security.[67,68] Since Korea possesses cutting-edge technologies in the fields of information technology, smartphones, shipbuilding, and automobile manufacture, and is under the threat of North Korea's nuclear weapons development, Korea cannot be free from these risks.[69] The Foreign Trade Act is a general law on foreign trade, and in certain cases, Article 5 stipulates the basis for import and export restrictions. This provision is important for the performance of obligations under international treaties in relation to international trade security.[70,71]

[66] The Coordinating Committee for Multilateral Export Control (COCOM) established by the US during the Cold War is seen as the starting point for modern import/export restrictions. The US pursued a blockade strategy of preventing the transfer of munitions and military technology through international cooperation with its allies to control communist countries after World War II, and export controls were one such means. That led to threats by rogue states and non-state actors and export controls to block them and their access to weapons of mass destruction (WMD) from the 1990s. Eon Kyung Park and Sang Han Wang, 'Legal Issues on Illegal Exporting Case of Mugunghwa Satellite No 3 – With a Focus on the Export Control on Strategic Items under the Foreign Trade Act' (2017) 52 *Kyung Hee Law Journal* 545, 549.

[67] Since the 9/11 terror attacks in 2001, the implementation of such 'supply chain control' has emerged as a key issue in the international community. ibid 551.

[68] If such export restrictions belong neither to the state of *lex causae* nor *lex fori*, the question arises as to how to handle them. This is a question of how to treat the overriding mandatory rules of third countries. The *Borax* and *Borsäure* rulings of the German Federal Court of Justice, which are analysed in ch 5, II, B, also questioned how the US export controls and sanctions should be considered under *lex causae*.

[69] Sung-won Kim, Seungwoo Son and Hyunwoo You, 'A Legal Study on the Export Control of Technology – Focus on the National Core Technology and Strategic Technology' (2016) 6 *Korean Journal of Industrial Security* 80. The transfer of such technology is not only related to companies' industrial competitiveness but also affects national security. Eon Kyung Park and Sang Han Wang, 'Implementation of Export Control Regulations – Status and Prospects of the Legislation for the Intangible Transfer of Technology (ITT) Control on Nuclear Related Items' (2018) 53 *Kyung Hee Law Journal* 382.

[70] In Korea, the former Trade Act (abolished upon the enactment of the Foreign Trade Act on 31 December 1986 and enforced on 1 July 1987) stipulated that in principle the export and import of goods must be approved by the Minister of Commerce and Industry, a stance that has been maintained even after the Foreign Trade Act was enacted. Since then, as a matter of principle, the Foreign Trade Act (which was wholly amended and implemented on 30 December 1996) has allowed the free export and import of goods. Permission or approval from the Minister of Trade, Industry and Energy is required only in exceptional cases.

[71] Dong Jun Choi, 'The Legal System for Protecting Technical Information in Korea – Focused on the Definition of Technical Information, the Types of Infringement, and the Legal Protection Methods of Relevant Laws' (2021) 72 *Kyoungpook National University Law Journal* 275, 320; Eon Kyung Park and Sang Han Wang, 'A Study upon the Legal System Regarding the Export Control of Strategic Items – The Controls on Transit or Transshipment of the Foreign Trade Act' (2020) 10 *Sogang Journal of Law and Business* 3, 6.

Article 19(2) of the Foreign Trade Act and Article 32 of the Enforcement Decree of the Foreign Trade Act provide that permission for exports shall be obtained from the Minister of Trade, Industry and Energy or the head of an administrative agency with respect to permission for the export of goods that require restrictions and the transfer of technology (strategic items)[72] that meet certain requirements to maintain international peace and security and national security. This is in accordance with the principles set forth in the Wassenaar Arrangement on Export Controls for Conventional Arms and Dual-Use Goods and Technologies (WA), Nuclear Suppliers Group (NSG), Missile Technology Regime (MTCR), Australia Group (AG), Chemical Weapons Convention (CWC), Biological Weapons Convention (BWC)[73] and the Arms Trade Treaty (ATT). Furthermore, Article 19(3) provides that non-strategic items that are highly likely to be diverted to the manufacture, development or use of weapons of mass destruction, missiles (and other delivery systems), and conventional weapons shall be subject to situational permission[74] in cases where the exporter knew of or is suspected to have the intention of diversion.

Export and import restrictions are a typical example of overriding mandatory rules.[75] The EU regulation that requires permission for the export of dual-use goods[76] across its borders,[77] the German Foreign Trade and Payments Act (*Außenwirtschaftgesetz*) provisions that regulate contracts for import and export, and the German Weapons Act (*Kriegswaffenkontrollgesetz*) requiring permission for the export and import of goods listed in the war weapons list are deemed to be overriding mandatory rules.[78] However, it is difficult to find literature that discusses which provisions of the Foreign Trade Act are overriding mandatory rules, other than abstract references[79] to the act being an example

[72] Strategic goods are goods, equipment, materials and technologies that may give a strategic advantage to a particular country or increase the threat of war. Eon Kyung Park and Chul Won Suh, 'Appraisal and Reform of Regulations upon the Export Control of Strategic Items: Focusing on the Foreign Trade Act' (2018) 16 *Korean Journal of International Economic Law* 157.

[73] For details of the items subject to export control by export control system, see the Table in Kim, Son and You (n 69) 77, 84–86; Park and Suh (n 72) 161.

[74] This is referred to as 'catch-all control', a system that controls all items that may be diverted to the development of weapons of mass destruction and missiles or other delivery systems, regardless of whether the items are listed on the control list. Park and Wang (n 71) 12.

[75] For discussions on English law, see Paul Torremans (ed), *Cheshire, North & Fawcett: Private International Law*, 15th edn (Oxford University Press, 2017) 743; Jonathan Hill and Adeline Chong, *International Commercial Disputes*, 4th edn (Hart Publishing, 2010) para 14.3.2. For discussions on German law, see Kurt Rebmann (ed), *Münchener Kommentar zum BGB*, 4th edn (Verlag Beck München, 2006) EGBGB 34, Rn 77ff; Martiny (n 61) Rom I-VO, Art 9, Rn 58ff; Lisa Günther, *Die Anwendbargkeit ausländischer Eingriffnormen im Lichter der Rom I- und Rom II Verordnungen* (Verlag Alma Mater, 2011) 13; Paul Hauser, *Eingriffsnormen in der Rom- I Verordnung* (Mohr Siebeck, 2012) 46; section by Martin Zwickel in Dieter Martiny (ed), *Internationales Vertragsrecht*, 9th edn (Ottoschmidt, 2022) Rn 5.64. For discussions on Swiss law, see Vischer and Lüchinger (n 61) Art 18, Rn 5. Regarding Korean law, see Suk (n 29) 142; Changseon Shin and Namsoon Yoon, *New Private International Law* [Singukjesabeop je2pan], 2nd edn (Fides, 2016) 274–75; Shin (n 61) 134.

[76] Dual-use goods are industrial goods that can also contribute to the proliferation of weapons of mass destruction. Strategic items subject to export permission under the Foreign Trade Act are double-use goods. Park and Wang (n 66) 553.

[77] Council Regulation (EC) No 1334/2000 of 22 June 2000 set up a Community regime for the control of exports of dual-use items and technology.

[78] Section by Dieter Martiny in Kurt Rebmann, *Münchener Kommentar zum BGB*, 4th edn (Verlag Beck München, 2006) EGBGB Art 34, Rn 84; Martiny (n 61) Rom I-VO Art 9, Rn 62–67.

[79] Suk (n 29) 142; Shin and Yoon (n 75) 274–75; Shin (n 61) 134.

of an overriding mandatory rule in Korean legal literature. In recent years, KT exported *Mugunghwa 3*, a major strategic item, to a Hong Kong company without obtaining permission from the relevant authority, resulting in an international dispute.[80] Accordingly, this author will examine whether Article 19(2)–(3) of the Foreign Trade Act constitutes overriding mandatory rules.

Article 19(2)–(3) stipulate that if a person intends to 'export' goods that constitute strategic items or weapons of mass destruction, he or she shall obtain permission from the Minister of Trade, Industry and Energy or the head of the relevant administrative agency. The Foreign Trade Act does not stipulate that this provision applies irrespective of the governing law of the relevant legal relationship, but explicitly states the international scope of application (ie., export from Korea to overseas) for legal relationships with foreign elements. Therefore, the legislator intended for the provision to apply regardless of the governing law of the export contract, so long as the relevant facts constitute an 'export' under the provision.

Next, whether the legislative purpose of Article 19(2)–(3) of the Foreign Trade Act corresponds to the special legislative purpose of Article 20 of KAPIL is examined. The purpose of the Foreign Trade Act is 'to contribute to the growth of the national economy by promoting foreign trade, establishing a fair trade system, maintaining international balance of payments, and expanding commerce' (Article 1). In addition, the purpose of the requirements in Article 19(2)–(3) to obtain permission for exporting strategic items and weapons of mass destruction is to achieve national security in international trade by 'perform(ing) duties to maintain international peace and security under treaties on trade entered into and promulgated pursuant to the Constitution of the Republic of Korea and generally accepted international laws and regulations' (Article 5(4)). This is an important economic and political purpose of the state. In addition, requiring permission for exports in Article 19(2)–(3) of the Foreign Trade Act is an essential means to accomplish such important public interests. This provision protects a public interest that cannot be protected under the laws of other countries, meaning that there is no legal substitutability or equivalence to the Foreign Trade Act of Korea. If Article 19(2)–(3) of the Foreign Trade Act are violated, criminal punishment will be imposed in accordance with Article 53 of the Foreign Trade Act, which is also a basis for finding essential public purpose. Therefore, Article 19(2)–(3) of the Foreign Trade Act contains overriding mandatory rules.

[80] KT, a Korean company, exported *Mugunghwa 3*, a satellite (regarded as a strategic item), to Hong Kong Asia Broadcast Site (ABS) in September 2011 without permission from the Minister of Trade, Industry and Energy (then the Minister of Knowledge Economy), in violation of the Foreign Trade Act. As such, on 18 December 2013, the Ministry of Science, ICT and Future Planning notified KT SAT (a company in which KT owns 100% of the shares that was physically split off from KT on 4 December 2012) of the nullification of the agreement to sell *Mugunghwa 3*, which was believed to violate mandatory rules such as the Telecommunications Business Act, Radio Act, and Foreign Trade Act, and revoked the allocation of frequency bands for the satellite services. In December 2013, ABS initiated an ICC arbitration proceedings claiming against KT SAT for damages and sought declaration of the ownership of the satellite, where it prevailed. Subsequently, KT SAT filed a lawsuit in the Federal Court of New York to annul the arbitration award, but lost, and the decision became final as the appeal to the US Court of Appeals for the Second Circuit and the application for leave to appeal to the Supreme Court were dismissed in December 2019. For detailed facts, see Park and Wang (n 66) 547–58; Min-ji Choi, 'Low-cost Sale of "Mugunghwa 3" Concludes with International Lawsuit … KT Faces Final Defeat' [Heolgap maegak 'mugunghwa 3-ho' gukjesosong jonggyeol … KT choejong paeso] *Digital Daily* (12 March 2020).

ii. Employment Security Act

Article 33(1) of the Employment Security Act stipulates that 'No person shall engage in a labor supply business without obtaining permission of the Minister of Employment and Labor.' A 'labour supply business' is a business that facilitates the provision of employees to work for individuals or entities based on supply contracts (Article 2(2)). Since labour supply contracts concern the transaction or lease of labour provided by humans, they are prohibited in principle (unlike the transaction or lease of goods) and only permitted exceptionally, under strict conditions.[81] However, it is questionable whether this regulation applies to cases where the governing law of the relevant contract is foreign law. For example, it is uncertain whether Article 33(1) of the Employment Security Act applies to contracts in which foreign companies supply pilots to domestic airlines.[82] Hereinafter, the question of whether Article 33(1) is an overriding mandatory rule will be examined.

The Employment Security Act does not explicitly stipulate that Article 33(1) should be applied regardless of the applicable law in the relevant contract, and there is no extraterritorial application clause. However, Article 33(3)[83] categorises the labour supply business into domestic and overseas labour supply businesses according to the place where the workers being supplied intend to work. That provision defines the scope of persons eligible to obtain permission for such business as 'a trade union under the Trade Union and Labor Relations Adjustment Act' for domestic labour supply business and 'a person who operates manufacturing business, construction business, service business, or other services in Korea' for overseas labour supply business. This bases the international and spatial scope of the application of Article 33(1) of the Employment Security Act on the premise of legal relationships that include foreign elements. Therefore, the legislators' intent was for the Employment Security Act to apply regardless of the law applicable to the labour relationship.

Next up is the question of whether the Employment Security Act pursues a special purpose under Article 20 of KAPIL. Under Article 1, the purpose of the Employment Security Act is

> to secure the employment security of all workers, and to contribute to the balanced development of the national economy, by providing workers with an opportunity to find a job with which they may develop and display their individual ability, and by supporting the smooth supply of and demand for the workforce required for each industry, based on cooperation between the State and the private sector.

[81] Sunhee Kang, 'A Study on Labor Supply Service and the Safety of the Supplied Worker under the Employment Security Act' (2014) 12 *Labor Law Forum* 185, 192.

[82] See Supreme Court of Korea, Judgment of 25 June 2004, Case No 2002Da56130 and 56147. Here, a contract was signed under which a foreign airline hired pilots to dispatch to a domestic airline for the provision of services. The domestic airline paid a certain fee to the foreign airline in return in addition to the pilots' salaries. The applicable law to the contract was foreign law. These pilots filed a lawsuit against the domestic airline claiming severance pay, asserting that they were workers under the Korean Labor Standards Act. The Supreme Court ruled that a contract executed between the foreign and domestic airlines was invalid as it was executed in violation of Art 33(1) of the Employment Security Act, although the contract was governed by foreign law. Meanwhile, the Act on the Protection of Temporary Agency Workers was enacted on 20 February 1998, and the temporary work agency business was institutionalised separately from the labour supply business and was therefore excluded from the scope of application of the Employment Security Act. The facts in this Supreme Court ruling occurred before such an amendment was made, and therefore the Employment Security Act still applied. However, even after the enactment of the Act on the Protection of Temporary Agency Workers the text of Art 33(1) of the Employment Security Act is the same under the current law. Hence, the legal principles set forth in this Supreme Court ruling are still relevant.

[83] This provision was newly inserted in the amendment by Act No 9795 on 9 October 2009 and does not apply to Case No 2002Da56130 (ibid).

Article 33(1) in principle prohibits the labour supply business and allows it only for those who have obtained permission from the Minister of Labor. The primary objective of this approach is to prevent negative consequences arising from interfering in others' employment and unjustly capitalising on their profits or exploiting workers' wages and interests as a middleman. Additionally, it aims to foster job security and actively support the growth of the national economy by upholding the principles of workers' free will and pursuing their best interests.[84] In addition, Article 33(4) provides that

> the Minister of Employment and Labor shall, in granting permission for labor supply business, comprehensibly consider the scope of work by a trade union, supply and demand status of human resources for each relevant region or occupation, stability in employment relations, etc., in respect of domestic labor supply business, and supply and demand status of human resources for each relevant occupation, stability in employment relations, maintaining the order for employment of workers, etc., in respect of overseas labor supply business.

The wording of 'Providing workers with an opportunity to find a job with which they may develop and display their individual ability' in Article 1, stating a legislative purpose under the Employment Security Act, may be interpreted as a protection of private interests. However, the main purpose of the Employment Security Act is to prevent human rights violations and crimes related to the labour supply business[85] and maintain stability and order in the domestic labour market by facilitating the supply and demand of human resources in the market. Therefore, the legislative purpose of Article 33(1) is to protect the economic and social interests of the nation in a manner that transcends adjusting private interests. In addition, the requirement for permission under the same article is an essential means to achieve that purpose. The purpose of Article 33(1) cannot be achieved by foreign laws with similar purposes, so there is no equivalence or substitutability in the law. Furthermore, carrying out a labour supply business without obtaining permission in violation of Article 33(1) is subject to criminal punishment (Article 47(1)), from which strong public purposes can be inferred. To sum up, Article 33(1) of the Employment Security Act corresponds to an overriding mandatory rule.[86]

iii. Act on Contracts to which the State is a Party

Article 5-2 of the Act on Contracts to Which the State is a Party (hereinafter the 'State Contracts Act') states:

> In order to enhance transparency and fairness in contracts to which the State is a party, the head or contract officer of each central government agency shall require a tenderer or counterparty to promise that he or she will not offer or receive money, goods, entertainment, or any other benefit

[84] Supreme Court of Korea, Judgment of 11 June 1985, Case No 84Do2858; Supreme Court of Korea, Judgment of 25 June 2004, Case No 2002Da56130.

[85] Constitutional Court, Decision of 26 November 1998, 97Hun-Ba31.

[86] Kwang Hyun Suk, 'Comments on the Private International Law Cases of the Supreme Court of Korea in 2004' (2004) 10 *Korea Private International Law Journal* 429, 436–37 and Seoung Jae Yu, 'Retirement Benefit Entitlement for Illegally Dispatched Foreign Workers' (2004) *Labour Law Monthly* 19, 22 contend that Art 33(1) of the Employment Security Act is an overriding mandatory rule, respectively because (in Suk's view) the Article mainly serves public interests and because (in Yu's view) the Article concerns a public interest of a territorial nature at the request of economic and social policy and is closely related to the administrative bodies of the country.

> directly or indirectly in the course of making or accepting a tender or signing or performing a contract (and even after the completion of the relevant project or the delivery of goods) and enter into an agreement (hereinafter referred to as the 'integrity agreement') on condition that the relevant tender or tender acceptance may be revoked or the relevant contract may be cancelled or terminated, if the tenderer or counterparty fails to keep such promise.

The State Contracts Act does not have a clause explicitly stating that the provision shall apply when the governing law of the contract is foreign, nor does it have an extraterritorial application clause. However, Article 2 of the Act stipulates the scope of application as being 'government procurement contracts awarded through international tendering procedures and contracts to which a national of the Republic of Korea is the counterparty', and Article 4 of the same Act specifies the scope of government procurement contracts through international tendering. As such, the State Contracts Act stipulates the international scope of application for legal relationships with foreign elements, and it can be inferred that legislators intended for the statute to apply to state contracts regardless of their governing law.

Now, this author will examine whether the State Contracts Act has a special legislative purpose under Article 20 of KAPIL. One of the purposes stated in the State Contracts Act is 'to promote smooth administration of contracts by prescribing basic matters regarding contracts to which the State is a party' (Article 1). That suggests that even a contract with the state as a party is still essentially made between private persons[87] and that the State Contracts Act is intended to determine the necessary matters to be observed by public officials involved in state contracts. However, that does not necessarily mean that all provisions of the Act aim to adjust private interests. Article 5-2 has a strong public purpose in guaranteeing transparency and fairness in national contracts by suppressing corruption related to the execution of contracts and by taking stern legal action against forms of corruption such as collusion and bribery in government procurement contracts.[88] That is intended not only to fairly coordinate private interests in state contracts, but also to protect essential social interests that transcend private interests. Article 5-2 is an essential means to ensure transparency, integrity and fairness of state contracts. There is no equivalence or substitutability to foreign laws in that it protects interests that cannot be protected by foreign laws.[89] If a party to a state contract or a public official in charge of the state contract gives or receives money, goods or entertainment, directly or indirectly, in the course of bidding, awarding, executing or performing a contract in violation of Article 5-2, not only can the bid or contract be cancelled or terminated under Article 5-3, but that party or official will also be subject to criminal punishment for the crime of accepting or offering bribes.[90] This indicates a strong public interest in the regulation of state contracts. In short, Article 5-2 of the State Contracts Act is an overriding mandatory rule.

[87] Supreme Court of Korea, Judgment of 10 December 2004, Case No 2002Da73852.

[88] Section by Won Jung and Nam-wook Ryu in Won Jung (ed), *ONJU Act on Contracts to which the State is a Party* (Thomson Reuters, 2016) Art 5(2), § 2.

[89] Even if there is a provision in foreign law to punish the receipt of bribes by public officials, such a provision will be limited to the public officials of that foreign country in light of the scope of legislative jurisdiction, and the acceptance of bribes by foreign public officials will not be punishable under the domestic law.

[90] Art 35 of the State Contracts Act stipulates that a member of a certain committee who is not a public official is still regarded as a public official with regard to the crime of receiving or offering bribes.

C. Provisions with a Strong Public Purpose and their International and Spatial Scope of Application can be Ascertained by Interpretation

Even if a certain provision is not explicitly stated to apply extraterritorially and its international or spatial scope of application is not directly stipulated, there are cases where its applicability can be recognised regardless of the governing law of the relevant legal relationship: namely, where the provision in question has a strong public purpose and where interpretation can limit the international or spatial scope of application based on the connection (or proximity) to the forum (*Inlandsbeziehung*).

i. Laws Protecting Economic Interests

a. Fair Transactions in Subcontracting Act ('Subcontract Act')

In principle, the issues arising between a contractor and subcontractor in relation to a subcontract must be regulated by private law. However, in Korea, the dependence on subcontracted transactions in the construction industry, manufacturing industry and service industry has steadily increased under policies aimed at supporting export-driven economic growth and fostering large enterprises.[91] Accordingly, the abuse of the dominant position of one contracting party arising from subcontract transactions between large corporations and small and medium-sized enterprises has become more than an issue in individual contracts – it has established itself as an unfair transactional practice and type of economic misconduct that has emerged as a significant social issue.[92] The contractor's abuse of bargaining position was initially regulated under the Fair Trade Act in accordance with the 'Notice on the Designation of Unfair Trading Practices in Subcontracting Transactions' (Economic Planning Board Notice No 59), but the regulation was thereafter enacted as a separate statute to increase its efficacy.[93]

Article 3–4 of the Subcontract Act prohibits unfair special agreements, which are commonly found when contractors abuse their bargaining position.[94] By way of example, Article 3–4 mentions agreements under which a prime contractor requires a subcontractor: (1) to bear expenses for work not stipulated in the contract or the tender documents; or (2) to bear expenses related to settling civil complaints and industrial accidents; and (3) other agreements that restrict a subcontractor's interests; or (4) shift an obligation imposed upon a prime contractor to a subcontractor. In addition, the Fair Trade Commission's Notice of Unfair Special Agreements (Fair Trade Commission Notice No 2019-4) and Guidelines for Review of Unfair Special Agreements[95] specify the types and concepts of unfair special agreements.

[91] Jun-Gil Lee (ed), *ONJU Fair Transaction in Subcontracting Act* (2016) Art 1, §1. The construction industry, manufacturing industry and service industry were 70.9% dependent on subcontracted transactions in 1999.

[92] Jin Yul Ju, 'A Review on Some Legal Issues of Regulation on Unfair Subcontract Transactions' (2009) 30 *Kyoungpook National University Law Journal* 35.

[93] Dongjin Lee, 'A Study on "Action Directe" of the Subcontractor' (2009) 58 *Korean Lawyers Association Journal* 74, 75; Ju (n 92) 35; Lee (n 91) Art 1, §5.

[94] Kwang Bai Park, 'Reform the Production System for Construction Win-Win Development' (2014) 5 *Journal of Local Government Contracting* 81, 95.

[95] For the background on the enactment of the Guidelines for Review of Unfair Special Agreements and the main guidelines, see Eun-jin Choi, 'Current Status and Future Tasks of the Establishment of "Guidelines for

The Subcontract Act does not explicitly stipulate that Article 3–4 applies regardless of the governing law, nor does it have extraterritorial application clauses, nor directly stipulate the international or spatial scope of application. Therefore, I will examine whether the Subcontract Act has the special legislative purpose stated in Article 20 of KAPIL and infer the international or spatial scope of application from the relevant provisions.

The legislative purpose of the Subcontract Act is 'to contribute to the sound development of the national economy by establishing a fair order in subcontract transactions so that the prime contractor and subcontractor may complement each other and develop equally' (Article 1). Granting differences depending on the specific types of acts being regulated, the Subcontract Act is not simply designed to intervene in private legal relationships, but to correct unfair practices in the trade order and economic structure. An empirical study[96] on the abuse of bargaining position in subcontracting transactions has revealed that prime contractors' abuse of their position, which is prevalent in the construction industry, leads to gaps in performance between contractors. The research results also show that the superior status of large corporations stemming from their market dominance has consistently affected the structure of transactions. Accordingly, Article 3–4 of the Subcontract Act has a strong regulatory purpose, which admittedly may vary with the specific type and form of the behaviour in question, presuming that the behaviour is closely related to trade order such as the unfair trade practices under the Fair Trade Act. This can be seen as correcting economic misconduct under Article 119(2)[97] of the Korean Constitution,[98] which is intended to protect important constitutional values along with the economic interests of the state, thus constituting a strong public interest.[99]

The prohibition of such conduct by Article 3–4 of the Subcontract Act is an essential means to protect a strong public interest. Violation of Article 3–4 not only results in liability for damages (Article 35), but also corrective measures (Article 25(1)) and penalty surcharges (Article 25-3) as administrative sanctions and criminal punishment (Article 30(1)(1)). This is also grounds for inferring a strong public purpose, corresponding to the special legislative purpose of Article 20 of KAPIL.

The next step is to review the scope of the Subcontract Act. Regarding the *in personam* scope of application of the Subcontract Act, Article 2(2)–(3) stipulates that the prime contractors and subcontractors subject to the Act are domestic companies. In other words, Article 2(2) stipulates the scope of the prime contractors subject to the Act as 'small and medium business entrepreneurs (referring to those specified in the Framework Act on Small and Medium Enterprises, including small and medium enterprise cooperatives under the Small and Medium Enterprise Cooperatives Act)' and 'member companies of a business

Unfair Contract Examination" for Improving Subcontracting Transactions' [Hadogeupgeoraeui gaeseoneul wihan 'budangteukyak simsajichim'ui jejeong hyeonhwanggwa hyanghu gwaje] *Issue and Focus* no 1,682 (26 March 2020), Legislative Research Office of the National Assembly 2–3.

[96] Pyeong-ryang Wi, 'An Empirical Study on Unfair Exploitative Practices in Subcontracting Transactions' [Hadogeupgeoraee isseoseo bulgongjeonghan jiwinamyonghaengwie gwanhan siljeungyeongu III] (2010) 1 *Economy Reform Report* 1.

[97] Art 119: '(2) The State may regulate and coordinate economic affairs in order to maintain the balanced growth and stability of the national economy, to ensure proper distribution of income, to prevent the domination of the market and the abuse of economic power and to democratis the economy through harmony among the economic agents.'

[98] Ju (n 92) 35.

[99] According to Shin (n 27), the Fair Trade Act is the parent law of the Subcontract Act and the Subcontract Act falls broadly under competition law.

group subject to limitations on cross-shareholding under the Fair Trade Act'. Article 2(3) stipulates prime contractors to be 'small and medium business entities'.

Meanwhile, the Subcontract Act does not explicitly stipulate the spatial scope of application. However, from the standpoint of *in personam* application, the Fair Trade Commission prepared a standard contract on the premise that the subcontracting law applies to overseas construction contracts between domestic companies[100] and had issued corrective orders on such basis.[101] Therefore, it is necessary to examine whether the Subcontract Act applies to the manufacture of goods, repairs and construction in foreign countries.

Article 2(9) of the Subcontract Act only stipulates construction work that is being subcontracted out to be 'from his or her business' and does not limit it to domestic construction work.[102] Since the scope of the Subcontract Act covers Korean entities, applying it to subcontracts executed abroad, including overseas construction projects, would fall within the legislative jurisdiction according to the principle of *in personam* application. There also may be a need to regulate unfair subcontracting transactions overseas between domestic prime contractors and domestic subcontractors even in cases where the subcontract is performed in a foreign country. However, for the following reasons, this author is not convinced that the Subcontract Act's spatial scope of application is not limited to Korea.

First, Article 2(7) of the Subcontract Act stipulates that its application regards 'goods prescribed by Presidential Decree, [are] limited to regions prescribed by Presidential Decree, including Special Metropolitan Cities and Metropolitan Cities' in relation to the outsourcing of manufacturing. Therefore, there is a reason to assume that the Act's spatial scope of application is the territory of Korea. Secondly, it is worth noting that the Supreme Court ruling on *Graphite Electrode*[103] stated that illegal cartel conduct that is subject to the Act is not limited to domestic business entities, and that formed one of the grounds for the extraterritorial application of the Fair Trade Act.[104] Unlike the regulations on the prohibition of illegal cartel conduct under the Fair Trade Act, the Subcontract Act limits the scope of *in personam* application to *domestic* business entities and thus has a different starting point from the Fair Trade Act.

Thirdly, the Supreme Court recently held that in a case where a Korean national running a massage parlour in Japan hired a person who was not qualified as a massage therapist, the spatial scope of application of the relevant provision was limited to Korea. The Court held that

> a person who intends to engage in massage business outside the territory of Korea should not be regarded as having an obligation to obtain qualification from a Korean mayor/governor, given that

[100] Guidelines attached to the Fair Trade Commission's 'Standard Subcontract Agreement for Overseas Construction Business' (as of 28 December 2018).

[101] Fair Trade Commission decision 2007-493, delivered on 19 October 2007 (accessible at case.ftc.go.kr/ocp/co/ltfrview.do). The FTC based its decision on the premise that the Fair Trade Act applies to Daewoo E&C's subcontract agreement with Yujin ENC in relation to overseas construction work. Although Daewoo E&C filed a lawsuit to challenge the Fair Trade Commission's corrective order, the Supreme Court of Korea did not look into whether the Subcontract Act also applies to overseas construction work. See Supreme Court of Korea, Judgment of 30 September 2010, Case No 2008Du16377.

[102] In the view of Sung Hyun Hwang, 'A Study on Application of Subcontracting Act to Overseas Construction Projects and Violation of Subcontracting Act by Use of FIDIC Conditions of Contract 2021 International Trade Law' (2021) 151 *International Trade Law* 92, 97, this provides the basis for arguing that the Subcontract Act applies to overseas construction work.

[103] Supreme Court of Korea, Judgment of 24 March 2006, Case No 2004Du11275.

[104] The extraterritorial application mentioned here refers to foreign businesses entities' conduct overseas and is distinct from the question of whether the provision can be applied to domestic business entities' conduct overseas.

> the purpose of the above provision, which limits massage practice to visually impaired persons who are accredited by the mayor/governor, is to provide those persons with an opportunity to support their livelihood and participate in their vocational activities by monopolising the massage business.

The Court did not apply the penal provision on recognition of massage practice under the Medical Service Act (Article 82(1)[105] and Article 88(3)[106]) *in personam* extraterritorially.[107] This ruling limited the spatial scope of the provision's application by interpreting its legislative purpose. This rationale can also be applied to the Subcontract Act. It is more plausible to assume that the reason the Subcontract Act applies to domestic subcontractors and prime contractors is because it is intended to correct unfair practices in subcontract transactions in the Korean market.[108] Therefore, it makes more sense to view that the Subcontract Act as applying only to cases where the manufacture, repair and construction of goods are performed in Korea.

Thus, Article 3–4 of the Subcontract Act aims to protect the important constitutional value of achieving economic justice by correcting unfair practices in the trade order within the scope of acts that are themselves highly related to the trade order. In addition, the interpretation of the relevant provisions of the Subcontract Act can specify the spatial scope of application as subcontracting that takes place in Korea. Moreover, Article 3–4 is essential for achieving the legislative objectives. From these points, the legislators' intention to apply this provision to acts performed in Korea regardless of the governing law of the contract or tort can be inferred. Therefore, Article 3–4 of the Subcontract Act constitutes an overriding mandatory rule.[109]

b. Franchise Act

As a result of the spread of awareness of the so-called 'owner's tyranny' in subcontracting to other areas, the Franchise Act, the Fair Agency Transactions Act and the Act on Fair

[105] Art 82 (Massage Therapists): '(1) A massage therapist shall be a visually impaired person under the Act on Welfare of Persons with Disabilities, who falls under any of the following subparagraphs and who is accredited by a relevant Mayor/Do Governor: 1. A person who has completed physical therapy courses for a massage therapist as set forth in paragraph (4) at a special school under subparagraph 5 of Article 2 of the Elementary and Secondary Education Act, which provides education equivalent to a high school; 2. A person who has completed two-year or longer courses for massage therapy at a massage therapy institution designated by the Minister of Health and Welfare, as a person recognised to have the academic background equivalent to a middle school graduate.'

[106] Art 88 (Penalty Provisions): 'Any of the following persons shall be punished by imprisonment with labor for not more than three years or by a fine not exceeding 30 million won ...'.

[107] Supreme Court of Korea, Judgment of 8 February 2018, Case No 2014Do10051.

[108] Hwang (n 102) 105 opines that the extraterritorial application of administrative provisions should be limited to cases where there is a written extraterritorial application clause or where it is clear from interpretation that the provisions presuppose *in personam* extraterritorial application, as the Passports Act or the Nationality Act does, or where it is obvious that the purpose of the individual administrative provisions cannot be achieved without extraterritorial application. He takes the view that it does not seem reasonable to conclude that the Subcontract Act applies to overseas construction work merely to protect the interests of subcontractors.

[109] On the contrary, there is the view that the Subcontract Act does not constitute an overriding mandatory rule on the grounds that there is no reason to presume that the Subcontract Act applies to international transactions. Seungsoo Han, 'The Protection of the Franchisee of the International Franchise Contract and the Governing Law in the Litigation' (2017) 58 *Seoul Law Journal* 78, 100. While the fact that a certain statute has assumed international transactions (eg, the Foreign Trade Act) may be a factor to consider in determining the overriding mandatory nature of a provision, as examined in ch 3, it is not the only decisive factor. Even if a provision does not

Transactions in Large Retail Business were enacted with the aim of achieving 'fairness in transactions'.[110] As with the Subcontract Act, these laws enacted separately what had previously been regulated as a type of abuse of bargaining position under the Fair Trade Act. Unfair trade practices in the franchise business had been regulated in accordance with the Notice on Standards for Unfair Trade Practices in the Franchise Business and the Types and Standards of Unfair Trade Practices in International Contracts announced by the Fair Trade Commission and then enacted and enforced under the Franchise Act on 13 May 2002.

Article 12 of the Franchise Act prohibits unfair trade practices by a franchisor and governs the acts of 'unreasonably suspending or refusing the supply of commodities or services or business assistance to a franchisee or placing significant limitations thereon' (Article 12(1)), 'imposing unfair restraints or limitations on the prices of commodities or services that a franchisee handles, or on customers, business territory, or business activities of a franchisee' (Article 12(2)), 'putting a franchisee at an unfair disadvantage by abusing its position in transactions' (Article 12(3)), 'unreasonably imposing obligations to compensate for damage on a franchisee, imposing an excessive penalty compared with criteria prescribed by Presidential Decree, such as the purpose and contents of an agreement, and losses that will occur' (Article 12(5)), 'any act that does not fall under subparagraphs 1 through 3 and 5, which is likely to interfere with fair transactions in franchising, such as inducing franchisees of a competing franchisor to conduct transactions with the franchisor' (Article 12(6)). The specific contents of each subparagraph are stipulated in detail in Article 13(1) and Table 2 of the Enforcement Decree of the Franchise Act.

The question of whether the Franchise Act is an overriding mandatory rule arises, for example, in cases where a foreign franchisor enters into a franchise agreement governed by foreign law with a domestic business entity operating in Korea.[111] Currently, the Fair Trade Commission also takes action on franchise agreements between foreign franchisors and

specify an international scope of application, it may be an overriding mandatory rule if it defends a strong public interest and if the spatial scope of application can be specified, which allows one to identify the legislators' intention for the provision to apply regardless of the governing law. Art 3-4 of the Subcontract Act corresponds to such an example.

[110] Shin (n 27) 39.

[111] This is the case in Seoul Central District Court, Judgment of 1 April 2020, Case No 2018Na63343. In this case, defendant Subway International BV, a corporation headquartered in Amsterdam, the Netherlands, operated a restaurant franchise business under the name 'SUBWAY' and entered into a franchise agreement with the plaintiff on 29 October 2013 at SUBWAY Yatap in Bundang-gu, Seongnam. The governing law of the franchise agreement was Dutch law, and the franchise agreement contained an arbitration clause requiring disputes to be resolved by the US International Centre for Dispute Resolution (ICDR) in accordance with the UNCITRAL Arbitration Rules. Thereafter, the plaintiff filed a lawsuit against the defendant seeking compensation for damages on the grounds that the defendant violated the plaintiff's sales territory by opening another store in the vicinity of the plaintiff's store. The defendant invoked the arbitration clause, to which the plaintiff responded by arguing that the arbitration arrangement was invalid as a violation of Art 12(1) of the Franchise Act, which is an overriding mandatory provision under Korean law. The Court first analysed the formation and substantive validity of the arbitration arrangement in accordance with Dutch law. It then proceeded to assess whether Art 12(1) of the Franchise Act was in fact an overriding mandatory provision. The Court held that the provision was not of overriding mandatory nature on the grounds that 'the Franchise Act was enacted to establish a fair trade order in the franchise business and to contribute to the promotion of consumer welfare and the sound development of the national economy by ensuring that franchisors and franchisees develop mutually and harmoniously on an equal footing' and that 'we do not discover the legislators' intent to intervene in international transactions, nor is there any special provision related to extraterritorial application'. The Court did not accept the plaintiff's case because the arbitration agreement was valid under Dutch law (the governing law of the arbitration agreement) and because the Korean Frachise Act could not override the applicable law.

domestic business entities by applying the Franchise Act,[112] so a review of the overriding mandatory nature of Article 12(1) of the Act is relevant.

In the Franchise Act, there are no clauses stipulating that it should apply when the franchise agreement is governed by foreign law, nor are there any extraterritorial application clauses. In addition, the Act does not directly stipulate the scope of international or spatial application. Therefore, this author will examine whether the Act protects strong public interests and whether its scope of application can be determined through the interpretation of related provisions.

Under Article 1, the legislative purpose of the Franchise Act is

> to contribute to the promotion of the welfare of consumers and the sound growth of the national economy by establishing a fair trading order for franchise businesses and by ensuring the mutually complementary and balanced growth of franchisors and franchisees on an equal footing.

As can be seen from its legislative history, the prohibition of unfair trade activities under the Franchise Act shares the legislative purpose of the prohibition of unfair trade practices under the Fair Trade Act, just as with the Subcontract Act.[113] The purpose of the Franchise Act in prohibiting franchisors from engaging in unfair trade practices is not simply to rectify the imbalance of bargaining power between individual franchisors and franchisees, but also to eliminate unfair practices that have become customary in trade, with the strong public purpose of improving market competition conditions[114] and thereby to implement the important constitutional value of correcting economic misconduct. Therefore, the interests protected by Article 12 of the Franchise Act can be recognised as national and economic in nature. That corresponds to the special legislative purpose of Article 20 of KAPIL.

The prohibition in Article 12(1) of the Franchise Act is an essential means of realising such interests. The correction of economic injustice in the domestic market cannot be achieved by foreign laws, so there is no equivalence or substitutability of laws. In addition, a franchisor that engages in unfair trade practices in violation of Article 12(1) is liable to an extent not exceeding three times the amount of damages (Article 37(2)(1)–(2)) and is also subject to corrective measures (Article 33(1)). Furthermore, the franchisor may be required to publish the fact that it has received an order for correction or notify the counterparty of that fact (Article 33(3)) and is subject to penalty surcharges (Article 35(1)). If the corrective measures are not followed, the franchisor is then subject to criminal punishment. This is also a situation in which a strong public purpose can be inferred. Therefore, the following issues should be examined when determining whether the international or spatial scope of application can be inferred from the connection (proximity) to the forum, on the grounds of the strong public purpose of the Franchise Act. The legislative purpose of regulating unfair trade practices in the Franchise Act is not simply to adjust the imbalance of tangible status between franchisors and franchisees, but also to correct unreasonable practices that have become customary in the Korean market.

[112] Fair Trade Commission resolution No 2021-182, dated 29 June 2021.

[113] The Fair Transactions in Large Retail Business Act and the Fair Agency Transactions Act share the legislative purpose of the Fair Trade Act.

[114] Young Hong Choi, *ONJU Fair Transactions in Franchise Business Act* (Thomson Reuters, 2020) Art 1, § 3.

In relation to the spatial scope of application, if Article 12 does not apply because either party to the franchise transaction in the domestic market[115] is a foreign business entity or the governing law of the franchise agreement is foreign law, it would be difficult to achieve that legislative purpose.[116] Meanwhile, Article 2(12) defines 'sales territory' as 'an area where a franchisee sells products or services in accordance with a franchise agreement'. Therefore, it is possible to infer that the sales territory being in Korea is an implied requirement of the Franchise Act, which suffices the connection to the forum.

In relation to the personal scope of application, the Franchise Act does not limit it to domestic businesses, unlike the Subcontract Act. On the other hand, the Franchise Act in principle presupposes that it applies to all business transactions that meet the requirements of franchise agreements (Article 2(1)). Its application is only excluded when the franchise fee is small, or when sales are small and the number of franchisees is four or less (Article 3(1)).[117]

Prior to the enactment of the Franchise Act in 2002, unfair practices were regulated under the Fair Trade Act; at that time, Article 32 of the former Fair Trade Act (before amendment by Act No 14137 on 29 March 2016) was still restricting the execution of unfair international agreements. Back then, it was possible to read the legislator's intention to apply the provisions on unfair trade practices even in cases where foreign elements are in play.[118] As seen earlier,[119] the removal of Article 32 of the former Fair Trade Act does not mean that the current Fair Trade Act would not apply to contracts with international elements, and even though the Franchise Act was enacted as a separate Act, Article 12 of the Franchise Act cannot be deemed to have lost the nature of unfair trade practices under the current Fair Trade Act.[120] In light of the legislative history, arguably, the Franchise Act was intended to apply even when the franchisor is a foreign business entity if its trade practices in the domestic market are unfair and problematic.

Therefore, the Franchise Act is an overriding mandatory rule because it has a strong public purpose and because the scope of application can be ascertained based on the connection to the forum.[121]

[115] While it may be asked whether the Franchise Act applies in cases where a domestic franchisor operates a franchise business overseas, it is reasonable to conclude the Act does not apply in such cases since its purpose seems to be establishing a fair trade order by preventing unfair trade practices in the domestic market. In this regard, see Choi (n 114) Art 3, §5 regarding the view that the Franchise Act should explicitly provide that it does not apply to a domestic business entity operating a franchise overseas.

[116] Fair Trade Commission resolution No 2021-182, dated 29 June 2021 purports the same. In this case, the Fair Trade Commission applied the Franchise Act to the franchise agreement between Subway International BV, headquartered in Amsterdam, the Netherlands, and a domestic business entity, on the grounds that Subway International BV is a franchisor that operates a franchise business in Korea.

[117] Even in this case, however, Art 9 (Prohibition on Providing False or Exaggerated Information) and Art 10 (Return of Required Payments, with the exception of Art 10(1)(1)) are not excluded.

[118] Incidentally, the Subcontract Act was enacted on 31 December 1984, before Art 32 of the Fair Trade Act, which was introduced when the Fair Trade Act was amended by Act No 4198 on 13 January 1990.

[119] See ch 4, I, A. i. b.

[120] The Fair Trade Act does not apply where the Franchise Act applies (Art 38 of the Franchise Act). In this sense, the Franchise Act is *lex specialis* to the Fair Trade Act.

[121] Despite its wide-ranging discussion, Seoul Central District Court, Judgment of 26 August 2019, Case No 2018Gahap576876 acknowledged that Art 12 of the Franchise Act had the same purpose as the Fair Trade Act and could therefore be considered an overriding mandatory rule.

On the other hand, there is a view that the Franchise Act cannot be regarded as an overriding mandatory rule for two reasons: Unlike the Fair Trade Act, firstly, the Franchise Act does not presume international transactions and, secondly, Article 92(2) of the Commercial Act on the right for a commercial agent (which is similar to a franchise business) to claim compensation aims to adjust private interests and cannot be regarded as an overriding mandatory rule.[122] However, as seen above, the Franchise Act regulates acts that are regarded as unfair trade practices under the Fair Trade Act, and Articles 32 and 34 of the former Fair Trade Act were restricting the execution of international agreements at the time under the premise that they would apply to international transactions. Therefore, the Franchise Act was intended to apply to international transactions. In addition, unlike the right for commercial agents to claim compensation under the Commercial Act, the Franchise Act has the legislative purpose of protecting the economic order beyond private interests. Furthermore, unlike Article 92(2) of the Commercial Act,[123] which makes it difficult to infer the scope of international or spatial application from interpreting the connection to the forum, the Franchise Act's spatial scope of application can be limited by interpretation. Therefore, Article 92(2) of the Commercial Act and the Franchise Act simply cannot be compared to each other. It is not convincing to assume that the Franchise Act is not an overriding mandatory rule simply because Article 92(2) of the Commercial Act is not.

ii. Laws Protecting Social Interests

Examples of overriding mandatory rules that protect social interests include the Equal Employment Act and the Cultural Heritage Act.

a. Equal Employment Act

The Equal Employment Act prohibits discrimination between men and women in labour relations. The term 'discrimination between men and women' means unfairly discriminating against men or women solely because of their gender, without a reasonable cause. Article 8(1) of the Equal Employment Act provides that 'The employer shall provide equal pay for equal-value work within the identical business', and Article 11(1) provides that 'no employer shall discriminate on grounds of gender in age limit, retirement, and dismissal of employees'. It needs to be examined whether these regulations apply only when the governing law is Korean law, or even when the governing law of the employment contract is foreign.

The Equal Employment Act does not explicitly stipulate its applicability when the governing law of the employment contract is foreign, nor does it have extraterritorial application clauses, or define its international or spatial scope of application. Therefore, it is necessary to examine whether each of the above regulations has a strong public purpose and if the spatial scope of application can be identified.

Labour laws are mainly aimed at protecting workers who normally have less bargaining power than employers, and such laws generally have the purpose of adjusting private interests. However, if a provision protecting private interests simultaneously serves as a means of

[122] Han (n 109) 100.
[123] The overriding mandatory nature of Art 92(2) of the Commercial Act is reviewed in s II, B below.

implementing economic, social and political purposes, it can be recognised as an overriding mandatory rule. The Equal Employment Act embodies the principle of equality under the Constitution,[124] and under Article1, its purpose is

> to contribute not only to realising equal employment for both genders by guaranteeing equal opportunities and treatment in employment between men and women in accordance with the principle of equality proclaimed in the Constitution of the Republic of Korea, by protecting motherhood, and by promoting the employment of women, but also to improving the quality of all the people's lives by assisting the work-family balance of employees.

In other words, the Act seeks to protect workers who are socially vulnerable and, at the same time, abolish gender discrimination in the labour market to implement the constitutional value of equality (Article 11 of the Constitution) and the prohibition of discrimination against female workers (Article 32(4) of the Constitution).[125] Therefore, Articles 8 and 11 of the Equal Employment Act aim not simply to adjust private interests, but to protect the social order by achieving the superior values of the Constitution. In addition, Articles 8 and 11 constitute an essential means to protect that social order. Strong public purpose can also be inferred from the fact that a business owner who violates Articles 8 and 11 is subject to criminal punishments (Article 37(1)).

Next, whether the scope of application of the above provision can be specified through the interpretation of relevant provisions is examined. Article 3(1) of the Equal Employment Act applies 'to all sorts of business or business places that employ employees'. However, the Act may not be applied in whole or in part to businesses prescribed by Presidential Decree, and Article 2 of the Enforcement Decree of the Equal Employment Act provides that 'the whole of the Act shall not apply to businesses or workplaces consisting of only relatives living together under the proviso of Article 3(1) of the Act, or housekeeping employees'. Article 3(1) does not specify the location of the businesses subject to the application of these provisions to be Korea, but at least in the case of businesses or workplaces located in Korea, the legislative intent to apply the Equal Employment Act regardless of the applicable law of the employment contract can be derived, except where its application is excluded under Article 2 of the Enforcement Decree. This means, in other words, that the spatial scope of each of these provisions can be identified from the requirement of the connection to the forum (i.e. a business or workplace being located in Korea).[126]

In summary, Articles 8 and 11 of the Equal Employment Act constitute overriding mandatory rules.

[124] Kwi Cheon Park (ed), *ONJU Equal Employment Opportunity and Work-Family Balance Assistance Act* (Thomson Reuters, 2019) Art 1.

[125] Supreme Court of Korea, Judgment of 31 October 2019, Case No 2013Du20011.

[126] The former Equal Pay Act 1970 of the UK, which had a similar effect, is also considered an overriding mandatory provision. Art 1 of that Act states that the place of application is 'establishment in Great Britain' and stipulates that men and women should be treated equally in terms of working conditions. The former Equal Pay Act 1970 was repealed by the enforcement of the Equality Act 2010, which incorporated various labour laws. The Equality Act 2010 did not provide for a spatial scope of application, as the Equal Pay Act 1970 had. It is said that the legislator's intention was to decide on applicability through a court or arbitral tribunal in light of the relevance between the labor relationship and the UK. Collins (n 61) vol 2, para 33-290. Germany's § 19 AGG (*Algemeinen Gleichbarhandlungsgesetzes*), a regulation to the same effect, is also evaluated as being an overriding mandatory provision. Peter Kaye, *The New Private International Law of Contract of the European Community* (Dartmouth, 1993) 243; see section by Martin Zwickel in Dieter Martiny (ed) *Internationa gtrewles Vertragsrecht*, 9th edn (Ottoschmidt, 2022) Rn 5.78.

b. Cultural Heritage Act[127]

Cultural artefacts have value and meaning that goes beyond their status as mere property because they reflect the history, culture, identity and pride of a country. Historically, a wide range of cultural heritages were plundered in the process of wars, conquests and colonial rule, and heritages were frequently stolen or removed illegally,[128] which was encouraged by the existence of a market in which cultural artefacts were illegally traded. In Korea's Joseon Dynasty, many cultural properties were lost to other foreign countries through wars, invasions and Japanese colonisation.[129] Accordingly, countries around the world prohibit the export of cultural heritage and cooperate[130] for the return of stolen and illegally expatriated

[127] The new cultural heritage law regime came into force on 17 May 2024, replacing the previous regulations established by the Cultural Heritage Protection Act. Under the new regime, the Framework Act on National Heritage (Act No. 19591) introduces new terminology and classifications for cultural heritage to align with those set out in the Convention on the Means of Prohibiting and Preventing the Illicit Import, Export and Transfer of Ownership of Cultural Property (hereinafter UNESCO Convention). Accordingly, the following acts were introduced: the Special Act on Conservation, Management, and Utilisation of World Heritage (Act No. 20309), the Act on Conservation and Utilisation of Cultural Heritage (Act No. 20369), the Act on Preservation and Utilisation of Natural Heritage (Act No. 19690), and the Act on the Safeguarding and Promotion of Intangible Heritage (Act No. 19588). However, the core provisions of the old Cultural Heritage Protection Act remain in the Act on Conservation and Utilisation of Cultural Heritage, which will be referred to here as the "Cultural Heritage Act." For more information on the introduction of the new regime, refer to Kwang Hyun Suk, "Consistency between the National Heritage Law Regime Implemented in 2024 and the UNESCO System," 33 Korean Forum on International Trade and Business Law 169.

[128] Plundering and theft of cultural heritage is not a matter of the past, as can be seen from the case where a Buddhist statue that was likely stolen from the Korean temple of Buseoksa in the Joseon Dynasty was brought back to Korea from Japan. See Kwang Hyun Suk, 'Comment on the Judgment of the First Instance which Ordered Return of the Korean Buddhist Statue Stolen from the Tsushima Island: Issues on International Cultural Property Law' (2017) 23 *Korea Private International Law Journal* 3; and Ho Young Song, 'Who Owns the Goryeo Buddhist Statue?' (2019) 36 *Hanyang Law Review* 279 for the detailed facts of the case and related rulings.

[129] Boo-Keun Cho, 'An Examination into the Illegal Trade of Cultural Properties' (2004) 37 *Korea Institute of Science and Technology Information* 371, 397.

[130] Given the systematic loopholes resulting from differences in each country's regulatory stance, there have been attempts to move cultural heritages to jurisdictions that essentially render stolen cultural heritages legal. As such, international cooperation and collaboration have been necessary for the effective protection of cultural heritages. A representative example is the UNESCO Convention, established in 1970 by UNESCO, and the Convention on Stolen or Illegally Exported Cultural Objects (hereinafter UNIDROIT Convention), established by the International Institute for the Unification of Private Law (UNIDROIT) in 1955. The EU has developed Council Regulation (EC) No 116/2009 of 18 December 2008 on the Export of Cultural Goods and Council Directive 2014/60/EU of the European Parliament and of the Council of 15 May 2014 on the Return of Cultural Objects Unlawfully Removed from the Territory of a Member State and Amending Regulation (EEC) No 3911/92 1024/2012 (Recast) OJ L159/1. Such rules have resulted from the efforts of various countries to prevent the illegal export and removal of their cultural property and to secure the return of illegally taken cultural heritages. Korea is also a member of the UNESCO Convention, which focuses on public law and administrative sanctions to prohibit and prevent cultural heritages from being illegally taken or traded. For Korean literature on the UNESCO Convention, see Song, 'Who Owns the Statue?' (2019) 287 and thereafter; Chan-Ho Park and Hun-Je Suh, *A Legal Study on Stolen or Illegally Exported Cultural Objects – With Emphasis on the 1970 UNESCO Convention and the 1995 UNIDROIT Convention and Their Implementation in Major Contracting Parties* (Korea Legal Research Institute, 2007); Kwang Hyun Suk, 'Korea's Efforts and Role in Preventing Illicit Trafficking of Cultural Properties: Including Discussions on the Concept of Cultural Properties and Cultural Heritage' (2020) 26 *Korea Private International Law Journal* 221; Jong Hyeok Lee, 'Private International Law Issues of the Implementation Legislations for the 1970 UNESCO Convention' (2020) 26 *Korea Private International Law Journal* 343. For Korean literature on the UNIDROIT Convention, see Kwang Hyun Suk, 'Some Issues on Korea's Accession to the UNIDROIT Convention on Stolen or Illegally Exported Cultural Objects' (2009) 15 *Korea Private International Law Journal*; Boo-Keun Cho, 'Examination into Illegal Trade' (2004) 388 and thereafter; Geun Gwan Lee, *Final Report on Research on the Direction of Domestic Legal Amendments for Joining the UNIDROIT Convention* (Cultural Heritage Administration, 2007); Kyung Han Sohn, 'Introduction to 1995 UNIDROIT Cultural Objects Convention and Korea's Accession Thereto' (2009) 15 *Korea Private International Law Journal* 200.

cultural heritages while protecting them under domestic law.[131] Although domestic and foreign academics generally agree that the Cultural Heritage Act contains overriding mandatory rules,[132] little research has been done on exactly which provisions those are.[133]

Article 39(1)[134] of the Cultural Heritage Act of Korea prohibits the overseas export or removal of national treasures, natural folklore cultural heritage, although in exceptional cases they may be taken out of the country for a certain period of time on condition of return. Article 39(1) applies *mutatis mutandis* to Articles 60(1) and 74(1) on general movable cultural heritages, city/province-designated cultural heritages, and cultural heritage resources.[135] Article 66 of the Act prohibits in principle the transfer of state-owned cultural heritages or the establishment of private rights over those heritages. Article 87(5) excludes bona fide acquisition for cultural heritages designated by the administrator of the National Heritage Administration or a mayor/provincial governor (Article 87(5)(1)); cultural heritages publicly announced as stolen or lost articles (Article 87(5)(2)); and cultural heritages with an essential part thereof or record showing its source was deliberately misrepresented (Article 87(5)(3)). The same article stipulates that when a person who has taken over a business purchases a cultural heritage in good faith through an auction or from a cultural heritage dealer, the victim or the person who has lost the cultural heritage may claim the return of that heritage by paying to the transferee the price paid by the person who has taken over the business. Articles 39(1), 60(1), 66(1) and 74(1) of the Cultural Heritage Act concern the obligation law aspect of cultural heritage transactions. On the other hand, Article 87(5) concerns the property law aspect of rights regarding cultural heritage transactions. In order to assess if Article 87(5) is of overriding mandatory character, the relationship with the principle of *lex rei sitae* concerning property rights should be examined.[136] The conclusion may vary in the following cases depending on whether each of the above provisions constitutes an overriding mandatory rule.

[131] For a brief introduction to the cultural heritage protection acts of the US, China, Germany, UK, France and Japan, see Seungwoo Jung, 'A Legal Study on the International Trade of Stolen/Lost Artworks: Focused on Illegal Trafficking of Cultural Property' (2019) 51 *Korean Association of Arts Management* 191, 203–07.

[132] Martiny (n 78), EGBGB Art 34, Rn 122; Martiny (n 61) Rom I – VO, Art 9, Rn 101; Suk (n 29) 142; Shin and Yoon (n 75) 274; Suk (2009) (n 129) 330.

[133] In previous research, Kwang Hyun Suk, 'The Role of the Private International Law Act and the Cultural Property Protection Act of Korea as Means of Protecting Cultural Property from International Illicit Transactions and the Proposal for Improvement' (2015) 56 *Seoul Law Journal* 117, 147 believes that Arts 20 and 39(1) of the Cultural Heritage Protection Act are overriding mandatory rules. Phil-Bok Lee, 'International Transaction of Cultural Heritage and Overriding Mandatory Provisions – Focused on the Overriding Mandatory Provisions of *Lex Originis*' (2021) 27 *Korea Private International Law Journal* 119, 159–61 points out that Arts 66 and 87(5) of the Act are overriding mandatory rules, and more research is needed on which other provisions on cultural heritage protection are overriding mandatory rules.

[134] For the history of the enactment and amendment of the old Cultural Heritage Protection Act, see Cho (n 129) 371, 382–83.

[135] These provisions were adopted to implement the UNESCO Convention. Song (n 127) 279, 288.

[136] Art 20 of the old Cultural Heritage Protection Act provided for the protection of foreign cultural heritages and covers the Cultural Heritage Administration's custody, storage and management of foreign cultural heritages illegally taken from a foreign country and brought into Korea and the return thereof to that foreign country. Since that stipulates the obligations of one state to another and not concerned with private law contracts, this author has not reviewed it here. For discussions of the overriding mandatory nature of Art 20, see Suk (n 132) 147.

Example 4.1

A, residing in Korea, sells a designated cultural property to B, who resides in Country X, secretly takes it out of Korea for the purpose of performing the sales contract (the governing law of which was the law of Country X) and delivers it to B. Then A files a lawsuit in a Korean court against B seeking the return of the cultural property based on Article 39(1) of the Cultural Heritage Act, alleging the invalidity of the contract.

Example 4.2

After B steals a cultural heritage at A's home in Korea, it was transferred to C, a malicious cultural heritage dealer, and D purchases the heritage in good faith from C. The governing law of the sales contract between C and D is foreign law. After D exhibits the heritage in question, A becomes aware of this fact and files a lawsuit against D in a Korean court to claim the return of the heritage, while D makes a plea of bona fide acquisition. All the relevant parties reside in Korea.

Example 4.3

After B steals a cultural heritage at A's home in Korea, B secretly takes it out of Korea to Country X and transfers it to C, a malicious cultural heritage dealer residing there. D then purchases the cultural heritage in good faith from C in Country X, and the governing law of the sales contract is the law of Country X. After D brings the cultural heritage back to Korea and exhibits it, A becomes aware of this fact and files a lawsuit against D in a Korean court to claim the return of the heritage, while D makes a plea of bona fide acquisition. The laws of Country X recognise the bona fide acquisition of stolen cultural property.

The Cultural Heritage Act does not specify that each of the above regulations applies regardless of the applicable law to the relevant transactions, and there is no extraterritorial application clause. However, Articles 39(1), 60(1) and 74(1) stipulate the international or spatial scope of application by stating that the law applies to transactions of cultural heritages that involve the international elements of exporting or taking those heritages out of Korea. In addition, each of the above provisions has a strong public purpose as shown below.

On the other hand, Articles 66 and 87(5) of the Cultural Heritage Act do not stipulate the international scope of application but do have a strong public purpose, and their spatial scope of application can be ascertained by the interpretation of the relevant provisions. The purpose of the Cultural Heritage Act is 'to promote the cultural edification of Korean nationals and to contribute to the development of human culture by inheriting national culture and enabling it to be utilised through the preservation of cultural heritage' (Article 1). The purpose of Articles 39(1), 60(1) and 74(1) of the Cultural Heritage Act is to protect cultural heritages by preventing their illegal exportation and removal; the purpose of Article 66 is to prevent the transfer and the establishment of private rights of state-owned cultural heritages; and the purpose of Article 87(5) is to deny bona fide acquisition of transactions or exchanges for specific cultural heritages. Therefore, each of the above provisions is intended to protect the social interests of the state, representing an essential means to realise strong public interests. There is no equivalence or substitutability of the provisions, as countries' cultural heritage laws are mainly aimed at protecting their own cultural property.[137] The violation of Articles 39(1), 60(1) and 74(1) of the Cultural Heritage Act is also subject to criminal punishment (Article 90), which infers that there are strong public purposes.

Now, whether the international or spatial scope of application of each of the above regulations can be ascertained based on strong public purposes and the connection to the forum will be examined. Article 66 of the Cultural Heritage Act defines the scope of application as 'State-owned cultural heritage', and considering the strong public purpose seen above, we can infer the legislators' intent for Article 66 of the Cultural Heritage Act to apply even when the governing law of the contract is foreign law, as long as the relevant transaction concerns a state-owned cultural heritage. The requirement of 'State-owned cultural heritage' itself satisfies the requirement of the connection to the forum. Allowing this provision to be avoided by choosing foreign law as the governing law of the sales contract of the State-owned cultural heritage would undermine that legislative purpose.

Under Article 87(5) of the Cultural Heritage Act, the international scope of application may also be determined from the connection to the forum. Since a 'Cultural heritage designated by the Administrator of the National Heritage Administration or a Mayor/Provincial Governor' or a 'cultural heritage publicly announced as a stolen or lost article' under Articles 87(5)(1) and 87(5)(2) are cultural heritages designated or publicly announced in *Korea*, the connection to the forum is inherently recognised. Fulfilling the requirement under Articles 87(5)(3) that it must be a 'cultural heritage with an essential part thereof or record showing its source deliberately mutilated' requires actual observation of the cultural heritage and can be limited to a 'cultural heritage located in Korea at the time of the trade in question', leading us to a connection to the forum. If Article 87(5) of the Cultural Heritage Act does not apply regardless of the applicable law to real rights, the legislative purpose will be undermined as the parties to the illegal transaction of cultural heritage

[137] For example, although foreign cultural heritages can also be included in the definition clause of cultural heritages under the Framewrk Act on National Heritage (Article 3), the main focus of protection under the Act is Korea-registered cultural heritages, designated cultural heritages and state-owned cultural heritages.

might quickly transfer the cultural heritage to a jurisdiction in which the bona fide acquisition of the cultural heritage is recognised. Therefore, the legislator's intent for Article 87(5) to apply regardless of the governing law of the real rights aspect of the relevant transaction can be inferred. As such, Article 87(5) of the Cultural Heritage Act corresponds to the special rule of Article 33 of KAPIL,[138] which defines *lex rei sitae*,[139] requiring compliance with the law of the place where the object was located at the time of the acquisition, loss or change of rights to the movable property.

Another possible view is that Article 87(5) shall apply only to cases where the governing law of real rights as designated under Article 33 of KAPIL is Korean law. Such a view may be based on the fact that Article 87(5) of the Cultural Heritage Act provides that 'the provisions on bona fide acquisition under Article 249 of the Civil Act shall not apply', presupposing that Article 87(5) is a special rule of the Korean Civil Act. However, such a view is not desirable considering the aim of Article 87(5) of the Cultural Heritage Act, which is to exclude the bona fide acquisition of cultural heritages under certain circumstances, for the effective protection of Korean cultural heritages. In light of the fact that most cultural heritages are movable property and thus easy to move, and that Article 39(1) of the Cultural Heritage Act prohibits the export and illegal removal of cultural heritages, it is very unlikely that legislators intended to recognise bona fide acquisition of Korean cultural heritages that have been illegally removed from Korea to foreign countries and traded there.

[138] For a detailed discussion on *lex originis* compared to *lex rei sitae* and supporting views in the context of cultural heritage protection, see Ho Young Song, 'Study on the Legal Policy for Restitution of Illegally Exported Cultural Properties in Foreign Countries' (2004) 11 *Journal of Comparative Private Law* 229, 249–53. Ho Young Song, 'Einige zivil und internationales privatrechtliche Frage zur Rückgabe von Kulturgütern – unter besonderer Berücksichting von Regelungen der UNIDROIT-Konvention 1995' (2009) 15 *Korea Private International Law Journal* 298, 313–14; Ho Young Song, 'A Study on the Rule of *Lex Originis* for the Cultural Properties in the International Private Law' (2013) 30 *Journal of Property Law* 79, 85–95; Song (n 127) 279, 299–300. *Lex originis* is the view that in the context of cultural heritage laws, *lex rei sitae* should be revised and *lex originis* should be applied to real rights. That serves as the basis for presenting the following points: (i) if *lex originis* is adopted, it is impossible to manipulate the connecting point that leads to a law that allows 'cultural heritage laundery', unlike *lex rei sitae*, based on the location of the subject matter; (ii) the reason that Savigny used the location of the goods as the connecting point was that he presumed the location of the objects changed by the free will of the original owner, while cultural heritages are more likely taken out of a country against the owner's will; (iii) cultural heritages are not very frequently traded, unlike general goods, so adopting *lex originis* with respect to the real rights of cultural heritages would not significantly harm the predictability or stability of transactions; and (iv) the use of *lex originis* as governing law is more consistent with the spirit of international comity than *lex rei sitae* would be. This author supports *lex rei sitae* because if 'the country of origin of cultural heritage' is used as a connecting point to the real rights over the cultural heritage, legal stability and predictability may be undermined given the lack of a unitary definition of the 'country of origin'. The scope of protected cultural heritage differs according to international norms and the laws of each country. Therefore, *lex rei sitae* would be more conducive for legal stability. The country of origin of the cultural heritage can be included under 'close connection', and the purpose sought by *lex originis* can still be achieved without taking the *lex originis* approach or using international public policy, provided that the cultural heritage protection law of the origin state of the cultural heritage is applied or considered the overriding mandatory rule of a closely connected third country. In this way, it is possible to prevent the shortcomings of implementing only *lex rei sitae* while maintaining legal stability and predictability, which are the strengths of *lex rei sitae*. Suk (2009) (n 129) 358 and Lee (n 132) 128–29 also support *lex rei sitae*.

[139] Art 33 (Governing Law of the Real Rights): '(1) Real rights, or other rights subject to registration, with regard to movable and immovable property, shall be governed by the *lex situs* of the subject matter. (2) The acquisition or loss of, or changes in rights under paragraph (1) shall be governed by the *lex situs* of the subject matter at the time of the completion of the causal act or fact.'

Therefore, Articles 39(1), 60(1), 74(1), 66 and 87(5) of the Cultural Heritage Act constitute overriding mandatory rules. Applying this conclusion to the aforementioned examples, in Example 4.1, Article 39(1) applies notwithstanding the law of country of X that is the governing law of the sales contract, so the sales contract that violates the Korean law is invalid[140] and B must return the cultural heritage to A. In Example 4.2, Article 87(5) applies as the *lex rei sitae* in accordance with Article 33 of KAPIL. That excludes bona fide acquisition and forces D to return the cultural heritage to A. In Example 4.3, although *lex rei sitae* under Article 33 of KAPIL is the Country X's law which allows bona fide acquisition, bona fide acquisition is excluded as Article 87(5) of the Cultural Heritage Act takes precedence as an overriding mandatory rule of the forum. As a result, D must return the cultural heritage to Party A.[141]

II. Examples of Rules that are not Overriding Mandatory Rules

A. Act on the Regulation of Terms and Conditions

In Korean case law, there were many examples of international contracts being concluded as standard terms and conditions in which courts had to determine whether the Act on the Regulation of Terms and Conditions (hereinafter 'the Terms and Conditions Regulation Act') applied to cases where the governing law was foreign law. In such cases, a party would argue that such terms and conditions cannot be incorporated into the contract because the other party did not fulfil its duty to explain under Article 3(3) of the Terms and Conditions Regulation Act. For example, a party to a marine cargo insurance contract, governed by English law and using the Institute Cargo Clauses, would argue that the Institute Advance Payment Clauses are not incorporated into the contract because the insurer did not explain the critical part of those clauses.[142] Other examples include a case where a party to the distributorship agreement, governed by the laws of Ontario, Canada, claimed that the

[140] Song (2004) (n 137) 247.

[141] If the other facts in Example 3 remain the same, but Party A filed a lawsuit against Party D in the court of Country X to claim the return of cultural heritage, the question would be how to handle Art 87(5) of the Cultural Heritage Act of Korea in the court of Country X, ie, how to apply or consider the overriding mandatory rules of a third country. This is examined in detail in chs 5 and 6. In this case, if Country X and Korea are parties to the UNIDROIT Convention, the courts of Country X will bear the treaty obligations to respect Korea's cultural property. Hence it would be practically beneficial for Korea to join the UNIDROIT Convention. Korea is not yet a member of the UNIDROIT Convention, but if it were, and if the country in which the cultural property is located were a Contracting State, the owner could seek restoration from the possessor in accordance with Art 3(1) of the UNIDROIT Convention in the case of stolen cultural property. In such a case, the owner could also request the courts or other competent authorities of the other Contracting State to order the return of the illegally removed cultural property in accordance with Art 5 of the Convention. To this extent, if Korea joins the UNIDROIT Convention, the general theory on the handling of overriding mandatory rules in third countries among the Contracting States would be of less significance for cultural heritage protection, but it would not render the discussion of third countries' overriding mandatory rules in that area completely meaningless. More countries have not yet joined the UNIDROIT Convention than those that have, and even if many more were to join the agreement, it does not take effect retroactively, which means there are still many restrictions on resolving disputes through the Convention.

[142] Supreme Court of Korea, Judgment of 27 July 2001, Case No 99Da55533.

counterparty did not fulfil its duty to explain under the Terms and Conditions Regulation Act;[143] a case where it was claimed that the warranty provisions under the ship insurance contract governed by English law were not explained to the insured;[144] and a case where it was claimed that a governing law provision designating New York law could not be incorporated into the contract as it was not fully explained in a loan debt guarantee contract.[145] In these cases, whether the Terms and Conditions Regulation Act applies depends on whether Article 3(3) of the Act, which stipulates the obligation of a business entity to explain the terms and conditions, corresponds to an overriding mandatory rule. In most cases, the courts applied the Act without presenting any basis for that application.[146] The courts held in some precedents that the Act cannot always apply when the governing law of the relevant transaction is foreign law.[147] This section will examine whether Article 3 of the Terms and Conditions Regulation Act is an overriding mandatory rule.

There is no explicit provision in the Terms and Conditions Regulation Act stating that the Act applies even when the governing law is foreign law, and there is no extraterritorial application clause. In addition, the Act does not directly stipulate the international or spatial scope of application.[148] Now, whether Article 3 of the Act has a strong public purpose and if its international or spatial scope of application can be specified through the interpretation of the relevant provisions needs to be assessed.

Article 1 of the Terms and Conditions Regulation Act provides that the purpose of the Act is

> to establish sound order in business transactions, and thus to protect consumers and promote the balanced improvement of people's lives by preventing business persons from preparing unfair terms and conditions and using them in business transactions by taking unfair advantage of their bargaining position and regulating unfair terms and conditions.

This may be read as the Terms and Conditions Regulation Act aims to protect fair competition in the market, as with the prohibition of unfair practices under the Fair Trade Act, going beyond adjusting the private interests between the terms and conditions proposer and the counterparty. In determining whether this is an overriding mandatory rule, however, it

[143] Supreme Court of Korea, Judgment of 26 August 2010, Case No 2010Da28185.

[144] Supreme Court of Korea, Judgment of 9 September 2010, Case No 2009Da105383 and Judgment of 20 March 2015, Case No 2012Da11846, 118853.

[145] Seoul High Court, Judgment of 4 March 1994, Case No 92Na61623.

[146] Seoul High Court, Judgment of 4 March 1994, Case No 92Na61623; Supreme Court of Korea, 27 July 2001, Case No 99Da55533; Supreme Court of Korea, Judgment of 9 September 2010, Case No 2009Da105383.

[147] Supreme Court of Korea, Judgment of 26 August 2010, Case No 2010Da28185 and Judgment of 20 March, Case No 20152012Da11846, 118853.

[148] In this respect, the Terms and Conditions Regulation Act is different from the former Terms and Conditions Regulation Act of Germany (*Gesetz zur Regelung des Rechts der Allgemeinen Geschäftsbedingungen, AGBG*) and the Unfair Contract Terms Act 1977 in the UK. Art 12 of the former AGBG declared that there is applicability when 'the contract is formed based on the offer performed, advertisement performed, or similar business activities of the proposer within the scope of the application of this Act, and the other party has its address or residence within the scope of application of this Act at the time of the other party's expression of intent regarding the execution of the contract, and the expression of intent is made within the scope of this Act.' Art 27(2)(b) of the former Unfair Contract Terms Act of the UK provided that the Act has effect notwithstanding any contract term which applies or purports to apply the law of some country outside the UK, where 'in the making of the contract one of the parties dealt as consumer, and he was then habitually resident in the United Kingdom, and the essential steps necessary for the making of the contract were taken there, whether by him or by others on his behalf.' However, this regulation was repealed by the enforcement of the Consumer Rights Act 2015 on 1 October 2015.

is necessary to separately examine the legislative purpose of the specific provision. The legislative purpose of the duty of explanation under Article 3(3) of the Terms and Conditions Regulation Act and the incorporation control under Article 3(4) is to protect customers by ensuring that they enter into a contract with prior knowledge of the contents binding on each party and thus preventing them from suffering unexpected disadvantages.[149] Therefore, Article 3(3) of the Act is intended to adjust private interests, and there is insufficient evidence to believe that its purpose is to correct unfair trade practices that have become part of the trade order or to protect public interests that go beyond the adjustment of private interests.[150] In addition, the Terms and Conditions Regulation Act does not impose administrative or criminal sanctions in the event of a violation of Article 3(3); in the event of such a violation, only the incorporation control under Article 3(4) would be put into practice.

Furthermore, the interpretation of other provisions of the Terms and Conditions Regulation Act does not imply the international or spatial scope of application under Article 3(3). On the grounds that Article 15 of the Terms and Conditions Regulation Act and Article 3 of its Enforcement Decree provide that 'the application of Articles 7 through 14 shall be excluded with respect to terms and conditions of the transport business, financial business, and insurance business that are commonly used internationally, and terms and conditions of trade insurance under the Trade Insurance Act', some believe that legislators intended to apply the Terms and Conditions Regulation Act to contracts that contain foreign elements, including ones where foreign laws are applicable laws.[151] However, when considering that: (1) it is the general legislative practice that when an Act's international application is intended, it is stipulated so under the general provisions of the Act, rather than only listing what is exempted from application; and (2) it is common practice in the shipping, insurance and financial industries to use internationally accepted terms and conditions in domestic contracts without foreign elements, it is difficult to derive the legislators intention to apply the Terms and Conditions Regulation Act to in legal relations with foreign elements.[152] There is no suggestion in the other provisions of the Act that the scope of spatial application should be based on the location of the office of the business entity or the counterparty.

Therefore, Article 3(3) of the Terms and Conditions Regulation Act does not constitute an overriding mandatory rule. That view is held by the majority of Korean academics[153] on the grounds that: (1) the legislative intention to apply the Act irrespective of the governing law of the contract cannot be inferred; and (2) the spatial scope of application cannot be

[149] Supreme Court decision 2009Da105383, delivered on 9 September 2010.

[150] However, Hun Mook Lee, 'Elements to Determine Internationally Mandatory Provisions' (2014) 442 *Human Right and Justice* 99 states that Art 3 of the Terms and Conditions Regulation Act protects fundamental or essential public interests.

[151] Kyung Han Sohn, 'General Understanding of Dispute Resolution Agreement' (2012) 61 *Korean Lawyers Association Journal* 70; Sohn (n 41) 132, 140; Lee (n 149) 99.

[152] This is strikingly so in marine shipping and marine insurance contracts. For example, see Supreme Court of Korea, Judgment of 9 September 2010, Case No 2009Da105383.

[153] Kwang Hyun Suk, 'Is the Act on the Regulation of Terms and Conditions Overriding Mandatory Rules?' *Law Times* (21 March 2011) 13; Suk (n 29) 336; Suk (n 61) 208–09; Shin (n 61) 134; Jung Won Lee, 'A Study on the Insurer's Duty of Explanation and the English Governing Law Clause – Comments on the Korean Supreme Court Ruling Case No. 2009DA105383' (2011) 122 *Justice* 212, 221; Seung-Hyeon Kim, *International Construction Contracts: Laws and Practice*, 2nd edn (Seoul, Pakyoungsa, 2019) 405–06.

limited by the requirement of the connection to the forum. Furthermore, (3) since Article 47 of KAPIL provides consumers with protection in relation to consumer contracts only under the law of their habitual residence, granting overriding mandatory character to the Terms and Conditions Regulation Act, which may also be applied to consumers, would be excessive. This author agrees with the aforementioned first and second grounds. However, the third ground for the majority views cannot be a decisive criterion in determining overriding mandatory character of a provisions.

On the other hand, there is a view that the Terms and Conditions Regulation Act should be applied to cases closely connected to Korea irrespective of the relevant contract's governing law.[154] However, this seems to confuse the issue of the connection to the forum, which establishes a country's legislative jurisdiction, with the matter of the legislator's intent to enforce the provision irrespective of the governing law stated in the contract. Even in cases where the relevant facts are connected to Korea, the Terms and Conditions Regulation Act cannot be applied simply for that reason. To apply the Act, the such an intention of the legislator must be identified.

B. Article 92(2) of the Commercial Act

Article 92(2)(1) of the Commercial Act recognises the commercial agent's right to request compensation, that 'if a principal obtains new customers or his/her business transactions increase substantially through the activities of his/her commercial agent, and he/she receives profits therefrom even after the contract is terminated, the agent may request reasonable compensation from the principal'.[155] If a commercial agency contract was executed between a domestic commercial agent and a foreign principal, with the applicable law as foreign law, and if the commercial agent claims the right to compensation based on Article 92(2) of the Korean Commercial Act,[156] the application of Article 92(2) will depend on whether it is an overriding mandatory rule.[157]

There is no explicit provision in the Commercial Act that Article 92(2) applies regardless of the applicable law of the agency contract. There is no extraterritorial application clause,

[154] Sohn (n 150) 70; Sohn (n 41) 132, 140.

[155] The legal nature of the right for a commercial agent to claim compensation under this provision is not a right to claim compensation for torts due to the undue termination of the agency contract, nor the right to claim the return of unfair profits (restitution) incurred by the principal after the termination of the contract. It is perceived as a stautory right allowed by this specific provision. Section by Jae-beom Kim in Dong Yoon Jung (ed), *Annotation to Commercial Law* [Juseok sangbeop je4pan], 4th edn (Seoul, Korean Judicial Administration Association, 2013) Art 92-2 105.

[156] Seoul High Court, Judgment of 14 January 2005, Case No 2004Na14040 is an example.

[157] As to whether Art 92-2 of the Commercial Act constitutes a domestic mandatory provision, one view is that it is not a domestic mandatory provision based on how Art 92(2) does not specify that it is a mandatory provision, unlike Art 89b of the German Commercial Code, which the provision benchmarked. However, it is reasonable that the commercial agent's right to claim compensation is intended to compensate for the part that cannot be fulfilled through ordinary remuneration for the commercial agent and is intended to protect the commercial agent, an economically disadvantaged person, therefore constituting a domestic mandatory provision (Namsoon Yoon, 'International Trade and Protection of Commercial Agents' (2006) 17 *Journal of Business Administration & Law* 120; Kwang Hyun Suk, 'Protection of Commercial Agents in International Transactions – Scope of Application of Article 92bis of the Commercial Code' (2006) 55 *Korean Lawyers Association Journal* 32). Therefore, this discussion is conducted on the premise that Art 92(2) of the Commercial Act constitutes a domestic mandatory provision.

nor is there a provision in the Act that directly stipulates the scope of international or spatial application of Article 92(2). Therefore, whether Article 92(2) has a strong public purpose, and whether its international or spatial scope of application can be determined through the interpretation of relevant provisions, must be assessed.

The aim of Article 92(2) of the Commercial Act is to protect commercial agents, whose economic status may be vulnerable, by securing their rights to receive appropriate compensation for their efforts. This provision has the main purpose of adjusting the tangible imbalance between private parties.[158] However, since the European Court of Justice ruled in *Ingmar*[159] that provisions in the EU's Commercial Agent Directive was an overriding mandatory rule, there may be room to argue that Article 92(2) of the Commercial Act, which was enacted with reference to the Commercial Agent Directive, also constitutes an overriding mandatory rule. Nevertheless, as discussed in chapter three, the context of the Commercial Agent Directive's declaration to be an overriding mandatory rule in the EU is unusual: the Directive was supposed to create uniform conditions for competition within the European market by harmonising the domestic laws of the Member States. That is different from the circumstances of Article 92(2) of the Commercial Act, a domestic law that neither presupposes a larger community nor is aimed at the harmonisation of the market.

Per the *Ingmar* ruling, Articles 17–19 of the Commercial Agent Directive removed restrictions on the conduct of commercial activities 'in the European Community' as a means of unifying domestic laws and 'harmonis[ing] the conditions of competition in the European Community'.[160] Therefore, it can be seen that the EU's Commercial Agent Directive had the purpose of protecting the strong economic interests of the EU. However, Article 92(2) of the Commercial Act of Korea does not seem to have such a purpose, and there is no evidence that this provision aims to correct imbalances deeply rooted in the trade order or to protect important constitutional values. In addition, in light of the fact that laws in different jurisdictions have rules to protect commercial agents, there is equivalence and substitutability in regulations protecting commercial agents. On top of that, even when Article 92(2) of the Commercial Act is violated, it does not lead to administrative or criminal measures. Furthermore, there is no clue about the international or spatial scope of application in Article 92(2) such as the place of business of either the principal or the commercial agent. Therefore, Article 92(2) of the Commercial Act does not count as an overriding mandatory rule.

In opposition to this, there is a view that Article 92(2) of the Commercial Act corresponds to an overriding mandatory rule because it is designed to protect the constitutional economic order by correcting malpractice in the commercial agency market.[161] However, it is questionable whether there is empirical evidence that the imbalance between commercial agents' and principals' tangible bargaining power in the market has reached the extent that it affects the trade order, as seen in the examples of subcontracts or franchise transactions.

Another view is that as long as the EU recognises the Commercial Agent Directive as an overriding mandatory rule, Article 92(2) of the Commercial Act of Korea should also

[158] Suk (n 56) 25–27, 54–57.

[159] *Ingmar GB Ltd v Eaton Leonard Technologies Inc* Case C-381/98, ECLI:EU:C:2000:605, [2000] ECR I-09305 ('*Ingmar*'). See ch 3, II, A.

[160] ibid [23].

[161] Lee (n 149), 97, fn 64.

be regarded as an overriding mandatory rule.[162] This view contends that not doing so may lead to an imbalance between cases where a Korean company executes an agreement with a commercial agent of an EU Member State and where a Korean commercial agent enters into an agreement with a principal in an EU Member State.[163] While that may be true, and despite the potential need to resolve the issue through further legislation, the need itself cannot be a sufficient ground to regard Article 92(2) of the Commercial Act as an overriding mandatory rule when it does not meet the requirements of Article 20 of KAPIL.

C. Article 799 of the Commercial Act

Article 799(1) of the Commercial Act states:

> No special agreement between the parties to reduce or exclude any obligation or liability of a carrier contrary to the provisions of Articles 794 through 798 shall be valid. The same shall also apply to an agreement to transfer to a carrier the benefit of insurance concerning the cargo, or a similar agreement.

This reflects Article III–8 of the Hague-Visby Rules (Protocol signed at Brussels on 23 February 1968, inclusive of 1979 Amendments).[164] However, the Commercial Act did not accept the provisions on the scope of application of the Hague-Visby Rules (Article X),[165] rendering the scope of application of Article 92(2) of the Act ambiguous.

Therefore, it is questionable whether Article 799(1) of the Commercial Act applies when the carriage contract is governed by a foreign law, like Article X of the Hague-Visby Rules does, or whether it would only apply when the governing law of a shipping contract or bill of lading is Korean law. Specifically this would be whether Article 799(1) applies in relation to the carrier's breach of its duty of care and grounds for indemnification in cases where the

[162] Yoon (n 156) 120.

[163] ibid.

[164] Jung Won Lee, 'A Study on the Relationship Between the Himalaya Clause and Article 799 of the Korean Commercial Act' (2010) 51 *Pusan National University Law Review* 563. After the enactment of the Commercial Act, provisions on maritime law in the Commercial Act was revised several times. Instead of joining the international treaty on international maritime shipping, the Commercial Act incorporated the contents of the treaty during its amendment in 1991. The 1924 Hague Rules (International Convention for the Unification of Certain Rules of Law Related to Bills of Landing, signed at Brussels on August 25 and major clauses of the1968 Hague-Visby Rules were adopted, and the 1978 United Nations International Convention on the Carriage of Goods by Sea, adopted in Hamburg on 31 March 1978 (Hamburg Rules) were also partially incorporated. Thereafter, the Commercial Act amended in 2007 was one step closer to the Hague-Visby Rules and Hamburg Rules. See Dong Yoon Jung (ed), *Annotation to Commercial Law* [Juseok sangbeop je2pan], 2nd edn (Korean Judicial Administration Association, 2015) Art 799, 475–76; Jong Hyeon Choi, 'Focusing on the Liability of a Carrier – Status of a Carrier under the Amended Maritime Law' (2008) 30 *Korea Maritime Law Journal* 49, 57.

[165] In the process of amending the Commercial Act in 2007, it was proposed to adopt a provision on the scope of application of Art 799(1) of the Commercial Act in Art 817, with the intention of tailoring the Maritime Law to international standards, as the applicability of Art 779(1) of the Commercial Act was frequently challenged in the case of transportation between Korea and foreign countries. However, that provision in the draft law was eventually deleted due to over excessive restrictions on the principle of freedom of contract and the reduction of the jurisdiction of the Korean courts. See also Kwang Hyun Suk, 'Several Choice of Law Issues in Maritime Matters' (2009) 31 *Korea Maritime Law Journal* 89, 113–14 and In-hyeon Kim, '2007 Revised Maritime Law Section of Korean Commercial Code' (2009) 31 *Korea Maritime Law Journal* (2009) 99, 149–50 for details of the amendment process and proposed amendment.

applicable law of a carriage by sea contract is designated as the 'Carriage of Goods by Sea Act of the United States and the Hague Rules' where the carrier decides to bear a significantly lower level of responsibility than it would under the Korean Commercial Act.[166] The same question arises where the applicable law of a carriage by sea contract is designated as the 'Hague Rules and Hague-Visby Rules'.[167] In such cases, since the limitation of liability under the contract varies significantly according to which law applies,[168] there would be practical benefits in reviewing the overriding mandatory nature of Article 799(1) of the Commercial Act.[169]

The Commercial Act does not stipulate whether Article 799(1) applies extraterritorially or whether it applies irrespective of the governing law of the shipping contract. Neither does the Act explicitly stipulate the international or spatial scope of application under Article 799(1). Therefore, this author will examine whether Article 799(1) protects strong public interests and whether the international or spatial scope of application can be determined through the interpretation of related provisions.

The law limiting compensation from carriers, which is unique to maritime laws, aims to protect businesses from the large scale of risks borne by carriers and the risks of sea.[170] In carriage by sea contracts, limitation of liability clauses have been widely used to reduce or exempt the carrier's liability for damages to goods that occur during voyage. However, Article 799(1) of the Commercial Act prohibits in principle terms and conditions that reduce or exempt the carrier's liability. The main purpose here is to protect consignors of individual shipping contracts who have less bargaining power and are at an economic disadvantage to carriers (unlike charterers, whose bargaining power is generally equal to that of shipowners).[171] This is the product of a compromise between the consignor's and carrier's conflicting interests and reflects the legal principle of consumer protection by seeking to protect the consignor, who can be regarded as the consumer of shipping services, whilst considering the inherent risks and nature of maritime shipping that the carrier must face.[172] Accordingly, Article 799(1) is a rule to adjust private interests, rather than one that is essential for the protection of the economic, political and social order. It would be difficult to conclude that Article 799(1) has the purpose of correcting unfair practices prevalent in the trade order or realising important constitutional values. Indeed, since international treaties such as the Hague-Visby Rules have been signed with respect to limiting the carrier's liability,

[166] Supreme Court of Korea, Judgment of 10 December 1999, Case No 98Da9038.

[167] Supreme Court of Korea, 10 January 2003, Case No 2000Da70064. In this case, the Supreme Court applied Arts 795, 796(6) and 799 of the Commercial Act which were in effect at the time, without providing any explanation as to why the Commercial Act of Korea applied, even though the governing law of the contract was not Korean law.

[168] Another example of discrepancies between national law is illustrated in Byung Suk Chung, 'Conflict of Laws Issues in Maritime Claims' (2010) 16 *Korea Private International Law Journal* 197, 199–200. He provides an example where the limitation of liability of the shipowner differs significantly depending on the governing law.

[169] If this is viewed as an overriding mandatory provision, the consignor can at least be protected according to the standards set by the maritime law of Korea.

[170] Lee (n 163) 2.

[171] Jung (n 163) Arts 799, 533, 535; Lee (n 163) 2, 7–8. In charterparties, however, if the carrier is in breach of seaworthiness requirements, and if a third party has issued the bill of lading, the special agreement to reduce or exclude the carrier's obligation and liability becomes invalid (Art 855(5)): Jung (n 163) 535.

[172] Lee (n 163) 8.

and shipping laws[173] have been enacted in each country with similar purposes, equivalence and substitutability of laws can be recognised; each country can therefore develop rules that suit its individual circumstances. Even when Article 799(1) of the Commercial Act is violated, administrative and criminal sanctions are not imposed.[174]

Furthermore, there are no indications of the international or spatial scope of application under Article 799(1) through the interpretation of other provisions of the Commercial Act. It might be assumed that the scope of application of Article 799(1) could be inferred from the place of issuance of the bill of lading or the place of receipt, loading, unloading and delivery based on Article 855[175] of the Commercial Act in cases where the bill of lading has been issued. However, Article 855 of the Commercial Act concerns charter-party agreements rather than shipping contracts. Taking such an approach would exceed the boundaries of interpretation and effectively constitute lawmaking.[176] In the 2007 Commercial Act amendment process, the Ministry of Justice proposed to include language in Article 817, stating that

> a special agreement to reduce or exempt the obligations or responsibilities of a carrier shall be null and void to the extent that that is not permitted by the provisions of this Section, irrespective of the applicable law of the carriage by sea contract for individual goods, if the place of either receipt, loading, unloading or delivery of the goods is the Republic of Korea.

However, this faced opposition for various reasons and was never introduced.[177] If such a provision had been introduced, it would have been possible to derive the legislator's intention for the provision to apply regardless of the governing law of the shipping contract, as it stipulates the spatial application under Article 799(1) of the Commercial Act. However, the Act's current provisions do not imply such a spatial scope of application of Article 799(1).

In sum, Article 799(1) of the Commercial Act does not constitute an overriding mandatory rule.[178] Without giving a specific reason, the Supreme Court held in the judgment of

[173] Examples are the Carriage of Goods by Sea Act 1971 of the UK and the Carriage of Goods by Sea Act of 1936 of the US.

[174] Jung (n 163) 533.

[175] Art 855 (Contracts by Charter Parties and Bills of Lading): '(1) When requested by a charterer, a shipowner shall issue a bill of lading under Articles 852 and 853 after the receipt of cargo. (2) When a bill of lading has been issued under paragraph (1), a shipowner shall be presumed to have received or loaded the cargo as stated in a bill of lading. (3) When a third party has acquired a bill of lading in good faith, a shipowner shall have the rights and obligations of a carrier under Article 854 (2). The same shall also apply when a shipowner has issued a bill of lading to a third party at the request of a charterer. (4) In cases falling under paragraph (3), a third party shall be deemed a consignor under Articles 833 through 835 and 837. (5) In cases falling under paragraph (3), no special agreement to reduce or exclude any obligation and liability of a carrier in violation of Article 799 shall be made.'

[176] Suk (n 29) 145 purports the same.

[177] Kim (n 164) 149–50.

[178] Therefore, it is unconvincing that the Supreme Court of Korea applied Art 799 of the Commercial Act in the Judgment of 10 January 2003, Case No 2000Da70064, where the relevant contract was governed by the Hague Rules and Hague Visbey Rules. It is the majority opinion in the Korean legal literature that Art 799(1) of the Commercial Act does not constitute an overriding mandatory rule, although on grounds somewhat different from those presented by the author. Suk (2009) (n 129) 112–13; In-ho Kim, 'Limitations by Mandatory Rules on the Dominance of Party Autonomy in International Contracts' (2012) 60 *Advanced Commercial Law Review* 110–133; and Jung Won Lee, 'Relationship between the Party Autonomy and Clause Paramount from the Viewpoint of the International Private Law (2019) 60(4) *Pusan National University Law Review* 137, 154 state that the legislative intent for the provision to apply irrespective of the governing law of the relevant contract is not in evidence because the Commercial Act excluded Article X of the Hague-Visby Rules.

10 December 1999, Case No 98Da9038[179] that Article 790(1) of the former Commercial Act (current Article 799(1)) does not constitute an overriding mandatory rule.[180]

III. Concluding Remarks

The results of the above analysis may be summarised as follows. First, it can be seen that the standard methods and factors to consider when determining an overriding mandatory character, as presented in chapter three, are useful. Provisions that constitute overriding mandatory rules reveal the legislator's intention for the provisions to apply to the extent that the relevant facts are within the international or spatial scope of application irrespective of the governing law of the relevant contract or tort (Fair Trade Act, Foreign Exchange Transactions Act, Foreign Trade Act, Employment Security Act and State Contracts Act), either through extraterritorial application clauses or clauses that define the international or spatial scope of application. Even in the absence of an extraterritorial application clause or direct stipulations regarding the international or spatial application scope, there are indicators that enable confirmation of the international or spatial scope of application. This can be achieved through the interpretation of the legislative purpose and related provisions, as seen in the Subcontract Act, Franchise Act, Equal Employment Act and Cultural Heritage Act. Provisions that were not overriding mandatory rules had the shared legislative purpose of adjusting private interests and lacked any indications of their international or spatial scope of application or protection of strong public interests that transcend private interests.

Secondly, the fact that there are legislative examples in different jurisdictions that recognise provisions similar to the Terms and Conditions Regulation Act and to Articles 92(2) and 799(2) of the Commercial Act as overriding mandatory rules from a comparative law perspective has implications for *de lege ferenda*.[181] Although this author believes that none of the above three provisions has the legislative purpose to be recognised as an overriding mandatory rule, legislative decisions whose values correspond to a strong national and public interest may vary with the times and circumstances. If the legislator determined that a certain provision has a strong public interest and there was indeed a need for the said provision to override the usual choice-of-law principles, it would be unfortunate for said rule to be denied the overriding mandatory character due to a legislative mistake or insufficient

[179] In the case, the Supreme Court denied the application of Art 790(1) of the former Commercial Act by stating that, 'The purpose of holding "the Hague Rules effective in the country where the court is located" is generally interpreted to mean that the Hague Rules are in themselves effective as a legal norm in the forum country. Since Korea is not a party to the Hague Rules, they do not have the effect of legal norms in Korea, and although it is true that the Commercial Act of Korea accepts most of the above Hague Rules, that by itself does not necessarily mean that the Commercial Act of Korea is the governing law of legal relations under the carriage of goods contract that is governed by the Hague Rules.'

[180] Suk (2009) (n 129) 112–13; Kim (n 177) 133.

[181] In the UK, the rules that domestically enact the Hague-Visby Rules, in the manner of Art 799(1) of the Commercial Act, are recognised as overriding mandatory rules. However, instead of considering Art 799(1) as an overriding mandatory rule, a more fundamental solution would be to adopt the Hague-Visby Rules directly. If the legislator intended to incorporate the effect of the Hague-Visby Rules into the Commercial Act, there should have been a provision introduced regarding the scope of application. The UK, which enacted the Hague-Visby Rules as part of domestic law, also included a provision specifying the scope of the Hague-Visby Rules' application.

consideration for private international law. As seen earlier, even if there is no extraterritorial application clause or stipulation of the international or spatial scope of application, there are cases where the relevant provision can be recognised as an overriding mandatory rule by interpreting its legislative purpose and related provisions. However, this is limited to cases when the scope of application can be ascertained through interpretation based on the requirement of the connection to the forum. That being said, such a process would be impossible when there are no hints about how to limit the international or spatial scope of application. Therefore, this must be taken into consideration in the legislative process. In the future, legislators ought to give sufficient consideration to the scope of the law's application and make an effort to explicitly demonstrate such consideration.

Thirdly, even when there is a strong regulatory purpose, a provision should not be too readily introduced or recognised as being an overriding mandatory rule. Considering that overriding mandatory rules not only limit parties' freedom of contract at the substantive law level but also their freedom to choose the applicable law, legislating and recognising certain provisions as overriding mandatory rules must be strictly and carefully done. Furthermore, when introducing provisions that are applied extraterritorially, it is also necessary to consider whether there are any overlapping foreign regulations and how to resolve such an issue.

Fourthly, among the provisions reviewed, there were only a few examples of recognised overriding mandatory rules that stipulate the private law effect of their violation. We must recall that the discussion of overriding mandatory rules in private international law is focused on their private law effect on the relevant legal relationships. Even if a certain provision is recognised as an overriding mandatory rule, it would be difficult to determine its effect on a contract following the violation of a rule if the provision does not stipulate whether the contract should be invalidated. The distinction between what is and is not a crackdown provision is also a difficult issue in substantive law, and for predictability, it is necessary to establish clear standards for determining the private law effect of violations of overriding mandatory rules.

The book has thus far discussed the issue of what provisions are overriding mandatory rules, an issue that is common to the overriding mandatory rules of the forum, the country to which the applicable law belongs, and third countries. In chapter five, as a matter peculiar to the overriding mandatory rules of third countries, we will turn to the question of under what conditions the overriding mandatory rules of third countries should be considered or applied.

5

Comparative Research on the Treatment of Overriding Mandatory Rules of a Third Country

The overriding mandatory rules of a third country refer to the overriding mandatory rules of a country that is neither the forum nor the country to which the applicable law belongs. One may ask how frequently the overriding mandatory rules of third countries will pose problems in international contracts, and whether this discussion is actually necessary. However, overriding mandatory rules of third countries have been problematic in various types of international contracts, as seen in the German and English case law in section II below and the Swiss case law in section III. In particular, recent examples of the overriding mandatory rules of third countries include economic sanctions by the EU or US, and particularly secondary boycotts[1] and laws with extraterritorial application adopted by different countries, such as data protection laws or consumer protection laws.

There is great controversy in private international law as to whether to consider or apply the overriding mandatory rules of a third country, and if so, how to do so, and there are no established theories.[2] Not only does the application of foreign public law pose a problem in relation to territoriality, but with the need for the judge of the forum country to interpret laws of various jurisdictions and cultures in order to take into account the overriding

[1] The US has imposed a wide range of economic sanctions on enemies since World War II. Its economic sanctions are divided into primary sanctions prohibiting transactions between the US and sanctioned persons, and secondary boycotts against third parties when a third country or a third-country national trades with sanctioned persons. The US has introduced secondary boycotts to block Cuba, Iran, Russia and Libya from international transactions and recently opened the possibility of secondary sanctions against North Korea. For details of the types of economic sanctions taken by the United States and their legal basis, see Dong-Eun Lee, 'The International Legal Dimension of Unilateral Economic Sanctions and the Implications on the Sanctions Against North Korea – Focused on the U.S. Secondary Sanctions' (2020) 65 *Korean Journal of International Law* 191, 193–99. *Libyan Arab Foreign Bank v Bankers Trust Co* [1989] QB 728 of the UK, introduced in s II below, is another case in which American sanctions against Iran were an issue. Since secondary boycotts by the US also regulate transactions with sanctioned countries by non-sanctioned third countries or third-country nationals, it is highly likely that such sanctions will be treated as overriding mandatory rules of a third country, from the perspective of third countries and sanctioned countries. Sanctions by the US are of particular significance in the economic structure of Korea, which is highly dependent on exports overseas, a large portion of which is to the US (according to the Bank of Korea's 'National Account' data, the export/import ratio against GDP for Korea reached 82.9% in 2018, 80.1% in 2019 and 72.9% in 2020. National Bureau of Statistics, among national development indicators, data on export/import ratio (against GDP) (9 June 2021) accessible at www.index.go.kr/unify/idx-info.do?idxCd=4207&clasCd=7. The portion of the total value of exports for Korea taken up by the US was 13.5% in 2019, 14.5% in 2020 and 14.9% in 2021. Korea International Trade Association, 'Korea Trade Statistics', www.index.go.kr/unify/idx-info.do?pop=1&idxCd=5010.

[2] Kurt Rebmann (ed), *Münchener Kommentar zum BGB*, 4th edn (Verlag Beck München, 2006) EGBGB Art 34, Rn 3.

mandatory rules of third countries, the overriding mandatory rules of third countries were considered to hinder the efficiency of the procedure, party autonomy, legal certainty and harmonisation of decisions in different jurisdictions.[3]

There is no provision in KAPIL on how to deal with the overriding mandatory rules of third countries. Section I of the chapter, as preliminary work for developing the theories of interpretation and legislation for KAPIL, first examines the theoretical basis for the consideration or application of the overriding mandatory rules of third countries and conduct comparative legal research. As a theoretical basis, the reasons for considering or applying the overriding mandatory rules of third countries and the interests to be weighed when considering or applying the overriding mandatory rules of third countries will be analysed.

With respect to how to treat the overriding mandatory rules of third countries, there is tension between the position that these rules should be considered as facts under the general provisions of the applicable substantive law (substantive law approach) and the position that they should be considered or applied based on the conflict of law of the forum (conflict-of-laws approach). Therefore, comparative legal research is conducted by distinguishing the respective approaches, set out in sections II and III. Following this is an assessment of whether each approach appropriately reflects the relevant interests. The resulting argument would be that considering or applying the overriding mandatory rules of a third country from a conflict-of-laws approach is more predictable for the parties than doing so based on the substantive law approach, and that the relevant interests can be better weighed by so doing. Among the conflict-of-laws approaches, there are different views on whether the scope of a third country should be limited to the place of performance or to a country closely connected to the contract. This author suggests that the latter reflects the relevant interests in a more balanced manner.

I. Theoretical Basis

A. Grounds for Considering or Applying Overriding the Mandatory Rules of Third Countries

It is clear that the interests of a third country to which the overriding mandatory rules belong are served by considering or applying its overriding mandatory rules. However, from the point of view of the forum country, there may be doubts as to why the overriding mandatory rules of a third country should be considered or applied. The following are feasible explanations.

The first discusses the necessity of taking into account the interests of other countries to achieve consistency in decisions.[4] This is based on Savigny's position that foreign law and domestic law are equal. The law most appropriate for legal relations should be identified and

[3] Ivana Kunda, *Internationally Mandatory Rules of a Third Country in the European Contracts Conflict of Laws: The Rome Convention and the Proposed Rome 1 Regulation* (Rijeka, 2015) 332.

[4] Paul Hauser, *Eingriffsnormen in der Rom- I Verordnung* (Mohr Siebeck, 2012) 53; Lisa Günther, *Die Anwendbargkeit ausländischer Eingriffnormen im Lichter der Rom I- und Rom II Verordnungen* (Verlag Alma Mater, 2011) 22.

applied regardless of the forum to prevent forum shopping and contribute to international harmonisation in judgments. In addition, a foreign judgment should be recognised and enforced unless it is contrary to the public policy of the forum. If foreign judgments can be frequently recognised and enforced internationally, the overriding mandatory rules applied in those foreign judgments will also be indirectly approved. Therefore, there is no reason not to consider the overriding mandatory rules of a foreign country unless they are contrary to public policy.

Second, in accordance with the principle of international comity and reciprocity, foreign sovereignty should be respected, and the overriding mandatory rules of third countries should be considered or applied.[5] Due to the internationalisation of commercial transactions, legal relations governed by domestic laws have increasingly been contested in foreign courts, and in order for domestic laws to be applied in foreign countries, the assistance of foreign courts is necessary. If a foreign court applies domestic laws, domestic courts must also apply foreign law to the legal relationships governed by that foreign laws in accordance with the principle of reciprocity.

Third, considering or applying the overriding mandatory rules of third countries makes it possible to protect shared interests.[6] This is a valid argument not only in regard to preventing terrorism but also in situations where international efforts and cooperation are needed to protect interests accepted worldwide, such as fair competition, cultural heritage protection and prevention of the spread of diseases such as COVID-19. If the overriding mandatory rules of a third country are not considered or applied, it may lead to an unjust outcome.

B. Relevant Interests in the Consideration or Application of the Overriding Mandatory Rules of Third Countries

Under which conditions the court should apply the overriding mandatory rules of a third country is largely a question of whether to prioritise the governing law of the contract, the forum law, or the law of the third country. Therefore, it is useful to analyse and evaluate related interests when solving this problem.[7] In private international law, there have been attempts to categorise and analyse relevant interests in general in the context of applicable law. However, such attempts did not specifically concern relevant interests in the context of a third country's overriding mandatory rules.

Professor Gerhard Kegel classified various interests that should be considered generally in private international law,[8] and his classifications have been introduced

[5] Günther (ibid) 23; Hauser (ibid) 54.

[6] Section by Dieter Martiny in Kurt Rebmann (ed), *Münchener Kommentar zum BGB*, 4th edn (Verlag Beck München, 2006) EGBGB Art 34, Rn 47.

[7] Andrea Bonomi, 'Mandatory Rules in Private International Law – The Quest for Uniformity of Decisions in a Global Environment' (1999) 1 *Yearbook of Private International Law* 215, 235 argues that the question of under which conditions the court will apply the overriding mandatory rules of a third country can only be resolved by interest analysis. As shown in s III below, legislative examples that stipulate the conflict-of-laws approach are based on interest analysis.

[8] Gerhard Kegel and Klaus Schurig, *Internationales Privatrecht*, 9th edn (Verlag CH Beck, 2004) 128ff. Professor Kegel classified private international legal interests as 'interests of parties', 'transaction interests' and 'order interests'. 'Interests of parties' are interests determined according to a legal order closely integrated with the party and

in Korea.[9] Kegel states with respect to the overriding mandatory rules of third countries that 'we must decide whether they are based on private-international-law interests that may be made our own (*Umgekehrt müssen wir bei solchen Normen aus dritten Rechtsordnungen selbst entscheiden, ob sie auf kollisionrechtlichen Interessen beruhen, die wir uns eigen machen kann*)' and that 'because of the diversity of the interests involved, there is no master key (*Passpartout*) for all interfering norms'.[10] However, this explanation is not particularly useful in classifying and weighing the interests involved in specific circumstances, such as the consideration or application of the overriding mandatory rules of third countries. When considering or applying the overriding mandatory rules of a third country, it is necessary to determine whether to prioritise the applicable law of the relevant legal relationship, the law of a third country or the forum law by weighing the relevant interests. However, according to Kegel's classification, it is not clear which law should apply.

On the other hand, Professor Brainerd Currie, who led the revolution in American private international law in the twentieth century, argues that applicable law should be determined by balancing the policy objectives pursued by relevant provisions; in other words, that governing law shall be selected by weighing the interests in applying domestic law for the implementation of policy by the state.[11] Currie's theory is that the policy objectives of all substantive laws that can be applied in an overlapping manner should be weighed to clarify the principle of connection unique to each substantive law, and that all judicial disputes reflect the policy objectives of the state.[12] However, this view also has limitations in that it emphasises only policy objectives among the various interests surrounding the overriding mandatory rules of third countries. Another problem is that the predictability for the parties regarding the choice of law is undermined because this principle is based on individual specific provisions and fails to present a general connection principle.

Meanwhile, Professor Andrea Bonomi classifies interests relating to the consideration or application of the overriding mandatory rules of a third country as 'the interests of parties', 'the interests of a third country', 'the interests of the forum state' and 'multistate interests'.[13] 'Interests of parties' refers to interests in choosing the law most closely connected to the party.

corresponds to the interest of the party to be governed by the applicable law to which the parties have agreed. 'Transaction interests' are in the safe and smooth conduct of transactions. 'Order interests' refer to how laws should be applied in a uniform and harmonised manner. Kegel explains that outside private international legal interests, there are public law/national interests (public law interests regarding political and economic interference by the state and interests in the survival and prosperity of the state) and substantive law interests. In exceptional cases, he contended, private international legal interests should yield to substantive law interests. For example, in cases where the results of applying the applicable foreign law would go against the concept of justice under the substantive law, such results should be corrected.

[9] Professor Kegel's view is followed by Ho Jeong Lee, *Private International Law* (Kyungmoonsa, 1985) 16 and thereafter, Choon Soo An, *Private International Law* (Bobmunsa, 2017) 53ff.

[10] Kegel and Schurig (n 8) 156.

[11] Brainerd Currie, 'Married Women's Contracts: A Study in Conflict-of-Law Method' (1958) 25 *University of Chicago Law Review* 227, 237ff; see Junhyok Jang, 'A Study on Brainerd Currie's Governmental Interest Analysis' (Master of jurisprudence thesis, Seoul National University, 1994), a Korean-language study introducing Currie's theory.

[12] The so-called 'government interests analysis theory' as put forward by this view is not limited to the context of the overriding mandatory rules of third countries, but rather concerns the general connection principles in private international law. The government interest analysis was reflected in Art 7(1)(2) of the Rome Convention, Art 9(3) of the Rome I Regulation and Art 19 of the Swiss Federal Act on Private International Law (FAPIL). These regulations determine whether to apply the law of a third country through interest-weighing based on policy considerations.

[13] Bonomi (n 7) 236ff.

These are the interests in a party's expectation that a particular legal system will be applicable. The advantages or disadvantages to a party following the application of governing law in specific cases are not included in the interests of the party discussed herein. 'The interests of a third country' are its interests in applying its laws to implement its policies from the standpoint of a third country, and 'the interests of the forum state' mean the interests of the forum or the values the forum intends to protect, which may be infringed by applying the overriding mandatory rules of a third country. 'Multistate interests' refer to the pursuit of international uniformity and harmony in decisions.[14] Bonomi argued that the three aforementioned interests do not play a decisive role in the consideration or application of the overriding mandatory rules of third countries and that the interests of multiple countries are important.

Bonomi's classification of interests is persuasive. However, this author disagrees with his assertion that the interests of parties, the interests of third countries and the interests of the forum state are not important factors. Rather, these three interests may conflict with each other and that these three interests should also be considered in a balanced manner. However, contrary to Bonomi's intended meaning, the term 'multistate interests' may be misunderstood as the common interests of various countries; thus, instead of 'multistate interests', it would be clearer to use the term 'interests of international harmony in decisions'. The following is based on Bonomi's classification of interests, but I would like to explain why the interests of parties, the interests of the forum state and the interests of third countries are also meaningful.

'Interests of parties' mean a party's legitimate expectation that the subjective or objective governing law of the relevant legal relationship will apply.[15] Accordingly, it can be understood that the 'interest of the party' is the predictability for a party as to which norms will govern the contract, including the governing law chosen by the parties. The contractual rights and obligations of the parties shall be determined in accordance with the applicable law of the contract. This outcome naturally arises from the parties' careful consideration and deliberate actions, taking into account the benefits to be gained from the contract and the associated risks, given that they anticipated the contract would be governed by the relevant applicable law.[16] However, the laws of a third country are less expected by the parties than the chosen law or the law of the forum. In addition, when considering or applying the overriding mandatory rules of a third country, the interests of the parties may be limited in that unanticipated norms affect the relevant legal relationship.

'Interests of the forum state' mean the interests in controlling the impact on the forum's legal system from the point of view of the forum.[17] The consideration or application of third-country law should not infringe upon the fundamental value protected by the forum.

[14] Per Kegel's classification, this corresponds to the 'order interests' of international uniformity or harmony in decisions.

[15] This corresponds to the interests of parties as stated by Kegel.

[16] This should be distinguished from the application of specific provisions contended by the parties in concrete cases, as Bonomi explains, which results in disadvantageous or advantageous outcome for one party. Bonomi (n 7) 236.

[17] 'The interests of the forum state' correspond, according to Kegel's classification, to the 'order interests', and in particular, 'the interests in the consistency of internal judgments', which require maximum uniformity in regulations without contradictions, deficiencies or conflicts of legal norms when applying foreign law at the forum. This is distinguished from what Kegel classifies as 'interests in consistency in external judgments', on the harmony and consistency in decisions in various jurisdictions at an international level. This would correspond to multistate interests and the interests of international harmony in decisions under Bonomi's classification.

Most countries recognise that the overriding mandatory rules and public policy of the forum apply, which demonstrates that the interests of the forum state are important. 'Interests of a third country' mean the interests of a third country in achieving its important policy objectives.[18] It is important to recognise and consider these interests, which pertain to the sovereignty of a third country. They should not be disregarded or underestimated. The 'interests of international harmony in decisions' reflect the ideal of private international law. In the following section, on the premise of such a classification of interests, various views on the consideration or application of overriding mandatory rules of third countries will be assessed.

II. Substantive Law Approach

Hereinafter, this author will introduce and critically assess the substantive law approach. German theories[19] such as the *lex causae* rule, the Territoriality Principle, the Theory of Power, and the case law of the German courts and English courts.

A. The *Lex Causae* Rule, Territoriality Principle and the Theory of Power

The following examples clarify the practical benefits of the conflicting theories.

Example 5.1

Party A is the owner of a statue designated as a cultural heritage in Country X, and Party B is a collector in Korea. However, at the time of the sales contract, the Cultural Heritage Act of Country X prohibited the export and removal of the cultural property. Nevertheless, Party A enters into a sales contract to sell the statute to Party B. The governing law of the sales contract was agreed to be Korean law, and the statue was to be delivered in Korea. At the time of the sales contract's execution, the statue was in Country X, and even afterward, Party A continues to keep the statue in Country X. Party B files a lawsuit against Party A in Korean court seeking the delivery of the statue based on the sales contract.

[18] 'The interests of a third country' correspond to 'substantive law interests', 'public law interests' or 'national interests' according to Kegel's classification.

[19] For an introduction of the German theories, see the section by Ulrich Magnus in Julius Von Staudinger and Norbert Habermann (ed), *Staudingers Kommentar Zum Bürgerlichen Gesetzbuch Mit Einführungsgesetz Und Nebengesetzen: Einführungsgesetz zum Bürgerlichen Gesetzbuche/IPR* (Sellier-De Gruyter, 2002) 630ff; Martiny (n 6), EGBGB Art 34, Rn 40ff; Günther (n 4) 57–66; Hauser (n 4) 96–100; Kwang Hyun Suk, 'The Role of the Private International Law Act and the Cultural Property Protection Act of Korea as Means of Protecting Cultural Property from International Illicit Transactions and the Proposal for Improvement' (2015) 56 *Seoul Law Journal* 117, 150 and thereafter; Kwang Hyun Suk, 'The Application of Foreign Exchange Control Law and Other Internationally Mandatory Rules of Third Countries in International Financial Transactions: Including Article VIII2(b) of the Articles of Agreement of the International Monetary Fund' (2020) 26 *Korea Private International Law Journal* 353, 379–81; Choon Soo An, 'International zwingende Bestimmungen im IPR – Theorien und die Bedeutung von

Example 5.2

Although the other facts are the same as in Example 5.1, Party A takes the statue out of Country X and into Korea after the execution of the sales contract to fulfil the obligation of delivery, without reporting to the competent authorities in Country X, and the cultural heritage is currently stored somewhere in Korea. However, upon arrival in Korea, Party A meets with a person who offers a higher purchase price for the statue, executes another sales contract and refuses to perform the sales contract with Party B. Accordingly, Party B files a lawsuit against Party A with the Korean court seeking the delivery of the above statue based on the sales contract.

According to the *lex causae* rule (or the fact theory, *Datumstheorie*[20]), since all laws of the country to which the governing law belongs exclusively regulate contractual relationships, the violation of the overriding mandatory rules of a third country can only be considered as facts under contract law provisions, such as the impossibility or infringement of good morals, and need not be considered at conflict-of-laws level.[21] According to the *lex causae* rule, in the case of Example 5.1, if Party A and Party B attempted to export a cultural heritage by deceiving the competent authorities of Country X, the sales contract may be invalidated for violating good morals or public policies under Article 103 of the Civil Act of Korea, the governing law of the sales contract. If the contract is valid, Party A may terminate the contract on the grounds of impossibility. In the case of Example 5.2, the contract may be invalidated in accordance with Article 103 of the Civil Act. However, if the contract is valid, the impossibility of performance cannot be found as the statue is located in Korea.

Various criticisms have been raised regarding the *lex causae* rule. *Lex causae* does not sufficiently respond to the need to consider third-country laws in a globalised world where cross-border transactions are thriving and the global economy is becoming integrated.[22] In a situation where contracts may affect several countries and there may be an essential public interest for several countries to regulate them, the *lex causae* rule is not desirable in that it does not provide the requirements under which the overriding mandatory rules of a third country may be considered.[23] That could undermine the predictability of international transactions for the parties. In addition, if the country to which the applicable law belongs is different from the forum law, the forum must first approve the content of the

Artt. 6, 7 IPR Koreas' (2011) 23 *Kookmin Law Review* 189, 195–205; An (n 9) 149–54; Changseon Shin and Namsoon Yoon, *New Private International Law* [Singukjesabeop je2pan], 2nd edn (Fides, 2016) 279–87. The confrontation of theories was triggered by Wengler in Germany in the 1940s, but was at its peak during the preparation for the Rome Convention and the amendment of German private international law in 1986.

[20] *Datumstheorie* is described as a type of the *lex causae* rule (Martiny (n 6), EGBGB Art 34, Rn 41). Although it is also explained as a view adjacent to or a variation of the *lex causae* rule (Magnus (n 19), EGBGB Art 34, Rn 134; Hauser (n 4) 97), the *lex causae* rule and the *Datumstheorie* share the basic purpose of dealing with the laws of a third country as facts under the requirements of applicable substantive law.

[21] Section by Frank Vischer and Corinne Widmer Lüchinger in Markus Müller-Chen (ed), *Zürcher Kommentar zum IPRG*, Bd I-1, 3rd edn (Schulthess, 2018) Art 19, Rn 11.

[22] Martiny (n 6), EGBGB Art 34, Rn 47; Günther (n 4) 59.

[23] Magnus (n 19), EGBGB Art 34, Rn 134.

law of the third country before the overriding mandatory rules of a third country can be considered or applied. However, under the *lex causae* rule, the applicability and application requirements of the overriding mandatory rules of the third country are entrusted only to the applicable law (eg substantive law rules of the governing law such as 'impossibility' or 'good morals'), thereby lessening the forum's control.[24] Since the consideration or application of the overriding mandatory rules of third countries may depend on specific facts, it would not contribute to uniform decisions across jurisdictions. In short, the *lex causae* rule is an unsatisfactory view in consideration of the parties' interests on the predictability of the governing law, the interests of the forum to protect its values, the interests of the third country to enforce its policies and the interest in harmonising judgments around the world.

The Territoriality Principle (*Territorialitätsprinzip*) is the view that the public law of a country applies only within that country.[25,26] The overriding mandatory rules of a foreign country apply to property and rights located in that country and to acts to be performed in that country (so-called 'positive effect of territoriality'), and the private law effect (eg nullification of contract, etc) of acts in violation of those rules shall be determined in accordance with the applicable law of the contract. Therefore, foreign overriding mandatory rules do not apply outside the territory of a foreign country (so-called 'passive effect of territoriality'). On the other hand, if the foreign country is in a position where it can enforce its overriding mandatory rules, such as in cases where the debtor resides or owns property in that country, the foreign law may be considered under the applicable substantive law.

According to the Territoriality Principle, in Example 5.1, the statue is located in Country X, so the law of Country X applies. The legal effect of a contract violating the law of Country X is determined in accordance with Korean law, the governing law of the contract. Under Korean law, the impact to the contract could be evaluated in the same manner as agreements that are in violation of the Cultural Heritage Act of Korea, or it could amount to a violation of Article 103 of the Civil Act or impossibility, depending on the specific facts. In Example 5.2, since the statue is located in Korea, the law of Country X cannot be considered or applied. Neither violation of Article 103 of the Civil Act nor impossibility of performance is a problem. The Territoriality Principle differs from the *lex causae* rule; while *lex causae* considers the underlying facts under the applicable substantive law, the Territoriality Principle directly applies foreign law as law within the territory of the country and evaluates the 'effect of violation of law' in foreign countries under the applicable substantive laws.

The Territoriality Principle holds that 'the public law of a country applies only within that country'. It is better than the *lex causae* rule for the interests of parties as it allows them to predict, to a certain extent, under which circumstances the third country's overriding mandatory rules will apply. In addition, the Territoriality Principle may not be very disadvantageous in terms of the interests of the forum state. If foreign public law does not apply outside the territory of the foreign country, the effect of foreign public law on the legal order of the forum state can be minimised.

[24] Hauser (n 4) 98 and Günthe (n 4) 57 purport the same.

[25] Martiny (n 6), EGBGB Art 34, Rn 42 explains that 'territoriality' embodies a special connection (*Sonderanknüpfung*).

[26] This is related to the principle of the non-application of foreign public law. See ch 2, III, B on the principle of the non-application of foreign public law.

However, while the Territoriality Principle may be meaningful in public international law, it may not be as useful under private international law. It is clear that foreign public law cannot be enforced directly outside its territory. However, the concern of private international law is not whether the foreign public law is directly enforceable in another country, but the effect of such rule on relevant private legal relationships (the so-called 'reflective effect', *Reflexwirkung*). The weakness of the Territoriality Principle is that it overlooks this problem.[27] The Territoriality Principle is also problematic in that it does not sufficiently reflect the interests of third countries; in Example 5.2, the Territoriality Principle does not consider or apply the law of a third country. Nevertheless, if we consider, for example, the perspective of the third country that is the country of origin of the cultural heritage, it has an interest in preventing illegal exports, both where the cultural heritage has already been illegally exported and where the cultural heritage has not yet been exported. In other words, the Territoriality Principle treats these two cases differently, which cannot be justified. In addition, the Territoriality Principle also fails to sufficiently reflect the interests of international harmony in decisions, in the sense that in cases where the forum state would not apply the third country's overriding mandatory rules under the Territoriality Principle, the court in the third country may have applied it.

The Theory of Power (*Machttheorie*) disregards the overriding mandatory rules of a third country as a principle, but exceptionally considers those rules to the extent that the said countries can enforce their powers. This refers to situations where a legal relationship is subject to the legislative and coercive authority of that foreign country. A case where a debtor owns property in a foreign country or resides there or where performance is carried out within the territory of that country could be examples. If a foreign law does not meet this requirement, it may be considered or applied if and when the political and economic purpose of that foreign law is consistent with the interests of the forum state (*Grundsatz der Interessenidentität*).[28] This can be seen as consistent with the interests of the forum state. According to the Theory of Power, the cultural heritage in Example 5.1 is within the scope that Country X can enforce its power because the statue is still located within Country X, meaning that the law of Country X can be directly considered or applied as facts under Korean law. In Example 5.2, as long as the cultural heritage has already been removed from Country X, it cannot be said that the cultural property is within the scope of Country X's power. However, the law of Country X may be considered or applied because the protection of the cultural heritage is a shared value in Korean law, the law of the forum.

However, since it may be difficult to determine which provisions are in fact enforceable,[29] the Theory of Power fails to sufficiently reflect the interests of the parties in terms of the predictability of the applicable law. That is not the only problem here: it is also inappropriate to decide whether to consider the overriding mandatory rules of a country based mainly on legal reality,[30] a stance that fails to properly reflect the interests of third countries. Considering that the court of a third country would apply its overriding mandatory rules

[27] Martiny (n 6), EGBGB Art 34, Rn 50 purports the same. Therefore, as long as it concerns the direct application of foreign public law, it can be said that the principle of non-application of foreign public law is still maintained (for example, acknowledging the obligation to obtain authorisation and permission under foreign public law, or imposing public law sanctions for violation thereof). See ch 2, II, B for details.

[28] Martiny (n 6), (2006) EGBGB Art 34, Rn 43.

[29] ibid, Rn 51.

[30] Suk (2020) (n 19) 380 and Hauser (n 4) 99 purport the same.

while the forum state may not apply the third country's overriding mandatory rules due to their lack of enforceability, the Theory of Power also does not sufficiently reflect the interests of international harmony in decisions.

The theoretical composition of each theory and the conclusions applied to Examples 5.1 and 5.2 are shown in Table 5.1.

Table 5.1 The *lex causae* rule, territoriality principle and the theory of power

		***Lex causae* rule**	**Territoriality principle**	**Theory of power**
Example 5.1	Theory	Apply Korean law	Apply Country X's law and consider the effect of its violation under Korean law	Consider or apply Country X law
	Conclusion	Invalidity of contract or impossibility	Invalidity of contract or impossibility	Invalidity of contract or impossibility
Example 5.2	Theory	Apply Korean law	Does not consider or apply Country X's law	Apply or consider Country X's law if its purpose is in line with Korean law interests
	Conclusion	Invalidity of contract	No possibility of the contract being invalid	Invalidity of contract

Except for the results of applying the Territoriality Principle in Example 5.2, it can be seen that the results of applying each theory to Example 5.1 and Example 5.2 are generally similar. However, this does not mean there is no real benefit of the respective theories.[31] Each theory takes a different stance as to how and under which conditions to consider or apply the overriding mandatory rules of a third country, which affects the predictability of the applicable law for parties to international transactions and the outcome of such application. It is problematic that the *lex causae* rule does not present any requirements for the consideration or application of the overriding mandatory rules of third countries and relies only on the applicable substantive law. The Territoriality Principle and the Theory of Power present their own standards, but those are not satisfactory for the aforementioned reasons. This issue is particularly evident when considering the German and English case law, which are explored in detail below.

B. Germany

Prior to the Rome I Regulation, the Federal Court of Justice of Germany divided the overriding mandatory rules of a third country into public law and private law. It did not apply

[31] For example, in Example 5.1, the *lex causae* rule and the Theory of Power reach the same conclusion. Following the *lex causae* rule, the law of a third country is considered as a mere fact under the governing law and therefore, the parties cannot predict which country's law will be considered. On the other hand, the Theory of Power narrows the scope of the laws of the third country subject to consideration to 'the law of the country that can exert power' and considers that a fact under the governing law. That makes the applicable law more predictable.

public law in accordance with the principle of non-application of foreign public law,[32] but developed the principle of considering foreign public law as a fact under the governing law, which is to say substantive German law (*materiellrechtliche Berücksichtigung*), when public law intends to protect wholly or mainly private interests or adjust interests between private persons.[33] The German courts determined whether a violation of foreign law is immoral and renders the contract invalid for the violation of good customs in Germany, ie, Section 138 of the German Civil Code (*Bürgerliches Gesetzbuch*, hereinafter BGB), or whether a contract cannot be performed due to the factual effect of a violation of foreign laws (Section 275 of BGB). Section 134 of BGB stipulates that 'a contract that violates a mandatory rule' is invalid, but 'the mandatory rule' referred to in the Article means only a mandatory rule under domestic law and does not include foreign mandatory rules and thus cannot be resolved under Section 134 of the German Civil Code.[34]

i. Cases Considering Good Customs

a. *Borax*[35]

The defendant, a German company, decided to sell 100 tons of the chemical borax to the plaintiff, a German company. The raw materials of borax were imported from the US. However, the US granted export permission under the condition that borax was not taken into socialist countries. The parties conspired to hide borax's final destination, while being well aware that it was East Germany. According to US law, the plaintiff, the buyer, was also obligated to sign a statement that he would not sell borax to socialist countries. When the plaintiff refused to sign the letter, the defendant refused to deliver the borax, and the plaintiff claimed damages against the defendant for breach of contract. The Federal Court of Justice of Germany held that a contract in which a party intends to export the chemical borax to a socialist country in fraudulent violation of the US export control was against the good morals (Section 138 of BGB) of Germany, as long as the party's intention to deceive the authorities is clear. Since the political purpose of the US export ban is consistent with the policy of maintaining the peace and freedom of Western European countries, including Germany, and protects not only the interests of the US but also the interests of free Western countries, including Germany, the German court ruled that the contract was invalid.

b. *Borsäure*[36]

This case also challenged US export regulations. The US prohibited the export of boric acid to socialist countries. However, after entering into a contract to sell boric acid to a German company, the buyer, the US seller obtained export permission by fraudulent means, knowing

[32] BGHZ 31, 367, 371. This is based on the Principle of Territoriality of public international law: namely, that foreign public law applies only within its territory. However, it was believed that if a foreign country has the authority to enforce the overriding mandatory rules of the public law (if a debtor has a residence or property in its territory), they should be considered. In this case, the German Federal Court of Justice did not apply the East German Foreign Exchange Regulation Act.

[33] BGH VersR 1976, 678; BGHZ 64, 183, 190.

[34] BGHZ 34, 169, 176.

[35] BGHZ 34, 169–79.

[36] BGH NJW 1962, 1436–38.

that the final destination of boric acid was Poland. Thereafter, the seller entered into a contract with a German shipping company to transport boric acid from the US to Germany, and the buyer entered into a marine insurance contract with the defendant, a German insurance company. The above insurance contract included an Institute War Clause, which refers to seizure. However, export permission was thereafter temporarily revoked, and the boric acid was seized in New York.

Meanwhile, the buyer transferred the insured subject matter and the bill of lading to the plaintiff, a German bank, which issued the letter of credit. Accordingly, the plaintiff filed a lawsuit for insurance claims against the defendant German insurance company. The German Federal Court of Justice cited the *Borax* ruling and held that the US export ban is intended to maintain peace and free order in the West, as well as the interests of the US. The sales contract between the seller and the buyer that violates such a regulation is invalid because of its violation of public policy under Section 138 of the German Civil Code; therefore, the court ruled, there was no insurable interest under the insurance contract.

c. Nigerian Mask Case[37]

This decision is considered the German Federal Court of Justice's leading case regarding the overriding mandatory rules of third countries. In this case, a Nigerian company entered into an agreement to export masks and statues that are Nigerian cultural heritages from Nigeria to Hamburg, Germany, in violation of the Nigerian laws on cultural heritages. The Nigerian company entered into a marine insurance contract with the defendant, a German company, after entering into a carriage of goods by sea contract with a carrier. However, six statues were destroyed during the voyage. Accordingly, the plaintiff claimed insurance money against the defendant after taking over the rights under the insurance contract from the Nigerian company.

The governing law of the sales contract was German law, but the German Federal Court of Justice ruled that a sales contract that violated the Nigerian laws on cultural heritages was invalid as it infringed good morals under Section 138 of BGB. The Court's view was that since foreign mandatory rules are not binding on Germany, Section 134 on Germany's violation of mandatory rules could not be applied, but whether Germany's good morals would be indirectly infringed should be analysed. The Nigerian Cultural Heritage Act was enacted before the execution of the contract, corresponding to an international trend to protect cultural heritage, as can be seen in the UNESCO Convention on the Means of Prohibiting and Preventing the Illicit Import, Export and Transfer of Ownership of Cultural Property. The Court found that all countries that intend to protect their cultural heritages require foreign cooperation and held that the sales contract was invalid and that there were no insured interests under the insurance contract. In both *Borax* and *Bräusere*, the determining factor was whether Germany shares the value that a third country's overriding mandatory rule seeks to protect, in this case, the court adjudged on the basis of 'value shared by all countries'.[38]

[37] BGHZ 59, 82–87.

[38] Ho Young Song, 'Study on the Legal Policy for Restitution of Illegally Exported Cultural Properties in Foreign Countries' (2004) 11 *Journal of Comparative Private Law* 229, 248 explains that regardless of whether the German

d. Prohibition of the Receipt of Bribery by Public Officials[39]

The German Federal Court of Justice recognised the validity of foreign laws prohibiting the acceptance of bribes by foreign officials. An agency contract governed by German law whose main purpose was to bribe Nigerian officials in violation of Nigerian law was at issue. The court held that in cases where a foreign ban is recognised because it aligns with the dominant legal and moral perspectives in Germany, contracts in violation of that ban would generally be invalid under generally accepted moral principles.

ii. Cases Considering Impossibility[40]

In the past, the German Federal Court of Justice considered the practical impossibility of performance of the contract due to the overriding mandatory rules of a foreign country as an impossibility under German law. A British company sold goods to a German company, after which a war broke out, making it impossible for the British company to transport goods to Germany under the UK's Trading with the Enemy Act. Accordingly, the German company claimed compensation for damages against the UK company due to its failure to deliver goods. The Court considered that the UK's Trading with the Enemy Act should not be applied because it is contrary to German interests and German public policy. However, as the Court cannot ignore the existence of illegality itself because a party violating the law would be subject to heavy sanctions, the Court found that the British party's obligation to deliver became de facto impossible to perform. In this case, the Court did not apply English law but considered its practical effect and held that the contract was rendered impossible under German law.

iii. Cases Considering Interference with the Basis of the Transaction (Section 313 of BGB)

In consideration of the de facto effect of overriding mandatory rules, there are cases in which the German Federal Court of Justice modified contracts on the grounds that the basis of the contracts has been interfered with (*Wegfall der Geschäftsgrundlage*).[41] An Iranian company based in Tehran entered into a contract with a German liquor company, governed by German law. The specifics of the contract were to resolve a previous dispute between the two companies, with the German company paying damages to the Iranian company and supplying beer at a favourable price for a certain period of time. However, as a result of Iran's enactment of laws prohibiting alcohol imports, it subsequently became impossible for the German company to ship beer to Iran. When the Iranian company filed a lawsuit seeking the payment of damages as per the contract, the German Federal Court of Justice ruled that the obligation to pay damages was not rendered impossible, but the fundamental basis of

courts have acceded to the UNESCO Convention, they have regarded the basic spirit of the Convention as some kind of public policy under international law and used this as the criterion for determining the public policy of German domestic law.

[39] BGHZ 94, 268, 271.

[40] RGZ 93, 182ff.

[41] IPrax 1986, 154.

the above settlement contract was lost, and the contract should be changed for both parties to share the risks caused by the Iranian ban on alcohol imports. Therefore, it was held that the German company was obligated to pay half of the above damages and half of the profits the Iranian company would have acquired by having the beer supplied.

iv. Evaluation

The German Federal Court of Justice, starting with the principle of non-application of foreign public law, considered the overriding mandatory rules of third countries as facts under the general provisions of the applicable substantive law (in all cases of the above precedents, the governing law of the contracts was German law). As previously mentioned, the principle of non-application of foreign public law based on territoriality cannot be a decisive solution in private international law.[42] As with criticisms against the *lex causae* rule, this position fails to sufficiently reflect the interests of the parties because it makes the applicable law less predictable for the parties by failing to indicate under which conditions the overriding mandatory rules of third countries can be considered. Furthermore, the interests of the forum state cannot be properly reflected either. Under this position, it is difficult to determine whether the interests protected by the overriding mandatory rules of a third country conform with the forum's values, unless the forum's public policy is applied to the case.

Additional reasons why the German court's view is not desirable are as follows. First, the delimitation between consideration of foreign law as a fact under the applicable substantive law and recognition of its normative effect is ambiguous. In this respect, considering foreign law in the normative context constitutes 'application' anyhow, and the conflict-of-laws approach applies.[43] The principles of substantive law (such as the doctrines of violation of good morals, impossibility, and change of circumstances) are matters of domestic law, so applying such principles to situations related to foreign law may be inappropriate.[44] Doing so would be essentially converting a conflict of laws issue to a substantive law issue, making it more difficult to find an adequate solution.[45] For example, if a specific movable property that is the subject matter of a contract is seized or confiscated in accordance with the overriding mandatory rules of a third country, the governing law of the contract may make performance impossible. However, as in the German case where the UK Trading with Enemy Act was at issue,[46] it is questionable whether the obligor's refusal to perform on the grounds of the mere 'existence' of the foreign mandatory rules without a disposition such as confiscation made under that law could be considered a 'fact'. Rather, it can be seen that the German Court recognised the normative effect of the foreign law when it considered the potentially serious sanctions following a violation of the foreign law.

Second, in order to determine whether the violation of the overriding mandatory rules of a third country infringes good morals of German law in the above cases, it was first

[42] See ch 5, II, A.

[43] Frank Vischer, 'General course on private international law' (1992) 232 *Recueil des Cours* 21, 177; Martiny (n 6), EGBGB Art 34, Rn 48–50, Kerstin Ann-Susann Schäfer, *Application of Mandatory Rules in the Private International Law of Contracts* (Peter Lang, 2010) 217.

[44] Vischer (ibid) 21, 177.

[45] Martiny (n 6), EGBGB Art 34, Rn 48–50, Schäfer (ibid) 217.

[46] See RGZ 93, 182. See s ii above.

necessary to examine whether the factual matrix fits into the rule's scope of application. This inevitably involves a process of examining the requirements and effects of the third country's provision, which amounts to considering foreign law as law.

Thirdly, it is worth noting that in the German Federal Court of Justice's decision[47] to prohibit the receipt of bribes by public officials, the Court held that the relevant foreign provision was in accordance with the prevailing legal and ethical perspective in Germany and therefore a violation of the foreign provision constituted a violation of good morals in Germany. In order to explain why the violation of a third country's overriding mandatory rules constitutes a German law violation, the logical structure followed was to review the content of the law of the third country and the legal interests protected by it first and then incorporate them into the legal interests of German domestic law. The same logic formed the basis of the *Nigerian Mask*, *Borax* and *Boräuser* rulings,[48] which held that the overriding mandatory rules of the third country in question protect universal values or are in line with the interests of Germany. The German courts examined whether the content of foreign law is legitimate from the point of view of the law of the forum. This is more of a process under private international law than a review under substantive law, as it is similar to examining public policy grounds in recognition of a foreign judgment or in application of a foreign applicable law. Kegel also deems the German Court to have given effect to the interests of Nigerian law, considering that the private international legal interest of Nigeria law was worthy of protection under German law.[49]

Lastly, the German Court's approach increases the burden of fact-finding for the courts. Unless there is a private international law principle established under which a third country's overriding mandatory rules are considered or applied, the facts must be first established for the court to determine whether there is indeed a violation of the relevant applicable law. For example, in order to determine whether the violation of an overriding mandatory rule of a third country constitutes an infringement of good morals under German law (applicable law), one must examine whether the parties fraudulently intended to violate the relevant foreign law. This may increase the courts' burden of examining indirect facts to ascertain such intentions. That may be even more true in cases where the applicable law is foreign law, as the judges may not be as familiar with that as they are with domestic law. On the other hand, if the conditions for the consideration or application of a third country's overriding mandatory rules are set out in private international law, such difficulties can be avoided.

C. England

Prior to the Rome I Regulation, the English courts had also taken the substantive law approach. In principle, under common law, only the applicable law regulate the validity of the contract,[50] and it was generally considered that the application of the mandatory

[47] See s i, d above.

[48] See ss i, a, b and c above.

[49] Kegel and Schurig (n 8) 156. Kegel asserts that the German Court should have invalidated the contract, having applied not Section 138 of BGB but Section 134 of BGB, which adjudges the nullification of contracts based on the violation of German mandatory rules, and criticises the ruling as being a 'smokescreen tactic' (*Vernebelungstaktik*).

[50] *Kleinwort, Sons & Co v Ungarische Baumwolle Industrie AC* [1939] 2 KB 678 (CA).

provisions of certain countries could be avoided by the agreement of the parties.[51] However, there were exceptions, where a claim that is unlawful under the law of a third country was not accepted. These can be divided into two categories: (1) an infringement of comity and English public policy (hereinafter the 'public policy-comity rule'[52]); and (2) an illegality rule or *lex loci solutionis* rule (hereinafter *lex loci solutionis* rule).[53]

i. Public Policy-Comity Rule

The public policy-comity rule is the 'principle of declaring a contract null and void when it is feared that the contract will be contrary to the national interests of the UK or harm peaceful relations with the UK's allied countries.[54] It is contrary to comity and public policy[55,56] for the courts of England to assist the violation of the laws of its friendly nations.[57] Therefore, the intent and purpose of the parties to commit unlawful acts under the laws of a friendly country is an important requirement for this rule.[58] If the true purpose and intent of the parties are to perform an act in violation of foreign law in a friendly foreign country, the contract is invalidated.[59] It is contrary to public policy to reach an agreement to harm the government of an allied state.[60] However, the contract cannot be rendered void by public policy when the contract merely involves activities prohibited under the laws of a third country without any such 'wicked intention'.[61]

[51] *Vita Food Products Inc v Unus Shipping Co Ltd* [1939] AC 277.

[52] This is not an established term under English law. However, under English law, it is explained that consideration of the laws of allied nations works together with the comity rule under the concept of public policy (Collins (ed), *Dicey, Morris & Collins: The Conflict of Laws*, 15th edn (Sweet & Maxwell, 2012) vol 1, para 5R-001 and vol 2, para 32-190; Peter Kaye, *The New Private International Law of Contract of the European Community* (Dartmouth, 1993) 240; Paul Torremans (ed), *Cheshire, North & Fawcett: Private International Law*, 15th edn (Oxford University Press, 2017) 753; Schäfer (n 43) 233. Therefore the term 'public policy-comity rule' shall be used in this book. Schäfer 244 also refers to this rule as the 'public policy-comity rule'. Kaye 240 uses the term 'the doctrine of public policy comity'.

[53] Collins (ibid) vol 1, para 32-094; Schäfer (n 43) 233–34.

[54] Collins (n 52) vol 1, para 1-016.

[55] The issue of public policy in English law emerges when (1) the nature and content of foreign law are repugnant in light of English legal conceptions and could never be admitted in England, or (2) the English courts want to refrain from doing a particular act. The public policy-comity rule falls under (2) to the effect that the English courts should reject any behaviour that could significantly harm the UK's national or international interests. Jonathan Hill and Adeline Chong, *International Commercial Disputes*, 4th edn (Hart Publishing, 2010) paras 14.3.25–14.3.26.

[56] Unlike KAPIL or French law's distinction between international and domestic public policy, English literature generally does not distinguish these two. According to comparative legal research in the context of international contracts, international public policy under French legislation attaches importance to subjective criteria, while English law values objective standards; otherwise, however, they are said to be considerably similar. See Adeline Chong, 'The Public Policy and Mandatory Rules of Third Countries in International Contracts' (2006) 2 *Journal of Private International Law* 27, 29.

[57] *De Wutz v Hendricks* (1824) 2 Bing 314; *Foster v Driscoll (*1929); *Regazzoni v K C Sethia* (1958).

[58] *De Wutz v Hendricks* (ibid). Kaye (n 52) 19 explains that it is not enough to simply violate the public or criminal laws of an allied country and that the relationship between England and the allied state must be at risk if the English courts assist in the violation as a result of a particularly serious infringement of the legal order of the allied state.

[59] *Foster v Driscoll* (1929) 1 KB 470, 521.

[60] *British Nylon Spinners Ltd v Imperial Chemical Industries Ltd* (1955) Ch 37, 52; *Bodley Head Ltd v Flegon* (1972) 1 WLR 680, 687–88.

[61] *British Nylon Spinners Ltd* (n 60).

More scholars believe that the public policy-comity rule is not a conflict-of-laws rule, but a substantive legal principle of English law.[62] However, since the public policy rule applies irrespective of governing law, this rule is believed to apply to contracts with foreign applicable law.[63]

a. *Foster v Driscoll*[64]

A contract was concluded to trade whiskey that would be smuggled into the US, violating the overriding mandatory rule of the US. Under the contract, the place of performance of the contract was set to Scotland in order to avoid British customs, and whiskey was to be placed on smuggling boats and taken out of the UK. The contract was governed by English law. The Court of Appeal held that the contract was unenforceable under English law because if the courts recognise a contract whose purpose is earning profits through a criminal act in the US, an allied nation, there will be complaints from the government of the US, which would go against international comity as well as English public policy. The Court of Appeal found that if the true purpose and intent of the parties was to violate foreign laws, the performance of the contract would be contrary to public policy, even if the behaviour in question was not illegal elsewhere.[65]

b. *Regazzoni v K C Sethia*[66]

This case concerned a contract for a British company to sell jute bags, which would be transported to Genoa. The governing law of the contract was English law. On the surface, the contract was not in violation of the laws of any country. Although the contract did not specify the origin and destination of the goods sold (that is, the jute bags), both parties to the contract knew that jute was produced only in India, and the seller knew that the buyer wanted to resell the bags in South Africa. In addition, both the seller and the buyer knew that India prohibited trade with South Africa and that exporting jute produced in India to South Africa would be subject to criminal punishment. When the seller failed to perform the contract, the buyer filed a lawsuit in the English court for breach of the contract.

The House of Lords did not accept the plaintiff's claim on the grounds that both parties knew that performance of the contract was in violation of Indian law and was in fact

[62] Collins (n 52) vol 2, para 32-193. The Court of Appeal also considered this as a substantive legal principle in *Isphani* v *Bank Melli Iran* (1998) Lloyd's Rep (Bank) 133. Another view understands English public policy as a special conflicts rule that stipulates conditions that are subject to the mandatory rules of third countries. Torremans (n 52) 754; Schäfer (n 43) 245.

[63] Richard Plender and Michael Wilderspin, *The European Contracts Convention: The Rome Convention on the Choice of Law for Contracts* (Sweet & Maxwell, 2001) para 9-05; *Royal Boskalis Westminter NV v Mountain* (1999) QB 674(CA), 691, 692.

[64] (1928) All ER Rep 130.

[65] Similarly, if the parties did not have a wicked intention to violate or aid a violation of the third country's law, carrying out an act prohibited by that law cannot be seen as a violation of English public policy. *British Nylon Spinners* (n 60), *Toprak v Finagrain* (1979) 2 Lloyd's Rep 98 (CA). In contrast, if a contract is executed for the purpose of violating foreign law and that foreign law itself violates English public policy, the performance of the contract does not violate English public policy. *Regazzoni v KC Sethia Ltd* (1958) 1 AC 301, 322, 328ff.

[66] (1958) AC 301(HL).

intended to violate it. The House of Lords ruled that it would be contrary to the public policy to have contracting parties perform the contract if they knew that the law of an allied country would be violated to perform the contract. As seen in this case, a contract violating foreign laws may be invalid because public policy is linked to respect for comity. This principle has been applied not only to foreign export and import regulations,[67] but also to exchange control laws[68] and tax laws.[69]

c. *Lemenda Trading Co v African Middle East Petroleum Co*[70]

The defendant, a British company, wanted to renew the oil supply contract with a state-owned company in Qatar. The plaintiff, a Bahamian company, entered into a lobbying agreement with the defendant to assist the defendant in renewing the oil supply contract through the influence and efforts of the plaintiff's major shareholders, and the defendant was to pay a commission to the plaintiff upon the renewal of its oil supply contract with the Qatari state-owned company. The governing law of this contract was English law, and the place of performance was Qatar. However, when the defendant refused to pay commission to the plaintiff after the oil supply contract was renewed, the plaintiff filed a lawsuit against the defendant with the English court seeking payment.

Although there are no explicitly written provisions prohibiting lobbying contracts under English law or Qatari law, the Court reviewed whether the contract violates English public policy. Under English law, contracts to secure benefits from public officials are contrary to public policy, but it was asked whether lobbying with foreign governments would also be contrary to English public policy. The Court held that although the public policy under English law challenged in the case – namely, that benefits cannot be assured by persons in public office – is a moral principle to be applied generally, that does not necessarily prevent the performance of a contract regardless of the stance taken by the *lex loci solutionis*. After finding evidence that the lobbying contract is contrary to the public policy of Qatar, the Court found the lobbying contract unenforceable on the basis of comity and the public policy of England. In short, where English law is the governing law of a contract, if (1) a contract does not violate any written law, but violates English public policy based on general moral principles, and (2) a public policy identical in substance is applied in the country where the contract is performed and thus the contract cannot be enforced there, enforcing the contract would be contrary to comity and English public policy such that English courts will not enforce such contracts.

d. *Euro-Diam v Bathurst*[71]

In this case, Euro-Diam, a British diamond seller, sold diamonds to a German buyer and recorded a lower price on the invoice than the actual price, as per the buyer's request. The seller would have become aware of the fact that the buyer intended to deceive the German

[67] *Soleymany v Soleymany* (1999) QB 785 (CA).
[68] *Isphani v Bank Melli Iran* (1998) Lloyd's Rep (Bank) 133.
[69] *Re Emery's Investment Trusts* (1959) Ch 410.
[70] (1988) 2 WLR 735.
[71] (1990) 1 QB 1.

customs authority in doing so. However, the diamonds were stolen before the risk was transferred to the buyer, and the seller had previously executed an insurance contract using the actual price of the diamonds as the insurable value and paid an insurance premium calculated accordingly. The seller's delivery of a false invoice to the buyer is subject to criminal punishment under German tax law, and in this case, it was asked whether the insurance contract should be rendered void for violating German tax law.

The Court ruled that ordering the performance of an insurance contract was not contrary to public policy because the seller's delivery of a false invoice was not related to the theft of the diamonds and would not be an act of deception against the insurer. In this case, the court expressly rejected the claim that English public policy was not related to a violation of foreign law.[72]

e. *Royal Boskalis Westminster NV v Mountain*[73]

The plaintiff, a Dutch company, while owning and operating dredging vessels, entered into an insurance contract with the defendant, an insurance company, to cover risks caused by war. The governing law of the insurance contract was English law. Thereafter, the plaintiff entered into an agreement with the Iraqi Government to conduct dredging work at a port in Iraq. The governing law of the dredging contract was Iraqi law, and the parties agreed to arbitrate in Paris. Dredging work was ongoing when Iraq invaded Kuwait in August 1999. The UN imposed sanctions prohibiting payments to Iraq, and those sanctions were also implemented in the Netherlands. In retaliation, the Iraqi Government seized a ship owned by the plaintiff and detained its crew. In order to release the dredger and repatriate the crew, the plaintiff agreed to pay large sums to the Iraqi Government through deposit accounts in Switzerland and Austria, in violation of UN sanctions, and to waive future claims based on the dredging contract. The plaintiff filed a lawsuit against the defendant, the insurer, to claim insurance money equivalent to the damage incurred by waiving the claim under the dredging contract.

In this case, the Court dismissed the plaintiff's claim on the grounds that the agreement violated English public policy and could not be enforced, meaning the plaintiff had neither lost its claim based on the dredging contract nor incurred any damages and accordingly could not claim insurance proceeds based on the premise that the agreement was valid.

ii. The Lex Loci Solutionis *Rule*

The *lex loci solutionis* rule refers to the 'principle that a contract is generally invalid if the performance of the contract is illegal in the country where the contract is to be performed,

[72] Professor Trevor Hartley takes the view that if the insurance contract and the violation of the tax law were more directly related, the insurance contract would have been invalidated. For example, presuming that a person exported a work of art from a foreign country in violation of the laws of that country and entered into an insurance contract for the artwork, which was thereafter lost, the English court would likely not accept a request to perform the insurance contract. Trevor Hartley, 'Mandatory rules in international contracts: the common law approach' (1997) 266 *Recueil des Cours* 345, 393.

[73] (1999) QB 674(CA).

regardless of the illegality of the contract under governing law'.[74] In cases where a contract had initial or subsisting illegality under foreign law from the time of its execution, the aforementioned public policy-comity rule would apply. The *lex loci solutionis* rule is different in that it is a principle to be applied if the contract becomes subsequently illegal after its conclusion, due to *lex loci solutionis*. The law of a country other than the place of performance is not considered under the *lex loci solutionis* rule.[75] The dominant view is that the *lex loci solutionis* rule is a principle of contract law.[76]

a. *Ralli Bros v Compania Naviera Scotta y Aznar*[77]

This is the leading case concerning the *lex loci solutionis* rule.[78] A London-based British company entered into a shipping contract with a Spanish shipowner to transport jute from Kolkata, India, to Barcelona, Spain. The British company agreed to pay half of the freight when the ship departed from India and half when it arrived in Spain. The contract was governed by English law, and at the time of conclusion, the contract was legal under the law of all the countries concerned. After the ship left, the British company paid half of the freight to the Spanish shipowner. However, before the ship arrived in Spain, Spain enacted a law regulating freight that was in force by the time the remaining freight was due to be paid. The parties agreed to pay the remaining half of the freight in Spain, but the contractual freight (£50) exceeded the upper limit set by the Spanish law (£10). Therefore, if all the remaining freight was paid, the Spanish law would be violated. The British company tried to pay the Spanish shipowner only the amount corresponding to the upper limit prescribed by the Spanish law. As a result, the Spanish shipowner filed a lawsuit in England to claim the payment of the outstanding freight. The Court of Appeal rejected the plaintiff's claim that the British company is obligated to pay the remaining freight because Spanish law is not the applicable law.[79]

[74] Collins (n 52) vol 2, para 32-094.

[75] *Kleinwort, Sons & Co Ungarishce Baumwolle Industrie AG* (1939) 2 KB 678; *Trinidad Shipping Co Alston* (1920) AC 888 (PC); *Toprak* (n 65); *Libyan Arab Foreign Bank v Bankers Trust Co* (1989) QB 728, 745; *Euro-Diam Ltd v Bathurst* (1990) 1 QB 1, 15.

[76] Hugh Beale (ed), *Chitty on Contracts*, 33rd edn (Sweet & Maxwell, 2020) para 23.027; Collins (n 52) vol 2, para 32-100; Hill and Chong (n 55) para 14.4.45; Andrew Dickinson, 'Third Country Mandatory Rules in the Law Applicable to Contractual Obligations: So Long, Farewell, Auf Wiedersehen Adieu?' (2007) 3 *Journal of Private International Law* 53, 78. See Chong (n 56) 64; Adrian Briggs, *Private International Law in English Courts* (Oxford University Press, 2014) para 7.251 for the view that this is a conflict-of-laws principle. English precedents have taken conflicting positions on the nature of the *lex loci solutionis* rule. In *Kahler v Midland Bank Ltd* (1950) AC 24, 48ff, (1949) 2 All ER 621, it was believed to be a contract law principle, while in *Zinostenska Banka v Frankman* (1950)AC 57, 78ff, (1949) 2 All ER 671, 681, it was seen to apply regardless of the applicable law of the contract. *De Béeche and Others v South American Stores (Gath and Chaves) Ltd and Others* (1934) All ER Rep 284. At [288] in this ruling, Lord Sankeys held that UK law does not enforce the performance of obligations if the performance is illegal under foreign law, which is the place where the obligations are performed. Since then, it was continuously held in precedents that this is a principle of English law. *Haugesund Kommune v Depfa ACS Bank* (2010) EWCA Civ 579 (2012) QB 549 at [99]; *Dana Gas PJSC v Dana Gas Sukuk Ltd* (2017) EWHC 2928 (Comm) at [79]; *Deutsche Bank AG v Unitech Global Ltd* (2013) EWHC 2793 (Comm), (2014) 2 All ER (Comm) 268 at [99].

[77] (1920) 2 KB 287(CA).

[78] This is evaluated as the adoption by the Court of Appeal of the rule established by Dicey and Morris. Collins (n 52) vol 2, para 32-097.

[79] The rationale for this ruling (*ratio decidendi*) is unclear. According to English law, the contract cannot be performed if the contract becomes subsequently illegal, and the court treated Spanish law as grounds for the

b. *Vita Food Products Inc v Unus Shipping Co Ltd*[80]

It was questioned whether the defendant, a Nova Scotian company, was obligated based on a bill of lading issued in Newfoundland. The bill of lading stipulated the applicable law as English law, but the issue to be determined was which law applies to the defendant's liability for damages due to cargo loss. According to the laws of Newfoundland, where the contract was concluded, the bill of lading was void because it did not meet the conditions set forth in the Carriage of Goods by Sea Act 1932, but the bill of lading was valid under English law. The Privy Council found that the bill of lading would be valid under English law, which is the governing law of the bill of lading, without considering Newfoundland law.

c. *Kleinwort Sons & Co v Ungarische Baumwolle Industrie AG*[81]

In this case, the foreign exchange regulations of a third country not subject to the IMF Agreement were at issue. The plaintiff, London-based bank Kleinwort Sons, agreed that the defendant, a Hungarian company, Ungarische Baumwolle Industrie AG, would be able to issue a bill of exchange, to be paid in London in sterling, after three months of maturity, with Kleinwort Sons as the payer; it was also agreed that the defendant would pay the bill of exchange to the plaintiff by the due date. At the time of conclusion, the contract was lawful in all relevant jurisdictions. However, before the payment was made, Hungary introduced foreign exchange laws that necessitated permission from its central bank for payments to be made overseas, and the defendant failed to obtain permission and was thus unable to pay. Accordingly, the plaintiff filed a lawsuit against the defendant seeking payment under the contract, and the Court did not accept the defendant's defence that the payment was prohibited under Hungarian law. The Court stated that the law governing the contract is not Hungarian law, but English law, and that because the place of performance is not in Hungary, *lex loci solutionis* would not apply, and it would be unfair to impose on the obligee the obligation to investigate the obligor's residence and the law of that place if interpreted

frustration of performance, citing a precedent in which the subsequent illegality under English law was challenged (*Metropolitan Water Board v Dick, Kerr & Co* [1918] AC 119 (HL)). All three judges on the Court of Appeal cited the principle that a contract (whether lawful by its proper law or not) is, in general, invalid in so far as the performance is unlawful by the law of the country where the contract is to be performed' stated in Collins (n 52) as the basis for the *lex loci solutionis* rule. Although Lord Justice Scrutton stated that this principle is to be understood as an obligation based on international comity, he joined Lord Justice Warrington in finding that the contract includes an implied term of continuing validity, ie, a condition that, if a contract is to be performed in a foreign country, the acts to be performed there shall not be unlawful under the laws of that foreign country, unless there are special circumstances. In terms of interpreting the contract, that is, it should be assumed that the parties did not intend to enforce the contract if it became unlawful under the law of the place of performance or under the laws of another country. At the time of this ruling, however, the basis of the legal principle of frustration was explained as the implicit condition of the contract, so his opinion could be interpreted as what developed into the legal principle of frustration, ie, a situation where a contract would subsequently be rendered impossible under English law. Meanwhile, since Lord Justice Scrutton mentioned comity as the grounds for the *lex loci solutionis* rule, this can be interpreted as the declaration of the conflict of law principle. This has raised a controversy about whether the *lex loci solutionis rule* is a conflict of laws principle or a contract law principle. William Day, 'Contracts, illegality and comity: *Ralli Bros* revisited' (2020) 79 *Cambridge Law Journal* 64, 67.

[80] (1939) AC 277 (PC).

[81] (1939) 2 KB 678.

otherwise. In this case, the English Court confirmed the principle that English law does not consider the overriding mandatory rules of a third country other than the place of performance, outside the context of comity and public policy.

d. *Rossano v Manufacturer's Life Insurance Co*[82]

In this case, the plaintiff, an Egyptian national residing in Egypt, entered into a life insurance contract with a Canadian company headquartered in Toronto. This contract was entered into at the Cairo branch office of the Canadian company. At the time of the conclusion of this contract, it was lawful in all relevant jurisdictions. However, several years later, and before the payment of the insurance proceeds was due, the Egyptian Government enacted a law prohibiting the payment of insurance proceeds without the consent of the Egyptian foreign exchange authorities. The plaintiff, who was residing in Italy at the time, filed a lawsuit in the English court to claim insurance proceeds against the Canadian company. The Canadian company argued that according to Egyptian law, it was illegal for it to pay insurance proceeds without consent from the foreign exchange authorities.

However, the Commercial Court did not accept the Canadian company's defence on the grounds that the contract was governed by the law of Ontario and recognised the plaintiff's right to claim life insurance payments outside Egypt. The Court refused to apply the subsequently enacted Egyptian law because the contract was governed by Ontario law, even though the contract had been concluded in Egypt and the plaintiff had been residing in Egypt as an Egyptian national when signing the contract.

e. *Libyan Arab Foreign Bank v Bankers Trust Co*[83]

The plaintiff, a Libyan Bank, held bank accounts at the London and New York branches of the defendant, a British bank. According to the deposit contract, the plaintiff agreed to make a remittance between the New York and the London branches at 2pm every day so that the defendant's New York branch account could maintain a certain balance. Thereafter, on 8 January 1986, the President of the US issued an order[84] to freeze all assets of Libya in the US, and two days prior to the order, the plaintiff's New York branch deposit account held an amount in excess of the specified amount (in US dollars). The excess should have been remitted to London, but due to the above sanctions, the remittance failed. The plaintiff required that amount to be returned by the defendant's London branch, but the defendant countered that the payment to the plaintiff would be illegal.

The Commercial Court did not accept the defendant's argument that it was exempt from the obligation to perform because the contract was illegal under the governing law of the contract or *lex loci solutionis*. In that case, the law governing the claim for return of deposit was English law and even if the US dollar was paid in New York through the normal Clearing House Interbank Payments System, New York cannot be deemed the place

[82] (1962) 2 All ER 214(QB); (1963) 2 QB 352.
[83] (1989) QB 728.
[84] This is not included in the meaning of 'exchange control regulations' in Art VIII, Section 2(b) of the IMF Agreement, so the Court did not apply that paragraph to the asset freezing order. See Suk (2020) (n 19) 363–69 for details on the requirements for application of that paragraph.

of performance unless there is a contractual provision that the deposit must be paid in New York. The Court held that the place of performance is England and that the defendant can pay in London using other possible means.[85,86]

iii. Evaluation

Taking into account the *lex loci solutionis* rule, in principle, English courts do not consider the law of a third country which is not the place of performance. However, English courts have considered the laws of third countries based on the public policy-comity rule if the contract was concluded by the parties with the purpose of violating the law of a foreign friendly country by deceiving its competent authorities. The public policy-comity rule may be useful to explain the ideological basis for considering or applying the overriding mandatory rules of third countries. In addition, the interests of the forum state may be sufficiently reflected, as it uses the public policy of the forum as the general criteria whether to consider the third country overriding mandatory rules. However, for the following reasons, the public policy-comity rule is not an apposite basis for considering or applying the overriding mandatory rules of third countries.

First, the public policy-comity rule's requirement that the contract is contrary to the British interests of states or likely to undermine friendly relations with allied nations is too vague and unclear. The scope of allies may change depending on the time, and another issue is that, conceptually, the laws of allied nations could include any type of laws. Although this may be appropriate as a principle of diplomacy, it does not provide clarity on the requirements to be met for applying the overriding mandatory rules of a third country and instead undermines the predictability and legal certainty for the parties. It therefore fails to properly reflect the interests of the parties.

Second, since the forum's public policy should be interpreted restrictively,[87] it is not appropriate to draw a general principle on overriding the mandatory rules of third countries from the public policy-comity rule. The forum's public policy functions to reject the

[85] Under English law, the place of performance of monetary obligations is the place where the debtor must perform his/her obligation and where the creditor will have the right to receive contractual payments, not where the debtor must make remittance. The place of performance is distinct from the place of governing law of the currency or place where any payment may be commonly cleared through the international banking system. Accordingly, even if the debtor has to remit funds to a creditor in a foreign country in order to repay his/her debt and the remittance cannot be made in accordance with the foreign exchange regulations of the country where the debtor resides, such cannot be a valid defence in English proceedings when the governing law is English. Charles Proctor, *Mann on the Legal Aspect of Money*, 7th edn (Oxford University Press, 2012) para 16.32; Collins (n 52) vol 2, para 37-065.

[86] If, in the case of an interbank euro/dollar deposit, the recipient bank's obligation is understood to be subject to account transfer through New York's clearing system (ie, specific performance), the obligation can only be fulfilled in New York, and there would be no alternative means. However, performance in New York became unlawful and impossible by the freeze on assets ordered by the President of the US, and hence the English court would not have ordered the return of the deposit. This is related to the legal nature of the euro/dollar deposit. Kwang Hyun Suk, 'Legal Issues in International Arbitration Related to International Guarantees That Are Unauthorized for Foreign Exchange' [Oehwanheogareul badji anihan gukjebojeunggwa gwallyeonhan gukjesabeopsangui munjejeom] (1994) *429 Korean Lawyers Association Journal* 142 385. This case is also an important judgment in that it declared where the place of performance of the obligation to pay was in international financial transactions. For Korean literature introducing this ruling, see Suk (2020) (n 19) 384.

[87] Collins (n 52) vol 1, para 5-003, and vol 2, para 32-182.

application of foreign law if the result of its application is contrary to public policy (passive function of public policy), and in the case of the public policy-comity rule, public policy functions to apply foreign law. However, this positive function of public policy is not recognised today,[88] so it is not appropriate as a theoretical basis for considering or applying foreign law.

Third, as with the stance taken by the German Federal Court of Justice, the public policy-comity rule also considers the intention of the parties in violating the law, and the court's burden of fact-finding increases as a result. Depending on the evidence presented in specific cases, the consideration or application of third-country law may vary. Therefore, the public policy-comity rule is not satisfactory in terms of the interests of the third country or of the interests of international harmony in decisions.

Although the *lex loci solutionis* rule is a principle of substantive law, it can be seen to be more advanced than the public policy-comity rule or the general provisions of substantive law, such as the doctrines of impossibility, infringement of good morals and interference with the basis of transaction used by the German Federal Court of Justice, as it stipulates more specific requirements. Therefore, the *lex loci solutionis* rule may allow greater predictability on governing norms for parties, therefore better reflects interests of the parties.

However, the *lex loci solutionis* rule does not sufficiently reflect the interests of the forum state in that it does not examine whether the *lex loci solutionis* shares the values of the forum law unless it violates the public policy of the forum. In addition, the rule limiting the consideration of third-country law to the place of performance does not properly reflect the essential regulatory interests of third countries in cases where the third country is not the place of performance but is instead (for example) the country of origin of a cultural heritage in the illegal cultural heritage trade. In this respect, the rule of *lex loci solutionis* does not properly reflect the interests of international harmony in decisions in that the law of the third country will be applied if tried by the court of the third country.

In addition, issues arising from the application of both the public policy-comity rule and the *lex loci solutionis* rule cannot be disregarded. Under English law, the dual application of the excessively restrictive *lex loci solutionis* rule and the excessively ambiguous and unclear public policy-comity rule generally undermines the predictability of the consideration of the overriding mandatory rules of third countries. This is undesirable in terms of the interests of the parties.

D. Concluding Remarks

This section has examined substantive-law approaches. From my analysis, the overriding mandatory rules of third countries has faced difficulties in providing specific conditions for their consideration or application. Furthermore, these approaches failed to adequately address the relevant interests of the parties, the third country, the forum and the need for international harmony in decisions.

[88] Torremans (n 52) 753.

III. Conflict-of-Laws Approach

A conflict-of-laws approach stipulates the conditions for the consideration or application of the overriding mandatory rules of third countries under conflicts-of-law rules. Some examples are the Special Connection Theory (*Sonderanknüpfungstheorie*), the Rome Convention, the Swiss FAPIL, the Hague Convention on the Law Applied to Agency Trusts and on their Recognition (hereinafter Hague Trust Convention), the Hague Principles on Choice of Law in International Commercial Contracts, the Rome I Regulation, and the Theory of Two-sided Conflict-of-laws rule. The last is critical of the Special Connection Theory. The following sections will assess whether the theories are appropriate in terms of the interests of the parties, the interests of the forum state, the interests of the third country and the interests of international harmony in decisions.

A. Special Connection Theory and the Theory of Two-sided Conflict-of-Laws Rule

The Special Connection Theory emerged in response to the principle of non-application of foreign public law; namely, that foreign public law cannot be applied. The Special Connection Theory believes that private international law is a principle of designating private law related to the relevant legal relationship, solving the conflicts in private legal relationships. Therefore, it suggests that there should be a separate special connection rule for overriding mandatory rules pursuing public interests. The person who first claimed the Special Connection Theory in Germany was Wilhelm Wengler, who argued that the overriding mandatory rules of a foreign country apply under the following conditions: (1) when they 'intend' to be applied regardless of the governing law of the relevant legal relationship; (2) when the foreign law is closely connected to the relevant legal relationship; and (3) when the public policy of the forum does not prevent such application.[89]

A variety of views are broadly categorised as belonging to the Special Connection Theory, differing on specific connection principles and connecting factors, but the majority view in Germany is that the law of a country sufficiently close to the legal relationship in the case should be considered or applied.[90] The Special Connection Theory generally requires, as Wengler argued, the legislator's intention for the provision to apply regardless of the applicable law in the relevant legal relationship, a close relationship between the law of the third country and the case, the non-violation of the public policy of the forum, or the foreign law's conformity with the legal system of the forum.[91] Some of the criteria for close connection are place of performance, the location of property, the residence or nationality of the parties,

[89] Yong Dam Kim, 'The Governing Law of the International Contracts and Mandatory Rules' (1986) 33 *Trial Reference* 6, 16 for an introduction of the theory by Wengler and 19–24 for an introduction of the Special Connection Theory developed in Germany.

[90] Magnus (n 19), Rn 115–118.

[91] Martiny (n 6), EGBGB Art 34, Rn 133; section by Mächler-Erne and Wolf-Mettier in Pascal Grolimund (ed), *Basler Kommentar Interntionales Privatrecht*, 4th edn, (Helbnig Lichtenhan Verlag, 2021) Art 19, Rn 7. However, there are conflicting views as to whether the requirement that the 'foreign law conform to the legal system of the forum' is to be understood as included in the requirement not to be contrary to the public policy of the forum or as a separate requirement. Martiny (n 6), EGBGB Art 34, Rn 158.

the place of employment or workplace, the affected market location and the applicable law.[92] If these conditions are met, the third-country law may be considered or applied.

Let us consider the examples presented at the beginning of section II according to the Special Connection Theory. In the case of Example 5.1, the legislative intent of Country X for the cultural heritage protection law to apply so as to prohibit the export of cultural heritages, regardless of the applicable law of the sales contract can be inferred.[93] The law of Country X, where the seller has his/her habitual residence and is the origin of the cultural heritage being sold, is closely connected to the case, and the purpose of Country X's law (that is, to protect cultural heritages) is consistent with the legal system of Korea,[94] and the result of application of Country X's law is not contrary to the public policy of Korea. Accordingly, Country X's law may be considered or applied. Likewise, in Example 5.2, Country X's law will be considered or applied as the law of a closely connected country.

In resolving Example 5.1 and Example 5.2, the difference between the Special Connection Theory and Territoriality Principle or the Theory of Power is that, unlike the latter two theories, the Special Connection Theory is considered or applied in both Example 5.1 and Example 5.2 regardless of whether the cultural property has been illegally taken out of Country X. Compared to the *lex causae* rule, the Special Connection Theory can enable the consideration or application of the overriding mandatory rules of a third country under the same conditions (ie, regardless of the requirements under the governing law of the sales contract), allowing international harmonisation of decisions and protecting parties from conflicting interests. Therefore, the Special Connection Theory neatly reflects the interests of international harmony in decisions.

Moreover, the Special Connection Theory is well positioned in terms of predictability for the parties and the legal certainty of international transactions, as it can clearly define the conditions of considering or applying the overriding mandatory rules of third countries and therefore meets the interests of the parties. In addition, the Special Connection Theory may reflect the legitimate regulatory interests of third countries by considering or applying the overriding mandatory rules of closely connected third countries. Furthermore, from the point of view of the forum state, its interests can be balanced by analysing whether the law of a third country conforms to its legal system or pursues shared interests.[95] In short, the theory of special connection is satisfactory in terms of the interests of the parties, the forum state, the third country and of international harmony in decisions.

On the other hand, the Two-sided Conflict-of-laws Rule Theory[96] is critical of the Special Connection Theory. Its supporters argue that it is not desirable to start by examining whether legislators in a third country intended for overriding mandatory rules to apply regardless of the applicable law of the legal relationship.[97] This view argues that

[92] Martiny (n 6), EGBGB Art 34, Rn 140.

[93] The provisions of the Cultural Heritage Act that prohibit the export of cultural heritages usually correspond to overriding mandatory rules. See ch 4, I, C, ii for a review of the overriding mandatory nature of the Cultural Heritage Act of Korea.

[94] At the stage of assessing the values protected by Country X's law, it should be examined whether the value of 'cultural heritage protection', which is the legislative purpose of Country X's law, corresponds to the values of Korean law.

[95] Martiny (n 6), EGBGB Art 34, Rn 47; Hauser (n 4) 103; and Günther (n 4) 74 support the Special Connection Theory.

[96] Changseon Shin and Namsoon Yoon, *New Private International Law* [Singukjesabeop je2pan], 2nd edn (Fides, 2016) 287.

[97] ibid 282–83.

the overriding mandatory rules of third countries should be applied when they are most closely connected to the case under the general connection principles in private international law.[98] According to this view, the third-country law that is most closely connected to the case should be applied. However, it will not be applied unless it is found that the legislators of the third country intended for the rules to apply regardless of the applicable law of the legal relationship.

According to the Two-sided Conflict-of-laws Rule Theory, in the case of Example 5.1, the specific connecting principle is unclear; but if the law of the country most closely connected to the case is that of Country X, the next step should then be to determine whether the legislators of Country X's law intended for it to apply regardless of the governing law of the sales contract. The legislative intent for the prohibition of the export of cultural heritages to apply can be recognised regardless of the applicable law of the sales contract. In this way, the use of the Two-sided Conflict-of-laws Rule Theory also reaches the same conclusion as the Special Connection Theory. The outcome in Example 5.2 would be similar to that in Example 5.1.

Table 5.2 shows how each viewpoint under the substantive law approach would attempt to handle the examples, in addition to the Special Connection Theory and the Theory of the Two-sided Conflict-of-laws rule.

Table 5.2 The *lex causae* rule, territoriality principle, theory of power, special connection theory and the theory of the two-sided conflict-of-laws rule

		***Lex causae* rule**	**Territoriality**	**Theory of power**	**Special Connection Theory**	**Theory of two-sided conflict-of-laws rule**
Example 5.1	Theory	Apply Korean law	Apply Country X's law and consider the effect of its violation under Korean law	Consider or apply Country X's law	Consider or apply Country X's law	Apply Country X's law
	Conclusion	Invalidity of contract or impossibility	Invalidity of contract or impossibility	Invalidity of contract or impossibility	Invalidity of contract or impossibility	Invalidity of contract or impossibility
Example 5.2	Theory	Apply Korean law	Neither consider nor apply Country X's law	Consider or apply Country X's law if its purpose is in line with the Korean law's interests	Consider or apply Country X's law	Apply Country X's law
	Conclusion	Invalidity of contract	No possibility of the contract being invalid	Invalidity of contract	Invalidity of contract	Invalidity of contract

[98] ibid.

However, the Two-sided Conflict-of-laws Rule Theory is not desirable for the following reasons. First, there are difficulties in practical application as it fails to present specific connection points and connection principles. This is also admitted by a commentator who supports that theory.[99]

Second, the methodology that the Two-sided Conflict-of-laws Rule Theory takes is not appropriate. When comparing the Two-sided Conflict-of-laws Rule Theory with the Special Connection Theory, the ideological basis may differ. But in determining whether the overriding mandatory rules of a foreign country should apply, they both require a close connection between the third-country law and the case and the legislative intent of a third country's legislators for the provision to apply regardless of the applicable law to the relevant legal relationship.

However, the Special Connection Theory first determines whether it was the intention of the third country's legislators for the relevant provision to apply regardless of the applicable law to the relevant legal relationship and next looks at whether that provision is closely connected to the case. On the other hand, the Two-sided Conflict-of-laws Rule Theory is different in that it first looks for laws closely connected to the case and does not apply them when no intent of application is found; in short, the order of examination is different. It is questionable whether this results in a substantial difference in the outcome of which country's law will be applied. However, in terms of methodology, there would be fewer laws that the legislators intended to apply regardless of the applicable law of the relevant legal relationship than laws closely connected to the case, so it would be easier first to find legislation with that intention, rather than starting with a close connection. Therefore, from a methodological perspective, it is considered easier to look for the legislator's intention first, which would be like starting with a finer filter.[100]

Third, the essential public interest pursued by one country through overriding mandatory rules cannot be protected by the laws of another country. Overriding mandatory rules need to be treated differently from ordinary legal norms because they do not have equivalence or substitutability to foreign law. Hence, the approach starting with finding the legislator's intention for the relevant laws to apply regardless of the applicable law of the relevant legal relationship can be justified. In addition, the Special Connection Theory does not suggest that a third country's overriding mandatory rule should be applied just because the legislators intended for the rule to apply regardless of the applicable law of the relevant legal relationship. As previously seen, the Special Connection Theory requires that the law of a third country conform to the legal system of the forum state. Thus, while reviewing this condition, it is possible for the judiciary of the forum to determine whether to consider or apply the law of a third country. It is untenable to argue for the Two-sided Conflict-of-laws

[99] Ralf Michaels, 'Towards a private international law for regulatory conflicts?' (2016) 59 *Japanese Yearbook of International Law* 175, 191–95.

[100] It would be very difficult to define the scope of 'closely connected provisions' as referred to in the Two-sided Conflict-of-laws Rule Theory because conceptually, all laws of the country with a close connection would be included. On the other hand, even if no statute explicitly states that it 'applies regardless of the governing law of the relevant legal relation,' it would be easier to clarify the provisions that 'the legislators intended to apply regardless of the governing law of the legal relationship' based on the criteria set forth in ch 3, which would make it easier to find closely connected provisions, as mentioned in the Two-sided Conflict-of-law Rules Theory.

rule Theory that the Special Connection Theory acquiesces solely to the intention of foreign legislators.

In conclusion, the Special Connection Theory holds that to consider or apply the overriding mandatory rules of a third country under a conflict-of-laws approach if the third country is closely connected to the case concerned. In the following section, this author will examine specific legislative examples based on the Special Connection Theory.

B. Rome Convention

Article 7(1) of the Rome Convention provides that the court may give effect to the mandatory rules of a third country closely connected to the case, in consideration of their nature and purpose and the effect of their application or non-application. The basis of Article 7(1) of the Rome Convention can be found in the Supreme Court of the Netherlands' (Hoge Raad) *ALNATI* ruling[101] and the Dutch court's *Sensor*[102,103] In *ALNATI*, the Supreme Court of the Netherlands held that, in principle, the law of the country chosen by the parties is the governing law of the contract, but that the law of a foreign state may prevail over the law chosen by the parties if 'for a foreign state such great interests are at stake in the observance outside of its territory of particular rules of law'.[104] In *Sensor*, even if the governing law of the contract is Dutch law, it was held that the overriding mandatory rules of the foreign law should take precedence over it 'if there is a sufficient connection with the foreign country in question'.[105]

i. Requirements

In order for Article 7(1) of the Rome Convention to be applied, (1) the country to which the overriding mandatory rules of a third country belong must be closely connected to the case, (2) the overriding mandatory rules of that country must be applied regardless of the

[101] 13 May 1966. *Van Nievelt, Goudriaan and Co.'s Stoomvaartmij NV v NV Hollandische Assurantie Societeit and Others* (1967) 56 Rev.crit.dr.int.priv. 522.

[102] *Cie Européenne des pétrôles SA v Sensor Nederland BV*, 1982, The District Court at The Hague (1983) 22 *International Legal Material* 66.

[103] Collins (n 52) vol 2, para 32-084; Plender and Wilderspin (n 63) paras 9-03-9-05.

[104] In this case, potatoes, which were the subject matter of the carriage-by-sea contract, arrived damaged during their transportation from Belgium to Rio de Janeiro, and the consignor's insurer claimed damages from the carrier. The governing law was specified in the bill of lading as Dutch law. Nevertheless, in this case, it was asked whether Belgian commercial law requiring 'the carrier to prove that the damage occurred outside his control' would be applied. The Court, while recognising that the law governing the bill of lading would be Dutch law, declared the legal principle that if a foreign country has an important interest in compliance with its mandatory provisions outside its territory, the Dutch court should respect it. In this case, however, the Dutch court decided that Belgian law did not have that extent of an important interest in its application.

[105] The Dutch subsidiary of an American company entered into a contract to sell equipment for pipes to a French company, after which the US enacted legislation regulating exports of American companies (including their European subsidiaries) in relation to a pipeline along the Trans-Siberian Railway. The Dutch subsidiary of the American company refused to perform on the basis of the regulation. The Dutch court ruled as above, while also recognising that Dutch law would be the governing law of the contract. Although the Dutch court did not specify which cases would show some sufficient connection, it found the contract could be enforced because this requirement was not met.

applicable law, and (3) judges have discretion as to whether to give effect to such a rule, and when a judge exercises discretion, the purpose and nature of the rule and the consequences of application or non-application shall be considered.

In the course of drafting the Rome Convention, the initial draft did not mention any close connection but only 'connection'. However, this was revised as 'close' connection based on concerns that an excessively large number of countries' laws may have to be considered under the broad provision, that there may be delays in the proceedings due to conflicts among those laws, and that the parties could use such as a delay tactic.[106] As to the meaning of close connection, it is suggested that the contract as a whole.[107] On the other hand, some commentators argue that the close connection should be to the issues in question in the dispute.[108] As a basis for determining close connection, the place of performance of the contract, the place of habitual residence and the place of business of the parties,[109] the law determined by Article 4(1) of the Rome Convention when the parties have not agreed on one for the contract,[110] the place of work, the place of conduct, nationality, and the centre of business may be used.[111]

Article 7(1) of the Rome Convention recognises the broad discretion of judges on whether to give effect to the overriding mandatory rules of third countries. The exercise of such discretion should be justified by the purpose and nature of the provision or the effect of its application or non-application. In this regard, in the process of drafting the Rome Convention, a draft proposed that the nature and purpose of the regulation should be justified by internationally recognised standards, or in other words, generally recognised legal interests in other countries. However, this proposal was not accepted, based on the objection that such standards do not exist and will only aggravate the difficulties the courts face.[112] Another view asserts that considering the nature and purpose of a provision is to consider whether it specifies the local spatial scope of application, whether it protected the parties or the state, the number of competing mandatory rules, and the general commercial or moral justifiability.[113]

However, since the factors presented in this view are already considered in determining whether the rule constitutes an overriding mandatory rule, it is unclear how these factors should be considered differently at the stage of assessing the overriding mandatory nature and at the state of exercising judicial discretion. In addition, the language of Article 7(1) of the Rome Convention, which takes into account the 'nature' of the regulation, is believed to be inappropriate since whether a certain provision is public or private cannot be a decisive criterion in determining whether it is an overriding mandatory rule.[114]

Therefore, a better understanding is that taking into account the nature and purpose of the regulation in exercising discretion should be seen as 'content control *(Inhaltskontrolle)*'

[106] Mario Guilano and Paul Lagarde, 'Report on the Convention on the Law Applicable to Contractual Obligations' (1980) C 282 *Official Journal* Art 7(2).
[107] ibid.
[108] Plender and Wilderspin (n 63) para 9-08; Chong (n 56) 60; Kaye (n 52) 254–55.
[109] Guiliano and Lagarde (n 106) Art 7(2).
[110] Plender and Wilderspin (n 63) para 9-09; Kaye (n 52) 251.
[111] Guiliano and Lagarde (n 106) Art 7(2); Kaye (n 52) 253–54.
[112] Guiliano and Lagarde (ibid) Art 7(3).
[113] Kaye (n 52) 251.
[114] See ch 3, II, D, (3).

of the overriding mandatory rules of third countries.[115] Under this view, the second sentence of Article 7(1) of the Rome Convention renounces the method of resolving conflicts of traditional laws and adopts a new method of selecting the applicable law based on policy considerations, similar to governmental interest analysis as suggested in the US.[116] This point will be considered in further detail in the discussion of the Rome I Regulation, which adopted the same text as the second sentence of Article 7(1) of the Rome Convention on the meaning of content control.

The discretion of the judge is also necessary for a situation where only one of the several conflicting overriding mandatory rules of several countries should be applied.[117] Non-application may be justified if there are adverse effects on the interests of other competing countries or parties.[118]

ii. Effect

Article 7(1) of the Rome Convention only stipulates that the 'effect may be given' to the overriding mandatory rules of third countries and does not define its specific meaning. In terms of its meaning, the persuasive view is that the overriding mandatory rule itself should be applied as law (Theory 1).[119] The grounds are that, if the overriding mandatory rules of a third country are considered under the applicable substantive law, the effect of the mandatory rules of the third country will depend on the remedies provided by the applicable substantive law concerning, inter alia, impossibility, illegality and good morals. If the substantive law does not provide such remedies, it is unclear how to give effect to the overriding mandatory rules.

There is another view (Theory 2),[120] which interprets 'effect may be given' to mean that a third country's overriding mandatory rule is considered as a fact under the applicable substantive law of the relevant legal relation. This view contends that 'giving effect' does not only mean application from a conflict-of-laws approach, but also includes any kind of approval for the said rule. Additionally, some argue that 'giving effect' is a concept weaker than the application (*Anwendung*) and that the judge does not recognise the effect according to overriding mandatory rules, but can recognise also other effects when needed (Theory 3).[121] According to Theory 3, the method of granting effect to overriding mandatory rules of a third country is not limited to either directly applying them or considering them as facts under substantive law; the effect provided by the law of the third country may be altered to draw a fair conclusion within the scope of the *lex fori* or the applicable law to the contract, for instance by considering only the purpose of the overriding mandatory rules.[122]

[115] Schäfer (n 43) 277.

[116] Chong (n 56) 61; Schäfer (n 43) 277; Hossein Fazilatfar, *Overriding Mandatory Rules in International Commercial Arbitration* (Edward Elgar Publishing, 2019) 137 (for details on governmental interest analysis, see 143ff).

[117] Guiliano and Lagarde (n 106) Art 7(3); Kaye (n 52) 251.

[118] Kaye (n 52) 251.

[119] Vischer (n 43) 13, 166–68; Chong (n 56) 42.

[120] See Martiny (n 6), EGBGB Art 34, Rn 70 introducing this view.

[121] Martiny (n 6), EGBGB Art 34, Rn 70, 71, Schäfer (n 43) 278. Meanwhile, Guiliano and Lagarde (n 106) Art 7(3) believe that the wording 'effect may be given' compels the courts to conduct a highly delicate exercise of combining the overriding mandatory rules of third countries with the governing law of the contract. This seems to resemble more closely Theory 3.

[122] The latter is a legal technique corresponding to adaptation under private international law. Schäfer (n 43) 334. Art 19 of the Swiss FAPIL, as seen in the following section, is of this stance.

iii. Evaluation

Corresponding to the conflicting views on the application or consideration of the overriding mandatory rules of third countries, there are also contradictory comments on Article 7(1) of the Rome Convention. Some believe that Article 7(1) has become a recipe of uncertainty and confusion, with its unclear wording and the granting of wide discretion to judges, and that consideration of the potential variety of overriding mandatory rules of third countries will delay proceedings, impose excessive burden on judges and unfairly restrict party autonomy.[123,124] On the other hand, there are other view refuting such points. First, Article 7(1) of the Rome Convention has established a unified methodology for the consideration or application of a third country's overriding mandatory rules and promotes the unity of judgments across jurisdictions,[125] conforming to international comity.[126] Second, the restriction on party autonomy inevitably arises due to the existence of overriding mandatory rules, not because of Article 7(1) of the Rome Convention.[127]

This author agrees with both of these arguments, with the following additional supporting points. In relation to the first argument, as can be seen from the positions taken by the German and English courts, domestic courts have considered the third country overriding mandatory rules under the concepts of infringements of good morals (*Sittenwidrigkeit*), impossibility, or public policy under applicable substantive law even before the enactment of the Rome Convention. However, it is difficult to establish in that way specific and consistent conditions under which third-country overriding mandatory rules are considered or applied. Accordingly, the Special Connection Theory and Article 7(1) of the Rome Convention based on this theory are a better approach than the substantive-law approach in that they guarantee the predictability of the applicable law, thus serving the interests of the parties. In relation to the second argument, the UK and Germany, which reserved the effect of Article 7(1) of the Rome Convention, also considered third-country overriding mandatory rules under substantive law, which shows that the party autonomy may be restricted due to the overriding mandatory rules of third countries, even in the absence of provisions like Article 7(1) of the Rome Convention.

The potential issue of 'delay in procedures and increased burden on judges due to the overriding mandatory rules of multiple third countries' can be tackled by limiting the scope of the third-country overriding mandatory rules to be applied or considered to countries closely connected to the relevant case. Rather, if the third-country overriding mandatory

[123] Collins (n 52) vol 2, para 32-086.

[124] The UK, Germany, Portugal, Ireland and Luxembourg have, from this view, reserved Art 7(1) of the Rome Convention.

[125] Kaye (n 52) 256–57 criticises the UK, which has reserved Art 7(1) of the Rome Convention, as follows: 'International contracts cannot be isolated within a conceptual vacuum. Convenient and just though it may be to apply a single applicable law to the main part of their regulation, whether on the basis of choice or closest connection, the fact that they have effects in other countries, which may be vitally important for the parties or those countries themselves – and not merely that of *objective* applicable law – cannot be simply be ignored in the name of sanctity of the applicable law. The latter doctrine is there to serve justice, not to be shaped and preserved in a pure forum so as to satisfy the predilections of theorists … Applied with appropriate reserve, therefore, Article 7(1) could prove an important additional influence for the cause of justice in the English courts – which the public policy doctrine, embodied in Article 16, may instead be called upon to exercise, involving some uncertainty. It seems churlish of the United Kingdom to have made the reservation.'

[126] Schäfer (n 43) 281.

[127] Kaye (n 52) 257 purports the same.

rules are to be considered under the general provisions of the applicable substantive law of the contract, indirect facts that serve as the basis for the factual requirements of the substantive law, such as 'the intent of the parties to violate the law', should be examined. This would place a greater burden on judges than what provisions such as Article 7(1) of the Rome Convention currently do.

However, it is worth noting the criticism on 'the broad discretion of the judge'. This criticism derives from the fact that the 'purpose and nature of the norm', a factor to be considered in exercising discretion under Article 7(1) of the Rome Convention, is hardly a clear criterion. If the factors to be considered in the exercise of discretion could be defined clearly, the interests of the parties could be better reflected, in terms of the predictability of the applicable law.

In short, regarding the overriding mandatory rules of third countries, the Rome Convention incorporated the interests of the parties by presenting consistent principles based on the conflict-of-laws approach and also reflected the interests of international harmony in decisions. It also duly reflects the interests of third countries by giving effect to the overriding mandatory rules of closely connected third countries. However, there are some weaknesses in terms of the interests of the parties because the criteria for exercising discretion are not clear. The second sentence of Article 7(1) of the Rome Convention only stipulates that the purpose and nature of the regulation, and the consequences of its application or non-application, be considered when exercising discretion, without explicitly providing criteria regarding the conformity of the overriding mandatory rules of third countries with the legal system of the forum state, which is also a shortcoming in relation to the interests of the forum state.

C. Swiss FAPIL

In 1987, Switzerland introduced a provision, based on Article 7(1) of the Rome Convention, on the overriding mandatory rules of third countries in its Federal Act on Private International Law (*Schweizerisches Bundesgesetz über das Internationale Privatrecht*, FAPIL), which is unusual in domestic laws. Article 19(1) of FAPIL provides:

> If interests that are legitimate and clearly preponderant according to the Swiss conception of law so require, a mandatory provision of a law other than the one referred to by this Act may be taken into consideration, provided the situation dealt with has a close connection with that other law.

Further, Article 19(2) stipulates:

> In deciding whether such a provision is to be taken into consideration, consideration shall be given to its purpose and the consequences of its application, in order to reach a decision that is appropriate having regard to the Swiss conception of law.[128,129]

[128] This translation is based on the German version of FAPIL and refers also to the French and Italian versions. This is referred to as '*Auffassung*' in the German translation, '*conception*' in the French translation and '*concezióne*' in the Italian translation.

[129] In the introduction of the above provision, the Swiss case law (BGE 68 II 203, BGE 76 II 33, BGE 80 II 49) that previously denied the application of the laws of third countries based on the theory of non-application of foreign public law, territoriality, and public policy of Switzerland were abolished.

i. Requirements

In order for Article 19 of FAPIL to apply, (1) a third country that enacted the overriding mandatory rules[130] must be closely connected to the case, (2) there must be legitimate and clearly preponderant interests of a party in accordance with Swiss legal conceptions, and (3) when a judge exercises discretion as to whether to consider the overriding mandatory rules of a third country, the judge must take into account whether it constitutes an appropriate decision based on Swiss legal conceptions in light of the purpose and effect of the provisions.

A close connection is recognised under the contract in accordance with other points of contact. For example, a close connection regarding the protection of lessees is found in the location of the leased property; for restrictions on the sale of land, it is the location of the land; and for restrictions on disposal of movable property (such as prohibition of cultural heritage exports), it is the location of the movable property. For occupational safety protection, the closely connected location is where the work is performed; for crew members, it is the flag state; for regulations protecting vulnerable contract parties, it is the place of residence of such parties; for the protection of currency, it is where the currency is used; for competition law, it is the market affected by competition; and for import restrictions, it is the place of performance.[131] However, in determining the presence or absence of a close connection, the location or territory is not the sole criterion, and the provision's direct effect on the position of the contracting party should also be taken into account.[132]

The requirement that there must be legitimate and clearly preponderant interests of a party in accordance with Swiss legal conceptions under Article 19(1) of FAPIL means that there must be some 'shared value' between the foreign country to which the challenged mandatory rule belongs and the forum.[133] This means that it is necessary to weigh interests through value judgment.[134]

On the other hand, while the German text in Article 19 of FAPIL stipulates that there must be clearly preponderant interests of 'a party (*einer Partei*)', the French text does not include 'of a party', and it is questionable whether the legitimate interests are limited to the 'interests of a party'. Some hold the view, true to the French text, limiting the relevant interests to the 'interests of a party' would be too narrow an approach.[135] Also, there may be cases where the third-country law should be applied against the interests of the parties. Thus, the most prominent view is that legitimate interests shall not be limited to the interests of a party, and that provisions protecting the national interests of the third country

[130] In relation to the laws of third countries, FAPIL does not specify that they are required to apply regardless of the governing law, unlike the Rome Convention, but this is interpreted to refer to overriding mandatory rules. Vischer and Lüchinger (n 21) Art 19, Rn 18; Schäfer (n 43) 272.

[131] Vischer and Lüchinger (n 21) Art 19, Rn 27.

[132] ibid Rn 29.

[133] Section by Dieter Martiny in Franz Jürgen Säcker (ed), *Münchener Kommentar zum BGB*, 8th edn (Verlag Beck München, 2021) Rom I-VO Art 9, Rn 142. Linguistically, 'in accordance with Swiss legal conceptions' modifies both 'legitimate' and 'clearly preponderant'. Mächler-Erne and Wolf-Mettier (n 91), Rn 22. Therefore, the question of whether a party's interest is 'clearly preponderant' is determined according to Swiss legal conceptions and is also related to shared values.

[134] BGE 136 III 392, E. 2.3.3.1.

[135] Schäfer (n 43) 274.

can also be applied.[136,137] That recognises the possibility of a party invoking the overriding mandatory rules of a third country only in its favour and failing to do so when the party is ignorant or intending to avoid the application of the third-country law, leading to abuse of the requirement of 'interests of a party'.[138] Therefore, when weighing interests under Article 19(1) of FAPIL, the interests of a party should not be given sole consideration, and the legal community's interests, the interests of the entire country, legal certainty, the principle of contract compliance (*pacta sunt servanda*), and international harmony in judgments should be considered comprehensively.[139] Although the Federal Supreme Court of Switzerland has not drawn a clear conclusion as to the meaning of the 'interests of a party', Federal Supreme Court precedents and academic theories agree that foreign law can be applied against the interests of the parties to the extent that the content of the foreign law can be recognised as an international public policy.[140,141] The Federal Supreme Court cited prohibitions of drug trafficking, the abduction of women and receipt of bribes by public officials as examples of international public policy.[142]

Weighing interests to determine whether they are clearly preponderant should be based on Swiss legal conceptions, which include the value structure (*Wertgefüge*) in Swiss law and international law, the protection of fundamental human rights and the economic order of Switzerland,[143] and the fundamental value of the legal order of Switzerland.[144] Therefore, the application of the overriding mandatory rules of third countries should be worth protection in light of Swiss legal conceptions, and this should be clearly preponderant to the interests in applying *lex causae*.[145] The third-country law need not be similar to that of Switzerland, and

[136] Vischer (n 43) 21, 174.

[137] *Schweizerische Bundesrat, Botschaft zum Bundesgesetz über das internationale Privatrecht* (IPR-Gesetz) vom 10 November 1982 (1983), 82.072 para 213.54, a commentary on the draft at the time of the development of Art 19 of FAPIL in 1987, also indicates that 'the interests in applying overriding mandatory rules of a third country are clearly preponderant to those in non-application' and does not mention the interests of the parties. BGE 136 III 620 left the question of which text should be the basis of determination unanswered, while disclosing the legislative history as follows. In the legislative process, the Standing Committee (*ständerätliche Kommission*) of the state council proposed the 'interest of one party', but the national congress committee (*Kommission des Nationalrat*) explicitly refused this proposal. However, the reporter of the state council (*ständerätliche Berichterstatter*) and the national congress (*Nationalrat*) later adopted it unknowingly.

[138] Mächler-Erne and Wolf-Mettier (n 91) Art 19, Rn 23. In this regard, the 'interest of the parties' in Art 19(1) of FAPIL is different from the interests of the parties as this author has classified them. The interests of parties according to my classification means the parties' legitimate expectations or predictability of the governing law of the contract and does not mean whether the result of the application of specific provisions would be advantageous or disadvantageous to the specific parties.

[139] Mächler-Erne and Wolf-Mettier (n 91) Art 19, Rn 24.

[140] Vischer and Lüchinger (n 21) Art 19, Rn 32; Mächler-Erne and Wolf-Mettier (n 91) Art 19, Rn 22.

[141] However, the Federal Supreme Court of Switzerland tends to regard the overriding mandatory rules of third countries as infringements of good morals under Art 20(1) of the Swiss Debt Enforcement and Bankruptcy Act, rather than Art 19 of FAPIL, to the extent that the content of those rules, including violations of UN resolutions, correspond to international public policy. Mächler-Erne and Wolf-Mettier (n 91) Art 19, Rn 5, 31. BGer 4A_263/2019 E. 2.3. also confirmed this legal principle. BGer 4C.172/200 E. 5 held that an arms sale contract was invalid for violating the good morals of the Swiss Debt Enforcement and Bankruptcy Act, as it violated a UN embargo.

[142] BGE 119 II 380, E. 4b.

[143] Mächler-Erne and Wolf-Mettier (n 91) Art 19, Rn 21.

[144] BGE 136 III 392, E. 2.3.3.1.

[145] ibid; BGE 138 III 489, 495. E. 2.3.3. The 'interests in applying *lex causae*' referred to herein mean, according to this author's classification, the interests of the parties.

it is sufficient that it pursues values that conform to Swiss legal conceptions.[146] The content of the third-country law should be reviewed at this stage. This can be seen as 'content control (*Inhaltskontrolle*[147])', which is contrary to how the outcome of applying the overriding mandatory rules of third countries is taken into account under Article 19(2) of FAPIL. First of all, it is necessary to examine whether the law of a third country conforms to the general principles of international law and the fundamental values of the constitutional state.[148] Thereafter, in the process of weighing interests, it is necessary to examine how oppressive the norms prohibiting the debtor's performance are to the parties.[149]

The Swiss Federal Supreme Court, without mentioning the 'interests of a party' in the following decisions, held that 'clearly preponderant interests' were not recognised. In Swiss Federal Supreme Court decision BGE 130 III 620, a married couple entered into a post-nuptial property agreement (*ehegüterrechtliches Post Nuptial Agreement*) under which property located outside the US would be owned by the wife. Before signing the contract, the wife opened a bank account in Switzerland, under the name of both herself and her husband. Afterwards, in the husband's insolvency proceedings, the American trustee requested the Swiss bank to provide information in accordance with the US insolvency law; under American law, a bank could be criminally prosecuted for disposing of the husband's property. When the wife filed a lawsuit against the Swiss bank for the return of deposits, the lower court found that there were clearly preponderant interests for the Swiss bank to apply the US Bankruptcy Act in accordance with Article 19 and ruled that, in principle, the obligation of the Swiss bank to return deposits to the wife should be changed in accordance with Article 19 of FAPIL and that the bank's obligation to pay would be postponed due to the risk of criminal prosecution and double payment.

However, the Swiss Federal Supreme Court said that it is not necessary to decide whether the judgment should be based on the clearly preponderant 'interests of a party' or simply on the basis of 'clearly preponderant interests'. The Supreme Court pointed out that the original ruling did not weigh interests, such as public interests, other than the interests of the parties,[150] and held that it was not clear whether there were clearly preponderant interests for the Swiss bank.[151] The rationale there was that the US was expected to request mutual legal assistance under Article 166 of FAPIL on recognition of foreign bankruptcy proceedings in accordance with the principles of international law, rather than directly use compulsory means against the defendant bank that operates in Switzerland.

The Swiss Federal Supreme Court found in BGE 136 III 392 that the law of Panama, which provides for the payment of compensation in case of unfair dismissal of crew

[146] BGE 136 III 392, E. 2.3.3.1.

[147] An example of the use of 'contents control' in the context of the Rome Convention, Schäfer (n 43) 277. Vischer and Lüchinger (n 21) Art 19, Rn 40 also uses the term '*Inhaltskontrolle*'.

[148] Mächler-Erne and Wolf-Mettier (n 91) Art 19, Rn 19.

[149] Vischer and Lüchinger (n 91) Art 19, Rn 31.

[150] Looking at the factual grounds, the grounds for this ruling seem to purport that because the clearly preponderant 'interests of a party' cannot be recognised, no issues arise as to whether the determination under Art 19(1) of FAPIL should be based on clearly preponderant interests or clearly preponderant interests 'of a party'.

[151] The Swiss Federal Supreme Court also pointed out that the lower court's decision overlooked the exceptional nature of Art 19 of FAPIL. Since Art 19 has the nature of a general provision, it does not apply if there is a special connecting principle under FAPIL. Since Swiss FAPIL is equipped with a provision on recognition of foreign bankruptcy proceedings (Art 166 of FAPIL), the issue of recognising foreign bankruptcy proceedings is not a matter of foreign law but a matter of Swiss law (E. 3.4.2-3.2. of the judgment).

members of deep-sea fishing vessels, is not required to be applied by 'the legitimate and clearly preponderant interests under Swiss legal conceptions' because Swiss law, which is the governing law of the employment contract, also permits compensation under similar but more restrictive requirements. Therefore, it was held that the provisions of the above Panama law need not be considered under Swiss law.[152]

In BGE 131 III 418, the Swiss Federal Supreme Court ruled on whether the security agreement entered into between the Swiss branch of a French bank and the companies controlled by the descendants of the Hyderabad Kingdom of India was invalid, as it relates to ancient gold coins taken out of India without the permission of the Indian Government in violation of the Indian Antiquities and Art Treasures Act 1972. In this ruling, the Swiss Federal Supreme Court ruled that 'legitimate, clear interests under Swiss law' could not be seen to request the consideration of the Antiquities and Art Treasures Act.[153,154]

Article 19(2) of FAPIL stipulates that the purpose of the provision and the appropriateness of the outcome of its application according to Swiss legal conceptions should be considered when judges exercise their discretion. In other words, the result of applying the overriding mandatory rules of third countries to specific cases must conform to Swiss legal conceptions, which corresponds to result control (*Ergebniskontrolle*).[155] This means

[152] However, the Swiss Federal Supreme Court stated in this ruling that the difference between the French, Italian and German texts of Art 19 have not yet been tackled and that the wording 'clearly preponderant interest' in the French text is meant to encompass 'interests of a party'.

[153] The reason is that 'there is no obligation to apply foreign public law within Swiss territory'. The Federal Act on the International Transfer of Cultural Property (*Kulturgütertransfergesetz*) regarding the UNESCO Convention was enacted in 2003, and according to this Act, 'the regulations of the country of origin of the illegally expatriated cultural heritage can be considered in the claim for return as a claim under public law, but such regulations under the public law of foreign countries need not be considered in private claims'. But in its ruling, the Court explained that 'Although the plaintiff argues that the security agreement is invalid for its violation of Indian law, it cannot be acknowledged that the gold coins in this case were taken out of the country in violation of Indian law. Even if the gold coins were taken out in violation of Indian law, the security agreement for gold coins in this case does not become void even if the Indian law is considered pursuant to Art 19 of FAPIL because Indian law does not provide that a security agreement for cultural heritage illegally taken out is invalid. Therefore, the security agreement cannot be deemed invalid in accordance with Swiss law, which is the applicable law, or the mandatory rules of India that could have been considered in accordance with Art 19 of FAPIL.' Accordingly, it is unclear whether this judgment purports that the Antiquities and Art Treasures Act of India, which prohibits the removal of cultural heritages, cannot be considered at all pursuant to Art 19(1) of FAPIL. Jong Hyeok Lee, 'Cultural Property Transfer Act of Switzerland – Main Contents and Implications for the Perspective of Private International Law' (2017) 23 *Korea Private International Law Journal* 59, 103 offers the following criticism of this judgment: 'By presenting the principle that the application of foreign public law concerning the protection of cultural heritages is recognised exclusively in relationships with countries that have entered into bilateral treaties with Switzerland, the ruling shelled Art 19 of FAPIL on the consideration of the overriding mandatory rules of a third country in the scope of cultural property protection.' However, in light of the above reasoning, it is unclear whether the Swiss court has definitively declared such a legal principle.

[154] On the other hand, BGer 4C.32/2001 is an example of how the Swiss Federal Supreme Court takes into account foreign overriding mandatory rules in accordance with Art 19. In this case, the plaintiff entered into a distribution agreement with the defendant whereby the plaintiff would exclusively sell the defendant's products in the Netherlands, Belgium and Luxembourg and the defendant would pay penalties for any violation of the non-competition provisions of the agreement. Thereafter, the plaintiff filed a lawsuit against the defendant seeking penalties for the violation of the non-competition provisions. In this case, it was contested whether the exclusive distribution agreement and, in particular, its penalty clause was invalid for violating the competition law of the European Union. The Swiss Federal Supreme Court held that the lower court's ruling, in accordance with Art 19 of FAPIL, was justified, taking into account the competition law of the European Union. BGer 4C.32/2001 E. 4. In this case, however, the Court did not make a separate reference to the 'clearly preponderant interests'.

[155] Mächler-Erne and Wolf-Mettier (n 91) Art 19, Rn 25.; BGE 130 III 620, E. 3.5.1.

weighing both the interests of the third country and Switzerland, the forum, in relation to the outcome of applying the overriding mandatory rules of the third country.[156] In this process, the impact on the contractual relationship and legal status of the parties should be taken into account. Here, the degree to which the interests of the third country correspond with those of Switzerland becomes an important criterion for judgment: and the higher the degree, the greater the likelihood that the law of the third country will be given effect.[157] Swiss law does not need to have mandatory rules similar to the overriding mandatory rules of the third country, and it is sufficient that the foreign rules conform in their purpose to the legal conceptions of Switzerland.[158] But even when the provisions of the foreign law are contrary to the public policy of Swiss law, that law must inevitably be considered in cases when the parties cannot avoid the application of that law or when it creates difficulties for performing the contract.[159]

ii. Effect

If the requirements under Article 19(1) of FAPIL are met, the overriding mandatory rules of a third country may be given effect. Article 19 gives judges the discretion to consider or not to consider foreign laws, and the factors considered in exercising that discretion are also to be considered in weighing interest, as mentioned above.[160] Therefore, if the protected legal interests of foreign law are legitimate from the perspective of Swiss law, the judges' discretion focuses on *how* the foreign law shall be considered, rather than *whether* it should be.[161]

The reasons why Article 19 of FAPIL stipulates that foreign laws may be 'considered' without stipulating that they should be 'applied' are as follows:[162] (1) Since Article 19 is not a provision on the direct effect of foreign public law, but on how foreign public law affects a private law relationship, it is not an 'application' of the public law. (2) Even if the requirements of Article 19 of FAPIL are met, the legal effect prescribed by foreign law is not always recognised. Article 19(2) of FAPIL states that 'consideration shall be given to its purpose and the consequences of its application, in order to reach a decision that is appropriate', enabling a judge to form a legal effect in order to appropriately reach a decision (*Gestaltungsmöglichkeit*). For example, as a result of the court's consideration of foreign law, the court may find that the contract is partially invalid, performance should be suspended, (*Stundung der Erfüllung*), it is impossible to enforce the contractual obligation (*Nichtdurchsetzbarkeit*, including Article VIII(2)(b) of the IMF Agreement), contract be terminated or amended. This amounts to the judges' discretion on which legal effect is to be recognised. If the court determines that a contract is invalid by applying the overriding mandatory rules of a foreign country, the subsequent effect of the nullification of the contract is determined by the applicable law of the contract.[163]

[156] Schäfer (n 43) 275 asserts that this is similar to policy weighing in the US.
[157] BGE 136 III 398, E.2.3.3.1.
[158] BGE 138 III 489, 495, 2.3.3.
[159] Vischer and Lüchinger (n 91) Art 19, Rn 35.
[160] ibid Rn 15.
[161] ibid Rn 50.
[162] ibid Rn 45–49.
[163] ibid Rn 49.

iii. Evaluation

The FAPIL, like the Rome Convention, defines the scope of the law of a third country that should be considered or applied as the law of a country closely connected to the facts. Article 19 of FAPIL provides clearer guidance than the Rome Convention (Article 19(1)) on what should be considered in the stage of examining whether the law of a third country is worthy of consideration or application in general, as well as in specific cases (Article 19(2)). Article 19(1) provides a specific criterion of 'the interests of the parties that are legitimate and clearly preponderant in accordance with Swiss legal conceptions', in weighing the interests of the third country and the interests of the forum state. In addition, Article 19(2) provides that the court should consider 'the purpose' of the overriding mandatory rules of a third country and whether a 'decision that is appropriate in regard to the Swiss conception of law' is reached should be considered. This is more helpful than Article 7(1) of the Rome Convention, which has the court take into account 'the nature and purpose and to the consequences of their application or non-application' when giving effect to the overriding mandatory rules of a third country.

It is appropriate to examine whether there are values shared between the overriding mandatory rules of a third country and the forum state based on 'legitimate interests according to Swiss legal conceptions'. This approach reflects the interests of the forum state. However, the consideration of the interests 'of a party' in finding the clearly preponderant interests is questionable. First of all, to prevent confusion due to the use of terms, the party interests referred to in FAPIL are different from the interests of the parties categorised here. The interests of the parties according to my classification refer to the predictability of the applicable law and do not mean the advantages or disadvantages to the parties resulting from applying specific provisions to specific facts. However, the interests of the parties under Article 19(1) does include the advantages or disadvantages to the parties upon applying specific provisions to the specific facts, in addition to the predictability of the applicable law.[164]

However, in applying or considering the overriding mandatory rules of a third country, content control and result control of the law of the third country must be distinguished. Methodologically, it is more efficient to control the contents first and the results afterward. As mentioned earlier, in determining whether the 'interests of one party' is clearly preponderant under Article 19(1) of FAPIL, the court should consider the extent to which the parties would be affected if the third country's overriding mandatory rule were to be applied.[165] However, it is more appropriate to consider the advantages or disadvantages to a party, including 'oppressive circumstances against the party', at the stage of control of the specific results, rather than the stage of reviewing the abstract contents of the provision in question. This is because the advantages or disadvantages to a party due to the application or non-application of a third country's overriding mandatory rules are premised on specific facts and issues. The degree of oppression on the party exerted by the provision and the advantages or disadvantages to the party following its application only become clear when the outcome of the application or non-application of the third country's overriding

[164] Vischer and Lüchinger (n 91) Art 19, Rn 31. This is true considering that the lower court which ruled on the BGE 130 III 620 decision mentioned the risks of double payment and criminal prosecution of Swiss banks as the interests of the parties.

[165] ibid.

mandatory rules is analysed in regard to specific facts. Therefore, at the stage of content control, I believe it would be sufficient to examine whether the abstract content of the law of a third country is legitimate from the perspective of the forum law.

In addition, considering that (1) the wording 'of a party' were inserted in error in the drafting process of Article 19 of FAPIL, (2) they were not included in the original French text of FAPIL, (3) a significant number of the decisions by the Swiss Federal Supreme Court[166] did not refer to the interests 'of a party', and (4) there is an discussion in Switzerland about amending the law to delete those words,[167] the criterion considering 'the interests of a party' is not decisive when considering or applying the overriding mandatory rules of a third country under FAPIL.

On the other hand, it seems fair to determine whether the consequences of application of the overriding mandatory rules of a third country is 'appropriate having regard to the Swiss conception of law' under Article 19(2) of FAPIL, as a means of result control. However, it is not apposite to take into account the 'purpose' of the provision again at this stage. In accordance with Article 19(1) of FAPIL, the purpose of the overriding mandatory rules of a third country should already be considered when examining whether those rules are legitimate in accordance with Swiss legal conceptions. It is unclear how re-examining the purpose of the overriding mandatory rules of a third country in Article 19(2) differs practically from the evaluation of their legitimacy under Swiss legal conceptions in Article 19(1). Examining the 'purpose' of the provision once again fails to provide meaningful guidance on result control. As mentioned above, it is sufficient to examine, at the result control stage, how oppressive the circumstances will be to the parties when the relevant provision is applied, what advantages or disadvantages there will be for the parties, and whether the application will violate the public policy of the forum.

In short, Article 19 of FAPIL comprehensively considers the interests of the parties in terms of the predictability of the applicable norms, the interests of third countries by examining closely the connected third-country laws, and the interests of the forum state and the interests of international harmony in decisions by observing whether the contents and results of the application of the overriding mandatory rules of third countries are legitimate from the perspective of the forum. However, it falls short to require consideration of the oppression suffered by the parties in the content control stage (Article 19(1)) and 'purpose' in the result control stage (Article 19(2)).

D. Hague Agency Convention, Hague Trust Convention and the Hague Principles on Choice of Law in International Commercial Contracts

There are several international norms based on the Special Connection Theory that take a similar stance to the Rome Convention and FAPIL. Conventions adopted at the Hague

[166] BGE 138 III 489, BGE 131 III 418.

[167] Mächler-Erne andWolf-Mettier (n 91) Art 19, Rn 3. The basis for this revision is that decisions should be made not based on the 'interests of one party' but the 'interests of the general public'.

Conference on Private International Law include provisions on the overriding mandatory rules of third countries.[168]

The Hague Convention of 14 March 1978 on the Law Applicable to Agency (Agency Convention) reflected a view similar to the one in the Netherlands Supreme Court's *ALNATI* ruling. According to Article 16 of the Convention, the mandatory rules of a country with a 'significant connection' to the matter may be given effect if applied, regardless of the law established under the private international law of that country.[169]

According to Article 16(2) of the Convention of 1 July 1985 on the Law Applicable to Trusts and on their Recognition (Hague Trust Convention), if a third country's overriding mandatory rule has a 'sufficiently close connection', it may be given effect 'in exceptional circumstances', which is a stricter requirement than those under the Rome Convention or the Hague Agency Convention. However, this may be criticised for failing to present clear criteria on the conditions for applying overriding mandatory rules, since it does not clarify the meaning of 'exceptional circumstances'.

Meanwhile, the Hague Principles on Choice of Law in International Commercial Contracts, adopted on 19 March 2015, do not directly stipulate the conditions for applying the overriding mandatory provisions[170] of a third country, and rather provide that the forum law[171] shall determine whether to apply or consider the provisions of a third country (Article 11(2)). What is peculiar about the Hague Principles on Choice of Law in International Commercial Contracts is that, in accordance with forum law, the public policy of the country to which the objective governing law belongs can be considered or applied (Article 11(4)[172]).[173] Taking into account the public policy of the country to which the objective governing law belongs is based on the idea that the public policy of a country closely connected to the case should not be ignored. However, considering that the common law system does not strictly distinguish between public policy and overriding mandatory rules[174] and that public policy and overriding mandatory

[168] However, unlike the Rome I Regulation, they do not define overriding mandatory rules.

[169] This Convention differs from the Rome I Regulation or the Rome Convention, which prioritises the overriding mandatory rules of the forum, in that it treats foreign overriding mandatory rules like the overriding mandatory rules of the forum. Kunda (n 3) para 64.

[170] It is probable that the scope of overriding mandatory provisions will be limited to the definition under Art 9(1) of the Rome I Regulation. HCCH (2015) paras 11.5, 11.20.

[171] The forum law referred to here includes the private international law of the forum. Kwang Hyun Suk, 'The Hague Principles on the Choice of Law in International Commercial Contracts' in *Commemorative Book in Honor of Professor Jinmu Hun-Je Suh's Retirement* (ChungAng University Press, 2015) 304; Hong Sik Chung, 'A Study on Hague Principles on Choice of Law in International Commercial Contract' (2015) 125 *International Trade Law* 3, 42.

[172] Art 11(4): 'The law of the forum determines when a court may or must apply or take into account the public policy (*ordre public*) of a State whose law would be applicable in the absence of a choice of law.'

[173] This reflects the attitude of s 187(2)b of the US Restatement (Second) on Conflict of Laws and aims to harmonise common and civil laws. HCCH (2015) para 11.20; Suk (n 171) 305. The US leaves the role of the law limiting party autonomy (*lex limitativa*) to objective governing law rather than the law of the forum. Therefore, the parties' selection of the applicable law cannot avoid the public policy of the country to which the objective governing law belongs. There are provisions to the same effect in the laws of Oregon and Louisiana. Further details are in Symeon Symeonides and Neil Cohen, 'United States of America' in Daniel Girsberger, Thomas Kadner Graziano and Jan Neels (eds), *Choice of Law in International Commercial Contracts* (Oxford University Press, 2021) para 68.35ff; HCCH (2015) para 11.20.

[174] This is well demonstrated in the public policy-comity rule in England. Before the Rome Convention was adopted, the term 'mandatory rules' was not well known in England, but the concept and functions corresponding

rules overlap,[175] giving consideration to the public policy of the country to which the objective applicable law belongs appears similar to how the Special Connection Theory gives effect to the overriding mandatory rules of a third country closely connected to the case.[176]

E. Rome I Regulation

The Rome I Regulation is the successor of the Rome Convention. Since the Rome Convention was a 'convention' in its form, some countries, including the UK and Germany, were able to reserve Article 7(1) of the Rome Convention. However, since the Rome I Regulation is a Council Regulation to be uniformly applied throughout the EU, it was not possible to reserve certain provisions. Therefore, in the process of drafting the Rome I Regulation, opinions greatly differed among Member States on how to handle the Special Connection Theory regarding the overriding mandatory rules of third countries. Initially, the draft Rome I Regulation had a provision similar to Article 7(1) of the Rome Convention, but the UK expressed its intention not to participate in the Rome I Regulation, asserting that provisions such as Article 7(1) of the Rome Convention would result in uncertainties in international finance and undermine its status as an international finance hub.[177] In the end, Article 9(3) of the Rome I Regulation, which incorporated the English *lex loci solutionis* rule, was drafted in order to induce the participation of the UK, the courts of which were handling many cross-border commercial disputes.[178] What distinguishes the Rome I Regulation from Article 7(1) of the Rome Convention is that the scope of the third countries whose provisions should be applied or considered was limited to the place of performance, rather than countries closely connected.[179] The next sections review the requirements of Article 9(3) of the Rome I Regulation before examining whether this is a desirable approach.

to those of 'mandatory rules' in civil law had been referred to as public policy. Likewise, US laws and precedents did not use the term 'overriding mandatory rules', used public policy to restrict party autonomy, and applied the public policy of the forum or the objective governing law. That is because most states have introduced ss 90 and 187 of the Restatement (Second) on Conflict of Laws. Daniel Girsburger, Thomas Kadner Graziano and Jan Neels, 'General Compartive Report' in Daniel Girsburger, Thomas Kadner Graziano and Jan Neels (eds), *Choice of Law in International Commercial Contracts* (Oxford University Press, 2021) para 1.458.

[175] See ch 3, II, D, (4).

[176] A similar explanation can be given about how the public policy of the country to which the objective governing law belongs should be considered under KAPIL. Under KAPIL, it is not commonplace to consider the public policy of the country to which the objective governing law belongs, rather than that of the forum. However, the public policy of the country to which the objective governing law belongs could be indirectly considered by (1) applying the overriding mandatory rules of the country to which the objective governing law belongs, if such protect the principles of the fundamental legal system of that country and overlaps with its public policy and (2) applying Korean public policy when the public policy of the country to which the objective governing law belongs is identical to Korean public policy.

[177] Dickinson (n 76) 74.

[178] For details of the Rome I Regulation drafting process and the stance taken by the UK, see Gralf-Peter Calliess (ed), *Rome Regulations: Commentary*, 2nd edn (Kluwer Law International, 2015) 25; Michael Hellner, 'Third Country Overriding Mandatory Rules in the Rome I Regulation: Old Wine in New Bottles?' (2009) 5 *Journal of Private International Law* 447, 451–54; MOJ, 'Rome I – Should the UK Opt In?' Consultation Paper (2008) 32, accessible at data.parliament.uk/DepositedPapers/Files/DEP2009-0185/DEP2009-0185.pdf.

[179] Martiny (n 133) Rom I-VO, Art 9, Rn 6; Briggs (n 76) paras 7.251, 7.305. In this regard, English law welcomed Art 9(3) of the Rome I Regulation. ibid, 7.306.

i. Requirements

In order for the overriding mandatory rules of a third country to be given effect in accordance with Article 9(3) of the Rome I Regulation, (1) the regulations of the third country must be included in the definition of the overriding mandatory rules in Article 9(1) of the Rome I Regulation,[180] (2) the provision must be an overriding mandatory rule of the 'place where the contract is to be performed or where it was performed'[181] and (3) there must be overriding mandatory rules that render the 'performance of the contract unlawful'.[182,183] It is clear that they correspond to laws prohibiting smuggling/bribery, export/import controls and criminal law.[184] Provisions that render a contract void in whole or in part and provisions that alter contractual obligations, such as price controls and rules about minimum wages or maximum hours of work, are categorised as provisions rendering the performance of a contract unlawful.[185,186] However, provisions concerning only the method of contracting or the method of performance[187] would not render a contract unlawful, so

[180] See ch 3, I, C.

[181] There are conflicting theories about the meaning of the place of performance, including the following. Some commentators view it as where the performance has taken place in effect or will take place (Calliess (n 178) 257; Martiny (n 133) Rom I-VO, Rn 118, 126; Martiny (n 6) EGBGB Art 34, Rn 141). Others contend that it is the place of performance set out in the contract (Collins (n 52) vol 2, para 32-096; *Lemenda Trading Co Ltd v African Middle East Petroleum Co Ltd* (1988) QB 448, 455–56; *Tamil Nadu Electricity Board v ST-CMS Electric Co Private Ltd* (2008) 1 Lloyd's Rep 93, 104). There is also a view that it also includes the place of legal performance if the contract is yet to be performed. This author finds the last view most persuasive, following the interpretation of Art 5(1)(b) of the COUNCIL REGULATION (EC) No 44/2001 of 22 December 2000 on jurisdiction and the recognition and enforcement of judgments in civil and commercial matters (hereinafter 'the Brussels I Regulation') on the grounds that the language on defining the place of performance under Art 5(1)(b) ('the place … where the goods were delivered or should have been delivered, the place … where the services were provided or should have been provided') is similar to the wording concerning the place of performance under the Rome I Regulation. Under the Brussels I Regulation, there was a conflict between the view that the plaintiff can choose between the de facto place of performance and the place of performance under the contract, and the view that the place of performance is either where the contract was in fact performed or where it would have been performed under the contract (in the event that it has not been performed); the latter is the majority view. Hauser (n 4) 84.

[182] Hauser (n 4) 71ff explains that the legislators of the Rome I Regulation intentionally distinguished between 'unlawful' and 'illegal' and adopt a broader concept of 'unlawful' and that the 'illegality' of English law only means provisions prohibiting performance and does not include provisions that partially invalidate performance, such as a provision restricting interest rates (*Mount Albert Borough Council v Australian Temperance and General Mutual Life Insurance Society* (1938) AC 224). Hellner (n 178) 461–62 purports the same. However, the use of the concept or terms 'illegal' and 'unlawful' do not appear distinct in England in the context of the *lex loci solutionis* rule to be observed later in this book. Collins (n 52) vol 2, para 32-097. Hartley, 'Mandatory rules' (1997) 386–87 broadly interprets 'illegal' to include criminal law violations, torts and other breaches of contracts with third parties.

[183] Martiny (n 133) Rom I-VO, Art 9, Rn 118. As to the applicable law to determine the place of performance, a persuasive view is that the governing law of the contract should be followed based on Art 12(1) of the Rome I Regulation. On the other hand, see Hill and Chong (n 55) para 14.3.13 for the view that the place of performance should be determined in accordance with the forum law. See Martiny (n 133) Room I-VO, Art 9, Rn 118, for the view that if a contract has already been performed, the law of the country where the performance is actually performed should be followed, as with the interpretation under the Brussels I Regulation.

[184] Günther (n 4) 163.

[185] Hauser (n 4) 75; section by Renner in Calliess (n 178) 258; Günther (n 4) 163.

[186] See Michael Wilderspin, *The European Private International Law of Obligations*, 6th edn (Sweet & Maxwell, 2023) para 12-053 for the types of laws that English, French and German courts have found to be overriding mandatory rules.

[187] As an example of these regulations, there are regulations that impose an obligation to provide information before the execution of a contract. Hauser (n 4) 78. Hellner (n 178) 462 takes the view that when 'unlawful' is defined broadly, there would be no overriding mandatory rule that does not render implementation unlawful and that in effect, Art 9(3) of the Rome I Regulation does not differ significantly from Art 7(1) of the Rome Convention.

they will not fall under the definition set out in Article 9(1).[188] Where there are several obligations to perform, the place of performance is determined on the basis of the obligation being disputed.[189]

If the above requirements are met, the judge may give effect to the overriding mandatory rules of the place of performance. The second sentence of Article 9(3) of the Rome I Regulation, like the second sentence of Article 7(1) of the Rome Convention, stipulates that the nature and purpose of the rule, and the consequences of its application or non-application, should be taken into account at this stage. The meaning of such has been discussed in greater detail than the discussions made under the Rome Convention.

The second sentence of Article 9(3) of the Rome I Regulation is interpreted to instruct the judge to weigh the relevant interests after exploring why the provisions in question were enacted, in light of the legal and societal structures of the country where it was enacted, and having identified the type of the regulation.[190,191] Taking into account the 'purpose' of the regulation is for the judge to examine the legislative intent and the interests of the government.[192] The meaning of 'nature' under Article 9(3) is unclear. Recognising the uncertainty and broadness of the term 'nature', some commentators assert that if the enacting country distinguishes public and private law, the judge may consider whether the regulation is public or private.[193] Consideration of 'the consequences of application or non-application' is to contemplate whether the consequences of applying third-country law are consistent with the outcome of applying the applicable law, whether it contributes to unifying and harmonising international decisions and whether it can protect the legitimate expectations of the parties.[194]

Various views have been presented on the specific means of weighing interests.[195] One is that the provision in question should protect internationally recognised values, but since the scope of 'internationally recognised values' would be too narrow, interests of third countries may not be fully considered. Meanwhile, others believe that the second sentence of Article 9(3) stipulates an evaluation of the equivalence (*Äquivalenzprüfung*) of the forum law, applicable law and third country's provision and that if the three provide the same level of protection, only the provisions of the applicable law will apply. However, there is persuasive criticism[196] that it is difficult to find a basis to prioritise the applicable law in the Rome I Regulation. Moreover, adopting that view requires the constant comparison of at least three laws, causing a heavy burden in practice. This approach poses another problem in that, if the governing law, forum law and *lex loci solutionis* provide different types of protective measures, assessing the degree of protection may not be easy.

[188] Hauser (n 4) 78 purports the same.
[189] Section by Renner in Calliess (n 178) 258.
[190] Hauser (n 4) 117.
[191] Section by Renner in Calliess (n 178) 258; section by Andrea Bonomi in Ulrich Magnus and Peter Mankowski (eds), *Commentary: Rome I Regulation*, European Commentaries on Private International Law, vol 2 (Verlag Dr Otto Schmidt, 2017) Art 9(174).
[192] Section by Renner in Calliess (n 178) Art 9(29).
[193] Bonomi (n 191) Art 9(173).
[194] Section by Renner in Calliess (n 178) Art 9, para 29; Bonomi (n 191) Art 9(178).
[195] For an introduction of various views, see Hauser (n 4) 118–22.
[196] ibid 121.

It is suggested that the overriding mandatory rules of third countries can be applied as long as the interests protected by them are consistent with or at least not contrary to the interests of the forum state.[197] According to this view, the overriding mandatory rules of third countries are not rendered inapplicable by their mere non-compliance with *lex fori*. They are excluded from application only when they cause 'outrage' to some extent.[198] Examples of non-applicable provisions include rules that may cause economic and social impediments to the forum state or rules that discriminate against other countries or harm other countries.[199] However, even according to this view, consideration is likely if there is a provision in the forum corresponding to the overriding mandatory rule of the third country in question, or if the interests that the rule seeks to protect are consistent with the interests of the forum state.[200] Where the interests protected by the overriding mandatory rules of third countries are in accordance with internationally recognised standards, the rules are more likely to be considered.[201]

ii. Effect

Article 9(3) of the Rome I Regulation stipulates that, as in Article 7(1) of the Rome Convention, the overriding mandatory rules of third countries can be 'given effect'. In a narrow sense, the giving of effect can be understood as the direct application of the third-country law (*Anwendung*), and in a broad sense, it can be understood as consideration under the substantive governing law (*Berücksichtigung*, taking into account).[202] The discussion at the time of the enactment of the Rome I Regulation alone does not clarify whether the European legislators intended direct or indirect application with the wording 'giving of effect', but it does not exclude the possibility of direct application of the overriding mandatory rules of third countries as law.[203] Accordingly, as under the Rome Convention, opinions are divided as to whether the overriding mandatory rules of a third country should be applied directly or indirectly or whether both would be possible.

The view that overriding mandatory rules from the law of third countries should be applied directly (Theory 1) asserts that overriding mandatory rules that meet the requirements of Article 9(3) of the Rome I Regulation should be given direct effect.[204] Where the law of a third country is applied directly, those provisions only apply to matters regulated by the overriding mandatory rules of the foreign country, and the governing law of the contract applies to other matters.[205] On the other hand, the view that overriding mandatory rules under third-country law should be applied indirectly (Theory 2)[206] holds that foreign law

[197] Günther (n 4) 168. Martiny (n 6), EGBGB Art 34, Rn 159, 160; Martiny (n 133) Rom I-VO, Art 9 Rn 142, 143.
[198] Martiny (n 6) EGBGB Art 34, Rn 160; Martiny (n 133) Rom I-VO, Art 9, Rn 143.
[199] ibid.
[200] ibid Rn 121, 143.
[201] The value to be protected by the prohibition of slavery or treaties joined by many countries can be cited as examples.
[202] Martiny (n 133) Rom I-VO, Art 9, Rn 52. See ch 6, II, A for the relationship between direct and indirect application and considerations related to conflict of laws and substantive law.
[203] Section by Renner in Calliess (n 178) Art 9(30).
[204] Hauser (n 4) 109, 111; Günther (n 4) 170.
[205] Bonomi (n 191) para 181.
[206] This is the position taken by the German and English courts before the Rome I Regulation. See ch 5, II for the substantive-law approach including such a position.

can be considered as facts under the applicable substantive law. Under this view, unless there are special provisions in the Rome I Regulation, the contract is governed only by the applicable law, and the effect of considering the overriding mandatory rules of third countries is also determined by the applicable law of the contract. For example, a norm prohibiting certain acts in the place of performance may be considered based on the infringement of good morals, impossibility, or *force majeure* under the applicable substantive law.[207] It is also argued under this view that being 'given effect' is weaker than 'application'. The discretion recognised for the giving of effect can be exercised differently in each Member State,[208] and the judge does not necessarily have to follow the effect under the overriding mandatory rules of a foreign country, but can change or recognise the effect, depending on the case (Theory 3).[209]

However, the prevailing view under the Rome I Regulation is that the courts of Member States can choose either direct or indirect application (Theory 4), which this author finds persuasive.[210] It is believed that such a broad term, which allows both direct and indirect application, was used in the Rome I Regulation not with the intent of supporting any one of the aforementioned three theories, but rather to allow the national laws or the courts of Member Sates to determine the scope and conditions for considering or applying the overriding mandatory rules of a third country and the specific means of consideration and application. Considering the heated debate among the states during the drafting of Article 9(3) of the Rome I Regulation, Article 9(3) of the Regulation can be seen as having legislated[211] the 'minimum consensus' of the Member States. Accordingly, it is natural to see that the 'giving effect' under the Rome I Regulation was made to follow the practice of domestic law and the courts of the member states, without specifying the means of application.

The position taken by the European Court of Justice is also the same. The European Court of Justice ruled in *Nikifordis*[212] that the overriding mandatory rules of a third country that do not meet the requirements of Article 9(3) of the Rome I Regulation cannot be applied directly or indirectly as legal rules,[213] clarifying that both direct and indirect applications are possible under the Rome I Regulation.

iii. Evaluation

The results of comparing and evaluating the Rome I Regulation with other legislation can be summarised as follows.

Compared to the Rome Convention, the Hague Agency Convention and the Hague Trust Convention, the application and consideration conditions for third-country overriding

[207] BGH VIII ZR 254/82, NJW 1984, 1746.

[208] Martiny (n 133) Rom I-VO, Art 9, Rn 120.

[209] Hauser (n 4) 110; Martiny (n 133) Rom I-VO, Art 9, Rn 52; section by Martin Zwickel in Dieter Martiny (ed), *Internationales Vertragsrecht*, 9th edn (Ottoschmidt, 2022) Rn 5.137.

[210] Bonomi (n 191) para 180 explains that this view is predominant, but does not specify the supporters.

[211] Hauser (n 4) 113.

[212] *Republik Griechenland v Grigorios Nikiforidis* judgment of the court (Grand Chamber) of 18 October 2016 C-135/15 ECLI:EU:C:2016:774. In this decision, the treatment of overriding mandatory rules of third countries that fail to meet the requirements of Art 9(3) of the Rome I Regulation was questioned. This is discussed in ch 6.

[213] *Nikiforidis* (ibid) [50].

mandatory rules in the Rome I Regulation limit the third-country overriding mandatory rules' scope to the place of performance, as opposed to closely connected countries. Some commentators welcome the incorporation of their *lex loci solutionis* rule in the Rome I Regulation and believe that predictability has improved.[214] However, other commentators criticise that limiting the scope of the law of a third country to the place of performance is too narrow, and that the overriding mandatory rules of countries closely connected to the case should also be applied.[215] In support of that criticism, I present the following additional justifications.

First, the conflicting evaluation of the Rome I Regulation can ultimately be seen as a disagreement about how to balance the conflicting interests of parties, the interests of third countries, the interests of the forum state and the interests of international harmony in decisions. Article 9(3) of the Rome I Regulation has increased legal certainty and predictability by limiting the scope of third countries to the place of performance, and it can guarantee the interests of the parties better than the Rome Convention does.[216] On the other hand, the Rome I Regulation resulted in greater disregard of the interests of third countries. Whether this attitude is desirable should be approached from the perspective of whether it is necessary to respect the interests of a third country which may not necessarily be the place of performance, or in other words, whether disregarding the interests of a third country that is not the place of performance can be justified. However, third countries may have strong regulatory interests that it may be necessary to respect. The country of origin of the cultural heritage illegally expatriated or the country with a market affected by an unfair cartel are possible examples.

This is also apparent in how English law, being the origin of the *lex loci solutionis* rule, has respected the regulatory interests of a state that is not the place of performance, on the ground of the public policy-comity rule. The connections shown between the unlawful acts to a third country that is not the place of performance, such as the importation of prohibited goods to that third country (*Foster v Driscoll*[217]) or the exportation of prohibited goods from the third country (*Regazzoni v KC Sethia*[218]) was considered under the public policy-comity rule. These can be covered under 'close connection'. Therefore, it is difficult to find a persuasive reason why a 'third country' should be limited to the place of performance under

[214] MOJ (n 178) 32. Commentators in the UK also approve of the fact that the ambiguity about whether the *lex loci solutionis* rule is a substantive-law approach or a conflict of laws approach was resolved by Art 9(3) of the Rome I Regulation.

[215] Günther (n 4) 172–73; Hauser (n 4) 130. Hauser proposes that not only the place of performance but also the countries affected by the performance should be included.

[216] On the other hand, Hellner (n 178) 354–470 broadly interprets the meaning of the unlawful under the Rome I Regulation and states that if 'obligations arising from contracts' include not only contractual obligations but also obligations related to contracts, the difference between Art 7(1) of the Rome Convention and Art 9(3) of the Rome I Regulation becomes insignificant and rather creates uncertainty because of the failure to define how overriding mandatory rules that do not fall within the scope of Art 9(3) should be treated. Although this author considers it less desirable to limit the scope of a third country's law, the rules of which are subject to application or consideration, to the place of performance, this author is not convinced that the text of Art 9(3) of the Rome I Regulations can be interpreted as broadly as Hellner does. There are insufficient grounds to interpret 'obligations arising from contracts' broadly, considering the process of drafting Art 9(3) of the Rome I Regulation and the UK's *lex loci solutionis* rule, which is the basis thereof.

[217] (1928) All ER Rep 130.

[218] (1958) AC 301 (HL).

the Rome I Regulation, when even English law, which was the model of Article 9(3) of the Rome I Regulation, had a principle under which the overriding mandatory rules of countries other than the place of performance can be considered.

Second, limiting the scope of the third country to the place of performance has another shortcoming. There may be cases where it is difficult to determine the place of performance. In particular, in international financial transactions where payments and transfers are made between different countries, it may be challenging to determine the place of performance. This can be seen in *Libyan Arab Foreign Bank*,[219] where the English *lex loci solutionis* rule was applied. There may also be situations where there is no particular connection between the case and the place of performance. This issue is also raised in the context of foreign exchange regulations.[220]

Therefore, the scope of the overriding mandatory rules of a third country should be determined based on a close connection to the case, rather than where the performance takes place. In this regard, there may be criticism that the concept of close connection is ambiguous, causing legal uncertainty.[221] However, the concept of close connection is established in the Rome Convention and Rome I Regulation, as well as KAPIL. The concept cannot be reasonably called ambiguous because it has already been sufficiently discussed and ample examples have accumulated in domestic and foreign theories and precedents.[222]

As for the criteria for the exercise of discretion in the second sentence of Article 9(3) of the Rome I Regulation, compared to the Swiss FAPIL, it is still unclear what 'their nature and purpose and the consequences of their application or non-application' means and how such factors should be considered when discretion is being exercised. It is regrettable that the wording in Article 9(3) did not present specific guidance for the exercise of discretion and failed to distinguish between content control and result control on the overriding mandatory rules of third countries.

In short, four observations can be made regarding relevant interests. First, Article 9(3) of the Rome I Regulation is in line with the interests of the parties in that it specifies the conditions for considering or applying the overriding mandatory rules of third countries based on a conflict-of-laws approach. Second, although it is possible to examine whether the law of a third country conforms to the legal system of the forum at the stages of exercising the judge's discretion on considering or applying those rules, that is less desirable in consideration of the interests of the forum state, as the criteria for evaluation are not clearly identified in the wording of Article 9(3). Third, limiting the scope of third countries to the place of performance does not adequately reflect the interests of third countries.

[219] (1989) QB 728.

[220] Proctor (n 85) para 4.20.

[221] This is the reason why the UK and Germany reserved Art 7(1) of the Rome Convention.

[222] Richard Plender, *The European Contracts Convention: The Rome Convention on the Choice of Law for Contracts* (Sweet & Maxwell, 1991) para 9.08 also points out that the criticism that Art 7(1) of the Rome Convention causes uncertainty is unreasonable because the connecting point for assessing close connection is clear. Kyung Han Sohn, 'Recent Case Law Developments in Governing Law of Contractual Obligation in Korea' (2016) 22 *Korea Private International Law Journal* 103, 104 evaluates the principle of the closest connection as one of the two major principles of private international law, along with the principle of party autonomy. For an analysis of Korean precedents on close connection, see ibid 114. Recently, in arbitration, it has been argued that the closest connection test should be applied uniformly as a principle to determine the governing law of the merits of the dispute. Benjamin Hayward, *Conflict of Laws and Arbitral Discretion: The Closest Test* (Oxford University Press, 2017) paras 7.05–7.07.

Fourth, Article 9(3) falls short of reflecting the interests of international harmony in decisions. Under Article 9(3), the forum country will not consider or apply a third country's overriding mandatory rules unless the enacting country is the place of performance, but the court of the third country will apply such rules. That may cause inconsistent decisions across jurisdictions.

IV. Conclusion

The results of the above review may be summarised as follows. First, the conflict-of-laws approach is better than the substantive-law approach. The substantive-law approach fails to clearly define the conditions for considering or applying the overriding mandatory rules of a third country and does not serve the interests of the parties in terms of the predictability of applicable law. In addition, the applicability of a third country's overriding mandatory rules may depend on the facts of the case and the contents of the general provisions set out in the applicable substantive law of the contract. This may cause inconsistent decisions in different jurisdictions which may go contrary to the interests of the third country and international harmony in decisions. Furthermore, if the applicable law is foreign, the interests of the forum state cannot be properly reflected, evaluating whether the content and consequences of the application of third-country law conform to the legal system of the forum state will be even more difficult.

On the other hand, the conflict-of-laws approach based on the Special Connection Theory can resolve such issues with the substantive-law approach. The conflict-of-laws approach is in the best interests of the parties, as it clearly stipulates the conditions for considering or applying third-country laws. In addition, the interests of third countries can be better reflected because third-country laws closely connected to the case are applied or considered. It also serves the interests of international harmony in decisions because third-country laws would be considered or applied under consistent conditions across jurisdictions. In addition, in considering or applying third-country law, it is possible to examine whether there are protect-worthy values from the point of view of the forum; that approach therefore serves the interests of the forum state.

Second, when applying or considering the overriding mandatory rules of a third country, it is better to examine first whether the contents of the third-country law conform to the legal system of the forum, followed by an evaluation of whether the specific consequences of its application would also be in line with the legal system of the forum. In addition, the elements to be considered in content and result control should be clearly defined. At the stage of content control, it is not appropriate to consider the nature of the third country's law and oppressive circumstances arising for the parties from the application of the third country's law (the latter should be considered at the result control stage). Furthermore, is not helpful to consider the purpose of the third country's law at the stage of result control, as this has already been considered for content control.

Based on the results of the comparative legal research conducted so far, chapter six discusses the theories of interpretation (*de lege lata*) and future legislation (*de lege ferenda*) of KAPIL on the consideration or application of the overriding mandatory rules of third countries.

6

The Korean Act on Private International Law and Overriding Mandatory Rules of Third Countries

I. Pros/Cons of the Consideration or Application of the Overriding Mandatory Rules of Third Countries

The Korean Act on Private International Law (KAPIL) does not contain any provisions on the overriding mandatory rules of third countries. Furthermore, unlike Germany or England, it is difficult to find discussion in Korean academia on the consideration of overriding mandatory rules of third countries from a substantive law perspective. However, that does not mean that the consideration or application of the overriding mandatory rules of third countries is prohibited under KAPIL.[1] The reason there is no provision about such rules in KAPIL[2] is the present lack of an internationally established view on the handling of the overriding mandatory rules of third countries. This is an intentional legislative vacuum that seeks to leave the decision to academic theories and case law.

As discussed in chapter five, there have been lengthy debates[3] as to whether the overriding mandatory rules of third countries should be considered or applied. Those who are against the consideration or application of the overriding mandatory rules of third countries cite reasons including the undue restriction on party autonomy, undermined legal certainty and uniformity of judgment, decreased efficiency of litigation proceedings and increased costs. However, the arguments put forward by critics are not convincing. Party autonomy is limited by the existence of mandatory rules themselves, not by the consideration or application of overriding mandatory rules of third countries.[4] The application of overriding mandatory rules of third countries under consistent requirements only contributes to

[1] In-ho Kim, 'Limitations by Mandatory Rules on the Dominance of Party Autonomy in International Contracts' (2012) 60 *Advanced Commercial Law Review* 110, 133.

[2] Kwang Hyun Suk, *Annotation to Private International Law* [Gukjesabeop haeseol] (Pakyoungsa, 2013) 148; Choon Soo An, 'International zwingende Bestimmungen im IPR – Theorien und die Bedeutung von Artt. 6, 7 IPR Koreas' (2011) 23 *Kookmin Law Review* 189, 194.

[3] See, inter alia, a mixed evaluation of the Rome Convention. See ch 5, III, B, iii.

[4] The English and German courts before the Rome I Regulation, adopted the substantive law approach which considered the overriding mandatory rules of third countries based on the applicable substantive law of contracts. Even if a contract is to be governed solely by the applicable substantive law, third-country laws may impose restrictions on party autonomy. For the stance taken by the English and German courts before the Rome I Regulation, see ch 5, II, B, and C.

greater legal certainty and uniformity in judgments. Procedural delays and inefficiencies arising from the consideration of foreign laws do not arise from 'considering or applying the overriding mandatory rules of third countries' itself, but as a general rule in all cases that apply foreign law, which invalidates such an assertion.

The above debate can be raised in relation to the interpretive methodologies of KAPIL. As examined in chapter five, the *lex causae* rule, Theory of Power, and the Territoriality Principle asserted in Germany, and the English and German case law before the Rome I Regulation are similar in that they consider the overriding mandatory rules of third countries at the substantive law level. There was only a difference in what concepts and requirements were employed, such as good morals (*Sittenwidrigkeit*),[5] impossibility or public policy.

Therefore, the overriding mandatory rules of a third country can be considered or applied under KAPIL. This chapter examines feasible methodologies and demonstrates that, for the interpretation of KAPIL, the conflict-of-laws approach is indeed better than the substantive law approach. Thereafter, based on the comparative legal analysis in chapter five, as an interpretive methodology of KAPIL, the chapter will present the criteria of content and result control and factors to be considered for balancing the interests of the parties, forum state, and third countries. It will then propose draft legislation.

II. Handling the Overriding Mandatory Rules of Third Countries

A. Feasible Methodologies: Substantive Law Approach, Direct Application and Indirect Application

As seen in chapter five, the positions taken by international instruments, the legislative examples and precedents of each country can be divided into two categories. The conflict-of-laws approach[6] applies or considers the overriding mandatory rules of third countries under conditions set out in private international law (the Rome Convention, Rome I Regulation, Hague Agency Convention, Hague Trust Convention, and Swiss Federal Act on Private International Law). The substantive law approach considers the overriding mandatory rules as facts, following the general provision of the applicable substantive law of the contract (German and English courts before the Rome I Regulation, (A) in Table 6.1 below, hereinafter referred to as (A)).

The conflict-of-laws approach may be further divided into the direct application ((B) in Table 6.1 below, hereinafter referred to as (B)); consideration of the rules as facts, provided that the rules meet the consideration or application conditions stipulated in private international law ((C) in Table 6.1 below, hereinafter referred to as (C)); and other means of consideration ((D) in Table 6.1 below, hereinafter referred to as (D)).

[5] See ch 5, II, B, i.

[6] This refers to the conditions for application based on the conflict-of-laws approach for the overriding mandatory rules to be of a country that demonstrates a close connection to the case, as under the Special Connection Theory, and for the rules to be consistent with the legal system of the forum.

The former ((B)) can be referred to as 'direct application', and the latter two ((C), (D)) as 'indirect application'.[7,8]

The Rome Convention and the Rome I Regulation do not stipulate that the overriding mandatory rules of third countries are directly applied, but provide that they 'may be given effect'. As examined above,[9] it is clear that this is not limited to direct application ((B)). Article 19(1) of Swiss Federal Act on Private International Law (FAPIL) provides that the rules 'may be taken into account'; while this stipulates a conflict-of-laws requirement, it provides how a third-country law may be directly applied ((B)) or considered as facts under the applicable substantive law if the third-country law meets the conflict-of-laws requirement ((C)).[10] As in Article 19(2) of FAPIL, the judge may recognise and alter the consequences of third-country law application ((D)). Among other conflict-of-laws approaches, (C) differs from the substantive law approach, which only gives consideration under substantive law conditions without first requiring the fulfilment of conflict-of-laws conditions ((A)), since (C) considers under substantive law the overriding mandatory rules of third countries that do meet the consideration or application conditions under private international law. The practical benefit of distinguishing between (A) and (C) is that (A) is the methodology of interpretation under the applicable substantive law and cannot stipulate in a written format the conditions for consideration under private international law,[11] while (C), as a conflict-of-laws principle, can expressly provide such conditions for consideration or application. This is a significant difference in terms of predictability for the parties to international contracts. Although direct application ((B)) and indirect application ((C), (D))

[7] The term 'indirect application' is not established universally. The European Court of Justice's *Nikiforidis* ruling merely contrasts direct application (or taking into account directly) with indirect consideration (having indirect regard, taking into account indirectly, taking into account as a matter of fact) and did not use the words 'indirect application'. However, 'apply indirectly as a legal rule' in [50] of the *Nifkiforidis* ruling may be seen to refer to indirect application. Gralf-Peter Calliess (ed), *Rome Regulations: Commentary*, 2nd edn (Kluwer Law International, 2015) para 32; Phil-Bok Lee, 'International Transaction of Cultural Heritage and Overriding Mandatory Provisions – Focused on the Overriding Mandatory Provisions of *Lex Originis*' (2021) 27 *Korea Private International Law Journal* 119, 149–50 refers to 'indirect application' as the consideration, through conflict of laws channels, of the effect or the consequences in substantive law.

[8] Marc-Philippe Weller, 'Vom Staat zum Menschen: Die Methodentrias des Internationalen Privatrechts unserer Zeit' (2017) 81 *Rabels Zeischrift für ausländisches und internationales Privatrecht* 747, 774–78 argues that, since conflicts-of-law selection of governing law in private international law is limited to one legal order, consideration of foreign law (*Berücksichtigung*) should be treated as an important method, along with the recognition of foreign law. Weller, as an example of 'consideration', refers to Art 9(3) of the Rome I Regulation and the Theory of Fact or the *lex causae* rule, *Datumtheorie*. See ch 5, II, A. Weller explains that 'consideration' only treats foreign law as the facts that specify the required facts under applicable substantive law or local data and introduces the French case related to Daimler AG's insider trading as a specific example. This explanation appears similar to (C). See ibid 778–79 for more details. Although not about contracts, Art 17 of the Rome II Regulation requires consideration of the rules on safety and conduct that were in force at the time of the occurrence of the event for which liability is being considered. This is thought to reflect the *Datumtheorie*. Kwang Hyun Suk, 'The Application of Foreign Exchange Control Law and Other Internationally Mandatory Rules of Third Countries in International Financial Transactions: Including Article VIII2(b) of the Articles of Agreement of the International Monetary Fund' (2020) 26 *Korea Private International Law Journal* 353, 355, fn 3.

[9] See ch 5, III, B and E.

[10] The Federal Supreme Court of Switzerland contemplated the Indian Antiquities and Art Treasures Act from both conflicts-of-law and substantive law approaches.

[11] The *lex loci solutionis* rule, under which English courts considered overriding mandatory rules of third countries before the Rome I Regulation, has been evaluated as a principle under English contract laws by the majority theory of the UK. The principle announced in the German court's Nigerian cultural property ruling was also an interpretation of whether the good morals of the German Civil Code had been infringed. This was described as a methodology of interpreting substantive law, so it cannot be expressly written in law. See ch 5, II, B and C.

can both stipulate written conditions in private international law, they take different positions as to how to recognise the consequences of applying the overriding mandatory rules of third countries.

The direct application ((B)) of the overriding mandatory rules of a third country is the application of such laws in the way that the governing law or the overriding mandatory rules of the forum would be applied, as law. With respect to the matters regulated by the third-country law, the effect of their application is recognised under the third-country law,[12] such as damage claims and contract nullification. With respect to matters not regulated by the law of the third country, the applicable law of the relevant legal relationship applies.[13] For example, in a case where a Korean lender executed an agreement to lend money to a borrower in a third country that is not a member of the Articles of Agreement of the International Monetary Fund (IMF Agreement) and agreed to have English law as the governing law, if the foreign exchange regulation law of the third country provides that international financial contracts without foreign exchange approval are void, the contract becomes null and void if a Korean judge, in determining the validity of the loan agreement, applies directly the foreign exchange regulation laws of the third country. However, follow-up issues arising from the nullification of a contract, such as the return of unjust enrichment, are to be tackled in accordance with the law applicable to that unjust enrichment.

Here, it is possible to hypothesise two cases: first, where the provisions of a third country stipulate the legal effect; and second, where they do not. The first category involves situations where the provisions of a third country stipulate explicitly the effect on legal relationships under private law as the consequences of their application. For example, when third-country law recognises as an overriding mandatory rule that men and women have the right to claim the same wages for the same work, if the law of the third country is applied using the conflict-of-laws approach at the forum, the right to claim those wages will be recognised in the case. For another example, if the law of a third country prohibits the export of goods of which that country is the origin and provides that sales contracts violating the prohibition are invalid, a judge of the court applying the same based on the conflict-of-laws approach will find those sales contracts invalid.

However, if the law of a third country recognises any other effect that is not known to the governing law of the contract, the issue can be tackled in accordance with the legal principle of 'adaptation'[14] under private international law. For example, if the law of a third

[12] This is the dominant position in Germany of those who adopt the Special Connection Theory. Section by Ulrich Magnus in Julius von Staudinger and Norbert Habermann, *Staudingers Kommentar Zum Bürgerlichen Gesetzbuch Mit Einführungsgesetz Und Nebengesetzen: Einführungsgesetz zum Bürgerlichen Gesetzbuche/IPR* (Sellier-De Gruyter, 2002) EGBGB Art 34, Rn 145; section by Dieter Martiny in Franz Jürgen Säcker (ed), *Münchener Kommentar zum BGB*, 8th edn (Verlag Beck München, 2021) Rom I-VO Art 9 Rn 123; section by Frank Vischer and Corrinne Widmer Lüchinger in Markus Müller-Chen (ed), *Zürcher Kommentar zum IPRG*, Bd I-1, 3rd edn (Schulthess, 2018) Art 19, Rn 49.

[13] Junhyok Jang, 'Internationally Mandatory Rules – A Comparative Study of Article 7 of the Rome Convention, Articles 18 and 19 of the Swiss Private International Law, and Article 7 of the Korean Private International Law' (2007) 75 *International Trade Law* 87; the same problem arises when applying the overriding mandatory rules of the forum. In that context, see ch 2, III, A, ii.

[14] When multiple laws are applied to a case, such as when overriding mandatory rules of a third country are applied, there may be deficiencies or overlaps in norms due to differences in the legal system or the content of such laws, and the means of resolving this issue is 'adaptation'. Choon-Soo An, *Private International Law* (Bobmunsa, 2017) 167; Heung Sub Choi, *Korean Private International Law I* (Korean Studies Information, 2019) 186. Kerstin Ann-Susann Schäfer, *Application of Mandatory Rules in the Private International Law of Contracts*

country does not stipulate that a contract is invalid with respect to the private legal effect of a contract that violates the provision and recognises an effect that is not known by its governing law, judges can change the effect of the application of the third-country law to a kind that is recognised by the governing law of the contract.

If a provision of a third country is silent as to the legal effect of its application – if, for example, a provision of the third country concerns a prohibition of a public law nature and does not expressly provide for its private law effect – a judge when applying it directly will determine the effect of the prohibition on the contract in accordance with the interpretation of the law of the third country.[15] Let us return to the example of the Korean lender who entered into an agreement to lend money to a borrower from a third country that is not a member of the IMF Agreement and agreed to have English law as the governing law. If the foreign exchange regulations of the third country does not directly provide for the effect under private law of an international financial agreement unapproved for foreign exchange, but if it is rendered as invalid under the interpretation of that country's law, the judge may determine that the loan agreement is invalid as a result of the direct application of the foreign exchange regulation laws of the third country.

Indirect application may be divided into the following two types on whether the satisfaction of substantive law conditions would be required in addition[16] to the conditions for consideration or application under conflicts of laws.[17] First, if the application of the overriding mandatory rules of a third country is covered by the general provisions of the applicable substantive law, the effect may be recognised in accordance with the general provisions ((C)). For example, there may be a case where a Korean lender entered into an agreement to lend money to a borrower from a third country that is not a member of the IMF Agreement and agreed to have English law as the governing law. If the foreign exchange regulation law of the third country prohibits an international financial agreement that has not been granted foreign exchange approval, then we must first look at whether the foreign exchange regulations of the third country meet the conditions for direct or indirect application under the

(Peter Lang, 2010) 334, fns 127 and 128 introduce a variety of literature on adaptation issues arising from the application of overriding mandatory rules of third countries.

[15] As explained in ch 2, III, B, ii, the interests of private international law are not in sanctions under public law upon the application of foreign laws with a public law nature, but rather are in the effect of such provisions on private law relationships (the reflexive effect). However, when the overriding mandatory rules of a third-country concern prohibitions with a public law nature and only stipulate public law sanctions as the effect of their direct application, without clearly stipulating the private law effect of a legal act that violates the provisions, it may be questionable whether it is meaningful from the perspective of private international law to 'directly apply' the rules. Even in such a case, however, it is still possible and meaningful to directly apply the rules because of the 'reflexive effect', which is recognised as an effect of directly applying such provisions. In other words, there are practical benefits in discussing the impact of a rule on private law relationships only after it is applied directly. If the overriding mandatory rules of a third country do not apply directly, it will not be necessary to discuss the effect of the provisions on private law relationships.

[16] There is no reason to distinguish between direct application and indirect application in terms of the 'application conditions' on 'which the third country's overriding mandatory rules should be considered or applied'. However, there is a difference in terms of 'the effect of application', that is, 'the treatment', or whether it will be 'applied as law or considered otherwise'. However, there may be cases where direct application is more appropriate and cases where indirect application is more appropriate, which will be explained below.

[17] This is not an internationally recognised classification, but one used by the author based on the approaches of the Rome Convention, the Rome I Regulation and FAPIL.

conflicts-of-laws approach. That will lead to a review, for example, of whether the contract is invalid because of a violation of good morals or public policies of the applicable substantive law. The loan agreement will be null and void if the facts can be regarded to have been in violation of the public policy-comity rule of English law due to the intent of the borrower and the lender to violate the law. If this method is followed, the conditions are stricter than those of direct application. While direct application is allowed when the conditions for the application of overriding mandatory rules of third countries under the private international law of the forum are met, indirect application of this type can only be allowed when the conditions prescribed by the general provisions of the governing law of the contract are met, in addition to the conditions for direct application. In other words, this is a hurdle to considering the overriding mandatory rules of third countries, and consideration may depend on the general provisions under the applicable law and the established method of interpretation. In addition, if the law of a third country is considered under the general provisions of the applicable law, such as good morals, the degree of violation of the law by the parties may be an important condition, so whether or not the overriding mandatory rules of the third country are considered may depend on the degree of finding of indirect facts (hereinafter this type of indirect application is referred to as type (1) indirection application, (C)). This method can be useful when the law of a third country does not explicitly stipulate the private law effect on contracts or establish which private law effect is recognised by the interpretive methodology under the third-country law, or when there is not enough data for the judge of the forum to identify the interpretive methodology.

The second type of indirect application is when the law of a third country that meets the conflicts of law requirements, such as FAPIL, is not recognised in accordance with the applicable law of the contract, and the forum judge can change its effect ((D)). Using direct application ((B)) acknowledges, in principle, the effect determined by the overriding mandatory rules of a third country and recognises effects other than what was determined by the third-country law, only when there is a conflict or discrepancy between the third-country law and applicable substantive law. However, using (D), even if there is no conflict or discrepancy between the norms, a judge may recognise the specific validity of an effect different from that determined by the law of a third country.[18] In this regard, this appears similar to how a judge would adjust contractual terms by applying the doctrine of change in circumstances. Even if the third-country law stipulates the invalidity of the contract as its effect, under this indirect application, judges will be able to recognise other effects, such as cancellation of the contract or postponement of the implementation period.

For example, in a case where a Korean lender executed an agreement to lend money to a borrower from a third country that is not a member of the IMF Agreement and designated English law as the governing law of the contract, let us suppose that the foreign exchange control law of the third country provides that the loan agreement is null and void if the borrower fails to obtain foreign exchange approval. If the borrower did not obtain foreign exchange approval, the forum judge may decide that the time for implementation of the loan by the Korean lender has been postponed, so that the borrower can receive approval. The difference with the first type of indirect application is that this type does not have to follow the requirements and effects prescribed by the applicable substantive law as there are

[18] Even in this case, the legal principle of adaptation can be applied if there is a conflict or discrepancy between the norms of foreign law and the applicable substantive law.

no hurdles in terms of the general provisions of the applicable substantive law. Furthermore, although the requirements prescribed by third-country law would be applied, the effects need not be followed verbatim (hereinafter this type of indirect application is referred to as type (2) indirection application, (D)). Therefore, type (2) indirection application ((D)) can be seen as a compromise or a middle way between direct application ((B)) and type (1) indirect application ((C)). The differences in each methodology, including substantive-law approaches, are shown in Table 6.1 below.

Table 6.1 Substantive law approach, direct application and indirect application

	Substantive law approach	**Conflict-of-laws approach**		
Classification		**Direct application**	**Indirect application**[19]	
Methodology	Indirect consideration ((A))	Direct application ((B))	Type (1) indirect application ((C))	Type (2) indirect application ((D))
Conflicts of law application conditions	Not applicable	Must be met	Must be met	Must be met
Method of consideration and application	Third-country laws considered under applicable substantive law	Third-country laws applied directly as law	Third-country laws considered under applicable substantive law	Third-country laws considered under special substantive law developed by judges
Requirements defined under general provisions of applicable substantive law	Must be met	May not be met	Must be met	May not be met
Legal effect of application of third-country laws	Recognised under applicable substantive law	Recognised through expressly written provisions or interpretive methodologies of third-country laws. However, adaptation is used in case of conflicts or inconsistencies between the third country norms and the applicable substantive law.	Recognised under applicable substantive law	The application effect prescribed by third-country laws can be changed. Appropriate consequences are based on the specific case, just as judges apply the doctrine of changes in circumstances.

[19] For example, comparatively, the concept and term 'indirect application' was used to refer generally to type (1) indirect application. For instance, the term is used by those who assert that 'may be given effect' under the Rome Convention or the Rome I Regulation means that the rules can be considered under applicable substantive law. See ch 5, III, B and E. The European Court of Justice used the term 'indirect application' as a term contrary to direct application in *Nikiforidis*, but did not specify which of these two types of 'indirect use' it refers to. In my view, both types (1) and (2) of indirect application can fall under 'indirect application'.

With respect to the relationship between (A), (B), (C) and (D), if the substantive-law approach is taken, (B), (C) or (D) are not viable since they presuppose that requirements are established in conflicts of laws.

On the other hand, if a conflict-of-laws approach is taken, the relationship between (B), (C) and (D) and the relationship of (B), (C) (D) to (A) should be identified. First of all, with regard to (B), (C) and (D), it is a matter of policy for each country to decide whether to adopt one or more of (B), (C) and (D) while taking a conflict-of-laws approach. As seen above, Article 19 of FAPIL allows (B), (C) and (D). In addition, despite the dissensus on the 'giving of effect' between the Rome Convention and the Rome I Regulation, they can both be interpreted to allow each Member State to choose one or more of (B), (C) and (D).

All four methods of (A), (B), (C) and (D) presuppose a third-country provision that satisfies the conditions for direct or indirect application. Whether a provision that does not meet the conditions for the direct or indirect application of the overriding mandatory rules of third countries can be considered under the general provisions of the applicable substantive law of the contract[20] is examined in Section III, D, below.

For the interpretation of KAPIL, two major methodologies are that third-country overriding mandatory rules should be considered from the substantive-law approach[21] or the Special Connection Theory.[22,23] The following section will first examine under which specific provisions of Korean substantive law consideration can be made and then demonstrate why the conflict-of-laws approach is better.

B. Substantive Law Approach and its Limitations

If an international contract provides for how to deal with the effect of a third country's overriding mandatory rules, those overriding mandatory rules may be taken into account under such a clause in the contract. Examples of such clauses are the hardship clause and the sanctions clause, which takes into account economic sanctions in a third country.[24,25] The utility of such clauses cannot be disregarded as they allow the issues of consideration or

[20] This is the question of how to deal with the overriding mandatory rules of third countries that do not meet the application conditions under the conflict-of-laws approach in the first place. That is different from (C), which considers rules again from a substantive law perspective once the conflicts of law conditions are met.

[21] An (n 2) 208–09 argues, however, that the conflict-of-laws approach should be given priority and that the experience necessary to establish the application conditions must first be accumulated, taking into account the de facto effects of foreign mandatory rules based on a substantive-law approach.

[22] Yongjin Kim, 'External Effect of Mandatory Rules' (1998) 3 *Korea Private International Law Journal* 703, 718–19; Kyung Han Sohn, 'Recent Case Law Developments in Governing Law of Contractual Obligation in Korea' (2016) 22 *Korea Private International Law Journal* 103, 140; Lee (n 7) 153. However, Suk (n 8) 383 supports the Special Connection Theory, but opines that it is more practical at the moment to consider rules using a substantive-law approach.

[23] For other views supporting the Two-sided Conflict-of-rules Theory, see Changseon Shin and Namsoon Yoon, *New Private International Law* [Singukjesabeop je2pan], 2nd edn (Fides, 2016) 287.

[24] Such clauses define the economic sanctions of the United Nations, the EU or the US and provides that the contract will terminate if a particular country or person becomes subject to sanctions.

[25] The same applies to the so-called special risks clause, Office of Foreign Control clause and the Grain and Feed Trade Association (GAFTA) prohibition clause. See Vischer and Lüchinger (n 12) Art 19, Rn 40 for further details.

application of a third country's overriding mandatory rules to be tackled in the interpretation and application of a contract.

However, unless there is a special provision in the contract allowing the consideration of the effect of a third country's overriding mandatory rules, and presuming Korean law is the governing law, the overriding mandatory rules of a third country may be considered as the underlying facts of Article 103 (Juristic Acts Contrary to Social Order) or provisions under Article 390 (non-performance of obligation) and Article 537 (Burden to Bear Risk) of the Civil Act of Korea.[26] Unlike the German Civil Code, the Korean Civil Act does not have a provision on interference with the basis of transactions (Section 313 of the BGB).[27] However, since the Supreme Court of Korea has recently been rendering decisions[28] that recognise the doctrine of change in circumstances in non-continuing contracts, which it had not done previously, the overriding mandatory rules of third countries may be considered accordingly to the extent that the doctrine of change in circumstances is recognised.[29]

Let us look at how cases such as German rulings prior to the Rome I Regulation will be dealt with in Korean courts. As in the *Borax*[30] and *Borsäure*[31] rulings, if the parties intended to violate the overriding mandatory rules of a third country and acted fraudulently for this purpose, they may be in violation of Article 103 of the Civil Act. Although that Article is not about the violation of foreign laws, there is an example[32] of the Supreme Court of Korea declaring that a contract is invalid as a legal act against public policy based on the 'subjective malicious intent of a party who knew of the illegality'. If the governing law of a contract is Korean law, it should be reviewed whether the value that the foreign law seeks to protect can be included in the 'good customs and other public policy' of the Civil Act of Korea, as the case was in the *Borax* or *Borsäure* rulings, to review ultimately whether the intent to violate foreign law can be equated with the intent to violate domestic law.

However, if the applicable law of a contract is foreign law, it is necessary to examine whether the facts of the case meet the requirements of general provisions, such as good morals and other public policy violations, under the foreign substantive law. In that case, there is no room for the Civil Act of Korea to examine whether the foreign substantive law is worthy of protection. The only means to examine whether the foreign provisions should be protected is to rely on the public policy of Article 23 of KAPIL. However, as already emphasised, Article 23 does not examine the contents of foreign law, concerning itself with the consequences of applying foreign law on an exceptional and restrictive basis. That renders

[26] For specific cases, please refer to the solutions for Example 1 and Example 2 in accordance with the *lex causae* rule in ch 5, II, A.

[27] However, there are also provisions where the doctrine of change in circumstances is stipulated, such as Art 19 of the State Contracts Act.

[28] Supreme Court of Korea, Judgment of 29 March 2007, Case No 2004Da31302; Supreme Court of Korea, en banc Judgment of 26 September 2013, Case No 2012Da13637; Supreme Court of Korea, Judgment of 8 June 2017, Case No 2016Da249557; Supreme Court of Korea, Judgment of 10 December 2020, Case No. 2020Da25846, etc.

[29] For an analysis of the doctrine of change in circumstances revealed in recent precedents, see first Young Jun Lee, 'Änderung der Geschäftsgrundlage' (2018) 82 *Korean Journal of Civil Law* 3; Tuck-soo Song, 'How the Principle of Change in Circumstances Works in South Korea'[Sajeong byeonggyeongui wonchik <daehaminguke-seoui moseup>] (2018) 85 *Korean Journal of Civil Law* 569; Inyoung Cho, 'Shared Mistaken Motives as to the Future Event and the Change of Circumstances – A Study on the Supreme Court Decision 2020da254846' (2021) 96 *Korean Journal of Civil Law* 275.

[30] BGHZ 34, 169–79. See ch 5, II, B.

[31] NJW 1962, 1436–38. See ch 5, II, B.

[32] Supreme Court of Korea, Judgment of 13 December 1994, Case No 94Da31617.

Article 23 an inappropriate means of examining whether the purpose or contents of the overriding mandatory rules of a third country conform to the legal system of the forum.

Let us suppose that cases like the German court rulings on the Nigerian mask[33] or the prohibition of the receipt of bribes by government officials[34] are filed in the Korean court. In cases where the parties agree to a sales contract of a cultural heritage in violation of the cultural heritage protection laws of a third country (the country of origin), or in cases where parties agree to offer bribes to public officials of a third country in violation of that country's laws, these internationally shared values[35] can be seen as protected under the Civil Act of Korea, and therefore may be deemed to have been infringed upon. Thus, the contracts contested in cases such as the German court's Nigerian mask case or the anti-bribery ruling on government officials can be found to be contrary to good morals and public policies under the Korean Civil Act.

Let us suppose that a claim similar to that in the German court's ruling on the ban on trade with enemy countries[36] has been filed in the Korean courts. A seller located in Country A enters into a sales of goods contract with a buyer located in Korea, the governing law of the contract being Korean law. However, a war breaks out between Country A and Korea, and Country A enacts a law prohibiting trade with Korea. The buyer files a lawsuit with the Korean court seeking delivery of the goods against the seller. In such a case, the court could recognise impossibility, among other types of non-fulfilment of obligation under the Civil Act of Korea. With the seller's duty to deliver goods not prohibited under Korean law, but prohibited by the overriding mandatory rules of Country A, a third country, impossibility will be found if the existence of such a provision makes it impossible for the obligor to perform his/her obligations (similar situations would be when goods cannot be taken out of a country due to the failure to obtain export permission or when the specific goods to be sold are seized or confiscated), or if the obligor will be subject to severe sanctions for performing his/her obligations in violation of the law. If the obligor refuses to fulfil the obligation on the grounds of the existence of overriding mandatory rules in a third country, it will be possible to recognise the refusal or delay of performance under the Korean Civil Act. If there is no negligence from either party and the overriding mandatory rule of the third country prohibiting the performance of the contract was enacted after the execution of the contract, it can be considered under the principle of the burden to bear risk (under Article 537 of the Korean Civil Act) or change in circumstances.

The benefit of taking a substantive law approach is that the judges in the forum country are familiar with their susbtantive law, and do not have to refer to the concept of third-country overriding mandatory rules or the Special Connection Theory. As examined in chapter five, however, such means reveal the weakness of the substantive law approach. First, it is a significant problem that the overriding mandatory rules of third countries may or may not be considered depending on the circumstances of each case, thereby damaging predictability and legal certainty. Whether or not the third-country law is considered may depend on the parties' intention to violate the law, negligence. This goes against the interests

[33] BGHZ 59, 82–87. See ch 5, II, B.
[34] BGHZ 94, 268, 271. See ch 5, II, B.
[35] Anti-corruption, anti-slavery, human trafficking and drug prohibition are some examples.
[36] RGZ 93, 182ff. See ch 5, II, B.

of the parties in relation to the predictability of the applicable law for the parties and also goes against the interests of third countries and the interests of international harmony in decisions.

Second, the 'substantive approach' still involves conflict-of-laws considerations. We can think about a contract for the export of cultural heritages executed in violation of the regulations prohibiting the export of cultural property in the country of origin (the Nigerian mask case), a contract executed for the purpose of bribery of government officials in a third country (the ruling on the prohibition of acceptance of bribery by public officials), or the enactment of laws by the third country, the country of origin of the goods to be sold under a sales contract, prohibiting exports to the place of performance of the duty to deliver, or the final destination of goods (*Borax* and *Borsäure* cases). In such cases, when the governing law of the contract is Korean law, deciding whether the values protected under the overriding mandatory rules of third countries can be included in the good morals and public policy under Korean law would be similar to a conflict-of-laws exercise: Evaluating whether the consequences of applying the governing law would be acceptable under the fundamental values of Korean law, in accordance with the public policy of KAPIL, or to assessing whether the consequences of recognition would go against public policy, in the context of recognising foreign judgments. Whether or not a third-country law is considered or applied is a question of whether the Korean legal system can recognise foreign law in legal relationships with foreign elements, and it is questionable whether this can be seen as a 'substantive law' approach.

Third, the forum court should have power to examine whether the consideration or application of the law of a third country is in the interests of the forum state and whether it aligns with the fundamental values of Korea. If the court takes a substantive law approach, however, it becomes difficult to fully reflect the interests of the forum state in considering the overriding mandatory rules of a third country, unless the governing law of the contract is Korean law.

On the other hand, the conflict-of-laws approach allows the examination of consistency with the legal system of the forum state. This serves the interests of the parties, third countries, the forum state and international harmony in decisions. Therefore, the conflict-of-laws approach is the better alternative.

III. Interpretation Based on the Conflict-of-Laws Approach

A. Selecting the Methodology

This section examines which of the three conflict-of-laws approach methods listed in Table 6.1 above – namely, direct application ((B)), type (1) indirect application ((C)), or type (2) indirect application ((D)) – should be used. I believe that direct application ((B)) is ideal in terms of the predictability of international transactions. If the overriding mandatory rules of a third country are applied using a conflict-of-laws approach, the legal effect recognised by the third-country law occurs, so the effect of third-country law application is more predictable from the perspective of the parties than would be provided using types (1) or (2) indirect application ((C), (D)). In contrast, type (1) indirect application ((C)) permits the overriding mandatory rules of a third country to be considered only if they meet substantive law requirements, in addition to conflicts of law requirements. Type (2) indirect application ((D)), which allows the court discretion on how to recognise the consequences of the application of third-country law, permits a case-specific approach. However, it may undermine the predictability of the governing law for the parties or the outcome of the application of that law.

However, insisting on the direct application of third-country overriding mandatory rules for legislation and interpretation under KAPIL may be somewhat radical. Unlike the EU or Switzerland, Korea has no written provisions on the conditions for the application of the overriding mandatory rules of third countries. Moreover, even when compared to the situation in Europe before the introduction of the Rome Convention or the Rome I Regulation, there is scarce precedent in Korea as to whether the overriding mandatory rules of a third country can be considered even at the level of substantive law,[37] and the issue has not been sufficiently discussed in academia. Considering that even the Rome Convention, the Rome I Regulation, and FAPIL, which expressly stipulate the conditions for considering or applying third-country overriding mandatory rules, do not yet provide direct application as the only approach and instead allow both direct ((B)) and indirect application ((C), (D)), it may be unrealistic to insist only on conflict-of-laws application ((B)) in the interpretation or future legislation of Korean private international law. Therefore, the interpretation and legislative methodologies under Korean private international law should not exclude indirect application ((C), (D)).

If the aforementioned substantive-law approach ((A)), direct application ((B)), type (1) indirect application ((C)) and type 2 indirect application ((D)) are listed by level of progression from a private international law perspective, the order is direct application ((B)), type 2 indirect application ((D)), type (1) indirect application ((C)), followed by the substantive-law approach ((A)). Therefore, direct application ((B)) and type (1) indirect application ((C)) appear appropriate as interpretive methodologies of KAPIL. Type (1) indirect application first confirms whether third-country laws may be considered or applied based on the conditions under the conflict-of-laws approach, and decisions are made under the general conceptions of substantive law (applicable law). This would be therefore an easier method for domestic legal experts, who are not very familiar with the overriding mandatory rules of third countries or the conflict-of-laws approach.

Furthermore, in Switzerland, which takes the position of type (2) indirect application ((D)), the basis for judges having the authority to recognise effects different from those under third-country laws is that Article 19(2) of FAPIL expressly stipulates that foreign overriding mandatory rules be considered, taking into account whether the consequences of their application would amount to an appropriate decision in accordance with Swiss

[37] Seoul Central District Court, Judgment of 17 August 2022, Case No 2021Gahap560147 is one of rare examples. In this case, the Court considered the possibility of US sanctions on a Korean bank that issued a performance guarantee (first demand bank guarantee) to a Russian company. The Russian company was listed as a Specially Designated National and Blocked Person under the Support for the Sovereignty, Integrity, Democracy, and Economic Stability of Ukraine Act of 2014. The applicable law governing the guarantee was Korean law. On the basis of the facts, the Court held that the Russian company's request for the performance guarantee would constitute an abuse of right under the Korean Civil Act. This was primarily due to the disproportionate impact of the sanctions on the Korean bank, leading to significant damages that outweighed any benefits the Russian company might gain from the guarantee.

legal conceptions.[38] Article 19(2) of FAPIL means that if the consequences of applying the law of a third country are not in accord with Swiss legal conceptions, a judge can find a different effect. However, since there is no express clause like Article 19(2) of FAPIL in KAPIL, there are no legal basis for the Korean court to generally change the legal effect of a third country's overriding mandatory rules, except for the cases where adaptation is allowed or necessary. There thus are difficulties in using type (2) indirect application ((D)) for interpretation under Korean law.

Based on this, following the interpretation of KAPIL, a judge can adequately adopt either the direct application ((B)) or type (1) indirect application ((C)) depending on the specific case. For example, if an overriding mandatory rule of a third country becomes the basis for a claim in private law or invalidates the private legal effect of a relevant contract, the judge would clearly apply that rule through a conflict-of-laws approach and recognise its effect. But even if the law of a third country expressly stipulates its application in writing, if it is an effect that is not known under the applicable substantive law, the judge may change the legal effect using the technique of adaptation. If the overriding mandatory rules of a third country are prohibitive provisions of a public law nature that do not state the private law effect of their violation, and if the law of a third country does not provide for an interpretation of the private law effect in the event of its violation, while the facts of the case can be easily incorporated into the general provisions of the applicable substantive law, the case may be resolved in accordance with type (1) indirect application ((C)).

In some cases, overriding mandatory rules of third countries that do not meet the conflict-of-laws conditions for consideration or application may be considered under the general provisions of substantive law ((A)).[39] Let us postulate a case where the overriding mandatory rules of a third country are unacceptable in light of the Korean legal order – for example, legislation that confiscates all property of homosexuals – and thus render the performance of a contract by its obligor impossible. Such provisions are not legitimate in light of the forum law and do not meet the conditions for consideration or application under conflicts of laws. While they therefore cannot be considered or applied using the conflict-of-laws approach, they should be considered as underlying facts that constitute impossibility of performance in substantive law.

However, as a future legislative methodology for KAPIL, this author believes it would be apposite to use type (2) indirect application ((D) in the table above), along with direct application ((B)). The author believes that the legislative methodology could be somewhat more progressive than the interpretive methodology of today. Type (2) indirect application is one step ahead of type (1) indirect application ((C)) from the perspective of private international law, and the introduction of written provisions such as Article 19(2) of FAPIL could develop the legal grounds for selecting type (2) indirect application. Type (2) indirect application does not rely on the concept of substantive law concerning the conditions for considering or applying third-country overriding mandatory rules, but rather has the judges recognise effects that may be different from those prescribed by the law of a third country. Even when direct application ((B)) is selected, consequences other than what was stipulated under the third-country law may be recognised, using the principle of adaptation

[38] See ch 5, III, C.

[39] See the following III, D.

under private international law, if the governing law is not familiar with the stipulated consequences. Therefore, the type (2) indirect application and direct application may not, at the end of the day, differ significantly. Furthermore, if the overriding mandatory rules of a third country do not directly stipulate the legal effect because they are prohibitive provisions in public law, taking type (2) indirect application ((D)), instead of direct application, could save the judges the burden of investigating the legal effect of that provision in the third county's law. Another advantage of this method is that it does not involve the concept of adaptation under private international law. If Korea can build experience in considering or applying the overriding mandatory rules of third countries through such legislative exercises, it may be able to legislate provisions that specify direct application in the future.

Based on this methodological perspective, in the following section this author will examine under which requirements the overriding mandatory rules of third countries should be considered or applied under Korean law.

B. Conditions

The Special Connection Theory as advocated in Korea supports the view that, as in Germany, the overriding mandatory rules of third countries can be considered or applied under the following conditions: (1) the rule must be closely connected to the case; and (2) the purpose of the mandatory rule must be legitimate under Korean law.[40] Hereinafter, based on the conditions presented in the domestic legal literature, this author will review the following points that have not been sufficiently dealt with therein.

First, in the context of the overriding mandatory rules of third countries, I will clarify the criteria for determining a close connection. The closest connection test has been a significant principle in determining the applicable law in private international law.[41] However, there has been little discussion in previous domestic studies on how to find close connections in the special context of the consideration or application of the overriding mandatory rules of third countries. Second, the criteria for determining whether the overriding mandatory rules of third countries are acceptable to the laws of Korea, the forum state, and the factors to be considered by judges when they exercise their discretion shall be explained for the stages of content and result control. Accordingly, I will present the conditions for considering or applying the overriding mandatory rules of third countries, which can adequately reflect in a balanced manner the interests of the parties, the forum state, third countries and international harmony in decisions.

i. Close Connection with a Third Country

As examined in the comparative legal study in chapter five,[42] on the one hand, there are instruments for considering or applying rules of a third country with a close connection (Rome Convention, FAPIL, Hague Agency Convention, etc) as well as an instrument that

[40] Kim (n 22) 720; Suk (n 8) 382; Lee (n 7) 151.
[41] Suk (n 2) 152.
[42] See ch 5, III.

only allows that for the place of performance (Rome I Regulation). However, there are reasons to support a close connection to the case. First, considering or applying the overriding mandatory rules of a closely connected third country may better serve the interests of the third country. Countries that are not the place of performance may still have strong regulatory interests in the case. Second, there may be difficulties in determining the place of performance, depending on the type of international transaction, such as in international financial transactions.

In reference to discussions under the Rome Convention,[43] there is a question about what should constitute a close connection to the third country. As under the Rome Convention, there may be different views on whether the connection should be to the contract as a whole, or to the issues in dispute. The latter is persuasive because if the connection is to the contract itself, the excessive number of foreign laws that would have to be reviewed would impose a great burden on the judge. Therefore, in a case where the buyer does not make a payment, for example, provisions that prohibit payment, invalidate the whole or part of the payment obligation, or alter such an obligation and provisions that justify non-payment would show a close connection.[44] Whether the third country and the matter being disputed show a close connection is determined based on the comprehensive consideration of the factors below:[45]

(1) *Place of performance or the place of preparation for performance*: place of performance can form a close connection. The law of the place of performance of a contract cannot be disregarded, as it may hinder the performance of obligations. Not only the place of performance, but also the place in which preparations for the performance take place may also be closely connected. This is a meaningful criterion in relation to foreign exchange control laws or export/import regulations. For example, if a third country prohibits exports to a particular country, and a party to a sales contract wishes to import raw materials from a third country and export them to the prohibited country, a close connection can be found.[46]

(2) Place of habitual residence and place of incorporation of the obligor: if the obligor is a natural person, he/she must obey the sovereignty of the country of his/her habitual residence; in the case of a company and a corporation, this would be the country of registration. Therefore, such third countries may also be found to be closely connected.

(3) *Location of property*: The state in which property is situated or disposed of may have overriding mandatory rules that apply to movable or immovable property. Provisions requiring permission to dispose of land or buildings may have a close connection with the disposal of a land or building as the law of the country in which it is located.

(4) *Place of provision of labour and location of business*: in labour relations, the overriding mandatory rules of the place of provision of labour or the relevant place of business of the employer can also be recognised as closely connected. In cases where a Korean

[43] See ch 5, III, B, i for discussions under the Rome Convention.

[44] One example would be a case when the buyer of a cultural property argues that the sales contract is void and null based on the rules under cultural heritage protection laws prohibiting the trade of cultural property and refuses to pay.

[45] Kim (n 1) 580; Martiny (n 12); Paul Torremans (ed), *Cheshire, North & Fawcett: Private International Law*, 15th edn (Oxford University Press, 2017) EGBGB Art 34, Rn 140–53; Martiny (n 12) Rom I-VO Art 9, Rn 125–37, 683.

[46] For example, the German court's *Borax* and *Borsäure* cases. See ch 5, II, B, i and ii.

company conducts a construction project and employs workers in a foreign country, even if the applicable law of the labour contract is Korean law, the law of that country may be closely connected to the labour contract.

(5) *Effect on markets*: According to the Effect Doctrine, one important criterion in the context of the fair trade law and the capital markets law is which country's market is affected by the violation. For example, illegal cartel conduct and business combinations in foreign countries may affect the markets of other countries.

(6) *Nationality*: nationality may be an important criterion if a rule is targeted at specific activities by nationals or foreigners. Germany has an overriding mandatory rule that restricts German citizens from trading in weapons,[47] and if an arms sales contract is concluded between a German citizen and a foreigner, the overriding mandatory rules of Germany would be considered the law of a closely connected country even if the applicable law of the arms sales contract is foreign law. That would also be the case when a worker protection law is designed to protect a specific group of individuals.

ii. Legitimacy of the Overriding Mandatory Rules of a Third Country in Light of the International Public Policy of the Forum

a. Consistency with the Interests of the Forum State

Based on the comparative legal research conducted in chapter five, we have seen that the Rome Convention, Swiss FAPIL and the Rome I Regulation, which take the conflict-of-laws approach, all grant judges discretion as to whether to consider or apply the overriding mandatory rules of third countries, and ask them to consider whether the legislative purpose of the third country's law is legitimate from the forum state's point of view when exercising their discretion.[48] This is a requirement that reflects the interests of the forum state (among the four interests to be weighed in the consideration or application of a third country's overriding mandatory rules). Even if a third country is closely connected to the disputed matter, its overriding mandatory rules should not be applied without any restrictions, and their consistency with the interests of the forum state must be confirmed.[49] To do so, there must be requirements that ensure the interests of the forum state are reflected.

As to the extent to which the legislative purpose of the overriding mandatory rules of a third country are consistent with the interests of the forum state, the prevailing view under the Rome I Regulation is that they should 'not be incompatible with or contrary to the interests of the forum state'.[50] On the other hand, some interpret Article 19 of FAPIL as requiring 'values that correspond to the legal conceptions of Swiss law',[51] 'the general principles of international law or the fundamental values of constitutional states'.[52]

[47] Art 5(5) of the German *Außenwirtschaftsgesetz* and Art 21 of *Kriegswaffenkontrollgesetz* are examples.
[48] See ch 5, III for details.
[49] Martiny (n 12) EGBGB Art 34, Rn 158; Martiny (n 12) Rom I -VO Art 9, Rn 141.
[50] See ch 5, III, E, i for details.
[51] BGE 136 III 392, E. 2.3.3.1.
[52] Pascal Grolimund (ed), *Basler Kommentar Interntionales Privatrecht*, 4th edn (Helbnig Lichtenhan Verlag, 2021) Art 19, Rn 19.

When comparing the standard of 'not being incompatible with or contrary to the interests of the forum state' to the standard required by the interpretation of FAPIL, the former provides both affirmative and passive standards, while the latter provides only affirmative standards. The latter also appears to have a wider scope than the 'fundamental value of the constitutional state', making it seem stricter. Here this author presents a compromise option for the overriding mandatory rules of a third country to be 'legitimate in light of Korea's international public policy'.

International public policy includes fundamental principles of law, underlying moral beliefs, fundamental values and concepts of justice, fundamental moral beliefs that the domestic legal order of Korea seeks to protect,[53] and the core values of the Constitution of Korea.[54] Whether something is 'legitimate in light of international public policy' would require that the overriding mandatory rules of a third country be consistent with, or at least not inconsistent with, the international public policy of Korea. There should be no reason to prevent the consideration or application of a third country's overriding mandatory rules if they do not affect the international public policy of the forum state.

Referring to the results of the comparative legal research in chapter five, the following criteria can be presented as 'being legitimate under Korean law': (1) whether the interests to be protected by the overriding mandatory rules of a third country are recognised worldwide (eg, prohibition of drug smuggling, terrorism, corruption, human trafficking, money laundering, and protection of cultural heritages);[55] (2) whether their protection would indirectly protect the interests of Korea;[56] (3) whether they are consistent with or at least not contrary to the interests of Korea;[57] (4) whether they present economic and social harm to Korea; and (5) whether they discriminate against other countries or intend to harm other countries. In the case of (1), (2) and (3), the third country's overriding mandatory rules could be applied or considered, but in the case of (4) and (5), they will not be.

b. Content Control and Result Control

According to the comparative legal findings in chapter five, the Rome Convention and the Rome I Regulation do not clearly distinguish between content control and results control concerning the overriding mandatory rules of third countries and their application. On the other hand, Article 19(1)–(2) of FAPIL is distinct, requiring analysis into the existence of legitimate interests in third-country overriding mandatory rules under Swiss legal conceptions in paragraph (1) and examination of the appropriateness of decisions to apply those

[53] Supreme Court of Korea, Judgment of 10 April 1990, Case No 89Daka20252. The ruling, in the context of the recognition of foreign arbitral awards, declared the meaning of 'international public policy'. In the context of recognising foreign judgments, Supreme Court of Korea, Judgment of 24 May, Case No 2012decision 2009Da22549 on compulsory drafts and Supreme Court of Korea, Judgment of 24 May 2012, Case No 2009Da68620 also present the same criteria.

[54] Supreme Court of Korea, Judgment of 24 May 2012, Case No 2009Da22549 on compulsory drafts.

[55] Ruling on the Nigerian Mask case by the German court. See ch 5, II, B.

[56] *Borax* and *Borsäure* rulings by the German court. See ch 5, II, B.

[57] Interpretation of Rome I Regulation and Art 19 of FAPIL.

rules based on Swiss conceptions of law in paragraph (2). Such a stance taken in FAPIL is desirable in that it clarifies that the interests of the forum state should be considered in both stages of content control and result control.

Therefore, interpreting KAPIL should also necessitate such an examination in the following two respects. First, abstract content control is the examination of whether the overriding mandatory rules of a third country are worth being considered or applied in themselves. Second (presuming that is the case), the specific result control will prevent applying the rules to specific cases from having consequences that are unacceptable from the perspective of the forum law. Even if there is no particular problem with content control, the results of the application may be unjust, so there will be practical benefits in also controlling for the results.

The content control stage reviews whether the purpose and content of the third country's law are legitimate in light of the international public policy of the forum. At this stage, the judge weighs both the interests of the parties, in terms of the predictability of applicable law, and the interests of the forum state. However, this author believes that the 'clearly preponderant interests of a party' standard adopted by FAPIL at the content control stage is not acceptable as a way of interpreting KAPIL for the following reasons.[58] First, considering the difference between the German text and the French text of FAPIL, it is unclear whether the standard of interests of 'a party' is actually established under Swiss law. Second, it seems that this standard has not played a very significant role in decisions by the Swiss Federal Supreme Court that have applied Article 19 of FAPIL, and there are currently calls within Switzerland to delete this standard.[59] Third, the 'clearly preponderant interests of a party' in Swiss law, as categorised in these cases, concern whether the results of applying third-country law to specific matters is oppressive to the parties, which would be more appropriately considered at the result control stage, as we will see below.

At the result control stage, the judge reviews whether the results of applying the overriding mandatory rules of third countries to specific cases are consistent with or contrary to the international public policy of Korean law. The legal basis for this is Article 23 of KAPIL, which excludes the application of foreign law where the result of the application violates international public policy. Through result control, the judge reviews whether the relevant provision would result in overly oppressive or harsh consequences for the parties. Another matter that can be considered at the stage of result control is whether the result of applying the overriding mandatory rules of third countries contributes to the international harmony and consistency of judgments.

Article 19(2) of FAPIL takes into account the purposes of the overriding mandatory rules of third countries at the stage of result control. However, since their purposes are also given consideration in determining their overriding mandatory nature, and once again in the content control stage, it is questionable whether reconsidering their purposes at the result control stage is of additional utility.[60] Therefore, I do not believe it is necessary to

[58] See ch 5, III, C for details.

[59] Mächler-Erne and Wolf-Mettier (n 52) Art 19, Rn 3.

[60] See ch 5, III, C for details.

further consider the purposes of the overriding mandatory rules of third countries at this stage.

Another criterion that has been proposed as one of the conditions for considering or applying the overriding mandatory rules of third countries[61] is 'how favourable the consequences of considering or applying those rules would be to the realisation of justice under private international law'. The idea is that whether to consider or apply the overriding mandatory rules of third countries should be determined by the impact of such application would have on the connecting principles established under the KAPIL, the relevance of the case to the country, and the importance of the public interest to be protected by the said rules. However, the meaning of 'the impact on the connecting principles established by KAPIL' is unclear. As discussed above, KAPIL has an intended legislative vacuum on the overriding mandatory rules of a third country, so even if those rules are applied, that could not be said to have an adverse effect on the connecting principles of KAPIL. I believe that the connection between the case and the country can be determined at the stage of finding a close connection, and the result of applying the overriding mandatory rules of a third country is more appropriately determined at the result control stage on the basis of 'whether there is legitimate interest to be protected according to the underlying values of the forum law'.

C. Effect

If the overriding mandatory rules of third countries are applied directly ((B)), the legal effect prescribed by those rules will occur (eg, nullification of contract), but the subsequent effects of decisions about the remainder of the contract (eg, return of unjust enrichment due to the nullification of the contract) are in accordance with the applicable substantive law of the contract.[62] If an overriding mandatory rule of a third country that is a prohibitive provision of a public law nature directly provides for the effect of private law relations as a result of its application, the effect should be given. However, if there are no such provisions, or if the applicable law does not recognise the stipulated effect, its effect will be modified by the principle of adaptation.[63] If the overriding mandatory rules of third countries give rise to claim rights under private law, such a right will be recognised accordingly.

If the overriding mandatory rules of third countries are considered by type (1) indirect application ((C)), the effect prescribed by the applicable substantive law will be recognised. In the absence of expressly written provisions such as Article 19(2) of FAPIL, it is difficult under Korean law for a judge to recognise an effect that is different from that prescribed by third-country law (type (2) indirect application, (D)), except in cases where adaptation is relevant.

[61] See Lee (n 7) 153, fn 111.
[62] See II, A above.
[63] See II, A, Table 6.1 above.

D. Overriding Mandatory Rules of Third Countries that Fail to Meet Conditions for Consideration or Application

It is doubtful whether third-country overriding mandatory rules that do not meet the conditions for consideration or application (ie, that fail to meet the conditions for consideration or application of (B), (C)) can be considered as facts under the applicable substantive law of the contract ((A)). The European Court of Justice, in its *Nikiforidis* ruling, held that the courts of Member States are not restricted from considering as facts overriding mandatory rules that do not meet the requirements of Article 9(3), on the grounds that the Rome I Regulation in principle seeks harmony between conflicting laws with respect to contractual obligations and does not seek unification of the substantive laws of contract laws.[64,65]

The above ruling under the Rome I Regulation cannot be adopted without changes as an interpretation of KAPIL. Considering that the Rome I Regulation outlines the conflict-of-laws principles of the European Community, a question arose whether a Member State was also bound by the Regulation in its substantive law. On the other hand, as a matter of principle, it would be possible to consider the overriding mandatory rules of a third country under the concept of substantive law in KAPIL since the Act does not have any explicit provisions regarding the overriding mandatory rules of third countries. However, what is possible and what is desirable are two different things. There would be practical benefits in examining this issue in preparation for the potential introduction of written provisions on overriding mandatory rules of third countries based on the theory of special connection in private international law in the future.

As previously discussed, the direct or indirect application of overriding mandatory rules of third countries is a better method than indirect consideration. In some cases, however, the practical effect of a provision that does not meet the conditions for considering or applying the overriding mandatory rules of third countries may inevitably have to be considered under substantive law. For example, there may be a case where an obligor's performance is rendered de facto impossible by a third country's overriding mandatory provision that is not deemed legitimate in light of the public policy of the forum. Specifically, that could be legislation that discriminates against other countries (eg, the refusal of Kuwait Airways to board Israelis because of Kuwait's boycott against Israel) or confiscates all property of a

[64] *Republik Griechenland v Grigorios Nikiforidis*, Case C-135/15, ECLI:EU:C:2016774 [43]–[49].

[65] In *Nikiforidis*, a school teacher, a Greek national, worked in a Greek public school in Germany. His employment contract was governed by German law. However, the Greek Government adopted a law to reduce the salary of the employees in the public sector. The German court asked the CJEU whether this Greek law could be given effect as the Greek law was not a law of the place of the performance under the meaning of Article 9(3) of the Rome I Regulation. Michael Wilderspin makes a valid point that if the German court would have considered the Greek law under the German contract law concerning alteration of the contract, it would not be very different from 'giving effect' to Greek law and thereby would allow the Member States to circumvent the strict requirement under Article 9(3) of the Rome I Regulation. Hauser expresses a view that in the cases where, third-country overriding rules cannot be considered even as facts under applicable substantive law; see Paul Hauser, *Eingriffsnormen in der Rom- I Verordnung* (Mohr Siebeck, 2012) 115–16. For a similar perspective, see the section by Martin Zwickel in Dieter Martiny (ed) *Internationales Vertragsrecht*, 9. Auflage (Ottoschmidt, 2022) Rn 5.38, which suggests that indirect consideration of a third country overriding mandatory rules under the substantive law is only permissible when it affects the performance of the relevant contractual obligation.

homosexual obligor. In such cases, the de facto effects resulting therefrom are bound to be considered under general provisions such as default and risk burden under the Korean Civil Act. Examining and handling this otherwise would have unfair results for the obligor.

IV. Draft Legislation

My suggested interpretation is possible under the KAPIL in its current form. However, there is a need to clarify, through future legislation, the requirements and effects of exercising discretion and the matters that should be taken into consideration. That will guarantee predictability and legal certainty for parties to international transactions and contribute to international uniformity and harmony in decisions.

Based on the discussion so far, I propose the following provision in Article 20-2 of KAPIL.

Article 20-2

(1) In light of the legislative purpose, effect may be given to mandatory rules of a third country, if they must be applied to the relevant legal relationship regardless of the applicable law, are closely connected to the disputed issue, and are legitimate in light of good morals and public order of the Republic of Korea.

(2) When the court gives effect to the overriding mandatory rules of a third country pursuant to paragraph (1), it may recognise effects different from those provided for in the law of the third country in light of the facts of the case.

Paragraph (1) of the draft legislation stipulates the content control of the overriding mandatory rules of third countries. 'Mandatory rules of a third country that must be applied regardless of the applicable law in light of the legislative purpose' are the overriding mandatory rules of third countries, which correspond to 'mandatory provisions of the Republic of Korea to govern the corresponding legal relationship, irrespective of the applicable law, in light of the purpose of legislation' under Article 20 of the current KAPIL, referring to the overriding mandatory rules of the forum state.[66] By using the same language as Article 20 of KAPIL, we can clarify that the criteria for determining whether the provisions of a third country are overriding mandatory provisions are the same as those under Article 20 of KAPIL on overriding mandatory rules of the forum. Even if the provisions of the third-country law in question are subject to extraterritorial application, their nature could be determined just as we would determine overriding mandatory nature under KAPIL, so no special clauses have been inserted concerning provisions applied extraterritorially.

[66] This draft legislation presumes that Art 20 of the current KAPIL on overriding mandatory rules of the forum would be retained. See ch 3, II, for the interpretation of 'mandatory provisions of the Republic of Korea to govern the corresponding legal relationship, in light of the purpose of legislation' in Art 20 of KAPIL. However, if provisions on the handling of overriding mandatory rules of third countries are to be newly established in KAPIL, it would be desirable to add a clause on the definition of overriding mandatory rules. If the legislators adopt the position that overriding mandatory rules are intended to protect public interests and that provisions in so-called special private law can be overriding mandatory rules if they protect public interests greater than adjusting private interests or fundamental constitutional values, Art 9(1) of the Rome I Regulation would be a good reference.

'Disputed issue' means an issue that is the subject of a dispute. In consideration of how the use of the term 'situation' under Article 7(1) of the Rome Convention led to conflicting views on whether the close connection must be with the contract as a whole, or the disputed issue, the author has selected 'disputed issue' to eliminate any uncertainties. FAPIL uses the term 'factual connection', and although it is unclear whether FAPIL intended a different meaning from that under the Rome Convention, I chose not to use 'factual connection' either as there may potentially be conflicting views on this.

The term 'good morals and public order of the Republic of Korea' means international public policy, using the same language as Article 23 of KAPIL. This includes fundamental legal principles, fundamental values and conceptions of justice, fundamental moral beliefs that Korea's domestic legal order seeks to protect,[67] and core values of the Constitution of Korea.[68] This is based on the Supreme Court of Korea's ruling on 'international public policy' in the context of the grounds for refusing recognition of foreign arbitral awards and foreign judgments. The Court refused to recognise foreign arbitral awards and foreign judgments when doing so would be contrary to 'good morals and public order of the Republic of Korea',[69] which is in the same language as 'good morals and public order' under Article 23 of KAPIL. However, the difference between the language in paragraph (1) of the draft legislation and Article 23 of KAPIL is the requirement that the third-country law in 'itself', rather than the 'consequences' of its application, not be contrary to the good morals and public order of Korea. In the context of recognising foreign arbitral awards and foreign judgments, international public policy is a standard for examining the results of approving or applying the governing law, and the decision may depend on the degree of the connection to the forum state (*Inlandsbeziehung*). However, examining whether a third-country law deserves protection according to the underlying values of the law of Korea does not concern the results of applying third-country law to specific cases, but is rather abstract control of the law's contents, and the connection to the forum state will not be a problem. Thus, in the draft legislation, this author phrased paragraph (1) as 'mandatory rules of a third country … are legitimate', without referring to the results of applying the overriding mandatory rules of a third country.

'Legitimate in light of good morals and public order of the Republic of Korea' means that the interests protected by the overriding mandatory rules of a third country are consistent with or at least not contrary to international public policy. This is a requirement for abstract content control over the overriding mandatory rules of third countries. I did not adopt the Swiss law's 'clearly preponderant interests of a party' criterion. Even without introducing that criterion, the oppressive or harsh consequences on the parties arising from the application of the overriding mandatory rules of a third country in specific cases can be considered at the result control stage.

In relation to the method of consideration or application, I additionally propose type (2) indirect application ((D)), along with direct application ((B)) and type (1) indirect

[67] Supreme Court of Korea, Judgment of 10 April 1990, Case No 89Daka20252. In the context of whether to recognise foreign arbitral awards, the Court defined 'international public policy' as a ground for refusal. In the context of whether to recognise foreign judgments, Supreme Court of Korea, Judgment of 24 May 2012, Case No 2009Da22549, and Supreme Court of Korea, Judgment of 24 May 2012, Case No 2009Da68620 presented the same criteria concerning forced labour during the Japanese occupation.

[68] Supreme Court of Korea, Judgment of 24 May 2012, Case No 2009Da22549.

[69] Art 39 of the Arbitration Act; Art 217(3) of the Civil Procedure Act.

application ((C)). The overriding mandatory rules of a third country that meet the requirements of paragraph (1) of the draft legislation allowing 'effect to be given' can either be directly applied as law ((B)) or considered under the general provisions of the applicable substantive law ((C)), and judges may also recognise an effect different from that stipulated in the third-country law ((D)).[70] In order to make it clearer that (D) is included, paragraph (2) of the draft legislation states that judges can recognise effects different from those prescribed by the law of a third country. Article 19(2) of FAPIL requires that the result of applying the overriding mandatory rules of a third country be taken into consideration to make appropriate decisions in accordance with Swiss legal conceptions and allows judges to recognise effects different from those determined by the law of the third country. However, since the wording of Article 19(2) of FAPIL is not common under Korean law, its intention might not be accurately communicated; I therefore explained the legislative intent specifically in Article 19(2) of KAPIL without adopting the same wording as Article 19(2) of FAPIL.

Compared to direct application ((B)), this may undermine the predictability for the parties to international transactions, as judges have discretion not only about whether to consider or apply third-country law, but also about the effect of applying third-country law. Nevertheless, I have two reasons for proposing type (2) indirect application ((D) in Table 6.1 above), along with direct application ((B) in Table 6.1 above) and type (1) indirect application ((C) in Table 6.1 above).

First, even if the third-country law is applied directly, there may be cases in which the effect of application should be altered through adaptation under private international law. In such cases, there may be no practical difference from recognising effects other than what is stipulated by third-country laws, in accordance with type (2) indirect application ((D)). Second, given the practical consideration that in Korea theories and precedents on the handling of the overriding mandatory rules of third countries have not been established, this approach is less burdensome and more flexible and workable in practice. Use of type (2) indirect application ((D)) will be much easier than direct application, as judges will be able to recognise the appropriate application effect for specific cases without needing to find a legal effect that may or may not be explicitly stated in the third country's law.

Unlike Article 19(2) of FAPIL, my draft legislation does not provide for result control. Article 19(2) of FAPIL provides that 'in deciding whether such a provision is to be taken into consideration, consideration shall be given to … consequences of its application, in order to reach a decision that is appropriate having regard to the Swiss conception of law', dealing separately for result control, in addition to content control under Article 19(1). However, it is not necessary to stipulate that the purpose of the overriding mandatory rules of third countries be considered at the result control stage, as that has already been reviewed during content control under paragraph (1) of the draft legislation. Whether such rules are applied directly or indirectly under KAPIL, control over the consequences of that can be sufficiently achieved by examining whether they are in violation of international public

[70] This is on the basis that the effect of applying the overriding mandatory rules of a third country should be determined in accordance with the law of that country. On the other hand, it is also possible to say that the effect of applying the overriding mandatory rules of a third country should be determined according to the applicable law of the contract. For a discussion of which law should determine the effect of applying the overriding mandatory rules of a third country, see ch 6, III, C.

policy, in accordance with Article 23 of the current KAPIL. Therefore, the draft legislation does not provide that the purpose of the overriding mandatory rules of third countries should be considered at the result control stage, as in Article 19(2) of FAPIL.

In determining the consequences of applying the overriding mandatory rules of a third country in accordance with the international public policy of Article 23 of KAPIL, we must consider not only whether the results of that conform to the underlying values of Korean law, but also whether they are excessively oppressive or harsh to the parties. Here, results may depend on the connection to the forum state according to the facts of the case.[71]

Unlike the Rome Convention and the Rome I Regulation, paragraphs (1) and (2) of the draft legislation do not specify the 'nature and the consequences of non-application' of the rules as factors to be considered when judges exercise discretion whether to give effect to the overriding mandatory rules of third countries. I did not mention the 'nature' of a rule because it was unclear what the language intended and because determining the public or private law nature of provisions cannot be a meaningful criterion.[72] Analogously, the consequences of non-application are the flip side of the consequences of application; since the consequences of application are considered in the examination of international public policy under Article 23 of KAPIL, such consequences do not need to be separately stipulated.

Next, this author will look at how this draft legislation reflects the interests of the parties, the forum state, third countries and international harmony in decisions. The interests of the parties refer to the predictability for the parties on the applicable norms of their legal relationship. Paragraph (1) of the draft legislation guarantees the predictability of the applicable norms for the parties by specifying in detail the conditions for considering or applying the overriding mandatory rules of third countries. This reflects the interests of the parties better than they would be through indirect consideration ((A)), which does not specify the conditions for considering the overriding mandatory rules of third countries on the level of private international law.

The interests of third countries consist of applying their laws to implement their essential policies. Paragraph (1) of the draft legislation takes into account the interests of third countries that are closely connected to the disputed case, better reflecting the interests of third countries than Article 9(3) of the Rome I Regulation, which only considers or applies the law of the place of performance.

The interests of the forum state are the values that the forum seeks to protect and the values of the forum that may be infringed by considering or applying the overriding mandatory rules of a third country. Paragraph (1) of the draft legislation protects the interests of the forum state by ensuring that the overriding mandatory rules of third countries with legitimate content and purpose in light of the international public policy of the forum are considered or applied. This reflects the interests of the forum state more effectively than Article 7(2) of the Rome Convention or Article 9(3) of the Rome I Regulation, which did not expressly require that the overriding mandatory rules of a third country meet the values of the forum, but only interpreted the same as a factor to be considered in the exercise of discretion.

[71] Suk (n 2) 176.

[72] For the same discussion under the Rome I Regulation, see ch 5, III, E.

The interests of international harmony in decisions refer to the interests in reaching a similar outcome for the same case whatever the jurisdiction may be. If the court of a third country decides on the same issue, the law of the third country will be applied as the overriding mandatory rule of the forum. Paragraph (1) of the draft legislation contributes to the global uniformity in decisions by considering or applying the laws of third countries that are closely connected to the case.

7

International Commercial Arbitration and Overriding Mandatory Rules[1]

I. Introduction

Overriding mandatory rules are relevant not only in litigation but also in arbitration. Whereas previous chapters discussed the treatment of overriding mandatory rules by the court of the forum state, this chapter considers how to solve various problems surrounding overriding mandatory rules in international commercial arbitration. I will first categorise the situations in which overriding mandatory rules are considered problematic, introduce and review the different views in academia, and present possible solutions under the Korean Arbitration Act (KAA).

A. The Necessity of Research on Overriding Mandatory Rules in International Commercial Arbitration

The increase in overriding mandatory rules affects the legal relationships of the parties to international transactions, and that is also true when disputes between the parties are resolved via international commercial arbitration. However, there has not been sufficient discussion on overriding mandatory rules in international commercial arbitration.[2] This is presumably not because there was no need for such research, but because of the

[1] This chapter is a revised and updated version of the author's article: 'Overriding Mandatory Rules in International Commercial Arbitration' (2021) 38 *Hanyang Law Review* 353, written in the Korean language.

[2] For previous research in Korea, see Kwang Hyun Suk, *Essays in International Commercial Arbitration Law*, vol 1 (Pakyoungsa, 2007) 177–83; Hong Sik Chung, 'Distributor's Indemnity Rights in International Commercial Arbitration' (2013b) 22 *Korean Forum on International Trade and Business Law* 319; Hong Sik Chung, 'Applicability of Overriding Mandatory Rules in International Arbitration' (2013a) 23 *Journal of Arbitration Studies* 3; Hun Mook Lee, 'Arbitrability in Terms of Internationally Mandatory Provisions' (2013) 22 *Korea Private International Law Journal* 21. For further references, see Marc Blessing, 'Mandatory Rules versus Party Autonomy in International Arbitration' (1997) 14 *Journal of International Arbitration* 23; Constantin Calavros, 'The Application of Substantive Mandatory Rules in International Commercial Arbitration from the Perspective of an EU UNCITRAL Model Law Jurisdiction' (2018) 34 *Arbitration International* 219; Alexander KA Greenwalt, 'Does International Arbitration Need a Mandatory Rules Method?' in George A Berman and Loukas A Mistelis (eds), *Mandatory Rules in International Arbitration* (Juris, 2011); Jan Kleinheisterkamp, 'The Impact of Internationally Mandatory Rules on the Enforceability of Arbitration Agreements' (2009) 3 *World Arbitration & Mediation Review* 91; Jan Kleinheisterkamp, 'Overriding mandatory laws in international arbitration' (2018) 67 *International & Comparative Law Quarterly* 903; Alan Scott Rau, 'The Arbitrator and the "Mandatory Rules of Law"' in Berman and Mistelis (ibid); Audley Sheppard, 'Mandatory Rules in International Commercial Arbitration: An English Law Perspective' in Berman and Loukas (ibid); Laurence Shore, 'Applying mandatory rules of law in international

characteristics of international commercial arbitration that set it apart from international litigation. In international litigation, it has been naturally accepted that the overriding mandatory rules of the *lex causae* or of the forum apply in accordance with the private international law of the forum state. On the other hand, international commercial arbitration is a private and alternative means of dispute resolution where party autonomy prevails.

There are two factors that make the problem of overriding mandatory rules in arbitration more complex. First, there is the question of whether arbitrators appointed by the parties can be expected to play the role of the guardians of public interest. Second, as arbitrators are not strictly bound by the conflict of laws rules at the seat of arbitration, it is unclear whether arbitrators should apply substantive overriding mandatory rules. Given the lack of uniform international norms on the choice of law in arbitration, there is no established theory as to how to handle overriding mandatory rules.

In international commercial arbitration, there are clearly situations in which overriding mandatory rules raise issues and, as we will explore below, there have also been precedents and arbitral awards in Europe and the US. For instance, in ICC Case No 4132 of the International Chamber of Commerce,[3] where a Korean company entered into a supply contract with an Italian company, the arbitrator considered the competition law of the EU *ex officio*, even though Korean law was the governing law of the supply contract. Accordingly, arbitration procedures to which Korean companies are a party, arbitration procedures for which Korea is the seat of arbitration, and the annulment, recognition and enforcement of arbitral awards in Korean courts are not free from the issues arising from overriding mandatory rules. Therefore, it is necessary to explore what kind of problems there are and how they should be resolved.

B. Types of Issues with Overriding Mandatory Rules in International Commercial Arbitration

As a specific situation in which overriding mandatory rules are problematic in international commercial arbitration, first, there are cases where claims based on overriding mandatory rules become the subject of litigation (hereinafter Type 1). An example of Type 1 would be when the commercial agent claims compensation under provisions of domestic laws (eg, English laws) enacted based on the EU law on the commercial agent's indemnity rights set out in the directive related to self-employed commercial agents, which are considered overriding mandatory rules,[4] even when the governing law of the commercial agency contract is the law of another country (eg, the state laws of California in the US). Let us presume that the governing law of the commercial agency contract was Californian law and that there was

commercial arbitration' in Berman and Loukas (ibid); H Smit, 'Mandatory Law in Arbitration' in Berman and Loukas (ibid); Jeffrey Maurice Waincymer, 'International Commercial Arbitration and the Application of Mandatory Rules of Law' (2009) 5 *Asian International Arbitration Journal* 1.

[3] ICC Case No 4132 (1983), ICC Year Book of Commercial Arbitration Vol X (1985) 49ff.

[4] Arts 17 and 18 of the European Union's Council Directive 86/653/EEC of 18 December 1986 on the Coordination of the Laws of the Member States Relating to Self-employed Commercial Agents provide that where a commercial agency contract is terminated, the commercial agent may claim compensation from the principal and that the parties cannot exclude Arts 17 and 18 against the commercial agent before the contract is terminated.

an arbitration clause designating the US as the seat of arbitration, but the commercial agent later files a lawsuit against the principal in an English court, claiming for compensation under English law. In this case, the principal put forward a defence of arbitration, and in this regard, the commercial agent may assert that its right to claim compensation under English laws constitutes an overriding mandatory rule and that there is no arbitrability in this dispute, or that the arbitration agreement is null and void because it is possible that the overriding mandatory rule may not apply in arbitration. Under Korean laws, a similar problem may arise in the case where damages are claimed due to a violation of the Monopoly Regulation and Fair Trade Act, Article 109.

The second type refers to a situation where some laws or regulations stipulate that disputes over overriding mandatory rules should be resolved exclusively in the courts (hereinafter Type 2). As I will explain in section II, B. below, Belgian law provides exclusive jurisdiction of Belgian courts over the indemnity rights of distributors, which raised a question of whether disputes over their indemnity rights can be resolved by arbitration.

Third, there may be cases where the legitimacy of the claim depends on the application of the overriding mandatory rules. This would include cases when a counterparty asserts that the contract is unenforceable for violating overriding mandatory rules of export control laws in relation to a party's contractual claim, or when the debtor asserts that the contract could not be performed due to restrictions on air transportation due to COVID-19,[5] or when, as in the above ICC Case No 4132, the validity of a supply contract is challenged for its violation of EU competition law (hereinafter Type 3).

Fourth, there is the issue of how courts should decide in regard to a claim for annulment or recognition/enforcement of an arbitral award when the losing party to the award asserts a lack of arbitrability or invalidity of an arbitration agreement with respect to disputes of Types 1, 2 and 3; in regard to a failure by the arbitral tribunal to make a decision on the overriding mandatory rules; or in regard to an error in the application of overriding mandatory rules.

Hereunder, I will discuss whether disputes of Types 1, 2 and 3 can be resolved by arbitration; that is, whether there is arbitrability and whether the overriding mandatory rules affect the validity of arbitration agreement (section II); whether the arbitrator may consider or apply overriding mandatory rules without the agreement of the parties (section III); and if so, which country's overriding mandatory rules should be considered or applied in arbitration (section IV); and as ex-post control of the court, how the court should decide on the grounds for annulment, recognition and enforcement in relation to overriding mandatory rules in proceedings Types 1, 2 and 3 cases (section V).

II. Arbitrability and Validity of Arbitration Agreements of Types 1, 2 and 3

The question of whether a dispute can be resolved by arbitration is referred to as 'arbitrability'.[6] If the dispute is mainly related to the public interest, arbitrability may be denied because

[5] See the section by Martin Zwickel in Dieter Martiny (ed), *Internationales Vertragsrecht*, 9th edn (Ottoschmidt, 2022) Rn 5.75.

[6] Suk (n 2) 26.

the country has a special interest in the dispute resolution.[7] There is a concern on whether the overriding mandatory rules enacted to pursue essential public interests can be properly applied or protected in arbitration. This was linked to discussions on the arbitrability of Types 1, 2 and 3, and whether arbitration agreements can be recognised as being capable of resolving these types of disputes. The KAA does not directly define 'arbitrability',[8] nor does it separately stipulate arbitrability for Types 1, 2 and 3 or the effect of an arbitration agreement. However, in foreign courts and academia, there are conflicts between the view that denies arbitrability, the view that allows arbitration on a conditional basis, and the view that recognises arbitrability but keeps it under the ex-post control by the courts. The differences in these views seem to be due to different perceptions as to whether the arbitral tribunal should apply overriding mandatory rules to the same extent as the courts, or whether, even supposing it does apply those rules, the tribunal would be capable of making proper decisions.

A. View Denying Arbitrability and its Review

The view denying arbitrability argues that disputes of Types 1, 2 and 3 should not be resolved by arbitration on the following grounds.[9] First, it is difficult for an arbitral tribunal to comply with the principle of due process because its procedural rules are less strict than in court proceedings. Second, unlike judges, arbitrators do not belong to the legal system of a particular country, so there is a possibility that they will not apply the overriding mandatory rules of a particular country. Third, even if an arbitrator does apply an overriding mandatory rule, the arbitrator may lack the ability to apply it as accurately as a judge of the country to which the overriding mandatory rule belongs.

However, arbitration rules of various arbitration institutions and the arbitration laws of each country ensure due process in arbitration proceedings. In addition, even if the arbitrator is not bound by the legal system of a particular country, it can't be assumed that the arbitrator would lack the ability to apply overriding mandatory rules, since there is no empirical evidence of such.[10] Some believe that arbitrators will use their best efforts while keeping in mind what decisions the courts would render in similar cases; and since arbitrators may continue to be appointed in other cases, there is also an incentive for them to

[7] ibid 26–27.

[8] However, the KAA stipulates that its purpose is to properly, fairly and expeditiously resolve 'disputes in private law' by arbitration (Art 1), and the definition of arbitration is a procedure resolving 'property right disputes and non-property right disputes that the parties may resolve by settlement' through an arbitrator's award (Art 3), and the interpretation of arbitrability has developed based on this. See first, as an interpretation of arbitrability under the KAA, Kwang Hyun Suk, 'Major Contents of Amendment of the Arbitration Act of 2016 and Several Comments Thereon' (2017) 53 *Chonbuk Law Review* 213, 217–28.

[9] Hossein Fazilatfar, *Overriding Mandatory Rules in International Commercial Arbitration* (Edward Elgar Publishing, 2019) 37–39.

[10] In arbitration proceedings, where the arbitrator is not familiar with a foreign applicable law, a legal professional of that country can be selected as an expert witness of foreign law. The majority opinion of the Supreme Court of the United States in *Mitsubishi*, as seen below, also stated that the premise that the Japanese arbitral tribunal has no intention or capability of dealing with disputes related to antitrust laws is unreasonable.

apply the laws accurately.[11] Therefore, to completely deny the arbitrability of Types 1, 2 and 3 would not only lack reasonable grounds, but also excessively restricts party autonomy.

B. View Permitting Arbitration on a Conditional Basis (Belgian and German Courts)

The Belgian and German courts believe that arbitration should be allowed on a conditional basis. In the Belgian Supreme Court's *Van Hopplynus Instruments SA v Coherent Inc*,[12] a Belgian vendor had entered into an exclusive sales concession with a Californian equipment supplier. The governing law of the concession was Californian law, and the arbitration clause indicated California as the seat of arbitration. Thereafter, when the supplier unilaterally terminated the sales concession, the distributor filed a lawsuit in the Belgian court to claim compensation in accordance with Belgian law.[13] In response, the supplier requested arbitration. However, the distributor argued that the Belgian courts have jurisdiction to protect its rights and that the arbitration agreement is invalid because Belgium's overriding mandatory rules, which stipulate the right of distributors to claim compensation, applies.

Belgian law states that if a supplier of a sales concession with no fixed period terminates the contract, the distributor's right of indemnity is recognised notwithstanding any contrary agreement concluded before the end of the sales concession; that if the sales concession is effective entirely or partially within the territory of Belgium, the distributor may sue the supplier with the Belgian court; and that in this case, the court must apply exclusively Belgian law. This qualifies as an overriding mandatory rule of Belgium, and the text of the legislation gave reason to consider that the right to file a lawsuit with the Belgian court could not be excluded even if the Belgian distributor entered into an arbitration agreement. Thus, the controversy was whether the arbitrability of the right of the distributor to claim compensation would be denied. The Belgian Apex Court ruled that even though the governing law of the arbitration agreement was foreign law, arbitration should be excluded when there is no arbitrability under *lex fori*.

In *Audi NSU v Adelin Petit SA*,[14] Belgium's Court of Cassation again held that the distributor's claim cannot be arbitrated before the termination of the contract, as that would have the aim and effect of avoiding the application of overriding mandatory rules in Belgium.

Since the above decisions, the position of the Belgian Court has been that, in principle, compensation claims by distributors are not arbitrable (Types 1 and 2), but as an exception, an arbitration agreement is valid if the party that invokes the arbitration agreement proves that the above provisions of Belgian law will apply.[15]

[11] Alan Scott Rau, 'The Arbitrator and the "Mandatory Rules of Law"' in George A Berman and Loukas A Mistelis (eds), *Mandatory Rules in International Arbitration* (Juris, 2011) 126–27.

[12] Cour de cassation 16 November 2006, 2007 Revue Belge de Droit Commercial 889.

[13] *Loi relative à la Résiliation Unilatérale des Concessions de Vente Exclusive à Durée Indéterminée* (Law on the Unilateral Rescission of Exclusive Sales Concessions Concluded for an Unlimited Period of Time) of 27 July 1961, Art 3, MONITEUR BELGE (5 October 1961) (Belgium).

[14] Cass, 18 June 1979, *Audi NSU v. Adelin Petit SA*, 1979 PASICRISIE I 1260. See Kleinheisterkamp (2009) (n 2) 91, 97–98 for a more detailed introduction of this case.

[15] Kleinheisterkamp (ibid) 99.

The German[16] courts take a similar approach, albeit with different principles and exceptions.[17] The Munich High Court in Germany ruled on a matter (Type 1) of similar factual grounds to those of the Belgian Supreme Court decision, in which the right of indemnity of the commercial agent was at issue. In this case, the party that claimed the validity of the arbitration agreement argued that Article 89b of the German Commercial Code (*Handelsgesetzbuch*), which stipulates the right of commercial agents to claim compensation by enacting the EU's directive on commercial agents, constitutes an overriding mandatory rule, which affects only the agreement on governing law and not the arbitration agreement. However, the Court held that arbitration agreements could be prohibited in order to ensure the application of overriding mandatory rules. In other words, an arbitration agreement is valid unless it is reasonably expected that German overriding mandatory rules will be applied in arbitration. In cases where there is an arbitration agreement or a jurisdiction agreement with a foreign court as the competent court, and German overriding mandatory rules may not be applied, the person who asserts the validity of the arbitration agreement bears the burden of proof.[18] This ruling was criticised as it was based on 'the risk that German overriding mandatory rules will not apply in arbitration', breaking with previously restrictive approaches in which the arbitration clause or the jurisdiction agreement with a foreign court as the competent court would not be enforced when it was against German public policy.[19] Now, German courts affirm the arbitrability of claims (Type 1) based on overriding mandatory rules and acknowledge the validity of jurisdiction agreements designating foreign courts. Those agreements are invalid in cases where the arbitral tribunal or foreign courts would not apply German overriding mandatory rules or foreign laws would not provide an equivalent level of protection.[20]

A similar view in Korea[21] is that the arbitrability of overriding mandatory rules should be determined through a fair comparison between public and private interests, such as

[16] Oberlandesgericht München, 17 May 2006, 2006 Wertpapier Mittelungen 1556, 2007 IPRax 322 (FRG). See Kleinheisterkamp (2009) (n 2) 100 and thereafter for a detailed introduction to this decision and the above Belgian decision. Chung (2013a) (n 2) 13–14; Chung (2013b) (n 2) 332–34 also introduces this decision.

[17] Kleinheisterkamp (2018) (n 2) 907.

[18] Kleinheisterkamp (2009) (n 2) 103.

[19] ibid 105. In other words, the previous precedents determined the validity of an arbitration agreement based on whether the potential outcome of foreign arbitration proceedings would go against German public policy. However, according to the standard of the 'possibility that overriding mandatory rules will not apply' presented by this judgment, the actual outcome is not considered, so this qualifies as a more relaxed criterion. See also, Karsten Thorn and Moritz Nickel, 'The Effect of Overriding Mandatory Rules on the Arbitration Agreement' in Franco Ferrari and Stefan Kröll s (eds), *Conflict of Laws in International Commercial Arbitration* (Juris, 2019) 120ff. Thorn and Nickel contend that an arbitration agreement avoiding an overriding mandatory rule may be reviewed under the public policy ground set out in the New York Convention, in cases where the arbitration agreement results in the non-application of an overriding mandatory rule and therefore constitutes a breach of the fundamental legal principles of the forum state. They insist that the courts can strike out the arbitration agreement only in cases where it is 'overwhelmingly likely and almost certain' that the overriding mandatory rule will not be applied in arbitration. ibid 138.

[20] BGH 5 September 2012 VII ZR 25/12 (2012) Betriebsberater 3103, (2012) Gesellschafts- und Wirtschaftsrecht 486. The factual grounds of this and similar rulings are mostly about the European Union's directive related to self-employed commercial agents, as seen in the *Ingmar* case. See *Ingmar GB Ltd v Eaton Leonard Technologies Inc*, Case C-381/98. Kleinheisterkamp (2018) (n 2) 907.

[21] Lee (n 2) 35–40.

'ensuring the application of overriding mandatory rules'. For example, an arbitration agreement reached in a vertical contractual relationship would mainly be based on the will of the party in a superior position, reducing the need for protecting that party; so advocates of this view believe that the party that asserts the validity of an arbitration agreement must prove that overriding mandatory rules will be applied in the arbitration proceedings, and that otherwise, there is no arbitrability and accordingly the arbitration agreement should be invalidated.

There is also a view that the invalidity of an arbitration agreement should be determined in accordance with the principle of proportionality.[22] The invalidity of an arbitration agreement is a restriction on party autonomy and must comply with the principle of proportionality in the restriction of basic rights, and as long as the applicable law agreement of the parties can be revised, the arbitration agreement need not be invalidated. This view holds that in the US Supreme Court ruling in *Mitsubishi* (see section C, below), the recognition of arbitrability was grounded in the finding that American overriding mandatory rules will apply in the arbitration to be held in Japan and that the US Supreme Court maintains the same position as German and Belgian courts. According to this view, if one of the parties to an arbitration agreement files a lawsuit despite an arbitration agreement, and the other party recognises in the lawsuit that overriding mandatory rules will be applied in future arbitration, this could be viewed as an agreement on governing laws. In addition, since the arbitrator will apply overriding mandatory rules in accordance with the agreement on applicable laws, there would be no need to invalidate the arbitration agreement in such a case.

The common ground of these views is that claims based on overriding mandatory rules are not arbitrable unless the overriding mandatory rule will be applied in arbitration. However, these views have shortcomings. First, it presupposes the lack of the ability of the arbitral tribunal to properly apply (or apply at all) overriding mandatory rules.[23] Such a premise may not necessarily be correct.

Second, if an arbitration agreement is deemed valid only when the parties acknowledge or consent to applying the overriding mandatory rules, the validity of the agreement will depend on circumstances that occurred after the agreement was reached, thereby undermining the predictability of the dispute resolution method. This would be contrary to the parties' desire to eliminate uncertainty about the venue of dispute resolution.

Third, it may not be easy for the parties to prove that overriding mandatory rules will be applied in arbitration, and even if they fail to prove this, the arbitrator will not necessarily fail to apply overriding mandatory rules in arbitration.

Fourth, suggesting that the parties' consent is needed to apply overriding mandatory rules in arbitration seems to have some logical flaws, as that would conceptually mean that overriding mandatory rules, the application of which must not be excluded, may or may not apply according to the parties' intention.[24]

[22] Kleinheisterkamp (2009) (n 2) 115–18; Kleinheisterkamp (2018) (n 2) 904–05.

[23] According to Lee (n 2) 38, it is difficult to find legal grounds for the arbitrator to apply the overriding mandatory rules of countries other than the country to which the applicable law belongs, and that the arbitrator is not in a better position to protect the public interest compared to the judges in the national courts. The arbitrator is bound to view overriding mandatory rules from a different perspective from the judge, and is therefore unlikely to apply the overriding mandatory rules.

[24] However, in Type 1, it is possible for the parties to exclude the dispute from the arbitration agreement or from submission to arbitration.

Ultimately, the fundamental concern held by in the views denying arbitrability or allowing arbitration on a conditional basis – namely, that overriding mandatory rules will not be applied properly or at all in arbitration – can be resolved by establishing a uniform standard for which overriding mandatory rules should be considered or applied by the arbitrator (see section IV, below). Therefore, the view advocating for arbitrability on a conditional basis excessively restricts party autonomy and fails to provide a fundamental solution.

C. Validity of the View Supporting Arbitrability and Ex-post Control by the Court: The European Court of Justice and the US Supreme Court

The European Court of Justice and the US Supreme Court recognise the arbitrability of Types 1, 2, and 3, but take the stance that the court can exercise ex-post control. The leading case of the European Court of Justice in this regard is *Eco Swiss China Time Ltd v Benetton International NV*.[25] Benetton International NV (hereinafter Benetton) entered into a licence agreement with Eco Swiss China Time Ltd (hereinafter Eco Swiss) to manufacture and sell watches bearing its trademark and later terminated the licence agreement, in which there was an arbitration clause. Eco Swiss sought arbitration and claimed damages due to Benetton's termination of the contract. The arbitral tribunal granted damages by applying Dutch law, the governing law of the licence agreement, and neither of the parties alleged any violation of EU competition law in the arbitral proceedings. Article 81 of the European Convention Treaty (EC Treaty) (currently Article 101 of the Treaty on the Functioning of the European Union) prohibits restricting or distorting competition among Member States. Benetton filed a lawsuit with the courts of the Netherlands to annul the arbitral award, arguing that the licensing agreement violates the competition laws of the EU and violates public policy. The Dutch court referred this case to the European Court of Justice, which ruled that, since Article 81 of the EC Convention, which prohibits anti-competitive acts, is the EU's overriding mandatory rule, the courts of the Member States can revoke an arbitral award against EU competition law on the grounds of a breach of public policy. Commentators regard this ruling as having affirmed the arbitrability of Type 3, stating that its reason for annulling the arbitral award was the violation of public policy, rather than a lack of arbitrability.[26,27]

The US Supreme Court also affirmed the arbitrability of Types 1, 2 and 3 following an arbitration-friendly policy. In *Mitsubishi Motors Corp v Solar Chrysler-Plymouth* Inc,[28] a leading case, Soler Chrysler Plymouth Inc (hereinafter Soler), an automobile dealer from Puerto Rico, entered into a distributorship contract with Mitsubishi Motors (hereinafter Mitsubishi), a Japanese car manufacturer. The contract was governed by Swiss law, and there was an arbitration clause providing that the Japanese Commercial Arbitration Association

[25] Case C-126/97 [1999] ECR 3055 (ECJ).

[26] Kleinheisterkamp (2018) (n 2); Fazilatfar (n 9) 69.

[27] For another example where the European Court of Justice ruled that the arbitral award that violated the EU's overriding mandatory rule should be annulled for its violation of public policy, see *Elisa María Mostaza Claro v Centro Móvil Milenium* SLC-168/05 (2006) ECR I -10421, 34–35.

[28] 473 US 614 (1985).

(JCAA) would resolve all disputes arising in connection with the contract. According to the contract, Solar was to sell Mitsubishi motor vehicles exclusively in Puerto Rico, but could not resell them outside the territory of Puerto Rico, particularly in the US. Thereafter, when a dispute arose between Soler and Mitsubishi regarding the vehicle sales price, Mitsubishi filed a lawsuit in a US federal court to enforce the arbitration agreement. Soler filed a counterclaim, claiming that the prohibition of sales under the distributorship contract violates the Sherman Act and that the dispute should not be resolved by arbitration because the US federal court has exclusive jurisdiction over disputes arising from Sherman Act violations. The majority opinion of the US Supreme Court affirmed the arbitrability of claims based on the Sherman Act and recognised the enforceability of the arbitration agreement, declaring the legal principle:

> Even if such dispute is resolved by arbitration, it would not constitute any waiver of statutory rights, but if both the arbitration clause and the applicable law clause serve as an advance waiver of statutory rights, such would be contrary to public policy,[29] and if the Sherman Act is incorrectly applied by the arbitrator, the courts could have their second look.[30]

However, the US Supreme Court stated that the substantive review of the arbitral award would be limited to whether the arbitrator recognised the claim under the Sherman Act and made a determination on it.[31] This ruling is significant in that it recognises the arbitrability and validity of arbitral awards for Types 1 and 3, and declares that rights based on overriding mandatory rules cannot be waived.[32]

The US Supreme Court thereafter affirmed the arbitrability of securities law violation cases in *Scherk v Alberto-Culver*[33] (Type 2) notwithstanding the provision of the Securities Act that US courts have exclusive jurisdiction over disputes of securities law violations. That was based on the premise that arbitrators can properly apply the overriding mandatory rules of the US.[34]

In light of the difficulties with the views denying the arbitrability of Types 1, 2 and 3 or allowing arbitration under certain conditions, it is a better approach to recognise

[29] 473 US 614, 637, n 19 (1985). There are contradictory views as to the meaning of this note. Based on the fact that the Court admitted that US law would be applicable in arbitration and stated the same to the arbitral tribunal, some view that the US court, based on the factual grounds of the case, recognised the arbitrability on the condition that Sherman Act would be applicable to arbitration. Kleinheisterkamp (2009) (n 2) 115. On the other hand, some opine that n 19 does not purport that arbitration is possible on the condition that the parties either acknowledge that US law should be applied or waive the agreement on the applicable law. Fazilatfar contends that as a result of the arbitration clause in this case being drafted with a broader scope than that of the applicable law clause, the Japanese tribunal could consider violations of the Sherman Act even if the applicable law of the contract was Swiss law. Fazilatfar (n 9) 166.

[30] 473 US 614, 638. The US Supreme Court stated that an intrusive inquiry is not necessary as to whether the arbitrator recognised the Sherman law provisions and made a decision thereon and that whether the arbitrator correctly applied the Sherman Act can be assessed at the enforcement stage of arbitral awards.

[31] 473 US 614, 638. Alexander KA Greenwalt, 'Does International Arbitration Need a Mandatory Rules Method?' in George A Berman and Loukas A Mistelis (eds), *Mandatory Rules in International Arbitration* (Justice, 2011) 152 states that if the arbitral tribunal had recognised and adjudged on a claim based on the Sherman Act, the court cannot re-examine it even if the arbitral tribunal misapplied the law.

[32] Greenwalt (ibid) 151.

[33] 417 US 506 (1974).

[34] H. Smit, 'Mandatory Law in Arbitration' in George A Berman and Loukas A Mistelis (eds), *Mandatory Rules in International Arbitration* (Juris, 2011) 22.

arbitrability, subject to the court's ex-post control.[35] This view is also consistent with the trend[36] of recognising a wider scope of arbitrability.

However, those opposing arbitrability or advocating for the validity of arbitration agreements on a conditional basis may argue that if the arbitrability and the validity of the arbitration agreement were to be recognised despite the high possibility that the overriding mandatory rules would not apply in arbitration, and if the courts examine the arbitral award only at the stage of annulment or recognition/enforcement of the arbitral award, then the parties would have gone through a futile procedure, resulting in the waste of time and money.[37] This criticism, for example, presupposes that overriding mandatory rules of Belgian law will not apply in the Californian arbitration. However, this situation could be avoided by establishing a framework that allows for the consideration or application of overriding mandatory rules of a country closely related to the subject matter of arbitration (see section IV, below). This approach is considered most suitable for achieving harmonious balance between party autonomy and the essential public interest protected by overriding mandatory rules.

D. Interpretation of the KAA[38]

On the premise that the requirements for arbitrability under Articles 1 and 3 of the KAA are met, the interpretation of the Arbitration Act would not deny the arbitrability of disputes of Types 1, 2 and 3 solely on the grounds that they are related to overriding mandatory rules.

For Types 1, 2 and 3, the question of the validity of an arbitration agreement is similar to the question of whether an exclusive choice-of-court agreement designating a foreign court should be deemed null and void on the grounds that the overriding mandatory rules of the country of the forum state may not apply in the designated court. When referring to the validity[39] requirements of an exclusive choice-of-court agreement presented by the Supreme

[35] Suk (n 8) 224; In-ho Kim, 'Reasonably-tailored Arbitrability to Promote the Development of International Trade' (2016) 23 *Journal of Comparative Private Law* 1153 purport the same opinion.

[36] Jeffrey Maurice Waincymer, 'International Commercial Arbitration and the Application of Mandatory Rules of Law' (2009) 5 *Asian International Arbitration Journal* 7.

[37] Kleinheisterkamp (2009) (n 2) 111–12; Chung (2013b) (n 2) 336.

[38] This discussion takes as its premise that the applicable law of arbitrability and the arbitration agreement is Korean law. The New York Convention does not specify the applicable law for arbitrability before the enforcement stage. In Korean legal literature, different views were suggested to apply either *lex fori*, *lex contractus* of arbitration agreements, *lex loci arbitri*, and the overlapping theory. For more details, see Kyung Han Sohn, 'Party Autonomy and Applicable Law in Arbitration Korea' (2011) 17 *Korea Private International Law Journal* 411, 426–28; In-ho Kim, 'Reasonably-tailored Arbitrability' (2016) 1155 and Suk (n 2) 275ff. The author supports *lex fori* theory for the following reasons. First, since Art 5(2)(a) of the New York Convention stipulates *lex fori* of the country of enforcement as the governing law of arbitrability, for the sake of consistency, *lex fori* should also apply before the arbitral award is rendered. For the enforcement state, the 'forum' court may be the court where the proceeding is brought despite an arbitration agreement. Second, since arbitrability is a principle for determining the allocation of jurisdiction between the arbitral tribunal and the court, the interests of the court deprived of jurisdiction should be considered. Therefore, arbitrability is to be determined in accordance with the *lex fori* of the court in charge of the review of the arbitral tribunal's competence, and that of the court in which the lawsuit was filed in violation of the arbitration agreement. However, if the court has not yet been requested to review the arbitral tribunal's jurisdiction, the law of the seat of arbitration should apply.

[39] As one of the requirements of validity for an exclusive jurisdiction agreement, the Supreme Court states that 'if an exclusive jurisdiction agreement is manifestly unreasonable and unfair, it will be against public policy and

Court of Korea, it may be too drastic a measure to invalidate an arbitration agreement solely because there is a possibility that an overriding mandatory rule may not be considered or applied in the arbitration, unless the arbitration agreement is significantly unreasonable, unfair and contrary to public policy.[40]

Therefore, the better interpretation of the KAA is to recognise the arbitrability and the validity of arbitration agreements of Types 1, 2 and 3, but to allow consideration or application of overriding mandatory rules in arbitration (see section IV below). However, since there is a view that the arbitrator cannot consider or apply overriding mandatory rules unless the parties agree, the feasibility thereof should be reviewed first.

III. Whether the Arbitrator May Consider or Apply Overriding Mandatory Rules without the Agreement of the Parties

A. A View that Overriding Mandatory Rules cannot be Considered or Applied by the Arbitrator Unless Agreed to by the Parties

There is a view that the arbitrator cannot apply overriding mandatory rules against the will of the parties on the following grounds.[41] Arbitration is based on party autonomy, and it is purely a product of a contract. The arbitrator, as a person appointed by the parties, plays a role in protecting private interests and does not play a public role such as a judge in the national courts.[42] Therefore, applying overriding mandatory rules against the parties' express or implied agreement contradicts the nature of arbitration and the role of the arbitrator. However, if the parties drafted an arbitration clause broadly to include claims concerning overriding mandatory rules, the arbitrator is permitted to consider or apply those rules. For example, if the arbitration clause provides that 'all disputes arising in connection with the contract shall be resolved by arbitration', claims under competition law related to the contract may also be included in the scope of the arbitration clause. If, on the other hand, claims under competition law are expressly excluded from the scope of the arbitration agreement, this will not apply.[43]

therefore invalid.' Supreme Court, Judgment of 9 September 1997, Case No 96Da20093. See Art 8 of the Korean Act on Private International Law for the validity requirements of a choice-of-court agreement.

[40] Suk (n 2) 181–82 purports the same. For a comparable view from Japan, see Kazuaki Nishioka, 'Choice of Court Agreements and Designation from Competition Law' (2020) 16 *Journal of Private International Law* 300.

[41] Pierre Mayer, 'Mandatory Rules of Law in International Arbitration' (1986) 2 *Arbitration International* 274, 280ff. According to this view, the overriding mandatory rules of the country to which the applicable law belongs can be applied if they meet the following two requirements: (1) that they were not excluded by the agreement of the parties; and (2) that the parties would have invoked them in the arbitration procedure. Fazilatfar (n 9) 84 also introduces such a view in fn 47 and references Yves Derains, 'Public Policy and the Law Applicable to the Dispute in International Arbitration' in Pieter Sanders (ed), *Comparative Arbitration Practice and Public Policy in Arbitration* (Kluwer Law International, 1987) 227–28.

[42] Lee (n 2) 38.

[43] Greenwalt (n 31) 158.

B. Evaluation

However, the above argument is unsatisfactory. First of all, it is possible to argue that overriding mandatory rules should not be excluded from arbitration merely because arbitration is a private dispute resolution. A dispute can be resolved by arbitration because the state's legal order and the courts that originally have inherent jurisdiction have accepted the arbitrator's jurisdiction;[44] arbitration itself cannot be deemed to exist in a legal vacuum. Although a unique principle of choice of law is allowed in arbitration, the freedom of choice of law is still restricted by overriding mandatory rules.[45] Overriding mandatory rules, by definition, cannot be excluded by agreement between the parties, and the absence of agreement between the parties cannot hinder the arbitrator from considering or apply such rules. Furthermore, considering that the New York Convention provides for a violation of public policy as one of the grounds for refusing recognition and enforcement of an arbitral award, it can be said that the arbitrator's rendering of an enforceable arbitral award that does not violate public policy is in line with the reasonable expectations of the parties,[46] and in that sense the arbitrator does play a public role in protecting public policy.[47]

On the other hand, unlike in litigation, there is no 'forum' in arbitration, and unlike judges, arbitrators are not bound by the legal system of a particular country or the private international law of the forum state. In arbitration, *lex causae* can be directly applied to the substance of the dispute by the arbitrators. That raises the question of whether they are not obligated to apply the mandatory provisions of a country other than the country to which the governing law belongs.[48] It is true that the connection between the seat of arbitration and the parties or the subject matter may not be as strong as that with the forum state in litigation. It follows that the substantive overriding mandatory rules of the seat of arbitration may not be applied or considered as a matter of course, in the way the overriding mandatory rules of the forum do in litigation. However, as we will explore below, this does not mean that overriding mandatory rules can never be considered or applied in arbitration, for three reasons.

First, if the applicable law to the merits has been designated in arbitration, overriding mandatory rules of the country of lex causae shall be applied as a part of that law.[49] In addition, if there is a principle in the *lex causae* that considers the law of a third country,[50] the law of that third country may be indirectly considered. In fact, there have been cases in which

[44] Constantin Calavros, 'The Application of Substantive Mandatory Rules in International Commercial Arbitration from the Perspective of an EU UNCITRAL Model Law Jurisdiction' (2018) 34 *Arbitration International* 233.

[45] Sohn (n 38) 419 also contends that the overriding mandatory rules can 'override' the parties' choice-of-law agreement.

[46] Art 41 of the ICC Arbitration Rules 2012 and Art 32(2) of the 1998 LCIA Arbitration Rules expressly stipulate that arbitrators are obliged to make an effort to render legally enforceable arbitral awards.

[47] Marc Blessing, 'Mandatory Rules versus Party Autonomy in International Arbitration' (1997) 14 *Journal of International Arbitration* 40 also states that arbitrators are not required to serve or submit to the parties and are not only obligated to them.

[48] Kim (n 38) 1169.

[49] See s IV, A, below.

[50] The English courts initially considered illegality under the laws of third countries in terms of the principles of illegality and public policy of the contract. *Foster v Driscoll* (1928) All ER Rep 130; *Ralli Bros v Compania Naviera Sota y Aznar* (1920) 2 KB 287 (CA). The German Court has also considered the validity of a contract that violates

the law of a third state that is closely related to the subject matter was considered a fact under the applicable law in arbitration. In ICC Case No 5622,[51] a French company entered into a contract to advise and cooperate with a UK company in connection with the execution of a contract to be performed in Algeria, the governing law of which was Swiss law. However, the law of Algeria, the place of performance, prohibited such a contract. Accordingly, the arbitral tribunal did not accept the French company's claim for payment based on the contract on the grounds that it violated Swiss public policy in its violation of the laws of Algeria. In *Northrop Corp v Triad International Marketing SA*,[52] the recognition and enforcement of an arbitral award was sought in US court in a case in which the plaintiff was a combat aircraft manufacturer in the US and the defendant was a Liechtenstein company wholly owned by a Saudi Arabian individual. The defendant signed a contract to help the plaintiff and the Saudi Air Force enter into a combat aircraft sales contract for fees from the plaintiff, and the governing law of the contract was Californian law. However, when the Saudi Government enacted a law prohibiting the payment of fees in connection with the execution of an arms sales contract, the plaintiff suspended the payment of fees, and the defendant initiated arbitration. In the arbitration proceedings, the arbitrator considered Saudi Arabian law as a fact under the governing law (being Californian law) and decided whether the contract became impossible due to Saudi Arabian law.

Second, depending on the national arbitration law or arbitration rules, the arbitrator may determine the applicable law with the guidance of private international law, which may stipulate the application of overriding mandatory rules. For example, Article 28(2) of the UNCITRAL Model Law on International Commercial Arbitration (hereinafter the Model Arbitration Law) provides that the governing law applicable to the substance of a dispute be determined in accordance with private international law rules the arbitral tribunal considers applicable. In this case, if the private international law deemed applicable by the arbitrator provides that the overriding mandatory rules of the *lex causae* or a third country may be considered or applied (eg, Article 9(3) of the Rome I Regulation), the overriding mandatory rules may be applied. It is also worth noting that Articles 1.4 and 3.3.1 of the UNIDROIT Principles of International Commercial Contracts (hereinafter UNIDROIT International Commercial Contract Principles) of the International Institute for the Unification of Private Law stipulate that arbitrators are obligated to apply overriding mandatory rules. Article 11(5) of the Hague Principles on Choice of Law in International Commercial Contracts also stipulates that the above principle does not prevent the arbitral tribunal from considering the overriding mandatory rules of laws that has not been chosen by the parties. That means that arbitration should respect overriding mandatory rules of other countries as much as it respects party autonomy. Arbitration should not be used as a means to evade the application of such mandatory provisions.[53]

the overriding mandatory rules of a third country as a fact according to good morals, the impossibility of performance, and the underlying basis of the transactions of German civil law. BGHZ 34, 169–79; NJW 15, 1436–38; BGHZ 59, 82–87; RG, RGZ 93, 182 ff. For English and German case law and other substantive-law approaches, see ch 5, II, B and C.

[51] ICC Yearbook of Commercial Arbitration (1994) 112.

[52] 811 F 2d 1265 (9th Cir 1987).

[53] Fazilatfar (n 9) 78.

Third, since the scope of arbitrable cases has expanded over time, it is necessary for arbitrators to consider or apply overriding mandatory rules. The reason for conventionally denying the arbitrability of cases involving public interest or national interest was to reserve such cases for the national courts.[54] However, arbitrability gradually increased, leading to the recognition of the arbitrability of Types 1, 2 and 3. The purpose of expanding arbitrability is not to allow the parties to avoid overriding mandatory rules in arbitration.[55] This point was also clearly present in the aforementioned US Supreme Court's *Mitsubishi* ruling.

It is necessary to distinguish between the fact that the parties cannot exclude the application of overriding mandatory rules and that the arbitrator's jurisdiction should be in accordance with the arbitration agreement.[56] If a party explicitly excludes a claim based on an overriding mandatory rule (Type 1) in an arbitration agreement, that agreement is valid because the parties do not renounce or exclude the application of an overriding mandatory rule, as the aim of that agreement is to resolve claims about an overriding mandatory rule through a court decision. Therefore, the arbitrator has no authority to decide on such a claim.[57] On the other hand, the parties cannot exclude overriding mandatory rules that should be applied in determining a specific claim by a choice of law, ie, explicitly agree to exclude overriding mandatory rules from the scope of applicable law (Type 3). Even if the parties have agreed to that, the arbitrator may ignore it and, *ex officio*, consider or apply overriding mandatory rules or refuse to arbitrate. That is because the parties cannot derogate from overriding mandatory rules and because applying the law is the obligation of the arbitrator.[58] The 2008 Report on Ascertaining the Contents of the Applicable Law in International Commercial Arbitration by the International Law Association's Arbitration Committee[59] also advises that, in disputes involving public policy or rules that require the agreement of the parties, the arbitrator may conduct an independent investigation to adequately determine the applicability and content of the overriding mandatory rules, give appropriate directions, or take other appropriate measures as necessary to comply with those rules and prevent the annulment of the award. Even in this case, however, the arbitrator should give the parties a reasonable opportunity to voice their opinions in accordance with the principle of due process.[60]

[54] At the time of the establishment of the New York Convention, it was considered that there was no arbitrability on the fundamental public policies of the forum. Kleinheisterkamp (2009) (n 2) 119.

[55] Fazilatfar (n 9) 78.

[56] Submission to arbitration means an independent agreement to submit existing disputes to arbitration. Suk (n 2) 286.

[57] This is equivalent to the 'principle of disposition' in litigation. The arbitrator does not have a jurisdiction to determine on the right to claim compensation under the aforementioned Belgian laws, if the Belgian distributors have not raised such a claim in arbitration, which is based on the overriding mandatory rules of Belgian law.

[58] Audley Sheppard, 'Mandatory Rules in International Commercial Arbitration: An English Law Perspective' in George A Berman and Loukas A Mistelis (eds), *Mandatory Rules in International Arbitration* (Juris, 2011) 204.

[59] ILA International Arbitration Committee, Report on Ascertaining the Contents of the Applicable Law in International Commercial Arbitration, presented at the ILA's seventy-third conference in Rio de Janeiro (August 2008) 23, Recommendation 13 (accessible at www.academia.edu/18695931/ILA_FINAL_REPORT_ON_ASCERTAINING_THE_CONTENTS_OF_THE_APPLICABLE_LAW_IN_INTERNATIONAL_COMMERCIAL_ARBITRATION_RIO_DE_JANEIRO_2008_).

[60] Fazilatfar (n 9) 101; Laurence Shore, 'Applying mandatory rules of law in international commercial arbitration' in George A Berman and Loukas A Mistelis (eds), *Mandatory Rules in International Arbitration* (Juris, 2011) 205.

IV. Scope of the Overriding Mandatory Rules Capable of Being Applied or Considered in Arbitration

Now we will look at the scope of the overriding mandatory rules that can be considered or applied in arbitration. In the context of litigation, overriding mandatory rules may be classified, depending on the country to which they belong, as overriding mandatory rules of the forum, overriding mandatory rules of *lex causae* and overriding mandatory rules of a third country.[61] However, in arbitration, the seat of arbitration does not correspond to the concept of the forum in litigation as that seat may be chosen for various practical reasons and therefore may not have a strong connection to the case. In other words, in arbitration, 'overriding mandatory rules of the forum'[62] cannot be recognised. Thus, the overriding mandatory rules of *lex causae* and of a third country are the relevant categories in arbitration.

A. Overriding Mandatory Rules of the State of *Lex Causae*

It is widely accepted that the overriding mandatory rules of the applicable law are applied in litigation.[63] Aside from those who contend that overriding mandatory rules themselves cannot be considered or applied in arbitration,[64] there seem to be no particular problems in applying in arbitration the overriding mandatory rules of the country to which the applicable law belongs.[65] The question is what requirements there should be in considering or applying the overriding mandatory rules of a third country.

[61] Suk (n 2) 148. See ch 2, III for the specific issues with different categories of overriding mandatory rules.

[62] An alternate view is that the place of arbitration plays a role corresponding to the forum in litigation. Calavros (n 44) 219–22 stipulates that in jurisdictions that accept the Model Arbitration Law, the scope of application of arbitration laws is arbitration conducted in its territory, and because, in particular, Art 28(2) of the Model Arbitration Law provides that the governing law applicable to the substance of a dispute can be determined in accordance with the principle of private international law that the arbitrator deems applicable, it is sufficient to say that the place of arbitration is a place corresponding to a forum. However, unlike Art 28(2) of the Model Arbitration Law, the KAA stipulates that the law of the country most closely related to the subject matter of the dispute be applied, so this position would not be plausible interpretation of Korean law, or any other law that states a direct application of the substantive law by an arbitrator. In interpreting the KAA, therefore, Korean overriding mandatory rules don't apply to the substance of a dispute for the mere reason that the place of arbitration is Korea.

[63] However, with respect to the basis for its application, there is a tension between *Einheitstheorie* and the Special Connection (*Sonderanknüpfung*) Theory. For an introduction, see the section by Dieter Martiny in Franz Jürgen Säcker (ed), *Münchener Kommentar zum BGB*, 8th edn (Verlag Beck München, 2021), Room I-VO Art 9, Rn 36 ff; Lisa Günther, *Die Anwendbargkeit ausländischer Eingriffnormen im Lichter der Rom I- und Rom II Verordnungen* (Verlag Alma Mater, 2011) 15; Kwang Hyun Suk, 'The Role of the Private International Law Act and the Cultural Property Protection Act of Korea as Means of Protecting Cultural Property from International Illicit Transactions and the Proposal for Improvement' (2015) 56 *Seoul Law Journal* 117, 142; Junhyok Jang, 'Conflict's Mandatory Character as the Key Element of Internationally Mandatory Rules' (2007) 19 *SungKyunKwan Law Review* 563, 571.

[64] Sheppard (n 58) 172 introduces this view, but does not reveal its supporters.

[65] However, even in this case, the factual grounds of the case should be within the scope of application of the overriding mandatory rules of the country to which the applicable law belongs. For example, the Housing Grants, Construction and Regeneration Act 1996, which is an overriding mandatory rule of the UK regarding construction contracts, applies regardless of the applicable law of construction contracts provided that the construction site is in the UK (Art 104(6)–(7) of the same Act). Therefore, even if the governing law of the construction contract was English law, the above law would not apply if the construction site was not in the UK.

B. Overriding Mandatory Rules of a Third Country

As discussed in chapter five, the issue of applying the overriding mandatory rules of a third country is one of the most controversial topics in private international law.[66] In the context of litigation, the Rome I Regulation and the Swiss FAPIL have explicit provisions. Although arbitrators may determine the applicable law without the guidance of conflict of laws principles, they are not blocked from being assisted by them.[67] Examining the discussion regarding litigation helps establish the criteria for determining the scope of applying overriding mandatory rules in arbitration. As I have discussed the pros and cons of different legislation in the context of litigation in chapter five, I will now review other suggested views in the specific context of arbitration.

i. Theories in the Context of International Commercial Arbitration

Various views have been presented on how to consider or apply the overriding mandatory rules of third countries in international commercial arbitration.[68]

(1) The transnational public policy approach is the view that an arbitrator is obligated to apply a law only when it reflects a transnational public policy.[69] Transnational public policy is distinct from the international public policy at issue in the recognition and enforcement of foreign arbitral awards, referring instead to the fundamental principles of natural law, the principles of global justice, *jus cogens* of international public law, and the principles of ethics generally recognised in civilised countries.[70] This view limits the arbitrator's discretion and contributes to the predictability and consistency of the outcome of the arbitral award by recognising the narrowest possible scope of a third country's overriding mandatory rules. However, it is difficult to define the contents and scope of transnational public policy,[71] and while we should not presume that international commercial arbitration is completely insulated from the regulations of a particular state, taking this view presents difficulty in its failure to consider the regulations of a country closely related to the matter. For example, even if the governing law was chosen to be the law of a country other than where the construction site was located, the construction company should comply with the overriding mandatory rules of the country where the construction site is located (eg, the 10-year

[66] Martiny (n 63), EGBGB Art 34, Rn 3. See ibid Rn 40ff; Günther (n 64) 57–66; Paul Hauser, *Eingriffsnormen in der Rom- I Verordnung* (Mohr Siebeck, 2012) 96–100; Suk (n 63) 150 and thereafter; Kwang Hyun Suk, 'The Application of Foreign Exchange Control Law and Other Internationally Mandatory Rules of Third Countries in International Financial Transactions: Including Article VIII2(b) of the Articles of Agreement of the International Monetary Fund' (2020) 26 *Korea Private International Law Journal* 379–81; Choon Soo An, 'International zwingende Bestimmungen im IPR – Theorien und die Bedeutung von Artt. 6, 7 IPR Koreas' (2011) 23 *Kookmin Law Review* 195–205; Changseon Shin and Namsoon Yoon, *New Private International Law* [Singukjesabeop je2pan], 2nd edn (Fides, 2016) 279–87. For different views before the Rome Convention, refer to ch 5.

[67] Suk (n 2) 168.

[68] In the following section, I classify the views I have encountered in the existing legal literature. For reference, Waincymer (n 36) 20 introduces the Special Connection Theory, transnational public policy approach, and legitimate expectations theory among these views.

[69] See Waincymer (n 36) 34–36 for a detailed introduction to this view. Calavros (n 44) 232 supports this view.

[70] Waincymer (n 36) 34.

[71] ibid 35.

defect warranty and subcontractors' direct indemnity for construction costs under the laws of France), but the transnational public policy theory would fail to explain such a situation.

(2) There is a view that overriding mandatory rules apply only when the parties legitimately expect that they will be applied.[72] However, this view does not accurately explain what the parties' legitimate expectations are.[73] It also overlooks the fact that overriding mandatory rules, by definition, cannot be excluded by the intention or expectation of the parties.

(3) The maximal approach states that, since the arbitration clause is generally drafted more broadly than the applicable law clause, the arbitrator has the authority and duty to examine mandatory rules other than the law designated by the parties as the applicable law.[74] In principle, the overriding mandatory rules of all relevant countries are applied, but the overriding mandatory rules of a particular country are not applied when the core interests they are intended to protect can also be protected by the overriding mandatory rules of other countries.[75] However, it may not be practical to expect the arbitrator to be aware of or to investigate all relevant overriding mandatory rules. This may also undermine the predictability of the applicable law.[76] This view is not desirable since it is little different from giving up on trying to establish criteria for applying overriding mandatory rules in arbitration.

(4) There is a view that the overriding mandatory rules of the place of performance and the place of enforcement should apply to ensure the efficacy of the arbitral award.[77] The main grounds for this view are that the arbitrator is obligated to make an enforceable arbitral award. However, if the party's property is located in several countries, it is difficult to accurately predict the place of enforcement at the arbitration stage. In addition, since there are many factors that may affect the effectiveness of the arbitral award, this should not be the only decisive criterion for the application of overriding mandatory rules.[78]

(5) A view that the *lex loci arbitri* should be applied argues that if the arbitral award violates the overriding mandatory rules of the place of arbitration, the arbitral award may be annulled, so *lex loci arbitri* must be given special status. This view contends that the overriding mandatory rules should be applied in accordance with the private international law of the place of arbitration.[79] However, although the violation of procedural mandatory rules in the seat of arbitration may constitute grounds for revoking the

[72] ibid 37–38; Shore (n 60) 140 for an introduction to this view. The former article cites Yves Derains (n 41) 228 as an opinion supporting this view.

[73] Shore (n 60) 140.

[74] For example, if the parties agreed that the applicable law of the supply contract of goods was English law, and that an arbitration agreement was made to resolve 'all disputes arising in connection with the contract'. If this agreement has an anti-competitive effect on the US market and either party claims damages against the other party for breach of the Sherman Act, English law applies only to the contract itself and does not apply to 'all disputes arising in connection with the contract'. Disputes arising from the violation of the Sherman Act are not governed by English law, but they are included in the scope of the arbitration clause as disputes arising in connection with the contract, so the arbitrator can make a decision on this. Accordingly, the arbitrator will resolve the dispute in accordance with American law, not the applicable law agreed upon by the parties.

[75] Greenwalt (n 31) 164–267.

[76] Fazilatfar (n 9) 164 also purports the same.

[77] ibid 156–58, 170.

[78] ibid 157 also recognises this.

[79] Shore (n 60) 131.

arbitral award, there are not sufficient grounds for applying the substantive mandatory rules of the place of arbitration even when the subject matter is unrelated to the place of arbitration.

(6) The Special Connection Theory, as asserted in the context of litigation, is a view based on Article 7(1) of the Rome Convention and Article 19 of the Swiss FAPIL. According to this view, it is possible to consider or apply the overriding mandatory rules of a country closely connected to the subject matter, taking into account the content of the rules and the consequences of their application or non-application.[80] The legal interests protected by laws and regulations must be worthy of protection as critical social and economic values (known as the 'shared values') Additionally, the outcomes of applying such laws and regulations must also be considered appropriate.[81] This view does not necessarily recognise the place of arbitration as being a close connection to the subject matter. Consequently, it may consider or apply the law of a country closely related to the matter even if it is not the place of arbitration.

Considering the weaknesses of the views explained earlier and the strengths of the Special Connection Theory, I believe that the Special Connection Theory is the most appropriate solution.[82] In this regard, it is worth paying particular attention to one of the following two drafts presented on the Law Applicable to International Contracts in 1980 by the International Chamber of Commerce Commission on Law and Commercial Practices.

Draft 1

Even when the arbitrator does not apply the law of a certain country as the law governing the contract he may nevertheless give effect to mandatory rules of law of that country if the contract or the parties have a close contact to that country and if and in so far as under its law those rules must be applied whatever may be the law applicable to the contract. On considering whether to give effect to these mandatory rules, regard shall be had to their nature and purpose and to the consequences of their application or non-application.

Draft 2

Even when the arbitrator does not apply the law of a certain country as the law applicable to the contract he may nevertheless give effect to the mandatory rules of the law of that country if the contract or parties have a close contact to the country in question especially when the arbitral award is likely to be enforced there, and if and in so far as under the law of that country those rules must be applied whatever be the law applicable to the contract.

[80] Blessing (n 47) 32–33; Waincymer (n 36) 30–33; Shore (n 60) 135–39.
[81] Blessing (n 47) 32.
[82] Sohn (n 38) 440 purports the same.

However, with regard to such a position, criticism has been raised that the scope of the overriding mandatory rules of a third country that are considered or applied in arbitration should be limited to the rules of the country that is the place of performance, as in the Rome I Regulation, because the criterion of close connection is vague and undermines predictability and legal stability.[83] The plausibility of such a challenge is to be reviewed in the following section.

ii. Whether the Scope of a Third Country's Legislation Should be Limited to Lex Loci Solutionis

a. Supposed Ambiguity of the Close Connection Requirement

The view that the scope of third countries' overriding mandatory rules should be limited to the place of performance faces the following challenges.

First, the concept of 'close connection' is widely recognised under private international law, including the KAPIL and KAA, as well as the Rome Convention and the Rome I Regulation. Since there are a lot of precedents on close connection across jurisdictions, it cannot be said that this concept is ambiguous. Recently, it has been argued that the closest connection principle should be uniformly applied in arbitration as the principle for determining the applicable law of the merits.[84]

Second, this view does not account for why the law of a country closely related to the matter (ie, the overriding mandatory rules of a country with essential regulatory interests) should not be considered or applied. In the case where a debtor is subject to the overriding mandatory rules of a country that is not the place of performance, but in which the debtor's residence or property is located, to prepare for the performance of the debt, it will be necessary to consider the hardship, at least under the substantive applicable law.

Third, there may be cases where it is difficult to determine the place of performance depending on the specific type of transaction. In particular, in international financial transactions where account transfers and payments are made among various countries, it may not be easy to determine the place of performance. Even in cases where the place of performance can be determined, it may not be particularly related to the subject matter.[85] In addition, due to the increase in international mobility, the expansion of online transactions, and the increase in work from home in foreign countries since the COVID-19 pandemic, it may be difficult to determine the place of labour or services under employment or consumer contracts.

Fourth, since the types of contractual obligations and overriding mandatory rules vary, it is insufficient for the place of performance to be the only decisive criterion.[86] Locational, functional and personal standards may be important depending on the case.

[83] Chung (2013a) (n 2) 23–24.

[84] Benjamin Hayward, *Conflict of Laws and Arbitral Discretion: The Closest Test* (Oxford University Press, 2017) paras 7.05–7.07.

[85] Charles Proctor, *Mann on the Legal Aspect of Money*, 7th edn (Oxford University Press, 2012) para 4.20; Suk (n 67) 376, fn 99. This article introduces the UK Court's *Libyan Arab Foreign Bank v Bankers Trust Co* (1989) QB 728 as a similar example.

[86] Martiny (n 63) EGBGB Art 34, Rn 138; Section by Dieter Martiny in Franz Jürgen Säcker, *Münchener Kommentar zum BGB*, 8th edn (Verlag Beck München, 2021) Rom I-VO Art 9, Rn 125 purports the same.

'Close connection' is a better criterion as it allows the incorporation of various standards, as shown in the following section.

iii. Criteria for Finding Close Connection

Potential criteria proposed for identifying close connection include the place of performance of the contract, the location of property, the residence of the party, the workplace or place of employment, the location of the affected market, and nationality.[87] It is necessary to consider such factors comprehensively to determine whether there is a close connection. Specifically, close connection can be found in the following circumstances:[88]

(1) Place of performance: Although it would not be appropriate to limit the scope of a third country to the place of performance, that can still be an example of a close connection. The *lex loci solutionis* of the place of performance can affect the performance of the contract. In the case of an international construction contract, one example might be the laws of the country where the construction site is located. Suppose that a Korean company has concluded a construction contract in France of which the governing law is English law, and executed the construction project accordingly. However, under the French Civil Code, the provisions on the contractor's 10-year defect liability constitute an overriding mandatory rule.[89] If a dispute arises in relation to defects in buildings constructed in France and arbitration begins, the 10-year defect liability must be considered, despite English law, which is the governing law of the contract, stipulating a shorter period of defect liability.[90]

(2) Place of residence of the debtor: Where the debtor is a natural person, he/she shall be under the sovereignty of the country of his/her habitual residence, and where the debtor is a company or a corporation, it shall be under the sovereignty of a country in which it was registered; hence, the overriding mandatory rules of such countries may show close connection.

(3) Location of property: The country in which property is located or disposed of may require that its overriding mandatory rules apply in relation to that property. The provisions of laws on land or location of housing that require permission to dispose of land or residential facilities as part of agricultural or residential policies are deemed to be closely related. In addition, although the law of the place of enforcement should not be necessarily considered or applied in arbitration, it may be included in the closely connected countries if the place of enforcement is where the debtor's property is located.

[87] Martiny (n 86) EGBGB Art 34, Rn 140; M Guilano and P Lagarde, 'Report on the Convention on the Law Applicable to Contractual Obligations' (1980) C 282 *Official Journal* Art 7(2); Richard Plender and Michael Wilderspin, *The European Contracts Convention: The Rome Convention on the Choice of Law for Contracts* (Sweet & Maxwell, 2001) para 9-09.

[88] For details, see ch 6, III, B.

[89] Kwang Hyun Suk, 'Laws Applicable to International Construction Contracts Using FIDIC Conditions and their Practical Consequences' (2014) 29 *Juris* 3, 54.

[90] See Seung-Hyeon Kim, *International Construction Contracts: Laws and Practice*, 2nd edn (Pakyoungsa, 2019) 395 for examples of overriding mandatory rules of a place of construction.

(4) Effect on the market: This is based on the Effect Doctrine, and in the context of monopoly regulations and competition law, a crucial criterion is which country's market is affected by the violation. That is important because unfair joint acts or corporate mergers in foreign countries may affect the markets of other countries. In ICC Case N. 8626,[91] even though the governing law was New York law, the arbitral tribunal considered the competition law of the EU because the contract in question affected the European market. If a contract between foreign companies constitutes an unfair joint act under the Korean Monopoly Regulation and Fair Trade Act and affects the Korean market,[92] the Korean Monopoly Regulation and Fair Trade Law may be considered or applied as the law of a country with a close connection.

(5) Transfer of value: This criterion is particularly meaningful regarding laws on foreign exchange and export and import controls. This may be especially relevant where the performance of the contract involves a transfer of value (eg, the payment of money or assignment of goods or property) and is supposed to take place in a country where such a transfer is partially or wholly prohibited. For example, if the country of origin of raw materials prohibits exports to a particular state, and the contract in question is expected to involve exports to the prohibited state, a close connection can be found in relation to the law of the country of origin.[93]

(6) In labour relations, the place of provision of labour, and the location of a company's business: The overriding mandatory rules of the place where labour was provided in labour relations and the location of the business of an employer may also be recognised as closely connected. If a Korean company conducts an overseas construction project and hires workers in a foreign country, the overriding mandatory rules on labour relations of the country where labour is being provided may be considered even if the applicable law of the employment contract is Korean law.

(7) Nationality: Where a regulation is imposed on a specific act of a citizen or foreigner, nationality may be an important criterion. For example, Germany has an overriding mandatory rule that restricts German citizens from handling weapons.[94] If an arms sales contract is entered into by a German citizen and a foreigner, Germany's aforementioned overriding mandatory rule may be considered as the law of a country showing close connection even if the governing law of the arms sale contract is foreign law. That is also true in cases where a particular group of individuals are to be protected under laws on the protection of workers.

iv. Concluding Remarks

Considering the discussion above, the most persuasive view is the one advocating the possibility of considering or applying the overriding mandatory rules of third countries

[91] *ICC International Court of Arbitration Bulletin* 14, no 2 (Fall 2003) 55.

[92] In this case, administrative and criminal regulations may be imposed in accordance with the offshore application provisions of Art 2-2 of the Fair Trade Act.

[93] In the context of international litigation, see BGHZ 34, 169–79. In this case, the German Supreme Court considered the ban (embargo) on the export of chemicals to Eastern European countries in relation to contracts between German companies.

[94] This corresponds to Art 5(5) of *Außenwirtschaftsgesetz* and Art 21 of *Kriegswaffenkontrollgesetz* of Germany.

that are closely connected to the matter under arbitration. Overriding mandatory rules are not mentioned in the UNCITRAL Model Law on International Commercial Arbitration, the KAA, the ICC Arbitration Rules or the Korean Commercial Arbitration Board's International Arbitration Rules. The KAA does not require the application of private international law in determining the applicable law to the substance of the dispute. However, this is a legislative lacuna and seemingly does not purport to exclude the consideration or application of overriding mandatory rules in arbitration. Significantly, there is no reason not to permit the consideration of overriding mandatory rules as 'facts' under the governing law of the contract anyway because it is part of applying the substantive applicable law. Therefore, the interpretation of the KAA could also allow for the consideration or application of overriding mandatory rules by the arbitrator. As with the Rome Convention and the Rome I Regulation, there are two options for the arbitrator: to directly apply the rules as laws or to consider them as facts under the substantive applicable law.

A likely counterargument[95] is that the parties will invoke overriding mandatory rules of multiple third countries, resulting in the delay of the proceedings and increasing costs and other practical difficulties. However, arbitration cannot be free from overriding mandatory rules, and an arbitral award may be annulled or denied if it does not consider or apply the overriding mandatory rules of a country closely related to the matter, as seen in the aforementioned *Eco Swiss* judgment of the European Court of Justice. In addition, as the arbitrator can first filter out the laws of countries without a close connection, it is unlikely the arbitrator would often have to investigate the laws of many countries. In cases where the law of a third country is considered a fact under the applicable law, investigating the third country's law may not incur additional costs.

In the long run, to ensure the predictability of the applicable law, it is desirable to establish legislative requirements for the consideration or application of overriding mandatory rules. Such attempts include the provisions under the proposal by the International Chamber of Commerce Commission on Law and Commercial Practices, the UNIDROIT International Commercial Contract Law Principles, and the Hague Principles on Choice of Law in International Commercial Contracts. Draft I proposed by the International Chamber of Commerce Commission on Law and Commercial Practices would be appropriate in terms of the detailed wording. These provisions may be further developed in the arbitration rules of major arbitration institutions, the Model Law, national arbitration laws, and international institutional rules, thereby establishing practice and forming a global consensus.

V. Ex-post Control by the Courts

Now, I will examine the ex-post control of the courts after arbitral awards have been rendered: where the parties to disputes of Types 1, 2 and 3 raise grounds related to overriding mandatory rules at the annulment or recognition/enforcement stage.

[95] Even in the context of litigation, objections to the same effect have been raised in relation to the consideration or application of the overriding mandatory rules of third countries. Ivana Kunda, *Internationally Mandatory Rules of a Third Country in the European Contracts Conflict of Laws: The Rome Convention and the Proposed Rome 1 Regulation* (Rijeka, 2015) 332.

A. Annulment of Arbitral Awards

i. Applicable Law

In cases where the seat of arbitration is in Korea and an application for the annulment of an arbitral award has been filed with a Korean court, the law governing the annulment of the arbitral award is Korean law.[96] Therefore, the annulment shall be determined in accordance with Article 36 of the KAA. Article 5(1)(e) of the New York Convention stipulates the same.

ii. Determination

The grounds for annulment that can be invoked by the parties in relation to overriding mandatory rules may be the lack of arbitrability, invalidity of an arbitral agreement, ultra vires by the arbitrator, omission of decision, and violation of public policy. As to arbitrability, Article 36(2)2-(a) of the KAA stipulates that the applicable law of arbitrability in an annulment proceeding is Korean law.[97] Therefore, decisions on arbitrability must be made in accordance with Korean law. The argument that the arbitration agreement is invalid as the dispute is not arbitrable under Korean law is a claim regarding arbitrability and can also be considered under Korean law.[98] For the interpretation of the KAA, if arbitrability requirements under Articles 1 and 3 of the KAA are satisfied, Types 1, 2 and 3 would be found arbitrable.

If the arbitrator makes a decision on a claim based on overriding mandatory rules (Type 1), despite its having been excluded from the arbitration clause or the submission to arbitration, it will be grounds for annulment due to ultra vires by the arbitrator, whose authority has extended beyond the scope of the arbitration clause or submission to arbitration.[99] For Type 3, if the parties agreed in the arbitration clause or the submission to arbitration that certain overriding mandatory rules do not apply with respect to the substance of the dispute (for example, if they decided not to apply the overriding mandatory rules),[100] but the arbitrator makes his/her decision by applying the overriding mandatory rules, the above agreement of the parties is ineffective and thus does not constitute grounds for setting aside the arbitral award.

On the contrary, when a submission to arbitration includes a claim based on overriding mandatory rules (Type 1) and an arbitrator omits to make a decision thereon, an additional decision under Art 34(1)3 of the Arbitration Act may be rendered due to the omission.

In cases where either party did contend that an overriding mandatory rule should apply in Type 3 but the arbitrator failed to decide upon that issue, affecting the outcome of the

[96] See Art 2(1) of the KAA.

[97] Art 34(2)(b)(i) of the UNCTIRAL Model Law also provides that it shall be judged in accordance with *lex loci arbitri*.

[98] The impact of the lack of arbitrability on the arbitration agreement should be determined in accordance with the applicable law of the arbitration agreement. However, it is questionable whether there is any practical benefit to acknowledging an arbitration agreement as valid for a dispute that does not have arbitrability, so even according to the applicable law of the arbitration agreement, it is likely that the same conclusion will be reached.

[99] Suk (n 2) 204.

[100] Examples are cases where a party that has entered into an export contract in violation of the export regulations of a particular country agrees to exclude the export regulations of the same country while reaching an agreement on the applicable law.

case, there are conflicting views on whether that would constitute grounds for challenging the award.[101] One view is that omitting such a determination is not in and of itself grounds for annulment, but may constitute such grounds, depending on the facts, under Article 36(2)1.(d) of the KAA. Another view is that such an omission should be treated in the same way as 'where the reasons for an arbitral award are not given' and therefore is grounds for annulment. A third view is that such an omission, in principle, should not be grounds for annulment, but in exceptional cases where the omission is obvious from the reading of the award, it may provide grounds for a challenge.

However, I am of the view that such an omission should not be treated as grounds for annulment under Article 36(2)1.(d) of the KAA. First, the old KAA, before amendment in 1999, stipulated that such an omission is grounds for annulment, but that provision was removed in the 1999 amendment of the law, which shows that legislators did not intend for such an omission to serve as grounds for annulment. Second, the current KAA provides an exhaustive list of grounds for annulment, following the UNCITRAL Model Law on International Commercial Arbitration, and the KAA does not explicitly list omission of a judgment as grounds for a challenge. Third, a distinction should be drawn between a decision has been made but the reasons for the decision reached are not given or contradictory, and not reaching a decision at all. Therefore, I hold the view that omitting a decision on overriding mandatory rules should not be equated to a situation where no reasons were given for a decision and thus cannot be grounds for annulment under Article 36(2)1.d of the KAA.[102]

In principle, the misreading and misapplication of overriding mandatory rules by the arbitral tribunal do not constitute grounds for annulment, but if the tribunal knowingly ignored the relevant overriding mandatory rules, it shall constitute ultra vires by the arbitrator and hence a reason for annulment under Article 36(2)1.(c) of the KAA.[103] It would not be easy to distinguish between simple errors in application and intentional disregard of the law, but I believe that such distinction can be made based on the parties' claim and defences, evidence, and the efforts of the arbitrator in the proceedings.

If it is contrary to public policy for the arbitral tribunal to recognise and enforce an arbitral award that omitted the application of overriding mandatory rules or that misinterpreted or misapplied those rules, that is reason for the award to be set aside under Article 36(2)2.(b) of the KAA. Here, public policy means international public policy, not domestic public policy (eg, a violation of Article 103 of the Civil Code and Korea's mandatory law).[104] If international public policy is understood as a concept that is narrower than overriding mandatory rules, this may be criticised for providing parties with insufficient relief because not all arbitral tribunal errors in the application or non-application of overriding mandatory rules can be considered a violation of public policy.[105] However, this will not be approached conceptually, and it is necessary to carefully assess on a

[101] For further details, see Min Kyung Kim, 'Annulment of Arbitral Awards – A Comparison of English and Korean Law and Practice' (Master of Law dissertation, Seoul National University, 2014) 83–84.

[102] ibid 84–85.

[103] Suk (n 2) 207; Kim (n 101) 76; Sohn (n 38) 443.

[104] Suk (n 2) 220; Supreme Court decision 89Daka20252, delivered on 10 April 1990.

[105] Kleinheisterkamp (2018) (n 2) 911 points out that, as a result of the prohibition of review of the merits of arbitral awards, the parties may avoid the application of overriding mandatory rules to some extent by choosing arbitration as a method of dispute resolution.

case-by-case, considering the impact of non-application of the said overriding mandatory rule to public policy. One must be careful about interpreting public policy broadly or allowing review of the merits to ensure that overriding mandatory rules are applied accurately in arbitration, as that is likely to undermine the effectiveness of the arbitration system itself.[106]

B. Recognition and Enforcement of Arbitral Awards

Since Korea has joined the New York Convention, arbitral awards should be recognised and enforced in accordance with the Convention. The grounds for refusing recognition or enforcement of an arbitral award may be argued at the enforcement stage for lack of arbitrability, invalidity of an arbitration agreement, ultra vires by the arbitrator, omission of decision and violation of public policy; and most of the discussion in the annulment stage above is valid in the enforcement stage. However, Article 5(2)(a) of the New York Convention explicitly stipulates the law governing arbitrability to be the law of the country that recognises and enforces the award, while Article 5(1)(a) of the New York Convention stipulates the law governing the arbitration agreement to be the governing law as agreed upon by the parties. Nevertheless, the argument, in the enforcement stage, that an arbitration agreement is invalid because there is no arbitrability is ultimately a question of arbitrability and should be determined in accordance with the KAA, the enforcing country.

VI. Conclusion

To summarise, the situations where overriding mandatory rules are at issue in international commercial arbitration can be divided into: (1) cases where a claim is based on overriding mandatory rules (Type 1); (2) cases where relevant laws and regulations provide that disputes regarding overriding mandatory rules should be resolved exclusively by the court (Type 2); and (3) cases where the appropriateness of the claim depends on whether overriding mandatory rules are applied (Type 3, ie, cases where overriding mandatory rules are used for defence).

The view denying the arbitrability of Types 1, 2 and 3 or denying the validity of an arbitration agreement presupposes that the arbitrator will not apply overriding mandatory rules properly or at all. However, these concerns may be resolved by prescribing the scope of the overriding mandatory rules that can be applied or considered in arbitration. Therefore, while acknowledging the arbitrability and the validity of the arbitration agreement, it would

[106] In general, errors in the application of law do not constitute grounds for the annulment of arbitral awards, and appeals on legal issues such as under the UK's Arbitration Act 1996, Art 69 are rather exceptional. On the other hand, if the arbitrator rejects the parties' express choice of law and applies another law, it may be ultra vires by the arbitrator and may constitute grounds for annulment or refusal of recognition/enforcement. See Franco Ferrari and Linda J Silberman, 'Getting to the Law Applicable to the Merits in International Arbitration and the Consequences of Getting it Wrong' in Franco Ferrari and Stefan Krölls (eds), *Conflict of Laws in International Commercial Arbitration* (Juris, 2019) 428–35.

be a better approach for the courts to exercise ex-post control at the stages of annulment or recognition/enforcement of the arbitral award.

With respect to the scope of the overriding mandatory rules that are considered or applied in arbitration, it is desirable to apply the rules not only of the *lex causae* but also of third countries closely related to the matter. Although it is possible to take such a position with the interpretation of the current arbitration law, in the long run, while carefully observing international discussions and legislative practices, it would be desirable for the predictability of international transactions to specify such in the arbitration law or arbitration rules based on language such as Draft I as recommended by the International Chamber of Commerce Commission on Law and Commercial Practices.

At the stage of annulling, recognising and enforcing arbitral awards, arbitrability should not be denied by the courts as long as Types 1, 2 and 3 are within the scope of arbitrability under Articles 1 and 3 of the KAA, and the validity of an arbitration agreement should not be denied. If the arbitrator misapplies or omits a decision on an overriding mandatory rule, the arbitral award may be revoked, or its recognition and approval may be denied, as the case may be, for ultra vires or the violation of public policy. However, one should exercise caution when reviewing an arbitral award on its merits when overriding mandatory rules have not been properly applied, as this may undermine the effectiveness of the arbitration system itself.

In conclusion, it is a better solution to consider or apply the overriding mandatory rules of a third country closely related to the matters and of the country to which the applicable law belongs rather than broadly interpreting the reasons for annulling or refusing to recognise or enforce the arbitral award and reviewing the arbitral award on its merits. Considering or applying those overriding mandatory rules under uniform rules would guarantee predictability for the parties and party autonomy, while also allowing to protect the essential public interest the overriding mandatory rules pursue.

A necessary task for the future is to identify in which case the omission of a decision on overriding mandatory rules or an error in the application of laws would constitute violations of public policy.

8

Conclusion

Party autonomy is an important pillar of modern private international law. Under the principle of party autonomy, parties are allowed to choose the applicable law for their contracts. Since domestic substantive laws differ, upholding party autonomy ensures the predictability of the applicable law in international transactions. However, overriding mandatory rules restrict party autonomy in that they apply regardless of the chosen law by the parties and may undermine such predictability. Against this backdrop, this book has tackled three main issues pertaining to overriding mandatory rules. First was how to ascertain if a certain provision of law has an overriding mandatory character. Second was how a third country's overriding mandatory rules should be considered or applied. Solving these two problems is of importance because otherwise parties and the courts would be left without guidance, generating uncertainty about the applicable law of the contract. On the other hand, establishing the criteria and considerations for determining overriding mandatory rules and the requirements under which a third country's overriding mandatory rules are considered or applied can help enhance the predictability of the applicable law. The third issue was what kind of problems overriding mandatory rules raise in international commercial arbitration and how they should be dealt with.

In relation to the first issue, an interpretation of Article 20 of KAPIL pertaining to what kind of legislative purpose an overriding mandatory rule must pursue was suggested. Considering relevant factors such as the historical background in which the concept of overriding mandatory rules was developed, as well as the wording and the legislative history of Article 20 of KAPIL, one must be cautious about too readily recognising a provision as an overriding mandatory rule. An overriding mandatory rule must aim to protect the essential political, economic and social interests of the state. In this regard, provisions that protect both public and private interests simultaneously can be overriding mandatory rules only if they protect public interests that transcend adjusting private interest. Even if a provision appears to be adjusting private interests, if it does not aim to simply intervene in individual legal relations to correct the imbalance between the parties, but has the purpose of correcting unfairness deeply rooted in the trade order or realising important constitutional values such as economic justice or gender equality, it may constitute an overriding mandatory rule. In addition, that provision must not have equivalence and substitutability to a provision in a foreign law; that is to say, it must not be possible for the specific goal of the provision to be protected by a similar provision in foreign law.

This book has suggested the methodology and the factors to be considered when determining which provisions are overriding mandatory rules. When making such a determination, it is better to first look at the factors that can be easily identified among the various factors to be considered. Thus, it would be more straightforward to examine whether there are explicit clauses about application regardless of the governing law of the legal relationship, whether there are extraterritorial application clauses or whether the scope of international or spatial application is defined. If such clauses exist, the next subject of analysis is whether there is a special legislative purpose. Where these factors are absent, one should examine whether there is a special legislative purpose, and whether the international or spatial scope of application can be specified by interpreting the legislative purpose in relation to the connection (proximity) to the forum state.

The book reviewed selected provisions of Korean law based on the suggested criteria to determine overriding mandatory rules. Articles 5, 9, 11, 40, 45 and 109 of the Monopoly Regulation and Fair Trade Act, Articles 6 and 15 through 18 of the Foreign Exchange Transactions Act, Articles 19(1) and (2) of the Foreign Trade Act, Article 33(1) of the Employment Security Act and Article 5(2) of the Act on Contracts to which the State is a Party, Articles 39(1), 60(1), 74(1) of the Act on Conservation and Utilisation of Cultural Heritage are of overriding mandatory character. These provisions apply irrespective of the applicable law of the relevant legal relationship, under the extraterritorial application clauses or in accordance with their stipulated international or spatial scope of application. Special legislative purposes are also recognised. Articles 66, 87(5) of the Act on Conservation and Utilisation of Cultural Heritage, Article 3(4) of the Fair Transactions in Subcontracting Act, Article 12 of the Fair Transactions in Franchise Business Act, and Articles 8 and 11 of the Equal Employment Opportunity and Work-Family Balance Assistance Act are of overriding mandatory nature although they do not apply extraterritorially and do not explicitly provide for the international and spatial scope of application. However, these provisions aim to achieve special legislative purposes, and their international or spatial scope of application can be identified by interpretation. On the other hand, Article 3(3) of the Act on the Regulation of Terms and Conditions and Articles 799 and Article 92(2) of the Commercial Act do not constitute overriding mandatory rules because special legislative purposes are not recognised and the international or spatial scope of application cannot be specified.

The provisions examined here are not an exhaustive list of overriding mandatory rules. Further provisions must be reviewed in the future to verify their overriding mandatory nature. One starting point could be the Act on Promotion of Information and Communications Network Utilisation and Information Protection and the Telecommunications Business Act, which have extraterritorial application clauses. It is also necessary to establish criteria for which regulations protecting consumers and employees correspond to overriding mandatory rules. Additional research questions for the future may include how to solve conflicts between multiple countries' overlapping provisions that are extraterritorially applied.

In relation to the second issue, the question of under which conditions the overriding mandatory rules of a third country should be considered or applied should be answered by weighing the conflicting interests of the parties (predictability for the parties of the governing law), the interests of the third country (interest in achieving policy objectives), the interests of the forum state (interests in protecting the values of the forum), and the interests of international harmony in decisions. Therefore, the conditions for consideration or application should be able to reflect these interests in a harmonious manner. One way to consider the overriding mandatory rules of a third country – the substantive law approach – fails to properly reflect all four of the above interests. On the other hand, the conflict-of-laws approach can reflect these four interests better than the substantive law approach. In terms of the interests of the parties, the conflict-of-laws approach, by stipulating the conditions for considering or applying the overriding mandatory rules of third countries at the conflict-of-laws level, guarantees the predictability of the governing law for the parties. Since the conflict-of-laws approach considers or applies third-country laws in accordance with consistent requirements, it is also in line with the interests of third countries and international harmony in decisions. Moreover, the interests of the forum state may be reflected through content control and result control over the laws of third countries. As for the scope of the third-country overriding mandatory rules to be considered or applied, limiting the scope to the provisions of the place of performance does not sufficiently reflect the interests of third countries.

In this regard, a task for future research is establishing more detailed standards for whether third-country overriding mandatory rules with various types and content should be applied directly or indirectly and in particular what effect different from that stipulated under third-country law would be recognised in the case of type (2) indirect application ((D)).

In relation to the third issue, there is some controversy regarding overriding mandatory rules in international commercial arbitration. Issues include the arbitrability of disputes involving overriding mandatory rules, the validity of arbitration agreement on such disputes, whether the arbitrator has the power to apply overriding mandatory rules without the parties' consent, which country's overriding mandatory rules are relevant, and how the national courts can have a 'second look' on the arbitral decisions regarding such rules. Although arbitration is grounded in the parties' consent, arbitration cannot and should not exist in a vacuum where overriding mandatory rules cannot be applied. Parties cannot, by definition, derogate from such rules, and an arbitrator has the power to apply relevant overriding mandatory rules above and beyond the agreed law between the parties. As to the scope of the rules to be considered or applied, this author proposes the rules of the governing law of the contract and of the countries to which the dispute has a close connection. The law of the seat, the law of the place of recognition and enforcement and the law of the place of performance are considered within the concept of close connection to the case.

National courts can review an arbitral decision on overriding mandatory rules in annulment, recognition and enforcement proceedings. In cases where the arbitrator's application or non-application of the overriding mandatory rules was erroneous, and recognising and enforcing the arbitral award would amount to the infringement of international public policy, courts can annul the decision or refuse recognition/enforcement.

Overall, this book contends that a restricted review by the court and a consistent standard for applying overriding mandatory rules in arbitration will serve as a better solution in terms of striking a balance between maintaining party autonomy and preserving the public interest reflected in overriding mandatory rules.

Ultimately, in order to develop the law and practice in relation to the issues discussed in this book, there needs to be greater interest in and further research of overriding mandatory rules, including those of third countries. Based on the methodologies of interpretation and legislation presented here, I expect and hope that overriding mandatory rules will be discussed more actively in both academia and legal practice.

BIBLIOGRAPHY

19th National Assembly of Korea, 340th National Assembly (Extraordinary Session), proposed by the chairman of the National Assembly on 2 March 2016, Bill No. 18638, Partial Amendment Act on Monopoly Regulation and Fair Trade (Original Bill).

An, Choon Soo, 'International zwingende Bestimmungen im IPR – Theorien und die Bedeutung von Artt. 6, 7 IPR Koreas' (2011) 23 *Kookmin Law Review* 189.

—— *Private International Law* (Bobmunsa, 2017).

—— 'Review of the Amendment Bill on the Private International Law – General Provisions and Corporations' (2001) 6 *Korea Private International Law Journal* 199.

Beale, Hugh (ed), *Chitty on Contracts*, 33rd edn (Sweet & Maxwell, 2020).

Blessing, Marc, 'Mandatory Rules versus Party Autonomy in International Arbitration' (1997) 14 *Journal of International Arbitration* 23.

Bonomi, Andrea, 'Mandatory Rules in Private International Law – The Quest for Uniformity of Decisions in a Global Environment' (1999) 1 *Yearbook of Private International Law* 215.

—— 'Overriding Mandatory Provisions in the Rome 1 Regulation on the Law Applicable to Contracts' (2008) 10 *Yearbook of Private International Law* 285.

Briggs, Adrian, 'The principle of comity in private international law' (2012) 354 *Recueil des Cours* 77.

—— *Private International Law in English Courts* (Oxford University Press, 2014).

Buxbaum, Hannah, 'RICO's Extraterritorial Application: Rebutting the Presumption?' in H Watt et al (eds), *Global Private International Law* (Edward Elgar Publishing, 2019).

Calavros, Constantin, 'The Application of Substantive Mandatory Rules in International Commercial Arbitration from the Perspective of an EU UNCITRAL Model Law Jurisdiction' (2018) 34 *Arbitration International* 219.

Calliess, Gralf-Peter (ed), *Rome Regulations: Commentary* (Wolters Kulwer, 2011).

—— *Rome Regulations: Commentary*, 2nd edn (Kluwer Law International, 2015).

Cho, Boo-Keun, 'An Examination into the Illegal Trade of Cultural Properties' (2004) 37 *Korea Institute of Science and Technology Information* 371.

Cho, Inyoung, 'Shared Mistaken Motives as to the Future Event and the Change of Circumstances – A Study on the Supreme Court Decision 2020da254846' (2021) 96 *Korean Journal of Civil Law* 275.

Choi, Bong-Kyung, 'A Consideration on the Proposal of Making §626 KCC Mandatory' (2012) 128 *Justice* 181.

Choi, Dong Jun, 'The Legal System for Protecting Technical Information in Korea – Focused on the Definition of Technical Information, the Types of Infringement, and the Legal Protection Methods of Relevant Laws' (2021) 72 *Kyoungpook National University Law Journal* 275.

Choi, Eun-jin, 'Current Status and Future Tasks of the Establishment of "Guidelines for Unfair Contract Examination" for Improving Subcontracting Transactions' [Hadogeupgeoraeui gaeseoneul wihan 'budangteukyak simsajichim'ui jejeong hyeonhwanggwa hyanghu gwaje], *Issue and Focus* no 1,682 (26 March 2020), Legislative Research Office of the National Assembly.

Choi, Heung Sub, *Korean Private International Law I* (Korean Studies Information, 2019).

Choi, Jeehyun, 'Standards of Extraterritorial Application of Competition Law: Case Study of Air Cargo' (2016) 15 *Korean Journal of International Economic Law* 35.

Choi, Jong Hyeon, 'Focusing on the Liability of a Carrier – Status of a Carrier under the Amended Maritime Law' (2008) 30 *Korea Maritime Law Journal* 49.

Choi, Kongwoong, 'Extraterritorial Jurisdiction and Private International Law' (1994) 3 *Korea Private International Law Journal* 152.

Choi, Min-ji, 'Low-cost Sale of "Mugunghwa 3" Concludes with International Lawsuit … KT Faces Final Defeat' [Heolgap maegak 'mugunghwa 3-ho' gukjesosong jonggyeol … KT choejong paeso], *Digital Daily* (12 March 2020).

Choi, Sung Jai, 'Analysis of the Supreme Court Cases on Antitrust Laws in 2018' (2019) 481 *Human Right and Justice* 127.

Choi, Young Hong, *ONJU Fair Transactions in Franchise Business Act* (Thomson Reuters, 2020).

Chong, Adeline, 'The Public Policy and Mandatory Rules of Third Countries in International Contracts' (2006) 2 *Journal of Private International Law* 27.

Chun, Changmin, 'A Brief Review of Scope and Entry Regulation of the Financial Consumer Protection Act' (2021) 14 *Korean Journal of Banking and Finance Law* 39.

Chung, Byung Duck, 'A Study on the Treble Damage Compensation System under the Korean Fair Trade Act' (2019) 43 *Dankook Law Review* 373

Chung, Byung Suk, 'Conflict of Laws Issues in Maritime Claims' (2010) 16 *Korea Private International Law Journal* 197.

Chung, Hong Sik, 'Applicability of Overriding Mandatory Rules in International Arbitration' (2013a) 23 *Journal of Arbitration Studies* 3.

—— 'Distributor's Indemnity Rights in International Commercial Arbitration' (2013b) 22 *Korean Forum on International Trade and Business Law* 319.

—— 'A Study on Hague Principles on Choice of Law in International Commercial Contract' (2015) 125 *International Trade Law* 14.

Collins, Lawrence (ed), *Dicey, Morris & Collins: The Conflict of Laws*, 15th edn (Sweet & Maxwell, 2012).

Currie, Brainerd, 'Married Women's Contracts: A Study in Conflict-of-Law Method' (1958) 25 *University of Chicago Law Review* 227.

d'Aspremont, Jean, 'The Implausibility of Coordinating Transborder Legal Effects of Domestic Statutes and Courts' Decisions by International Law' (2019) in H Watt et al, (eds), *Global Private International Law* (Edward Elgar Publishing, 2019).

Day, William, 'Contracts, illegality and comity: *Ralli Bros* revisited' (2020) 79 *Cambridge Law Journal* 64.

Day, William, 'Isn't Brexit frustrating?' (2019) 78 *Cambridge Law Journal* 270.

Dickinson, Andrew, 'Third Country Mandatory Rules in the Law Applicable to Contractual Obligations: So Long, Farewell, Auf Wiedersehen Adieu?' (2007) 3 *Journal of Private International Law* 53.

Fazilatfar, Hossein, *Overriding Mandatory Rules in International Commercial Arbitration* (Edward Elgar Publishing, 2019).

Freitag, Robert, 'Die kollisionsrechtliche Behandlung ausländischer Eingriffsnormen nach Art. 9 Abs. 3 Rom I-VO' (2009) 29 *Praxis des Internationalen Privat- und Verfahrensrechts* 109.

Fujikawa, Nobuo, 'Toward Unification and Order Formation of Extraterritorial Application Rules in International Transactions' (2013) 79 *Japanese Legal Studies* 1. (藤川信夫,「國際取引における域外適用ルール統一化ならびに秩序形成に向けて」, 日本法學 第79巻 第1号 (2013).) ['Kokusaitoryū ni okeru iki-gai tekiyō rūru tōitsu-ka narabini chitsujo keisei ni mukete', Nihon Hōgaku, Dai 79-kan Dai 1-gō (2013).]

Girsberger, Daniel, Graziano, Thomas Kadner and Neels, Jan (eds), *Choice of Law in International Commercial Contracts* (Oxford University Press, 2021).

Greenwalt, Alexander KA, 'Does International Arbitration Need a Mandatory Rules Method?' in Berman, George A and Mistelis, Loukas A (eds), *Mandatory Rules in International Arbitration* (Juris, 2011).

Grolimund, Pascal (ed), *Basler Kommentar Interntionales Privatrecht*, 4th edn (Helbnig Lichtenhahn Verlag, 2021).

Guilano, Mario and Lagarde, Paul, 'Report on the Convention on the Law Applicable to Contractual Obligations' (1980) C 282 *Official Journal*.

Günther, Lisa, *Die Anwendbargkeit ausländischer Eingriffnormen im Lichter der Rom I- und Rom II Verordnungen* (Verlag Alma Mater, 2011).

Han, Chan Sik, 'Legislation Study: Proceedings and Key Points of Conflict of Laws Act Revision' (2001) 50 *Korean Lawyers Association Journal* 151.

Han, Seungsoo, 'The Protection of the Franchisee of the International Franchise Contract and the Governing Law in the Litigation' (2017) 58 *Seoul Law Journal* 78.

Hartley, Trevor, 'Mandatory rules in international contracts: the common law approach' (1997) 266 *Recueil des Cours* 345.

Hauser, Paul, *Eingriffsnormen in der Rom- I Verordnung* (Mohr Siebeck, 2012).

Hay, Peter, Borchers, Patrick and Symeonides, Symeon C, *Conflict of Laws*, 5th edn (West, 2010).

Hayward, Benjamin, *Conflict of Laws and Arbitral Discretion: The Closest Test* (Oxford University Press, 2017).

HCCH, 'Commentary on the Principles on Choice of Law in International Commercial Contracts' (2015).

Hellner, Michael, 'Third Country Overriding Mandatory Rules in the Rome I Regulation: Old Wine in New Bottles?' (2009) 5 *Journal of Private International Law* 447.

Heo, Seon, 'Experience and Logic of Extraterritorial Application of Fair Trade Laws to International Cartels: Focusing on the Graphite Electrode Rod International Cartel Case' (2003) 9 *Journal of Competition Law* 207.

Hill, Jonathan and Chong, Adeline, *International Commercial Disputes*, 4th edn (Hart Publishing, 2010).

Hong, Dae-sik, 'Korean Competition Law from a Private Law Perspective – Focused on Abuse of Market-dominant Position' (2008) 18 *Journal of Competition Law* 203.

—— 'Revisiting the Standard for Determining Illegality of Unfair Trade Practices under the Monopoly Regulation and Fair Trade Act of Korea – Centered on Relevance to Competitive Order' (2018) 37 *Journal of Competition Law* 188.

—— 'Unfair Trade Practices in Relation to Public Order and Good Morals' (2007) 14 *Journal of Comparative Private Law* 109.

Hong, Myungsoo, 'A Study on the Determination of Illegality According to Types of Unfair Trade Practices – Focusing on Unfairness' (2015) 50 *Kyung Hee Law Journal* 43.

Hwang, Sung Hyung, 'A Study on Application of Subcontracting Act to Overseas Construction Projects and Violation of Subcontracting Act by Use of FIDIC Conditions of Contract 2021 International Trade Law' (2021) 151 *International Trade Law* 92.

ILA International Arbitration Committee, 'Report on Ascertaining the Contents of the Applicable Law in International Commercial Arbitration, presented at the ILA's 73rd conference in Rio de Janeiro' (August 2008).

Jang, Junhyok, 'Conflict's Mandatory Character as the Key Element of Internationally Mandatory Rules' (2007) 19 *SungKyunKwan Law Review* 563.

—— 'Internationally Mandatory Rules – A Comparative Study of Article 7 of the Rome Convention, Articles 18 and 19 of the Swiss Private International Law, and Article 7 of the Korean Private International Law' (2007) 75 *International Trade Law* 71.

—— 'A Study on Brainerd Currie's Governmental Interest Analysis' (Master of jurisprudence thesis, Seoul National University, 1994).

Jeon, Min Cheol, 'A Study on the Extraterritorial Application of Competition Law – Focused on Legislations and Judicial Decisions of US and EU' (2017) 29 *Yonsei Law Journal* 209.

Ju, Jin Yul, 'A Review on Some Legal Issues of Regulation on Unfair Subcontract Transactions' (2009) 30 *Kyoungpook National University Law Journal* 35.

Jung, Dong Yoon (ed), *Annotation to Commercial Law* [Juseok sangbeop je4pan], 4th edn (Korean Judicial Administration Association, 2013).

—— (ed), *Annotation to Commercial Law* [Juseok sangbeop je2pan], 2nd edn (Seoul, Korean Judicial Administration Association, 2015).

Jung, Seungwoo, 'A Legal Study on the International Trade of Stolen/Lost Artworks: Focused on Illegal Trafficking of Cultural Property' (2019) 51 *Korean Association of Arts Management* 191.

Jung, Won (ed), *ONJU Act on Contracts to which the State is a Party* (Thomson Reuters, 2016).

Kang, Minwoo, 'The Redesign of Enforcement System on the Violation of Foreign Exchange Transactions Regulation' (2016) 13 *Korea Financial Law Association* 139.

Kang, Sunhee, 'A Study on Labor Supply Service and the Safety of the Supplied Worker under the Employment Security Act' (2014) 12 *Labor Law Forum* 185.

Kaye, Peter, *The New Private International Law of Contract of the European Community* (Dartmouth, 1993).

Kegel, Gerhard and Schurig, Klaus, *Internationales Privatrecht*, 9th edn (Verlag CH Beck, 2004).

Kim, Hyun and Song, Sang-Hyun, *Principles of Maritime Law* [Haesangbeop wollon je4pan], 4th edn (Pakyoungsa, 2008).

Kim, In-ho, 'How to Revisit the Korean Private International Law Based upon the Rome I Regulation with Respect to the Objectively Applicable Law for International Contracts in the Absence of Choice' (2013) 19 *Korea Private International Law Journal* 543.

—— 'Limitations by Mandatory Rules on the Dominance of Party Autonomy in International Contracts' (2012) 60 *Advanced Commercial Law Review* 110.

—— 'Reasonably-tailored Arbitrability to Promote the Development of International Trade' (2016) 23 *Journal of Comparative Private Law* 1147.

—— 'Validity of an Unreasonably Unfavorable Arbitral Clause Contained in a Franchise Agreement' (2020) 27 *Journal of Comparative Private Law* 349.

Kim, In-hyeon, '2007 Revised Maritime Law Section of Korean Commercial Code' (2009) 31 *Korea Maritime Law Journal* 99.

—— 'Whether Warranty Clause with English Governing Law is Subject to Korean Law Regulating General Terms' (2013) 35 *Korea Maritime Law Journal* 373.

Kim, Jae Hyung, 'Contracts Infringing Mandatory Rules (2004) 26 *Journal of Private Case Law Studies* 1.

Kim, Min Kyung, 'Annulment of Arbitral Awards – A Comparison of English and Korean Law and Practice' (Master of Law dissertation, Seoul National University, 2014).

—— 'Overriding Mandatory Rules in International Commercial Arbitration' (2021) 38 *Hanyang Law Review* 353.

Kim, Seung-Hyeon, *International Construction Contracts: Laws and Practice*, 2nd edn (Pakyoungsa, 2019).

Kim, Sung-won, Son, Seungwoo and You, Hyunwoo, 'A Legal Study on the Export Control of Technology – Focus on the National Core Technology and Strategic Technology' (2016) 6 *Korean Journal of Industrial Security* 77.

Kim, Soojeong, 'Das Unterscheidungskriterium zwischen Effektsvorschriften und Ordnungsvorschriften' (2018) 85 *Korean Journal of Civil Law* 3.

Kim, Yong Dam, 'The Governing Law of the International Contracts and Mandatory Rules' (1986) 33 *Trial Reference* 6.

Kim, Yongjin, 'Choice of Law in International Antitrust Law' (2013) 44 *Journal of Legislation Research* 801.

—— 'External Effect of Mandatory Rules' (1998) 3 *Korea Private International Law Journal* 703.

—— 'Pro Opt In Class Action in Antitrust Law' (2014) 21 *Journal of Comparative Private Law* 157.

Kleinheisterkamp, Jan, 'The Impact of Internationally Mandatory Rules on the Enforceability of Arbitration Agreements' (2009) 3 *World Arbitration & Mediation Review* 91.

—— 'Overriding mandatory laws in international arbitration' (2018) 67 *International & Comparative Law Quarterly* 903.

Ko, Young Han, 'Extraterritorial Application of Fair Trade Law, Various Issues Economic Law' [Dokjeomgyuje-beopui yeokoejeokyong, gyeongjebeopui jemunje] (2000) 87 *Trial References* 765.

Korea International Trade Association, 'Korea Trade Statistics', Export Data by Country.

Kunda, Ivana, *Internationally Mandatory Rules of a Third Country in the European Contracts Conflict of Laws: The Rome Convention and the Proposed Rome 1 Regulation* (Rijeka, 2015).

Kwon, Youngjoon, 'The Philosophical Foundation of Contract Law – From the Perspective of Autonomy and Paternalism' (2011) 124 *Justice* 169.

Kwon, O Seung, 'Extraterritorial Application of the Korean Monopoly Regulation Act – With a Focus on the Air Cargo Cartel Case' (2011) 24 *Journal of Competition Law* 149.

Lee, Bong-Eui, 'Jurisdictional Issues of Extraterritorial M&A Regulation under Korean Competition Law' (2016) 33 *Journal of Korean Competition Law* 165.

Lee, Dong-Eun, 'The International Legal Dimension of Unilateral Economic Sanctions and the Implications on the Sanctions Against North Korea – Focused on the U.S. Secondary Sanctions' (2020) 65 *Korean Journal of International Law* 191.

Lee, Dong-jin, 'A Study on "Action Directe" of the Subcontractor' (2009) 58 *Korean Lawyers Association Journal* 74.

Lee, Geun Gwan, *Final Report on Research on the Direction of Domestic Legal Amendments for Joining the UNIDROIT Convention* (Cultural Heritage Administration, 2007).

Lee, Ho Jeong, *Private International Law* (Seoul, Kyungmoonsa, 1985).

—— 'Savigny's Private International Law Theories' (1981) 22 *Seoul Law Review* 92.

Lee, Hun Mook, 'Arbitrability in Terms of Internationally Mandatory Provisions' (2013) 22 *Korea Private International Law Journal* 21.

—— 'Elements to Determine Internationally Mandatory Provisions' (2014) 442 *Human Right and Justice* 83.

Lee, Jong Hyeok, 'Cultural Property Transfer Act of Switzerland – Main Contents and Implications for the Perspective of Private International Law' (2017) 23 *Korea Private International Law Journal* 59.

—— 'Private International Law Issues of the Implementation Legislations for the 1970 UNESCO Convention' (2020) 26 *Korea Private International Law Journal* 343.

—— 'Prospectus Liability in Cross-border Securities Offering: Focusing on the Choice-of-law Rules' (Doctorate degree dissertation, Seoul National University, 2019).

Lee, Jun-Gil (ed), *ONJU Fair Transaction in Subcontracting Act* (2016).

Lee, Jung-won, 'Relationship between the Party Autonomy and Clause Paramount from the Viewpoint of the International Private Law (2019) 60 *Pusan National University Law Review* 137.

—— 'A Study on the Insurer's Duty of Explanation and the English Governing Law Clause – Comments on the Korean Supreme Court Ruling Case No. 2009DA105383' (2011) 122 *Justice* 212.

—— 'A Study on the Relationship Between the Himalaya Clause and Article 799 of the Korean Commercial Act' (2010) 51 *Pusan National University Law Review* 563.

Lee, Phil-Bok, 'International Transaction of Cultural Heritage and Overriding Mandatory Provisions – Focused on the Overriding Mandatory Provisions of *Lex Originis*' (2021) 27 *Korea Private International Law Journal* 119.
Lee, Young Jun, 'Änderung der Geschäftsgrundlage' (2018) 82 *Korean Journal of Civil Law* 3.
Lehmann, Matthias, 'New challenges of extraterritoriality: superposing laws' in Ferrari, Franco and Arroyo, Diego P Fernández (eds), *Private International Law: Contemporary Challenges and Continuing Relevance* (Elgar, 2019).
Magnus, Ulrich and Mankowski, Peter (eds), *Commentary: Rome I Regulation*, European Commentaries on Private International Law, vol 2 (Verlag Dr Otto Schmidt, 2017).
Martiny, Dieter (ed), *Internationales Vertragsrecht*, 9th edn (Otto Schmidt, 2022).
Mann, Frederick Alexander, 'Conflict of laws and public law' (1971) 132 *Recueil des Cours* 115.
Mayer, Pierre, 'Mandatory Rules of Law in International Arbitration' (1986) 2 *Arbitration International* 274.
Michaels, Ralf, 'Towards a private international law for regulatory conflicts?' (2016) 59 *Japanese Yearbook of International Law* 175.
Müller-Chen, Markus (ed), *Zürcher Kommentar zum IPRG*, Bd I-1, 3rd edn (Schulthess, 2018).
Myung, Hwon, 'A Study of Distinctions Between Mandatory Provisions and Non-mandatory Provisions' (Master of Law dissertation, Seoul National University, 2019).
Nishioka, Kazuaki, 'Choice of Court Agreements and Derogation from Competition Law' (2020) 16 *Journal of Private International Law* 300.
Park, Chan-Ho and Suh, Hun-Je, *A Legal Study on Stolen or Illegally Exported Cultural Objects – With Emphasis on the 1970 UNESCO Convention and the 1995 UNIDROIT Convention and Their Implementation in Major Contracting Parties* (Korea Legal Research Institute, 2007).
Park, Eon Kyung and Suh, Chul Won, 'Appraisal and Reform of Regulations upon the Export Control of Strategic Items: Focusing on the Foreign Trade Act' (2018) 16 *Korean Journal of International Economic Law* 157.
Park, Eon Kyung and Wang, Sang Han, 'Implementation of Export Control Regulations – Status and Prospects of the Legislation for the Intangible Transfer of Technology (ITT) Control on Nuclear Related Items' (2018) 53 *Kyung Hee Law Journal* 379.
—— 'Legal Issues on Illegal Exporting Case of Mugunghwa Satellite No. 3 – With a Focus on the Export Control on Strategic Items under the Foreign Trade Act' (2017) 52 *Kyung Hee Law Journal* 545.
—— 'A Study upon the Legal System Regarding the Export Control of Strategic Items – The Controls on Transit or Transshipment of the Foreign Trade Act' (2020) 10 *Sogang Journal of Law and Business* 3.
Park, Iksoo (ed), *ONJU Monopoly Regulation and Fair Trade Act* (online, Thomson Reuters, 2015).
Park, Kwang Bai, 'Reform the Production System for Construction Win-Win Development' (2014) 5 *Journal of Local Government Contracting* 81.
Park, Kwi Cheon (ed), *ONJU Equal Employment Opportunity and Work-Family Balance Assistance Act* (online, Thomson Reuters, 2019).
Park, Seonuk, 'Standards of Extraterritoriality of US Antitrust Law: Applying the US Supreme Court's Analysis in RJR Nabisco to Foreign Component Cartels' (2020) 30 *Dong-A Journal of International Business Transactions Law* 227.
Peari, Sagi, 'Savigny's Thefory of Choice-of-Laws as a Principle of 'Voluntary Submission'' (2014) 64 *University of Toronto Law Journal* 106.
Plender, Richard, *The European Contracts Convention: The Rome Convention on the Choice of Law for Contracts* (Sweet & Maxwell, 1991).
Plender, Richard and Wilderspin, Michael, *The European Contracts Convention: The Rome Convention on the Choice of Law for Contracts* (Sweet & Maxwell, 2001).
Proctor, Charles, *Mann on the Legal Aspect of Money*, 7th edn (Oxford University Press, 2012).
Rau, Alan Scott, 'The Arbitrator and the "Mandatory Rules of Law"' in Berman, George A and Mistelis, Loukas A (eds), *Mandatory Rules in International Arbitration* (Juris, 2011).
Rebmann, Kurt (ed), *Münchener Kommentar zum BGB*, 4th edn (Verlag Beck München, 2006).
Ministry of Justice (UK), 'Rome I: Should We Opt In?' Consultation Paper CP05/08 (2009).
Riles, Annelise, 'Managing Regulatory Arbitrage: A Conflict of Laws Approach' (2014) 47 *Cornell International Law Journal* 63.
Samuel, Adam, 'The New Swiss Private International Law Act' (1988) 37 *International and Comparative Law Quarterly* 68.
von Savigny, Friedrich Karl, *System des heutigen römischen Rechts*, Band 8 (Veit, 1849).
Säcker, Franz Jürgen (ed), *Münchener Kommentar zum BGB*, 8th edn (Verlag Beck München, 2021).

Schäfer, Kerstin Ann-Susann, *Application of Mandatory Rules in the Private International Law of Contracts* (Peter Lang, 2010).
Schweizerische Bundesrat, *Botschaft zum Bundesgesetz über das internationale* Privatrecht (IPR-Gesetz) vom 10 November 1982 (1983).
Sheppard, Audley, 'Mandatory Rules in International Commercial Arbitration: An English Law Perspective' in Berman, George A and Mistelis, Loukas A (eds), *Mandatory Rules in International Arbitration* (Juris, 2011).
Shin, Changseon, 'The Objectives and Ideals of Private International Law: Focusing on the Relationship between Private International Law Justice and Substantive Law Justice' (2000) 5 *Korea Private International Law Journal* 86.
Shin, Changseon and Yoon, Namsoon, *New Private International Law* [Singukjesabeop je2pan], 2nd edn (Fides, 2016).
Shin, Chang Seop, *Private International Law* [Gukjesabeop je4pan], 4th edn (Sechang, 2018).
Shin, Young Su, 'Issues and Prospects for the Introduction of Punitive Damages under Fair Trade Act' (2017) 163 *Justice* 36.
Shore, Laurence, 'Applying mandatory rules of law in international commercial arbitration' in Berman, George A and Mistelis, Loukas A (eds), *Mandatory Rules in International Arbitration* (Juris, 2011).
Smit, Hans, 'Mandatory Law in Arbitration' in Berman, George A and Mistelis, Loukas A (eds), *Mandatory Rules in International Arbitration* (Juris, 2011).
Sohn, Kyung Han, 'General Understanding of Dispute Resolution Agreement' (2012) 61 *Korean Lawyers Association Journal* 40.
—— 'Introduction to 1995 UNIDROIT Cultural Objects Convention and Korea's Accession Thereto' (2009) 15 *Korea Private International Law Journal* 200.
—— 'Party Autonomy and Applicable Law in Arbitration Korea' (2011) 17 *Korea Private International Law Journal* 411.
—— 'Recent Case Law Developments in Governing Law of Contractual Obligation in Korea' (2016) 22 *Korea Private International Law Journal* 103.
Song, Ho Young, 'Einige zivil und internationales privatrechtliche Frage zur Rückgabe von Kulturgütern – unter besonderer Berücksichting von Regelungen der UNIDROIT-Konvention 1995' (2009) 15 *Korea Private International Law Journal* 298.
—— 'Study on the Legal Policy for Restitution of Illegally Exported Cultural Properties in Foreign Countries' (2004) 11 *Journal of Comparative Private Law* 229.
—— 'A Study on the Rule of *Lex Originis* for the Cultural Properties in the International Private Law' (2013) 30 *Journal of Property Law* 79.
—— 'Who Owns the Goryeo Buddhist Statue?' (2019) 36 *Hanyang Law Review* 279.
Song, Tuck-soo, 'How the Principle of Change in Circumstances Works in South Korea' [Sajeong byeonggyeongui wonchik <daehamingukeseoui moseup>] (2018) 85 *Korean Journal of Civil Law* 569.
Statistics Korea, 'Data on Export-Import Ratio (as a percentage of GDP) from National Development Indicators' (9 June 2021).
Staudinger, Julius von and Habermann, Norbert, *Staudingers Kommentar Zum Bürgerlichen Gesetzbuch Mit Einführungsgesetz Und Nebengesetzen: Einführungsgesetz zum Bürgerlichen Gesetzbuche/IPR* (Sellier-De Gruyter, 2002).
Stone, Peter, *EU Private International Law* (Edward Elgar Publishing, 2006).
Suh, Hun-Je, 'Extraterritorial Application of Fair Trade Act – Focusing on the Extraterritorial Application of Substantive Rules' (1998) 23 *International Trade Law* 6.
Suk, Kwang Hyun, *Annotation to Private International Law* [Gukjesabeop haeseol] (Pakyoungsa, 2013).
—— 'The Application of Foreign Exchange Control Law and Other Internationally Mandatory Rules of Third Countries in International Financial Transactions: Including Article Vf2(b) of the Articles of Agreement of the International Monetary Fund' (2020) 26 *Korea Private International Law Journal* 353.
—— 'Application of Korean Social Security Law to Aliens: Shift from Alien Law to Conflict of Laws Rules' (2021) 27 *Korea Private International Law Journal* 647.
—— 'Cloud Computing: Regulation, Jurisdiction, and Applicable Law' [Keullaudeu keompyutingui gyuje mit gwanhalgwongwa jungeobeop] (2011) 7 *Law & Technology* 3.
—— 'Comment on a Lower Court Judgment Dealing with Law Applicable to International Acquisition Agreement – Are the Provisions of the Korean Commercial Code Requiring Resolution of Special Shareholders' Meeting Internationally Mandatory Rules?' (2018) 53 *Kyung Hee Law Journal* 119.

—— 'Comment on the Judgment of the First Instance which Ordered Return of the Korean Buddhist Statue Stolen from the Tsushima Island: Issues on International Cultural Property Law' (2017) 23 *Korea Private International Law Journal* 3.
—— 'Comments on the Private International Law Cases of the Supreme Court of Korea in 2004' (2004) 10 *Korea Private International Law Journal* 429.
—— 'Comments on the Private International Law Cases of the Supreme Court of Korea in 2006' (2006) 12 *Korea Private International Law Journal* 569.
—— *Essays in International Commercial Arbitration Law*, vol 1 (Pakyoungsa, 2007).
—— 'Extraterritorial application of the Act on the Consumer Protection in Electronic Commerce and Consumer Protection in Private International Law' [Jeonjasanggeoraebeopui yeokoejeokyonggwa gukjesabeopsang sobijaui boho] *Law Times* (5 July 2021).
—— 'The General Contract Terms Control Act of Korea and Its Application to Hull Insurance Contract between Two Korean Companies Governed by English Law' (2015) 149 *Justice* 196.
—— 'General Issues with Amended Private International Law' [Gaejeong gukjesabeopui chongnonjeok munje] (2001) 536 *Korean Lawyers Association Journal* 5.
—— 'The Hague Principles on the Choice of Law in International Commercial Contracts' in *Commemorative Book in Honor of Professor Jinmu Hun-Je Suh's Retirement* (ChungAng University Press, 2015).
—— 'International Contract Law' (1999) 4 *Korea Private International Law Journal* 297.
—— 'International Employment Contracts and Protection of Employees under the New Conflict of Laws Act' (2001) 13 *Journal of Labour Law* 1.
—— 'Is the Act on the Regulation of Terms and Conditions Overriding Mandatory Rules?' *Law Times* (21 March 2011) 13.
—— 'Korea's Efforts and Role in Preventing Illicit Trafficking of Cultural Properties: Including Discussions on the Concept of Cultural Properties and Cultural Heritage' (2020) 26 *Korea Private International Law Journal* 221.
—— 'Laws Applicable to International Construction Contracts Using FIDIC Conditions and their Practical Consequences' (2014) 29 *Juris* 3.
—— 'Legal Issues in International Arbitration Related to International Guarantees That Are Unauthorized for Foreign Exchange' [Oehwanheogareul badji anihan gukjebojeunggwa gwallyeonhan gukjesabeopsangui munjejeom] (1994) 429 *Korean Lawyers Association Journal* 142.
—— 'Major Contents of Amendment of the Arbitration Act of 2016 and Several Comments Thereon' (2017) 53 *Chonbuk Law Review* 213.
—— 'New Swiss Private International Law' [Seuwiseuui gaejeonggukjesabeopjeon] in *Liberal Lee Ho Jeong's Life and Learning* [Jayujuuija leehojeongui salmgwa hakmun] (Hongmoonsa, 2019).
—— *Private International Law and International Litigation*, vol 1 (Pakyoungsa, 2001).
—— *Private International Law and International Litigation*, vol 5 (Pakyoungsa, 2012).
—— 'Private International Law of Switzerland Revisited' (2010) 26 *Korea Private International Law Journal* 571.
—— 'Protection of Commercial Agents in International Transactions – Scope of Application of Article 92bis of the Commercial Code' (2006) 55 *Korean Lawyers Association Journal* 19.
—— 'Review of the Bill to Amend Private International Law – General Provisions and Corporations' [Seopoesabeop gaejeongbeomnyulanui geomto-chongchikgwa beopin] (2010) 6 *Korea Private International Law Journal* 167.
—— 'The Role of the Private International Law Act and the Cultural Property Protection Act of Korea as Means of Protecting Cultural Property from International Illicit Transactions and the Proposal for Improvement' (2015) 56 *Seoul Law Journal* 117.
—— 'Several Choice of Law Issues in Maritime Matters' (2009) 31 *Korea Maritime Law Journal* 89.
—— 'Some Issues on Korea's Accession to the UNIDROIT Convention on Stolen or Illegally Exported Cultural Objects' (2009) 15 *Korea Private International Law Journal* 324.
—— 'A Study on the Revised German Private International Law' (2021) 27 *Korea Private International Law Journal* 631.
Symeonides, Symeon C, 'Party Autonomy in Rome I and II From a Comparative Perspective' in Boele-Woelki, Katarina (ed), *Convergence and Divergence in Private International Law – Liber Amicorum Kurt Siehr* (Shulthess, 2010).
Torremans, Paul (ed), *Cheshire, North & Fawcett: Private International Law*, 15th edn (Oxford University Press, 2017).
Vischer, Frank, 'General course on private international law' (1992) 232 *Recueil des Cours* 21.

Waincymer, Jeffrey Maurice, 'International Commercial Arbitration and the Application of Mandatory Rules of Law' (2009) 5 *Asian International Arbitration Journal* 1.

Weller, Marc-Philippe, 'Vom Staat zum Menschen: Die Methodentrias des Internationalen Privatrechts unserer Zeit' (2017) 81 *Rabels Zeischrift für ausländisches und internationales Privatrecht* 747.

Wi, Pyeong-ryang, 'An Empirical Study on Unfair Exploitative Practices in Subcontracting Transactions' [Hadogeupgeoraee isseoseo bulgongjeonghan jiwinamyonghaengwie gwanhan siljeungyeongu III] (2010) 1 *Economy Reform Report* 1.

Wilderspin, Michael, 'Overriding Mandatory Provisions' in *Encyclopedia of Private International Law* (Elgar Publishing, 2017).

Wilderspin, Michael, *The European Private International Law of Obligations*, 6th edn (Sweet & Maxwell, 2023).

Yoon, Namsoon, 'International Trade and Protection of Commercial Agents' (2006) 17 *Journal of Business Administration & Law* 97.

You, Jung Hwa, 'The Vaccine Purchase Agreement Signed by South Korea and the United Nations Convention on Contracts for the International Sale of Goods (CISG)' [Daehanminguki chegyeolhan baeksingumaegyeyakgwa UNtongilmaemaebeop(CISG)] *Law Times* (26 August 2021).

Yu, Seoung Jae, 'Retirement Benefit Entitlement for Illegally Dispatched Foreign Workers' (2004) *Labour Law Monthly* 19.

INDEX

www.ingramcontent.com/pod-product-compliance
Ingram Content Group UK Ltd.
Pitfield, Milton Keynes, MK11 3LW, UK
UKHW050944290926
15470UKWH00005B/1626